Politics and Markets

POLITICS AND MARKETS

The World's Political–Economic Systems

CHARLES E. LINDBLOM

Basic Books, Inc., Publishers

NEW YORK

Library of Congress Cataloging in Publication Data

Lindblom, Charles Edward, 1917-
  Politics and markets.

  Includes bibliographical references.
  1. Comparative economics. I. Title.
HD82.L475   330   77-75250
ISBN: 0-465-05957-0

To

Rose Winther Lindblom

With the breath, smiles, tears, of all my life
—Browning

CONTENTS

vii

Contents

PART V

The Close but Uneasy Relation between Private Enterprise and Democracy

PART VI

Communism Compared

PART VII

Other Alternatives

PREFACE

ASIDE from the difference between despotic and libertarian governments, the greatest distinction between one government and another is in the degree to which market replaces government or government replaces market. Both Adam Smith and Karl Marx knew this. Hence, certain questions about the governmental-market relation are at the core of both political science and economics, no less for planned systems than for market systems.

Both political science and economics have been to a degree impoverished by pressing the study of these questions on each other, consequently leaving the questions to fall between two stools. Thus, when political science turns to institutions like legislatures, civil service, parties, and interest groups, it has been left with secondary questions. The operation of parliaments and legislative bodies, bureaucracies, parties, and interest groups depends in large part on the degree to which government replaces market or market replaces government. In political science also, even ambitious attempts to refine democratic theory are marred by inattention to the functions of government or the state, functions that differ depending on the role of the market in political-economic life.

These, then, are the issues of this book: the fundamental questions about government and politics, about market systems, and about the relations between the two. The issues are pursued in an explicit progression from simplicity to complexity. We begin with elements of social systems, the understanding of which subsequently permits a grasp of complex systems in which the elements are combined in varied ways. The very simplest elements are exchange, authority, and persuasion.

The study pursues further some issues analyzed in *Politics, Economics, and Welfare* by Robert A. Dahl and Charles E. Lindblom (Harper & Brothers, New York, 1953). It does not, however, recapitulate the normative parts of the earlier book, and is instead more empirical. It also revises the theory of democracy of the earlier book, and it is greatly more explicit in connecting economic and political phenomena, especially in the analysis of the subtleties of the corporation in politics. The classification of basic processes (hierarchy, price system, bargaining, and polyarchy in the earlier book) are reconsidered, making more of a fundamental distinction between hierarchy and the other three, all of which represent forms of mutual adjustment rather than approximations to unilateral control.

Whereas the earlier book was largely concerned with liberal democratic systems alone, this is broadly comparative. It brings two well established fields of study, comparative economics and comparative politics, together within the covers of one book in the expectation that their juxtaposition will enrich both.

Parts of chapters 19 and 23 closely follow an analysis I earlier published as "The Sociology of Planning," in Morris Bornstein's (ed.) *Economic Planning, East and West* (Copyright 1975, Ballinger Publishing Company).

Most studies that attempt similar breadth ask Whence? and Whither? On the whole, I have relatively little to say about where the systems analyzed in this study came from, or where they are going. My attempt has been mainly to dissect and analyze those fundamental aspects of the systems that have been with us for at least several centuries and show every sign of persisting indefinitely. If we are to have any control over our futures, understanding our institutions well enough to reshape them is on some counts more necessary than predicting a future on the assumption that we are wholly powerless to form it.

Hence this book explores such questions as why governmental authority sometimes crumbles with astonishing abruptness, how it is that many nondemocratic governments seem to be as strongly motivated to guard the welfare of citizens as democratic governments, why "free" markets are sometimes as coercive as governmental authority, how businessmen play another role in politics different from and more influential than their interest-group role, why "industrial democracy" in the form of worker participation in management can develop more easily in a nondemocratic state than in a democratic society, and whether the Maoist tradition in communist China represents a fundamental or only secondary deviation from conventional communism.

It is a book of many themes rather than one. Among them, certain ones are given greatly extended treatment: for example, the "privileged position" of business in market-oriented systems, tendencies toward circularity in popular control in both government and market in the Western democracies, and some convergencies in working assumptions and aspirations between communists, on one hand, and Western advocates of scientific planning and management in corporation and government, on the other. Running through these themes and the whole book is a reconsideration of the validity of both classical liberal and pluralist thought. Both are found to be grossly defective, yet some core elements of them seem to remain firm.

I regret that acknowledgments will fail to do justice to the many persons who have given specific help in my years of work on this study. To many dozens of faculty colleagues and students, whose names I did not record, I owe thanks. In 1973 I tried out an earlier, much different version of the book on an undergraduate course and a graduate seminar, profiting greatly from the discussion of the material that arose in classes. For detailed reading and comment on parts or on all of the manuscript at one stage or another, I should like to thank especially Frederick C. Barghoorn, Robert E. Emmer, Martin Kessler, Everett C. Ladd, Robert E. Lane, Nicholas R. Lardy, Robert Z. Lawrence, Steven W. Lindblom, Harris N. Miller, J. Michael Montias, Richard R. Nelson, Raymond P. Powell, Arvid Roach, William Roth, Harold Stanley, Burton A. Weisbrod, and Edward J. Woodhouse.

For research assistance, I wish to thank Arvid Roach, Harris N. Miller, Robert Z. Lawrence, James Swiss, and Richard W. Smithey.

For editorial assistance, my thanks to Ann Collins, Richard W. Smithey, Eric N. Lindblom, and especially Janet Adami for her brilliant services in typing and steadily moving the manuscript forward to readiness for the press over a period of two years.

I also acknowledge with thanks a supporting grant from the Ford Foundation, as well as assistance from the Institute for Social and Policy Studies at Yale.

But it is Yale—a university—that I wish to single out in these acknowledgments. In expressing my thanks to a university, I address them not to a set of buildings or a place, but to a large number of people drawn together in such a way that, more than in any other kind of institution, they protect and stimulate inquiry.

Politics and Markets

Comparing Systems

RELENTLESSLY accumulating evidence suggests that human life on the planet is headed for a catastrophe. Indeed, several disasters are possible, and if we avert one, we will be caught by another. At present rates of population growth, another century will put 40 billion people on Earth, too many to feed. If industrial production grows at present rates during the next century, resource requirements will multiply by a thousand. And energy emission, some scientists say, will over a longer period of time raise Earth's temperature to a level unsuitable for human habitation. All this assumes that a nuclear catastrophe does not spare us the long anguish of degeneration.[1]

However fearful one may be that the fallible and dilatory intelligence of the human species will somehow either end human life or reduce it to unbearable squalor, the decline of the human condition is not inevitable. It is for us to decide whether we will continue to reproduce at disastrous rates, plunder the planet of resources, or burn ourselves from the face of the earth through either thermal pollution or a few quick blasts. The world is man's doing, not something done to him.

Assuming that men and women wish to give some thought to their futures, what are the fundamental politico-economic mechanisms they can employ in order to maintain—indeed greatly enlarge—the humane qualities of life on Earth? That is the question of this book. Some will doubt that political and economic mechanisms matter. They will say that man's future hinges on a moral regeneration. Or science and technology.

Or inner awareness. Or a new form of family or other small-group association. Or organic foods—the list is open to nominations. This book is for those who believe that politics and economics will turn out to matter.

Politico-Economic Systems

The political-economic mechanisms available for coping with present and future are, at a low level of abstraction, numerous beyond count. They include such varied devices as legislatures, jails, research institutions, armies, double-entry bookkeeping, national income accounting, business enterprises, bureaus, contracts, espionage agencies, secret police, international organizations like the United Nations and Comecon, elections, public opinion surveys, and municipal sanitation departments. These are endlessly reshuffled, and new ones are invented in all the countries of the world.

At a higher level of abstraction these various mechanisms can be grouped into a few categories that do not much change. For all the attention given a few years ago to Cuba's attempt to bring in a new day by substituting moral for conventional market incentives and for all the excitement of China's Great Proletarian Cultural Revolution, the fundamental politico-economic alternatives open to man make up only a very short list. One is social organization through the authority of government. One is social organization through exchange and markets. Another, I shall suggest, is social organization through persuasion, admittedly a less well defined possibility. And there are a few others. It is these few that man can combine and give specific form in multitudinous ways.

The fundamental alternative possibilities are most fully developed in the industrialized nations of the world and in China, Cuba, and Yugoslavia. Elsewhere in the world, the less developed countries are largely imitative of the industrialized systems. We shall consequently largely exclude the greatest number of less developed systems from our analysis; recognizing that in any case their particular problems and characteristics deserve a separate volume.

Misconceptions

The fundamental politico-economic mechanisms are still not well understood. For example, the myth is disseminated that the market is dead or dying.[2] How do we know that it is? Because it is obvious that planning is increasing. Planning is indeed increasing, but the logic of the argument is no better than the inference that if people jog for exercise then swimming must be on a decline, as if one cannot do both. A great deal of planning takes the form of steering or guiding the market rather than replacing it; and internally within a corporation, planning is a method of making the corporation a more effective participant in the market. Nor is the rise of big business evidence of market decline. Two Marxist economists, who might be expected to look for evidence of market decline, write: "The big corporations relate to each other, to consumers, to labor, to smaller business primarily through the market."[3] That we need achieve a better understanding of market systems is all the more important since Yugoslavia—and Hungary also to a degree—has, since the 1950s, established a socialist market system.

Not a myth but a misunderstanding is the common view of how liberal democratic government works. Except for some analysis of interest groups, democratic theory makes no place for the business enterprise. In American law the corporation is a "person"; and in all the democratic market-oriented systems, corporations and other business enterprises enter into politics. Their needs and preferences are communicated to lawmakers no less urgently than those of citizens. But these fictitious persons are taller and richer than the rest of us and have rights that we do not have. Their political impact differs from and dwarfs that of the ordinary citizen. Clearly democratic theory needs to be extended to take account of what we will call the privileged position of business.

In fact, we understand liberal democracy so poorly that we do not know —neither economists nor political scientists have produced more than speculative essays on the question—why it is that liberal democracy has arisen only in nations that are market-oriented, not in all of them but only in them.* The tie between market and democracy is on many counts an astonishing historical fact. We understand neither market nor democracy well if we cannot explain it.

We do not understand communist systems very well either. In some important ways, they are more humane than most market-oriented systems, showing a greater concern for income equality, for job security, and for minimum standards of health and other necessities. Appalled by the absence of the civil liberties in communist societies and by their despotic control of the mind, liberal democrats often forget that in history many of man's greatest excesses are the other side of some great

---

* To avoid unnecessary dispute over whether the industrialized mixed systems of the world, which once were called capitalist systems, are still capitalist, we shall avoid the term, referring to them instead as market-oriented systems, or, where they might be confused with socialist market systems, as private enterprise systems.

altruistic effort. In the French Revolution the Terror was paired with Liberté, Egalité, Fraternité; and in the American operation in Vietnam, a savage destruction of countryside and life itself was paired with what many Americans rightly or wrongly regarded as a noble aspiration to protect the liberties of a people.

The failure to understand fundamental politico-economic mechanisms and their potentials in new combinations is worldwide. India's difficulties in economic development are in part the consequences of her leaders' inability to understand that growth requires a growth mechanism: if not the market, which Indian policy cripples, then the authority of government, which India has never chosen to mobilize. It is as elementary an error as any in American, British, or Soviet policy. In the 1960s, the Soviet Union's realization that its rapid growth had been accomplished more through crude and massive transfer of labor and capital resources from agriculture to industry rather than through the intelligence and scientific quality of its planning, underscores elementary misperception of fundamental politico-economic mechanisms there.

Man's Instruments

In what way shall we try to raise the level of our understanding of these systems? One approach is to postulate that in all systems most people spend most of their time looking after themselves, which means that they either neglect or take advantage of other people. On such a postulate we can explain a great deal about social organization. It explains tyranny, when some persons in the society enjoy extraordinary authority to exploit their fellows. It explains gross inequity in the distribution of life's opportunities when the rights of property build a wall of privilege. It explains lesser ills too, like corporate exploitation of the consumer, labor racketeering, medical malpractice, and fee padding—there is no end to the story of man's aggressive abuse of his own kind.

Another approach is to consider each system as a mechanism through which people, all of whom do very badly, might in some sense do better— either toward each other or simply to save themselves from the impossible futures now predicted for them. In this book, we take the position that what we urgently need to know about the systems are those features of them that bear on how they might be made more useful and less destructive.

Such an analysis does not abandon values. To pursue it means that we take our general orientation from the traditional values of liberty, equality, democracy, and popular participation in policy making. Some similar commitment, either for or against some such values, is necessary to give

6

coherence to any analysis. Otherwise one only randomly and aimlessly observes the phenomena under study.

Yet our purpose is to describe rather than to evaluate politico-economic systems. The two processes cannot, however, be wholly separated. To ask whether Americans in fact control their government or whether a market system achieves a systematic allocation of resources can be either empirical or evaluative questions, depending on what is intended by the questions and their answers. Our general method, however, is to analyze characteristics of politico-economic systems that appear to be important for such widely accepted values as popular control, efficiency (of various kinds), liberty (however defined), and equality (again of various kinds) without then pressing on into an evaluative, normative, or philosophical analysis.

Our task, then, is to clarify the basic politico-economic mechanisms and systems. This is not the same thing as guessing the future, measuring trends, or examining the particular policies or developmental strategies of this or that nation. It is an examination of the fundamental politico-economic instruments through which the nations of the world can develop their futures. These are the instruments man has available to grapple with both his familiar problems of crime, poverty, war, and unemployment and the emerging problems of population, energy, and environment. They are what he has to work with in the less developed parts of the world, in the industrialized societies, and in the "postindustrial state" into which the wealthier nations are emerging.[4] They are his tools whether what Marxists call capitalism has a long life ahead of it or whether it is on the decline in a world of steady communist expansion.[5] For capitalists and communists alike, the fundamental alternatives are the same, though they may choose to combine them in different ways.*

Smith and Marx

The two heroes of this book are Adam Smith and Karl Marx. We no longer live in a Smithian world of atomistic competition; but the market remains one of the few institutions capable of organizing the cooperation of millions of people. We owe to his *Wealth of Nations*, written 200 years

---

* To two spheres of politico-economic life we give relatively little attention for no better reason than at some point breadth has to be sacrificed to depth. Small-group life is one, despite its importance for human well-being. See Robert A. Dahl and Charles E. Lindblom, *Politics, Economics, and Welfare* (New York: Harper & Brothers, 1953), pp. 519–21. The other is international relations. Except that the market system is itself international in scope, the special processes and problems of international politico-economic organization are distinctive and require their own independent parallel analysis.

ago, much of our understanding of what markets can and cannot do. We also owe to him our still quite imperfect understanding of the degree to which man accomplishes many of his ends as an epiphenomenon, a by-product of activities pursued for other purposes. Income distribution, resource allocation, and economic growth are accomplished as by-products of petty self-serving individual decisions to buy and sell. Sociologists subsequently picked up the idea of epiphenomenal effects in their concept of latent functions of social institutions. But the inquiry into epiphenomena begun by Smith remains to be completed.

To the genius of Marx we owe more than can be listed, despite the tediously listed errors of so ambitious an analysis as his. Even at this late date in the history of social science, we must still turn back to Marx to understand, for example, the adverse effects on democratic government of property rights and of their grossly unequal distribution. Property is a system of authority established by government, just as what we call government is itself a system of authority. In its preoccupation with problems of authority in government, liberal democratic thought remains insensitive to problems of that authority which is embodied in property rights.

Politics and Economics

For many good reasons, politics and economics have to be held together in the analysis of basic social mechanisms and systems. The principal activities of government are heavily economic: taxation, national defense, education, energy conservation and administration, transportation and communication, social security, economic stabilization, and promotion of growth.

To Thomas Hobbes we owe some confusion on the relation of politics to economics. Since the *Leviathan*, the study of politics has been largely the study of conflict and its resolution. But government is not merely or even primarily a conflict resolver. And when it does attend to conflict, it is not conflict, as Hobbes saw it, over land, wives, and cattle. It is conflict over the control of government itself, over the terms of man's cooperation in government, and over the purposes of that cooperation. Government engages in vast economic tasks—supporting an army, building railroads, stimulating business enterprises to produce, and taxing to finance the economic activities it undertakes. That is why there is so much to conflict about and such a great stake in the outcomes.

In all the political systems of the world, much of politics is economics, and most of economics is also politics. What then is the difference between the two? In common sense, "economics" refers to a certain kind of activity, whether it is undertaken by individuals, enterprises, or governments. More precisely, "economics" refers to activities, which may simultaneously be political activities, looked at in a particular way. Thus, if I ask questions about how an army is recruited from the nation's labor force, how it is equipped, and how it is paid for, I am looking at the army as an economic institution despite the obvious that the army is also a political or governmental institution. For what follows in later chapters it will be helpful to specify the distinctive characteristics of the economic view of processes and institutions, whether they are also political or not.

The Economic View of Things

A misconception to be avoided is that economics is wholly concerned with material goods. In actual fact the principal inputs in any economy are labor services, not materials; and material inputs are themselves largely a product of previous inputs of labor services. As for outputs, they include services no less conspicuously than material goods—outputs in the form of the personal services of doctors and dentists, entertainers, waiters, launderers, repairmen, teachers, judges, police, and clerks, as well as the many services of the housewife and householder performing maintenance work in the home. Even in marketable output alone, services loom large. After World War II the United States became the first nation in which over 50 percent of marketable output came in the form of services rather than commodities; other wealthy nations are now following.[6]

Another misconception is that there exists some category of man's goals or aspirations that can be labeled economic. People work, as well as buy and sell, in pursuit of goals as diverse as comfort, security, aesthetic pleasures, novelty, conformity, thrill, and diversion.* In economic life, individuals, groups, and nations deploy their material and nonmaterial resources—their energies, time, brainpower, and physical equipment— in the pursuit of every imaginable goal.

* Even at today's prices, in the United States an adult can meet his physical nutritional requirements for an expenditure of not more than 75 cents per day. What he spends beyond that is for variety, palatability, and other intangibles; and even the poorest persons in the society insist on the intangibles rather than a cheap synthetic diet for nutrition alone. For the calculations, see Victor E. Smith, "Linear Programming Models for the Determination of Palatable Human Diets," *Journal of Farm Economics* 41 (May 1959); and Paul Samuelson, *Economics,* 9th ed. (New York: McGraw-Hill, 1973), p. 19n.

These misconceptions aside, the economic view of things is one that sees in an activity or process an input-output relation. More specifically, to see a process as economic is to see it as accomplishing a conversion or transformation of goods and services from one form into another. Iron ore and labor are transformed into automobiles, refrigerators, and freight services on steel-using railroads. I can also look at trimming my fingernails as a similar conversion, whether I do it myself or hire the service. Trading an hour's baby-sitting for an hour in return at another time is a conversion.

We call these social processes economic, however, only on the additional assumption that we see in them a gain in value—for example, converting iron ore into finished steel products because the finished steel products are of more value than the original iron ore. Hence, we also see people choosing among alternatives and choosing in a particular way—choosing what is worth more rather than less. People make an economic choice only when, in order to get what they want, they choose to give up something else of value that they want—in other words, when a choice is costly.

To decide which of two pairs of shoes to wear for the day is an act of choice but not of economic choice unless one is so enamored of his shoes that it pains him to forego one pair while wearing the other. To choose to support one party or candidate instead of another is, again, an act of choice, but not an act of economic choice for most people unless they want both parties. To work for a party or candidate is, however, an act of economic choice if the time I spend working precludes my spending the time in other pleasurable ways. The other pleasurable uses of my time are the costs of my political activity. In many choice situations, to choose one objective, goal, or value is to forego another, that is, to incur a cost. Costly choice is obviously fundamental to the economic view of things.

Choices incur many costs beyond those that are represented in monetary terms. Everyone now knows that the cost of operating automobiles is greater than the money cost paid by those who operate them. Some of the other costs are the values of unpolluted air, of quiet, and the use for other desired purposes of resources now given over to traffic control. We look at social life from the economic point of view when we ask questions about who pays these costs, whether they are greater than should be borne, and whether society has social mechanisms for estimating them and bringing them to bear on decisions about automobile use.

Basic Methods of Social Control

How now to begin the analysis of politico-economic organization? One possibility is to hinge the analysis on the conventional distinction between administered, or command, systems and market systems. Family and household aside, the world's two big organizing institutions are indeed state and market. Slavery is almost gone, so also the manorial economy of feudal society. Although in Asia, Africa, and South America, millions of people in preindustrial milieus still engage primarily in subsistence agriculture, almost all of them are now caught up in market transactions, just as they are all now targets of, if not active participants in, their governments' development programs.

But striking similarities between state-directed systems and market systems confuse any simple distinction between the two. Some uses of the market system are indispensable even to centrally planned systems. One of the first ambitions of the Russian Revolution in 1917 was to abolish the market system along with money and prices. The Bolsheviks tried, and an extraordinary social disorganization ensued. Neither the Soviet system, nor any other communist system, has ever again tried to dispense with the market, although Castro at one time announced such an intention for Cuba. All the national systems of the world use the market among other devices to recruit and assign workers to their various tasks. All national systems provide for much of the distribution of consumer goods through market sales to willing buyers. All make use of money and prices. They all, of course, make heavy use of the state.

Distinctions are blurred on another count. In all industrial systems, production is directly organized not by market but by bureaucratic authority, either private or governmental: Unilever, General Motors, Hindustan Machine Tools, the U.S. Postal Service, the British Transport Commission, the Shih-ching-shan Steel Works, and a Soviet state farm are all bureaucracies. Whether the bureaucracy is enmeshed in a market system or in a governmental administration may be of little consequence to either employee or customer.

We need therefore to begin with surer concepts than complex abstractions like market and administered system. I propose to begin with the elemental mechanisms for social control that all politico-economic systems employ.*

The particular methods by which people control others seem countless.

*But this book will deal with these matters more simply and more precisely than Dahl and Lindblom's *Politics, Economics, and Welfare,* which also begins with some elementary mechanisms.

They are not limited to deliberate attempts at control, for people influence each other's behavior in many unintended ways. Scholars have frequently tried to make a definitive classification.[7] The first major distinction is usually between methods that actually change rewards and penalities and those that only change people's perceptions of the rewards and penalities. To control me, you can threaten to disadvantage me if I do not do what you want. Or you can, without any such threat or intention to harm, simply call my attention to reasons why I will be disadvantaged by not responding to your request.

Not all control methods fall into these two categories. For example, a distinctive though infrequent method of control is physical constraint, as when police bodily seize a drunk. Or through drugs or brain surgery, physicians try to alter a person's mental or emotional characteristics so that he thinks—that is, calculates rewards and penalties—in an altered way. Or A will manipulate B's resources, depriving him of the ability to do what A does not want him to do, or giving him new capacity—money, position, or even a weapon—to do what A wants him to do. Beyond these categories are many possibilities of restructuring the immediate environment or agenda of B (other than by altering his resources) so that some possible kinds of behavior are no longer open to his consideration. Although one way to keep children from nibbling at sweets is to punish them for doing so, another is simply not to have any sweets available.

Not to disregard any of these or the more complex methods to which they in turn give rise, we find three—exchange, authority, and persuasion —to be of such critical consequence for politico-economic organization as to require special attention at the outset of the analysis.*

Exchange is ubiquitous. We all exchange favors in order to get along with each other, and politicians exchange favors in order to facilitate cooperation among themselves. Exchange is also the fundamental relationship on which market systems are built.

The authority relationship is the basic relationship that characterizes membership in formal organizations like churches, clubs, lodges, corporations, and unions. When one says he belongs to any of these, he in effect says that he recognizes the authority of their officers to act for him or to

---

* We might have added a fourth: moral codes, which could be presented as an internalized control system. We single out only the three, however, not to slight the fourth—or to slight many other control methods to which we shall have to give attention from time to time—but to give them the sustained and meticulous attention they require in the analysis of politico-economic organization. The elaborateness of politico-economic organization, specifically the detail of division of labor and role specialization in complex politico-economic systems, is maintained by control systems that can draw distinctions that moral codes do not. One can explain, by reference to morality, why a people lives at relative peace with each other or why their relationships are generally abrasive. To explain the occupational structure or the complexities of government, however, one needs to give special attention to authority, exchange, and persuasion.

control him with respect to the functions of the organization. A government is a formal organization; consequently, the authority relationship is the bedrock on which government is erected. Authority is as fundamental to government as exchange is to the market system.

Persuasion is central and fundamental in all social systems. It does not, however, play in any existing politico-economic system the distinctive role that exchange plays in markets or authority plays in government. Nevertheless, it is a ubiquitous form of social control and is of special importance in the analysis of politico-economic systems on three counts. In the form of ideological instruction and propaganda, persuasion is a major method of elite control of masses, much more so in communist systems than in liberal democratic ones. In the form of commercial advertising, it is a major instrument of corporate control of masses of consumers in market societies. In the form of mutual persuasion in "free" societies—that is, in the form of "free competition of ideas"—it is fundamental to liberal democracy.

Maoist China may have been making such distinctive use of persuasion as a method of social control that its system for doing so warrants special attention. In any case, one can imagine a picture or model of a certain kind of control system like China's based on massive unilateral persuasion. We shall call such a system a preceptoral system. The preceptoral system bears, very roughly, the kind of relation to persuasion that market bears to exchange and government bears to authority. But only very roughly; one should not push the parallelism too far.*

* Why not tradition as another major category? For two reasons. One is that for our purposes we need categories especially pertinent to contemporary nontraditional societies. The other is that tradition is no more than an umbrella term that designates an unspecified variety of controls, including internalized norms, that are not administered through public policy but somehow "spontaneously" through family, kinship, status, and the like. If we were to need to refer to tradition, it would be necessary to identify the controls encompassed in the concept; and among them would be authority, exchange, and persuasion.

PART

I

THE ELEMENTS

Authority and State

ALTHOUGH it is obvious that market systems are based on the exchange relation, it may be less obvious that government is similarly based on the authority relation. For that matter, just what the authority relation is has never been wholly clear. In our earlier work, Dahl and I thought that authority could be identified with commands backed by prescribed penalties; but in the carpool we shared at the time we conferred authority on one member of the pool to set schedules for it, and he could neither have prescribed a penalty if we thereafter disobeyed him nor enforced one if he had tried.[1] Just what authority is and how government depends on it both need meticulous examination.

The Authority Relation

At the end of the war between Nigeria and secessionist Biafra in 1970, Colonel Effiong came to Lagos to surrender: "We accept the authority," he said, "of the federal military Government of Nigeria."[2] In effect he gave it permission to issue orders; he pledged a rule of obedience. That is the key relation to which, with ample precedent, we give the name authority. It exists whenever one, several, or many people explicitly or tacitly permit someone else to make decisions for them for some category of acts. Once I give permission to someone else to make decisions for me, then all that he need do in order to control me is to make his wishes known.[3]

People may grant such permission because they believe that there is someone who knows best what to do—someone, for example, who knows best when to plant the season's crops. Or because they want to shift to someone else the responsibility for making a troublesome decision—to decide, for example, whether to disconnect the dialysis machine and let the patient die. Or because they need to focus responsibility on some one person to coordinate the others, as when a carpool grants authority to some one member to set schedules. Authority also has a harsher side. Colonel Effiong granted authority because he and his associates were otherwise threatened with violence and death. And between the two extremes of voluntary and coerced authority, people also grant authority—employees grant authority to employer or job supervisor—because they are paid to do so.

What we are going to call authority is an ancient control mechanism: it was established, denied, then once more exercised in the Garden of Eden. At least 5,000 years ago rulers already knew how to use it on a large scale. In ancient Sumer authority allocated land, directed work gangs on canals and dikes, and coordinated a division of labor in agriculture.[4] A remarkable method of social control, it is perhaps ominously efficient, because unlike persuasion and exchange, it is a method of control that often works with extraordinary simplicity. Sometimes not even a word is needed; in an authority relation a docile person knows what is wanted of him and does it without being told.

Peoples of different cultures differ in their willingness to grant authority. Thus, Germans are often said to be more willing than the French, for example. Some studies document differences of this kind: the Flemish are more willing to grant authority than the Walloons, or, comparing two tribes in Kenya and the Sudan, the Gusii are more willing than the Nuer.[5]

One can use each of such diverse controls as indoctrination, legal and illegal threat of deprivation, offer of benefit, and persuasion, including deceit, to control another person either directly or by the indirect route of inducing him to grant authority to the controller, that is, to give permission, to accept a rule of obedience. *Every specific control can be used either as a method of direct control or as a method for establishing a rule of obedience (authority) which, once established, itself suffices for control as long as it stands.** And existing authority can assign new authority.

* Dahl and Lindblom (*Politics, Economics, and Welfare*) err in saying: "To command is to control the response of a subordinate exclusively by virtue of a penalty prescribed. . ." (p. 106).

Ever since Max Weber, many social scientists have argued that the authority relationship ordinarily requires legitimacy. It can exist only when someone obeys out of a belief that he ought to do so.[6] But people can also be simply coerced, as some were in Nazi Germany, to follow a rule of obedience even when they believe that the commands and the commander are illegitimate. That they grant authority because a moral code induces them to do so is only a frequent but not a necessary foundation of authority.

More often than not, people grant authority not directly because of the efforts of the person who exercises it but because of others: a father will intervene to maintain a distraught mother's authority over their child or a factory worker will obey his foreman because the payroll office pays him to do so. The authority, say, of a tax official is conferred upon him by a legislature (whose authority to do so is granted willingly or otherwise by the citizenry). His superiors in tax administration bring their authority to bear to support him. If necessary, the courts throw their authority to his support, and the authority of the judges rests on authoritative support from bailiff and police.

Political authority is also often supported by widespread indignation against dissidents. In most situations—in small groups, associations, and government alike—any one person practices a rule of obedience conditional on others doing so. Granting authority to the president of an association makes sense for any one member only if others also do so.

Control through exchange always requires that a person give up some value to induce another to do as he wishes, and control through persuasion takes time and energy. By contrast, control through authority is often costless, as when some people find it convenient to be authoritatively coordinated and someone else enjoys coordinating them. There is no denying, however, that the establishment and maintenance of authority is often costly, especially in government, where it requires guns, police force, military, and other specialized authority-maintaining organizations like courts. Once established, however, any single exercise of authority is often costless or nearly so. Thus the marginal cost of control is zero or nearly so. Indeed the repeated exercise of it often helps to maintain it.*

The exercise of authority on particular occasions is costless because grants of authority can be made long in advance of the occasions on which exercised, can be made stable and lasting, and can embrace large categories of acts. Then when a response is wanted, no reward, no penalty, no manipulation, not even the task of persuasion is required. All that is required is an indication of what response is desired. Some social scientists

---

* Occasionally, however, a particular exercise of authority can destroy the whole authority system by triggering a withdrawal of the grant of authority.

have made the mistake of looking, with respect to each occasion when one person authoritatively controls another, for a control device particular to the occasion—a persuasive communication, perhaps, or a threat or a payment of some kind. They cannot find it because in the authority relation it is not there.

That explains why authority becomes a major method of social control; it is cheap when the time comes to use it. The costliness of alternatives is often discouraging. Although parental authority was once well established in American family life, many contemporary parents, having either failed to establish authority or not wishing to, must now wheedle, cajole, entreat, and bribe, exercises that require time and money. Thus, the marginal costs of controlling their children have risen very high, sometimes so high that they give up trying.

Getting the cost of control down is sometimes essential—or considered to be. In Europe in World War II, to reduce the marginal cost of controlling American soldiers who had been increasingly testing the army's tolerance for desertion, General Eisenhower sanctioned the execution of Private Slovik.[7] The execution was defended as a method of "restoring authority."

In common speech, the word "authority" goes beyond its key use in designating forms of social control. We call Bernard Berenson an authority on art, Watson and Crick authorities on the structure of the DNA molecule. We also sometimes say of a person that he "speaks with authority," not meaning that we obey him but only that he seems confident. Set these usages aside as unnecessary for our purposes. We do need usages, however, like "The treasurer has authority to make payments," or "I authorize you to speak and vote in my name." In these cases, authority does not at first seem to refer to control over anyone. The treasurer appears not to control anyone but instead has permission to do things not permitted to others. Not everyone can disperse the funds that belong to a group. But when someone is permitted to do what others are not permitted to do, the permission has effect only because others follow a routine of making appropriate responses. To give someone the authority to spend the funds of an association requires that others must, for example, accept his checks drawn on the association's account, though they would accept no other person's checks drawn on that same account and might in fact jail anyone else for attempting to pass them. One thus sees authority in two lights—as two kinds of permission: a routinized permission to control; and a routinized permission to do things denied to others, to perform acts that only secondarily achieve control over others.

The Authority Relation in Formal Organization and Government

In philosophy, mythology, science fiction, and comic strip, men have imagined brighter and stronger creatures than themselves. They also create them in the shape of formal organizations that can do what men cannot do singly, entities that can build the Pyramids, administer the empire of the Incas, conduct an Inquisition, and put a man on the moon.

How to assemble the giant and make it move? The authority relation both structures it and breathes life into it. Authority subordinates ordinary members to the organization's officers, and officers of different functions to each other. Many authority relations, each connecting at least one member of the organization to others, tie individual members into a cooperating whole. In fact, one can define an organization as a purposive structure of authority relations. Like single individuals, formal organizations pursue purposes, even if like single individuals they are often torn by internal conflict. Some pursue profits, some educate, some lobby public officials, some hijack airplanes, and some arrange cooperative day care for children. Whatever the purpose, a network of authority is created to achieve it.*

Government as an Authority Network

One would think that an easy way to acknowledge the special character of government as an organization is simply to say that governments exercise authority over other organizations. But some nongovernmental organizations sometimes refuse a rule of obedience to government; Cuba's guerrillas granted authority not to Batista's government but to Castro.

To describe the difference between government and other organizations, we have to come to some such formulation as the following: For any given population, a government exists for them to the degree that one of the groups exercising authority over them exercises authority over all the others or claims, without challenge from a rival claimant, a generalized authority for its orders over those of every other organization. It may not make effective its claimed priority in case of conflict and in some cases

---

* In a representative attempt at definition, P. M. Blau and W. R. Scott write: where "the goals to be achieved, the rules the members of the organization are expected to follow, and the status structure that defines the relations between them (the organization chart) have not spontaneously emerged in the course of social interaction but have been consciously designed *a priori* to anticipate and guide interaction and activities," there we find the formal organization (*Formal Organizations* [San Francisco: Chandler, 1962]), p. 5.

may not even wish to enforce a priority. But the generality and uniqueness of its claim to priority distinguish it.*

The efficiency of authority—specifically, the low marginal cost of any single exercise of authoritative control—explains its central role in government. Governmental control through ad hoc deployment of rewards and penalties—say, a bargain struck with each individual citizen on each of repeated occasions—is hopelessly expensive and time consuming for the vast tasks of government. Even if a government could employ a battery of ad hoc methods of enforcement, it could do so only because a large group of people stand willing to administer these enforcements. Yet how to induce that group's cooperation, if not by authority? Lenin embarked on a revolutionary course for Russia when he perceived how small a force of army and police, because of the phenomenon of authority, controlled the Russian masses. He realized that a small revolutionary group might do so too.

Authority, the core phenomenon that makes government possible, explains how a congress or parliament can be more powerful than an army, how a Stalin can override the unanimous opinions of his colleagues in party leadership, and how a political boss can boss. Both the obvious features and the puzzles of politics are inexplicable except by reference to the authority relation and to the intricate network of relations that supports any specific authority relation. The great feats of political leadership and organization rest on the phenomenon of authority. So also do the crises that disturb political order. For authority can vanish with astonishing suddenness, as abruptly as people can change their minds about which rules of obedience they are willing to follow, as a long list of former rulers, including Haile Selassie and Isabel Perón, testifies.

Authoritative Rules in Government

Government officials sometimes issue individual orders, as when a judge declares at the conclusion of a civil trial that "defendant must pay to plaintiff the sum of $5,000." But authority usually operates through law and other general prescriptive rules. Similarly, grants of governmental authority by those subject to it typically take the form of rules specifying who can exercise what kind of control over whom in what

---

* To describe government as an authority system or as a formal organization seems to miss some of the most familiar aspects of the governmental process: the multiplicity of organizations within government, the occasional fervor of political activity, the complexities of maneuvering among interest groups or between interest groups and officials, political discussion and debate, party rivalry, and chicanery. We shall put them all in the picture, but only step by step in this and other chapters.

circumstances. "Communism," a Soviet writer says, "is the most organized society man has ever known." He then goes on to say it is organized by rules, and that it achieves "the habitual observation of these rules as a regular norm of conduct."[8] The same can be said for any government.

Even in the disorder of revolution, Lenin employed conventional rules of majority voting in the party Central Committee to decide on acceptance of the Brest-Litovsk Treaty.[9] Where formally announced rules, like those that forbid the Central Intelligence Agency to conduct domestic espionage, are disregarded, other tacit or informally announced rules take their place. People often impose rules on themselves. After the death of Stalin and the subsequent execution of Beria, Soviet leadership came to agree—no doubt for its own protection—on the rule that exile or death is no longer required for deposed Politburo members.[10]

In government, authoritative rules of the game are controlling in the same way that they are in a game of poker or basketball. That again explains the volatility of politics in some circumstances. Abruptly—as abruptly as they can change their minds—political leaders decide they no longer wish to follow an existing rule. It is then a new game.

Oblique and Extended Use of Authority

Oblique Authority

When an official wishes to direct subordinates or citizens, he does not always use his authority directly to give orders or to inaugurate rules that do so. He has at hand a variety of possibilities for using authority in oblique ways. To induce almost everyone to rise an hour earlier, officials announce daylight savings time rather than specifically instruct people to get out of bed. To increase a nation's supply of physicians, they can authorize draft deferments for medical students rather than authoritatively, order young people into medical training.

One of the major avenues for the oblique use of authority is authority to enter into exchange or to alter the terms of exchange in market systems. Instead of conscripting an army, a government can use its authority to hire it. Instead of directly forbidding imports, it can indirectly achieve the same effect by taxing imports to raise their prices. The common distinction between "direct" and "indirect" economic controls is a special case of the distinction between direct and oblique use of authority.

Extended Use of Authority

Caesar used his limited military authority to transform the government of Rome. Because there is no complex organization in which authority can be constrained within the limits intended by those who establish it, authority always becomes to a degree uncontrollable. Grant an official authority to do a job, and he will also use it to do other things not intended for him. Authority, both direct and oblique, can always be extended to gain powers beyond the original grant.

Some participants in government develop remarkable skill in making the extension. Through his authority as party secretary, Stalin appointed local party secretaries who would influence the selection of delegates to party congresses who in turn would sanction new powers he sought.[11] Often a superior will enlarge a subordinate's authority if the subordinate assents to the extended use of the superior's authority; hence, the cooperative or conspiratorial extended use of the authority of both is common. The Nixon–FBI cooperative illegal extension of the authority of both is an example.

"Wheeling and dealing," "playing politics," and "power plays" are colloquial terms that only imprecisely denote the many ingenious ways in which people in government control each other not directly by their authority but through its extended use. A municipal public works official has authority to organize street sweeping and snow removal. Because he can offer jobs to those who will do favors for him, he can extend his control beyond his grant of authority. He can require anyone he hires to campaign for his party. He can use his authority over contracts to compel businesses to contribute to his party, to himself, or to his allies. Taking these and other exploitable possibilities together, he may go further and demand to be recognized as a member of some of the top policy-making groups in municipal government. Perceiving him to be a member, other people will predictably seek to ingratiate themselves with him in the hope of future favors; and so his influence grows.

The same process can be seen at other levels of government. The president of the United States has no authority to regulate industrial prices. But to constrain price increases, President Johnson used his authority over military contracts, extending that authority in order to withdraw contracts from firms that raised prices. President Kennedy extended his authority in order to call for FBI and antitrust investigations against price-raising firms.[12] In short, authority is extended by using it where it is conferred in order to achieve control in an area in which it is not.

When we observe the proliferation of chains of power and influence in government, we sometimes mistakenly think we see forms of power distinct from authority. But if we see favors and kickbacks, they are in fact typically the products of grants of authority to hire and to contract. If we see an official coerced for fear of losing his job, it is because someone has the authority to fire him. If we see loyal henchmen gather around a figure who dominates them, his authority to offer benefits has been used to bind them together. When money talks most loudly in government, someone has authority to dispense it.

Extended Use to Create a New Authority Structure

The East India Company, given certain authority to do business in India in the seventeenth century, extended that authority until it became the actual government of parts of India. Persons with authority commonly extend their use of it not simply to win additional influence but to win new grants of authority itself. In his role as Senate Majority Leader, Senator Lyndon Johnson did so with widely admired skill. He used his authority to do favors for fellow senators so effectively as to build a new authority for himself that rivaled the president's, reducing the Senate, it was suggested with some exaggeration, to "a docile body ruled by a senior oligarch."[13] A political machine is an authority structure built on an extended use of prior authority. The public works official uses his authority over city contracts to extract, in exchange for a benefit, a grant of authority from each of the men who will constitute the core of his machine. Each then uses the benefit granted him to win concessions of authority from a subordinate group around him.

Real and Apparent Power

The simple concept of extended use of authority we shall call upon often in subsequent chapters. We can put it to use even at this point in the analysis in order to begin to dissipate a popular illusion that there lies mysteriously and secretly behind the facade of the authority of government officials a distribution of "real" power, an illusion that social power is a family and class structure to which the distribution of authority in government must correspond or yield.

Authority does not always lie where it seems to lie—that much is true. But if a group of authority relations is a facade, another group of authority relations, not some other set of social processes, lies behind it. One will not find "the truth" about political power by looking for it in disregard of authority; one finds it by uncovering the operative authority relations. If an oligarchy of "old families" runs a town, it is because the ostensible authorities have conceded authority to the old families. If a conclave of party leaders or bosses dominate, it is because each has established that particular form of control here called authority over a politically consequential following.

Some people believe that wealth or property is the underlying source of power. But property is itself a form of authority created by government. Property is a set of rights to control assets: to refuse use of them to others, to hold them intact, or to use them up. Property rights are consequently grants of authority made to persons and organizations, both public and private and acknowledged by other persons and organizations.[14] The wealthy are those who enjoy larger grants of authority than most people do. Just as ecclesiastical authority set limits on secular authority in medieval Europe, entrepreneurial authority today in the form of property rights limits governmental authority. But that is because governments authorize such an arrangement.

Sometimes democratic politics appears to be far removed from organization through authority and looks more like exchange. The president offers a higher minimum price for milk in return for a financial contribution from a dairy association, or a governor pledges his support to a presidential candidate in hope of the vice-presidential nomination. Identify, however, the counters in the play. The president can "sell" favors to dairymen only because he has authority over policy. A candidate can offer a vice-presidential nomination only because, by unwritten party rules, a presidential nominee has the authority to choose his running mate.*

Nevertheless, authority always mixes with other forms of control. A network of authority gives rise to a parallel network of persuasion. Commenting on the ease with which subordinates escape from obedience to authority unless also persuaded, President Truman said of his successor: "He'll sit here, and he'll say, 'Do this! Do that!' And nothing will happen. Poor Ike—it won't be a bit like the Army."[15] Authority, we have seen, also often takes the form of authority to buy or sell: President Jefferson claimed the authority to purchase Louisiana rather than conquer it.

It is not surprising that Hobbes, Rousseau, and others have tried to find the origins of government authority in a social contract. For the authority relation can, we have seen, be established by contract, and sometimes explicitly so, as in the Mayflower Compact. In the absence of an explicit

* What is fundamentally misguided about recent attempts to formulate an exchange theory of politics is the failure to see that what is exchanged in politics is not such personal favors as ordinary individuals can offer each other but favors of authority (as well as authoritative threats, which do not fit well at all into an exchange theory). In politics the benefits of the exercise of authority are the values moving in exchange. An exchange theory of politics has to begin, consequently, with authority. For examples of exchange theories, see R. L. Curry and L. L. Wade, *A Theory of Political Exchange* (Englewood Cliffs, N.J.: Prentice-Hall, 1968); and Warren F. Ilchman and Norman T. Upoff, *The Political Economy of Change* (Berkeley: University of California Press, 1969).

contract, it makes some sense to construe citizens as voluntarily granting authority in return for which the ruler pledges to protect them and to do other things for them that they cannot do for themselves. Where citizens accept a ruler's authority because he terrorizes or threatens them, we can still speak of a coerced contract. The ruler offers, on his side, release from terror and injury; and the intimidated offer, on their side, to obey.

Hierarchy and Bureaucracy

In the most familiar—but not the most frequent—pattern of authority in both private and governmental organizations, an official exercises authority over immediate subordinates, each of whom then exercises it over his own subordinates, and so on down to the bottom of a ladder. A hierarchical or pyramidal structure appears to achieve the efficiencies of a coordinated division of labor and functional specialization.

Pyramidal authority or hierarchy often shares certain characteristics that taken collectively are called bureaucracy. In both governmental and private organizations, bureaucracy is a powerful multipurpose tool. It routinizes problem solving to an extreme degree and frees it from dependence on any unusual skills or initiatives. For each category of problems, a bureaucracy stands ready to provide an appropriate category of solutions through an appropriate set of standardized skills. Specifically, its characteristics are:

1. Bureaucracy practices a high degree of specialization of tasks, on the assumption that specialization makes for efficiency (and at risk that it makes for narrow-minded functionaries who lose sight of the organization's purpose).
2. Each specialized authoritative assignment for a specific member or subunit is, more than in most other kinds of formal organization, prescribed in ways that make the discharge of function independent of the particular characteristics of the persons who hold office. In an ideal bureaucracy, no one is unique.
3. Problems, procedures, and solutions are all categorized. In a food rationing system, if I apply for an increase in my ration, I am asked to prove membership in an eligible category like the infirm, the aged, or nursing mothers.
4. Coordination of standardized assignments is considered to be a major task of those at the top (rather than their stimulation of the unique talents and resourcefulness of each of the participants).

5. A relatively stable structure of assignments and authority comes to be valued within the bureaucracy as necessary for organizational readiness (for whatever tasks may appear).
6. The organization therefore becomes to some degree an end in itself. Members of the bureaucracy will often develop loyalties to the organization stronger than their commitments to the particular ends of the organization. Rather than disband when polio is at last conquered, the March of Dimes bureaucracy looks for other diseases to fight. Freer to explore new functions than is a government bureaucracy, a corporate bureaucracy will take on increasingly diversified lines of production because officials prize the organization as an instrument of such great value that appropriate duties must be found for it.
7. Yet each bureaucracy tends to develop its own style and thereafter can only be bent so far, only partly adapted, to new tasks. Despite the availability of ostensibly appropriate old bureaucracies, high-level decision makers must therefore often create new bureaucracies to attack new tasks.
8. There is, consequently, no ideal structure for the many departments and branches of government; administrative reform is endless.[16]

Although hierarchy and bureaucracy are ancient in origin, in the contemporary world man is organized into bureaucracy as never before. In the early nineteenth century, four out of five Americans were self-employed; the number is now less than one in ten. Assuming all but the smallest corporations are bureaucratically organized, over half the gainfully employed work in bureaucracies. Another 13 million Americans work in the thousands of bureaucratic organizations that make up the federal government, fifty state governments, and 78,000 units of local government. Millions of people are also members of bureaucratically organized labor unions, employer groups, fraternal orders, veterans associations, and farm organizations; and their children are encouraged to sample bureaucracy in the Scouts and Little Leagues. Some of these bureaucracies are enormous. By numbers employed, the largest in the United States is the Defense Department with over a million civilian employees (and another 2 million in the armed forces), followed by American Telephone and Telegraph and General Motors, each with roughly 800,000.[17]

An unplanned revolution has been brought about by men who, without making a political issue out of their dimly perceived intentions, drew most of the work force out of small farming and small enterprise into the authority relations of the modern bureaucratic enterprise. It is a revolution that in industrialized systems has fundamentally changed the work patterns and other forms of human interdependence for most of the gainfully employed. Not a revolution pursued for egalitarian, democratic, or other humane motives, its motives are profit and power; and it succeeds for no more lofty reason than efficiency. But it is no less a revolution for that. It has altered politico-economic organization more than the French, the Bolshevik, or Mao's revolution. And it has established a new order in the U.S.S.R. and China no less than in the West.[18]

We shall see that both in communist systems and in the West the revolution has by now motivated a counterrevolution, in which are joined, remarkably, Yugoslav practitioners of worker self-management, Maoist energizers of the masses, Western advocates of participatory democracy, a new wave of professional industrial psychologists, and both corporations and unions now experimenting with alternatives to the assembly line. Although mankind has known bureaucracies for at least 3,000 years— from Hammurabi down to the modern nation-state, public school, and corporation—some people, we shall see, anticipate its disappearance from the earth, its replacement by forms of cooperation in which "people will be differentiated not vertically, according to rank and role, but flexibly and functionally. . . ."[19]

Mutual Adjustment among Authorities

Although habit of thought associates authority with hierarchy, the habit needs to be broken, for authority is probably more often than not exercised in other than a hierarchical pattern.

Certainly the pyramidal pattern is often imperfect. For example, the pyramid may have no apex. At the top are several or many authorities, interacting as members of a governing board, sometimes each with authority over a specialized group of subordinates. For a government as a whole, an apex is unusual. Mao was able to operate as an apex authority only for short periods of time, if at all. In democratic governments, authority is divided among a plurality of officials—a chief executive, members of a legislature, and sometimes a judiciary.

Some officials are outside the lines of pyramidal or hierarchical authority. The specialized authority of budget, personnel, or security officials cuts across the hierarchical lines of authority constituting the pyramid. Speer tells us that Hitler was thwarted by pension office bureaucrats in repeated attempts to qualify for a more liberal pension. Even in an ostensibly democratic system, a police department sometimes uses harassment, blackmail, and assassination to establish authority over its hierarchical superiors.

Interdependence—if not outright conflict—among authorities at any one level often requires mutual adjustment among them, as in the hundreds of interagency and interministerial coordinating committees of the U.S. and British governments. Mutual adjustment will sometimes be disorganizing, will create conflicts rather than solve them. Yet it carries much of the load of coordination in any government. For a hundred years during the nineteenth century the major world powers lived at relative peace with each other because they worked out effective mutual adjustment among themselves to settle their conflicts. In metropolitan areas, a complexity of governmental authorities is coordinated through mutual adjustment. In the New York City area, for example, the two state governments of New York and New Jersey, the city governments in the metropolitan area, and other specialized bodies like the Port of New York Authority work out their conflicts and arrange cooperation, in the absence of an authoritative overseer, through mutual adjustment among themselves.

Sometimes an authority adjusts to another by giving way. At an extreme one official may completely defer to another official, even going so far as to announce his allegiance or loyalty to him. Short of that, he may push only those activities that do not interfere with the work of another official. More often, officials actively exercise authority and other control over each other—for example, compelling the cooperation of another agency by threatening noncooperation on its projects. And for many reasons, lower authorities achieve influence, control, or power of some sort over higher. Superiors need advice from subordinates, or their willing cooperation, which they can win only by giving in to them on some issues. Or through the extended use of his authority, an official gains control over his superior.

In mutual adjustment among officials, all kinds of controls are practiced, including exchange and persuasion. Especially noteworthy, however, is the use of threats and other manipulation carefully designed to control particular officials. We might call these controls ad hoc to distinguish them from more routine controls such as issuing authoritative orders. Although officials cannot take the trouble to design ad hoc control for each citizen, they can design them for more important targets—each other. The U.S. Treasury and the Federal Reserve Board, for example, have often been in conflict over the short-term rate of interest. At one time the Treasury's strategy was to frustrate the Board's attempts to increase the rate by itself making early announcements of the rate at which it would undertake new borrowing. That left the Board in the position of going along with the Treasury decisions or facing widespread criticism for refusing to support the market for U.S. bonds on the Treasury's terms.[20] Mutual control among officials is thus even more intricate than officials' control over the population.

Reciprocal Obligation among Authorities

At any one time, an authority is locked into a network of obligations that requires him to use his authority to do favors for other officials who have used their authority to do him favors. And conversely he initiates favors for other officials in order to put them under obligation to him. When he initiates this distinctive and ubiquitous form of mutual adjustment, an official does not offer a contingent measured benefit to induce a response, as in an ordinary exchange of favors. Nor does he negotiate or bargain over the actual terms of an exchange. Instead he uses his authority to confer a favor, knowing that he has thereby created an obligation for a reciprocal favor sometime in the future, the exact character and size of which remains uncertain.*

Doing favors is like putting money in the bank. In 1969, Senator Clinton Anderson supported President Nixon in the antiballistic missile controversy. "Long-time observers of Anderson's activities speculated that he had won an IOU from the Administration that would fall due when he wanted some specific program for his constituency."[21] One can accumulate a vast store of credits. Some of them will be canceled by an unanticipated or unwanted return of favors. But the obligations sometimes also permit an official to ask for specified favors from those who owe him obligations. On these reciprocal obligations alliances are also built.

That reciprocal obligation is the foundation for extremely powerful controls is attested to by the frequency with which it corrupts public officials. Drawing on his own experience in the U.S. Senate, Senator Paul Douglas commented on reciprocal obligation between the public official and the private party, who also enter into mutual control. Of the latter, he said:

> He tries . . . by a series of favors to put the public official under such feeling of personal obligation that the latter gradually loses his sense of mission to the public and comes to feel that his first loyalties are to his private benefactors and patrons. What happens is a gradual shifting of a man's loyalties from the community to those who have been doing him favors.[22]

* * *

* A norm of reciprocity is perhaps "no less universal and important an element of culture than the incest taboo. . . ." It is recognized in Cicero's "There is no duty more indispensable than that of returning a kindness . . ." and Hobhouse's ". . . reciprocity . . . is the vital principle of society. . . ." (Alvin Gouldner, "The Norm of Reciprocity," *American Sociological Review* 25 [April 1960]: 161ff. See also his references to Becker, Thurnwald, Homans, Levi-Strauss, Firth, Durkheim, Marx, Mauss, Malinowski, von Wiese, and others.)

Hypothetically, we can say in partial summary, large-scale politico-economic organization is possible either through unilateral coordination in hierarchy-bureaucracy or through mutual adjustment among authorities who practice an extended use of their authority in order to control each other. One of the most common forms of mutual adjustment, but of a distinctively different kind, is exchange. Exchange in market systems, we shall now see, is another control system representing, compared to government, an extreme of mutual adjustment, and one in which most of the population engages.

3

Exchange and Markets

NO LESS than Mao in our time, Adam Smith in his day voiced a swelling antagonism to hierarchy and bureaucracy. As though shaking his head, he wrote of Louis XIV's great minister Colbert: "The industry and commerce of a great country he endeavored to regulate upon the same model as the departments of a public office."[1] *The Wealth of Nations* remains the classical argument that doing so is a mistake of such magnitude as to keep nations poor.

Historically the alternative to governmentalization of a national politico-economic system has been the market. And just as hierarchical, bureaucratic, and governmental systems arise from the authority relation, so market systems arise from the simple exchange relation.

Simple and Complex Exchange

The exchange relation on which markets are built is one of deliberate control. It is a relation between two (or sometimes more) persons each of whom offers a benefit in order to induce a response. The offer is, therefore, contingent on achieving the response.* A benefit is anything that the

---

* Exchange of positive benefits, with each offer contingent on receipt of a specified benefit, is an identifiable specific form of control. The same word "exchange" is some-

recipient perceives to be desirable, whether he perceives correctly or not.* In the simplest exchange, two people stumble onto the knowledge that each has or can do something that the other wants. Or one person finds that another person has or can do something he wants, and he casts about to find a benefit that he can offer to the other in order to induce the other to do as he wishes. Not merely a method for reshuffling the possession of things, exchange is a method of controlling behavior and of organizing cooperation among men. On the eighteenth- and nineteenth-century American frontier, exchange of services organized men to clear land and build barns. Exchange also recruited the energies which dug the Suez Canal, put men on the moon, and all but eliminated cholera from the earth, and which plow and continue to harvest the most productive of earth's acres.

A few fanciful possibilities aside, people will lack the capacity to grant (or withhold) a benefit unless rules grant it to them. Rules do so. In the form of laws on personal liberty and property, rules specify that people have authority to control their own labor and can claim certain assets as their own to withhold from or grant to other persons. And exchange is possible only in a society in which a moral code and authority keep social peace.

Money and Prices

Exchange can hardly become a significant method of social organization, however, if exchanges are only occasional and fortuitous. A weekly assembly for barter or the posting of public notices increases the frequency of exchange only modestly. Only with money and prices can exchange become the instrument of major instead of occasional very small-scale social organization. Prices are a device for declaring in standardized form the terms on which exchange is offered or consummated. With prices, it

---

times used by social scientists to embrace the exchange of words and other symbols, of injuries as well as benefits, and of the unspecified and delayed favors traded in networks of reciprocal obligation—indeed anything and everything that can be imagined in an interaction between people. On such a broad view of exchange, all human interaction is exchange. For one influential broader concept, see George C. Homans, "Social Behavior as Exchange," *American Journal of Sociology* 63 (May 1958). See also Peter Blau, *Exchange and Power in Social Life* (New York: John Wiley & Sons, 1964).

* Suppose A offers B the benefit of *not* injuring him if B does as he wishes? Is that a benefit to B? It is not a benefit to B if measured against his welfare if he and A had no relation at all with each other. The operative control is A's threat, not a benefit. For our purposes exchange is limited to exchanges of benefits other than those which consist of no more than the removal of threats and injuries that the parties would otherwise employ.

is no longer necessary for a person to announce tediously to each of many potential partners in exchange each of the services and commodities, together with the amounts of each, that he stands ready to take in exchange for his offer. He simply announces its price.

Without money and prices, exchange is obstructed by the need for a double coincidence: A has to find a B who has or can do just what he wants and B has to want just what A has to offer. What we ordinarily call money we easily care for, transport, and exchange. Because, therefore, almost anyone will take it in exchange and offer it in exchange, the need for coincidence vanishes, and exchange opportunities grow beyond count.

Although I am willing to watch my neighbor's house during his absence in return for his some day doing the same for me, I am unlikely to sell my services as a watchman to anyone. Nor can some people bring themselves to buy or sell a child. Yet the range of benefits exchanged for money is almost unlimited. Such an intangible as commercial "goodwill" is bought and sold. Loyalty, subservience, public recognition, votes, judicial decisions, party nominations—all are sometimes for sale, legally or not. Market exchange reaches into every aspect of life, with still unfold-. ing consequences.

Specialized Traders

With the help of money, another elaboration of exchange—the participation of the specialized trader—makes possible extraordinarily long chains of exchange relations. The trader sees the possibility of making a living—possibly a fortune—through making exchange his occupation rather than an occasional convenience. Americans want coffee from Colombian coffee growers, who in turn want various manufactured goods. Even with money, a direct exchange is impossible. Instead Colombian coffee growers sell to a trader, who is willing to buy because he knows that an American processor will buy from him. The processor will buy because he knows that a wholesaler will buy—and so on eventually to the American consumer.

The professional or full-time trader who makes it his business to provide an exchange "partner" for someone who needs one is identified by modest names like merchant, shipper, jobber, wholesaler—even used-car dealer and junk man. But some traders are great organizers. In the second millennium B.C., Babylonian merchants in both domestic and foreign trade laid a foundation for an emerging urban Mesopotamian society. New chains of market linkages have ever since effected major social change. In fourteenth to sixteenth centuries, just such long chains of linkages, created largely by merchants in a few dozen cities of Europe, especially those of northern Italy, organized Western Europe for the first time into an integrated economy, achieving a continental coordination still not even approximated in government.[2]

The Business Enterprise

One particular kind of specialized trader further transforms the exchange system—categorically and drastically. He does not simply facilitate a wider ranging exchange of existing commodities and tasks. Unlike the merchant who sells what he buys, this trader buys or hires inputs, organizes a production process, and then in turn sells the resulting products and services. He deals in human and other energies, seeking tasks to be done and organizing people to do them. He consequently becomes a leader, supervisor, or director of other men (indeed, sometimes a despotic one). If his enterprise is large, he—the entrepreneur—becomes in fact a kind of public official, though not a government or political official.

An entrepreneur exercises authority within a market system. In a limiting case, he can organize a labor force without asking his workers to accept his authority, for, like the organizers of the putting-out system of eighteenth-century England, he can simply pay workers for products of their labor. Or he can minimize his authority over them by putting them in his own workplace but paying exclusively by piecework, thus leaving speed and style of work for each worker to decide by himself. Overwhelmingly, however, an entrepreneur finds it efficient to pay employees neither for their products nor for specific tasks determined in advance. Instead he pays them to accept his authority for the duration of the working day, week, or month.

It is this specialist in the market system—the entrepreneur—who, even more than the trader or merchant, brings formal organizations into the market, and sometimes these organizations are extremely large. From the seventeenth through the nineteenth centuries, European entrepreneurs engaged in putting two resources to work on a scale never before attempted: machines of great variety, made possible by accelerated science and engineering; and coal as a source of power to run them. Just as the organization of the mines called for organized business enterprises, so also did the man-machine coordination necessary to take advantage of the productive potential of the new machines.

More than that, in the search for raw materials and customers for their outputs, these enterprises forged market links with every inhabited continent. In the eighteenth and nineteenth centuries for the first time in man's history the world finally became an integrated whole—not in language or government or culture but in coordination of work and use of the world's resources. In each inhabited continent, millions of people performed services for, and received benefits from, a large number of people in every other continent. Accordingly, in about 1900 for the first time in history millions of the world's inhabitants—the Western Europeans and North Americans—left illiteracy, plague, and famine behind them. Whatever may be said about colonialism and imperialism and the continued suffering of those millions left out of the new order, this first global integration represented a new level and complexity of social organization.*

The Three-Market System

The rise of the entrepreneur and the entrepreneurial organization transforms a once homogeneous kind of exchange into three distinct forms. People no longer directly exchange their labor or other assets for what they want to eat, wear, use, or otherwise enjoy. Instead they enter into one set of markets—the labor market and other factor markets—to offer their energies and assets for money. They enter into a second set of markets —consumer markets—to exchange that money for desired goods and services. Because in each of these two sets of markets they face a business enterprise, the enterprise sits astride the whole market system, a momentous development in social organization the implications of which are not yet wholly revealed.

In a third set of markets, business enterprises buy and sell with each other. In these intermediate markets, from which both individual consumers and individual suppliers are excluded, exchange is usually larger in volume than in the other two combined. Retailers enter into exchange with wholesalers and jobbers, who in turn do so with manufacturers. Manufacturing enterprises buy from other enterprises that supply component parts, raw materials, electric power, and business services, including accounting, equipment maintenance, and advertising. It is, incidentally, only this third set of markets, not the other two, that "planned" systems like that of the Soviet Union usually disestablish.

Just as government officials are distinguished from ordinary citizens, enterprise managers are distinguished from ordinary consumers and employees. In the market system, leaders or "officials" are further marked off from ordinary participants when formal organizations other than the enterprise become participants. In many market systems, trade union leaders take over the main tasks of negotiating wages and working conditions. And government officials, representing the military services,

* The internationalism of the market system is now greatly supplemented by the internationalization of the corporate bureaucracies within the market system, in the form of multinational corporations, which account for perhaps 15 percent of world gross product.

public works departments, and other government agencies, become major purchasers in market systems.

Related Forms of Control

Although market exchange is our main interest in this chapter, exchange is commonplace outside the market. It is, we have already seen, common in politics. A legislator, for example, offers to support his colleague's bill if his colleague will reciprocate by supporting him on his own bill. Often confused with exchange is another form of control that resembles it: an unconditional grant of a benefit intended to produce a response, but without the conditional quid pro quo of exchange. A tax reduction, for example, is an unconditional benefit to businesses who profit from it, and it may produce a response. But it is not offered only to those who promise a response. In the complex workings of the unconditional granting of benefits we shall find in later chapters a method of control that in some systems bids fair to rival exchange, authority, and persuasion in its central importance for politico-economic organization.

In Perspective

In *The New Industrial State*, some ambiguities in Galbraith's analysis may account for his being read as saying that exchange in the United States has been replaced by corporate authority as the principal coordinator of economic life.* It is either bad reading or bad writing. The big corporations are clearly not generally coordinated by a government plan or any other overarching governmental direction, but through market exchanges. They dispose of most of their products by selling. They get most of what they need for their productive processes by buying. If a firm's production plan requires a certain mixture of inputs—of labor of various grades, of electric power, of raw materials, of partially fabricated inputs and parts—they are drawn to the enterprise (and are drawn away from

---

* His specific points on decline of market are growth of vertical integration of firms, of market control by firms, and of long-term contracting. These points identify certain areas in which enterprise authority accomplishes what otherwise would be accomplished through exchange, but they do not establish the fact of a general decline in exchange and market, let alone the end or displacement of the market. They show only that in a sea of exchange some of the islands of authority are large. J. K. Galbraith, *The New Industrial State*, 2nd ed. (Boston: Houghton Mifflin, 1971).

other enterprises) not by a coordinating authority of any kind, private or public, but by purchase in an interlocked set of markets. And if, say, the total demands of American businesses for labor are roughly consistent with total supplies, the consistency is achieved through the selling and buying of labor, not through a manpower plan. (If the consistency is not quite so tight as one would wish—if, in short, there is unemployment—it is because market exchange is far from ideally efficient.) Corporations indeed employ authority for their "domestic" affairs—each is an authority system internally; but they conduct their "foreign relations" through buying and selling on the market.

It is easy to overlook the coordinating functions of market systems, so much do we take them for granted. Constant occupational reassignment is an example. In a seven-year period in the United States the number of airline stewardesses doubled; and stenographers, typists, and social workers went up 50 percent. At the same time, locomotive firemen fell by one-half, electrotypers and cabinetmakers fell by a third, and hundreds of other occupations rose or fell as much as 20 percent.[3] In a ten-year period in Britain, the number of workers in coal mining and cotton fell by more than a quarter, while in certain other occupations, including sports and entertainment, employment doubled; in still others, it trebled.[4] In a never-ending reshuffling of labor, consumer and occupational preferences are reconciled.

In describing how millions of buyers and sellers, each bent on nothing more than finding his own opportunities for exchange, give rise to a vast system of mutual coordination, Adam Smith, in his most famous passage, wrote that the individual is "led by an invisible hand to promote an end which was no part of his intention." Ever since then it has become common to speak of market forces as automatic, and sometimes as unconscious. The hint of mystery is unfortunate; there is nothing mystical about Smith's view of the world. All social controls have elements of the automatic, unintended, and unconscious. Most parents "automatically" teach their offspring to speak, whether they intend to, or are conscious of doing so, or not. In market life men are deliberate and conscious; but their acts accomplish feats of coordination of which they are not necessarily conscious and which they do not intend.

Coordination is achieved only at a price, however. A hypothetical pure unmodified market system would be extraordinary—and intolerable—in that it would strip the individual of all but one claim on other members of the society. He could not ask for their help in distress as he can in traditional premarket systems in which he is an accepted member of the tribe or clan and deserves their compassion. In a pure market system his claim on others would be established if and only if he had something to offer in exchange. Marx understood this earlier and better than most of us. In

The Communist Manifesto he observed that the market "resolved personal worth into exchange value"; it "has left no other bond between man and man than naked self-interest, than callous 'cash payment.'"

Although early nineteenth-century England and other countries at other times displayed some of the characteristics of just such a "satanic mill,"[5] all over the world market systems are intertwined in varying degrees with other methods of organization to soften the severity of market system alone. Even in early nineteenth-century England, the heyday of laissez-faire, both poor laws and private charity acknowledged the need for some minimum other than market claims.

Efficiency Pricing

It can be shown that, on certain assumptions, market exchanges approximate a certain kind of optimality or efficiency simply because people will have entered into exchange when they gain from it and otherwise not. A wrong set of prices, however, will block an efficient exchange. The idea of efficient pricing familiar to every economist is therefore indispensable to an understanding of market systems (as well as, subsequently, of communist systems, in which pricing problems are severe).

Suppose that I need food and you need the use of my muscles. You have grown some potatoes, and I have time on my hands. We agree on a price: if for an hour I help you, you will give me ten pounds of potatoes. We make the exchange, and we are consequently both better off. Suppose, however, that a government decree had intervened to require that no one offer an hour of his labor for less than twenty pounds of potatoes. You would rather keep your potatoes than surrender twenty pounds of them for one hour's work from me. So you decide to go without my help and I therefore go without the food. We are both worse off than we might have been.

In the language of theoretical economics the price that reflects our preferences is called an efficiency price, and the price that frustrated us is called arbitrary. An efficiency price is efficient for both of us. It is also called a scarcity price; it corresponds to your appraisal and mine of relative scarcities. To me, potatoes are more scarce than labor time; to you the labor time is more scarce. The agreed price is not dictated by weight, density, or any physical quality of the potatoes but by our preferences, which are preferences with respect to uses to be made of our scarce resources.

Look carefully at our thwarted exchange. One consequence of the arbitrary price is that although I stand ready to offer my labor to you, you are not willing to take it. That price fails to clear the market. Hence, one requirement for an efficiency or scarcity price is that it be such as to clear the market.

Strictly speaking, however, an efficiency or scarcity price is not defined when a single buyer or very few buyers face a single seller or very few sellers, since they might be able to do business with each other at any one of a number of prices. A price that blocks exchange among willing exchangers is clearly not an efficiency price, but which of the various prices that do not block it is the efficiency price? An answer sufficient for all purposes at this point is that the efficiency price is the price that would be established if sellers and buyers became so numerous that no single buyer or seller could manipulate the price.

One consequence of an arbitrary price is that you are informed that an hour's labor is available at the cost to you of twenty pounds of potatoes, although in fact at least one person is willing to make his labor available for half that cost. The arbitrary price misrepresents to you the cost (or alternative to be foregone) at which, but for the imposed price, you could have what you want. Hence a further criterion for efficiency or scarcity pricing is that each price correctly inform buyers and sellers of the cost (the foregone alternatives) at which goods and services can in fact be provided if people are free to make such offers as they wish.

What is a scarcity or efficiency price for a product made and sold by a business enterprise? Again, one that will clear the market and is not monopolistically controlled. It is a price not so low as to create a body of willing customers for whom supplies are inadequate nor so high as to finance the production of outputs for which there are no willing buyers. It is, again, also a price not so high as to overstate or so low as to understate the terms or costs at which the good or service can actually be made available if people are free to make whatever offers they wish. Thus it should not fall short of or exceed the sum of the various costs incurred in production.* But how is each of the costs to be measured? The answer is that each input has to be valued in the calculation of total costs according to its own scarcity price.

An enterprise selling price that is not an efficiency price puts the enter-

---

* The two conditions for pricing by an enterprise can be shown to be consistent with each other only if a third condition is met: that the enterprise expand production whenever sales can be made at prices higher than the cost of additional output and contract it whenever selling prices do not cover costs. That is of course just what a competitive enterprise will tend to do, because so doing will maximize its profits.

prise in the position of offering customers a product or service at a price less than or more than its marginal cost. If less than marginal cost, then the enterprise is offering the commodity or service even though the value of the inputs at the margin (as indicated by their use in alternative lines of production) is greater than the value of the output. If more than cost, then customers are in effect told that production uses up more real resources than is in fact the case. In either case, misinformation causes poor choices.

Approximations to efficiency prices can be established either through the play of demand and supply in competitive markets or by a price-setting authority. It is not who sets them or how that determines whether they are efficiency prices, but whether their levels meet or fail the three criteria.

Look at the rationale of scarcity or efficiency prices from the point of view of a hypothetical central planner. He will know that society needs, say, steel, foodstuffs, and transport services. But how much of each ought to be produced he cannot even begin to think about sensibly unless he knows trade-off ratios, because production of each can be expanded only by constricting the others. He needs to know, for example, what value of steel production has to be foregone in order to expand transport services by a given amount.

The trade-offs can be represented in prices. To say that steel costs $400 a ton is to say that $400 of other products have to be sacrificed to get a ton of steel. Prices that correctly represent the actual trade-off possibilities are efficiency or scarcity prices; any other prices are called arbitrary.

For measuring trade-offs, could such a planner simply assign a number (a price) to each unit of a commodity that corresponds to its tonnage, its length, or, in the case of personal services, the height in inches of the persons performing them? Prices of that sort, we would say, are obviously ridiculous. But why are they? Because weight or size of inputs is not related to cost: a ton of steel is worth less than three ounces of complicated electronic equipment. Why? Because much more labor goes into the electronic equipment? Then let the planner assign numbers or prices that accord with the amount of labor put into products.

If he does that, he will give the same number or price to two commodities that have equal labor inputs, even if one requires for its production enormously more equipment than does the other. That is just as unsatisfactory as pricing by weight without regard to labor input. It looks, then, as though he needs a number that combines a reflection of materials, labor, mechanical equipment used, and any other inputs used in production. He needs a common denominator for all of them.

What is the efficient way of combining the different inputs into a common denominator number or price? Should an hour of labor count for more or less than a pound of steel? More than five pounds of steel? A hundred pounds? The correct number—the efficiency price—depends not on any physical attribute but on the relative values of the inputs. But what does that mean?

It means that to the degree that an input can produce desired outputs elsewhere it is valuable and should be counted in that degree in the common denominator. At the extreme, if an input cannot produce any other desired outputs, it is not a valuable input—it is a free good—and should not be counted in the common denominator. How desirable other outputs are will depend on user preferences in relation to scarcity, including their preferences for leisure. Efficiency prices will therefore represent the preference-scarcity relation. To the degree to which real-world market systems approximate efficiency prices, their prices will represent that relation.

Inequality

Certain elementary connections between market system and common social values need a preliminary characterization at this point. No belief about market systems is more common, for example, than that they make a few men rich at the cost of poverty for many. On this score alone many of the new nations, we shall see, count very little on markets to aid their growth. By departures from the market system, Cuba and China have moved toward equality of income and wealth. Are market systems prevented by some internal logic from so doing?

Clearly a hypothetical pure form of market system would be highly inegalitarian in income earned through wages, rents, interests and profits, since every person's income would depend solely on what he could and would offer in exchange, and people differ in what they can offer. Real-world market systems, all modified by taxes and other redistributive devices, are another story. Neither logic nor empirical evidence shows the impossibility—even the improbability—of reconciling a real-world market system with a greatly more egalitarian distribution of wealth and income.[6]

It has sometimes been argued a priori that if income differentials are reduced, we will all lose our motive to be productive. A priori, that result is no more likely than its opposite: when extra income becomes harder to get, a person may work harder to get it.[7] What a person actually will do depends on the pattern of his work-leisure choice; and that in turn depends on culture, personality, and many specific patterns of social and job organization that bear on incentives.[8]

Empirical evidence reveals no clear association between degrees of income inequality and differences in work habits, or diligence. The more egalitarian market systems of Scandinavia, for example, do not show productivity losses when compared with the relatively more inegalitarian United States. Nor can we find in responses to decades of increasingly severe income taxation evidence of declining managerial incentives. Like other British, German, and American studies, an interview study of almost a thousand high-income Americans concluded:

> Seven-eighths of the high-income respondents explicitly stated that they had not curtailed their work effort on account of the income tax. Many of the tax disincentives reported by the remaining respondents seemed implausible in the light of other information.[9]

This evidence supports the hypothesis that high-income people are more motivated by the "scores" they make—their pretax income—than by the actual disposable income they receive.[10] Such a hypothesis opens up the revolutionary possibility that a market-oriented system might preserve work incentives through "scoreboard" incomes even though taxation wholly equalized disposable income.

Even if it could be established that a reduction of income inequality does in fact reduce work incentives, that would not prove the impossiblity of reconciling a market system with equalization of income. It would only demonstrate that in such a reconciliation market production would decline, a result neither obviously bad nor obviously good. Insofar as productivity may already be declining, later chapters will show that dissatisfaction with authority in the workplace and cultural change—for example, the decline of the work ethic—go further to explain it than does income equalization.

Historically, all societies, market or not, have preserved economic inequality. The barrier to greater income and wealth equality in real-world market-oriented systems is not any internal logic. It is instead, we shall see, a historically inherited and politically maintained inequality in individual assets, earning power, and income shares. In England, for example, the rise of the market system was accompanied and supported by enclosure movements that drove peasants off the land, leaving as future participants in the market system a well-to-do gentry and an impoverished working class. In principle, governments can redistribute income and wealth and repeat the redistribution as frequently as wished. Their disinclination to do so requires a political explanation rather than reference to market forces.

Liberty

The classical liberal case for market systems declares: Liberty through the market; no liberty without.[11] True? No one understands market systems until he appreciates how many good, though conflicting, answers can be given to that simple question. Beginning with parental control in infancy, no one ever escapes social control. "Freedom" and "liberty" denote situations in which controls are not absent but are in some sense acceptable.* Whether, then, the market supports freedom raises questions about its characteristic forms of control.

According to the liberal† argument in the tradition of Locke, Smith, the Mills, Spencer, and Dicey, in a market system one responds—for example, takes a particular job—only if the proffered benefits are attractive, hence only if one voluntarily chooses to do so. In an authority system one is required to work where assigned and obey any other command regardless of benefit. As some people see it, no more needs to be said to prove men freer in markets than in authority systems.‡

An immediate objection to that line of argument is that it simply ignores the effect of a transaction on persons not a party to it—those who must endure the smell of a new factory in the area, the noise of motorcycles breaking the quiet of their neighborhood, or the risk of accident in a nuclear power plant. In a market system, they make no free choice; these effects are imposed upon them.

Third-party or external effects aside, the argument does not hold even for the parties immediate to the transaction, who are regarded as voluntarily entering into exchange with each other. Let us see why.

Property

How much I can accomplish and how effectively I can protect myself through exchange depends in large part on what I own and can offer in

* Freedom and liberty are not synonymous with democracy, although certain kinds of freedoms are necessary to democracy, and democracy is necessary to certain kinds of freedoms.

† "Liberal in this book refers to the classical free-market individualism formulated largely in the eighteenth and nineteenth centuries, not twentieth-century reformism, though major components of the former carry over into the latter.

‡ The conventional liberal argument also holds that market liberties, together with the fragmentation of property and decision making that are characteristic of market systems, are necessary to political freedom and democracy, an allegation relevant to later chapters.

exchange. A hidden assumption in the conventional argument is that private property, on which exchange rests, does not itself constitute a barrier to freedom and is, in addition, noncoercively established and perpetuated. If one imagines a small society sharing assets collectively which is then transformed, by assignment of every asset to some one individual, into a society practicing exchange among owners of private property—and with grossly unequal distribution of the assets to individuals—it is not at all obvious that free exchange makes (or leaves) the less propertied members of that society free. And if the move from collective to private ownership is imposed by strong men who forcibly take the lion's share of the assets, clearly no simple argument leads to the conclusion that subsequent exchanges among them, however free, make those who have little property free. Nor if we are all born into a world in which property rights are already assigned, as indeed they are, does it follow that exchange supports our freedom unless we own a great deal.

This objection to the liberal argument does not depend on how in actual fact private property was historically established, how it is in fact maintained, or whether it is a good institution. The objection rests on logic. The traditional liberal argument is incomplete unless it defends private property as itself consistent with freedom, a point on which it is silent.[12] It is simply blind to the implications for freedom of Proudhon's "Property is theft!" as well as to implications of less extreme interpretations of how property is established and maintained.*

Another way to put the point is this. In liberal thought a world of exchange is conflict-free. Everyone does what he wishes. When all social coordination is through voluntary exchange, no one imposes his will on anyone else. But how, we ask, can such a happy state be possible? It is possible only because the conflicts over who gets what have already been settled through a distribution of property rights in the society. Was that distribution conflict-free? Obviously not. Was it noncoercively achieved? Obviously not. The distribution of wealth in contemporary England, for example, is a consequence of centuries of conflict, including Viking raids, the Norman Conquest, the early authority of Crown and nobility, two waves of dispossession of agricultural labor from the land, and the law of inheritance.

---

* Formally, the same objection can be brought against the liberal position that, leaving property aside, exchange of services makes men free because they will respond through exchange of services only when they voluntarily choose to do so. Some distribution of skills among persons would make some men greatly dependent on others— for an extreme example, if only a few persons could fight and thus defend themselves and others. The favored persons could extract, as a price for their services, concessions from the others inconsistent with their freedom, however freedom is defined. Again, whether historically this is or is not the case, the liberal argument simply fails to examine the implications for freedom of distribution of skills.

Authority in Exchange

In developed market systems, most gainfully employed people in fact spend their working hours in an authority system—typically an organized business enterprise. The consequent threat to freedom is all the more obvious in large corporations: an organization in which a few men command thousands of others in the standardized patterns of bureaucracy does not nourish freedom. Libertarians reply that employees accepting managerial authority are still free because they voluntarily accept that authority and are free to terminate it. Then whether authority permits men to be free depends on whether people choose to enter the authority system? If so, the liberal argument that men are free in exchange and unfree in authority systems is destroyed; it all depends.

It might be argued that the authority of the state, unlike employer authority, is invariably imposed by threat rather than voluntarily accepted. Although some citizens see all governmental authority in that light, we have seen that others do not. They voluntarily authorize officials to issue commands and voluntarily establish a rule of obedience (even if they sometimes also wish to evade the authority once established).

Impersonal Coercion

The classical liberal argument also forgets a point from the history of thought. In the eyes of the classical economists one of the great virtues of the market was that it forced people to work. Naturally indolent, people have to be coerced to work either by the force of law or, through the market system, by the "silent, unremitted pressure" of hunger.[13]

Those who identify market with freedom introduce a distinction at this point: Freedom is abridged only when one person can compel another to do his bidding. In a market system, no particular person compels anyone else to work. People are compelled to work only by the impersonal requirements of the system. For that matter, most people would probably argue that any social system must require that able-bodied adults work. That they must do so in market systems is hardly distinctive.

Livelihood

Yet when livelihood is at stake in exchange, as it has been in all market systems so far in history, personal coercion adds to impersonal. If jobs are scarce, anyone who has a job to offer can coerce job applicants: can compel a kickback of wages or personal services, a contribution to a political party, or a coercive relation on the job itself, among other possibilities. If coercion is rampant in labor markets with severe unemployment, even in years of "full" employment jobs in the right place and of the right kind are not so plentiful as to eliminate some of its forms. Only in a market system in which all persons are provided, through money income, with a generous basic livelihood whether they work or not would these coercive possibilities in exchange vanish.

Coercion through Termination of Exchange

The classical liberal argument postulates a population not yet engaged in economic cooperation and asks how they might be organized. By being drawn into mutually advantageous voluntary exchanges. Does such a method of organization impair their liberties? Not at all, for each enters into exchange for his own advantage, hence voluntarily. Societies, however, are in fact already organized through markets. How, then, today and tomorrow as needs change over time, are people drawn out of old assignments or tasks and into new ones? How does economic organization continuously adapt to changing circumstances? In two ways. First, by the opening up of new mutually advantageous exchange possibilities into which people move voluntarily. Second, by the termination by one party or another of existing exchange relations (for example, termination of jobs by a corporation).

The second method, terminations, is coercive. People must move, leave their homes, change their occupations—any of a number of possible major changes, none of their choosing. In addition the mere threat of termination can be as constraining, as coercive, as menacing as an authoritative governmental command. A person whose style of life and family livelihood have for years been built around a particular job, occupation or location finds a command backed by a threat to fire him indistinguishable in many consequences for his liberty from a command backed by the police and the courts.

In most societies the law broadly prohibits one person from inflicting injury on another: prohibits, for example, physical assault, theft, libel, and conspiracy to injure. Even threats are illegal. But it leaves one great exception: injury through termination of an exchange relation. It is easy to see why it must allow that exception if a market system is to persist. But it is an exception, one to which classical liberal theory on liberty seems blind.

Disparity in Attractiveness of Alternatives

Many of the coercive potentials in exchange can be subsumed under one generalization. Suppose A offers something of overwhelming value to B— say, a lifetime income—in return for which B must do something he abhors. Is he really free to refuse? Suppose A offers something that B must have—water when he is stranded in the desert—but at an exorbitant price. Is he not then coerced? Clearly freedom depends on the character of alternatives. The generalization, then, is that exchange best supports freedom when every party can choose among offers that do not greatly differ in value from each other or from no exchange at all.

The requirement can be met in either of two circumstances. One is that exchange is limited to small values (hence livelihood must not be at stake). The other is that, although important values are exchanged, no single act of exchange is greatly more advantageous to either party than other available exchange opportunities. In neither circumstance can anyone be coerced, since he can, without great loss to himself, easily refuse any offer.

Competition and Liberty

The second circumstance—no exchange opportunity is greatly more advantageous than any other—makes liberty depend on competition. On this the liberal argument is correct: liberty in market systems exists only if everyone is able to escape coercion at the hands of any one buyer or seller by turning to another. If that proposition holds out hope for enlarging man's freedom, it also tells us that poor labor markets stand as a worldwide enemy of freedom. Landless rural laborers in much of the world remain dependent for livelihood on land-owning employers too few to compete. That helps explain why, for example, during twenty-five years of democratic national government, millions of India's agricultural laborers often surrendered control of local government to the landlords, submitted to beatings and other indignities at their hands, and accepted exploitative work contracts.

Limited Capacity to Offer

Precisely why do inadequate labor markets count so heavily against freedom? For two interconnected reasons. One is, again that livelihood is at stake in market systems. The other is that hundreds of millions of people have nothing to offer in their pursuit of livelihood than their labor, an obvious truth the significance of which has long been obscured. Landless laborers, laborers without assets of any kind, must count on jobs alone to protect their freedoms in the market. So also millions of industrial workers. In a wealthy society like the United States, as of the early 1960s only about 3 percent of families had assets of as much as $50,000, and 75 percent had assets less than $5,000.[14]

Marx saw the staggering importance of that simple fact; classical liberal thought has been embarassed by it. Income-earning property is a bulwark of liberty only for those who have it!* Those who do not are vulnerable to coercion when jobs are scarce and insecure to the degree that jobs may become scarce. Unemployment compensation and other welfare programs are—by such a line of analysis—necessary to freedom in market societies.

Costliness of Control

Every attempt to control someone in an exchange system is costly because something of value has to be offered in order to induce the desired response. No one is in a position in which exercising control is easy and thoughtless, as it often is in an authority system, where the marginal cost of exercising control is often zero. In some authority systems indeed, we saw, authority can be maintained only by exercising it. Hence authority is sometimes costly not to use.

Pure Authority as an Extreme

One last perspective on liberty in market systems can be had in a view of a hypothetical national society without money and markets. Consider in such a system some characteristic problems in the allocation of housing to the population, for example. How to decide who gets what? Is every individual, regardless of age, to be allocated a room or some standard amount of floor space? Or is the allocation to depend on age and family structure? Is one's allocated space to be near one's place of employment, near one's friends and relatives, within a mixed socioeconomic group or within a stratified one? Or suppose one wishes to make a trip. Who is to be entitled to transportation? For what reasons? How often? By air or bus? Suppose that one wishes to publish a book or pamphlet. Who is to be allowed to call on the services of editors, typesetters, distributors, and shipping services? Who is to be allowed to play the role of artist, musician, publicist, clergyman, union organizer, or party official?

All these decisions, which the market leaves in the hands of individuals, must now be made by governmental authorities. Nothing we wish to do that requires expensive equipment, other resources, or help from others beyond the favors of family and friendship can be done without a request to and the cooperation of a government official. Call us free or not, in the absence of money and markets our way of living is transformed. For each of the decisions or results that we ourselves are accustomed to achieve

* The conventional liberal argument alleges, however, that because a system of private property disperses control over production, it guarantees the political liberties of the propertyless as well as the propertied (Friedrich A. Hayek, *Road to Serfdom*, Chicago: University of Chicago Press, 1944, p. 103). The allegation is silent on the effect of property on the market liberties of those who have very little of it or whose share of it they never voluntarily chose.

through exchange—dozens of decisions in a single day for any one person
—we must now ask for an official decision from a bureaucracy.

*　*　*

This, the most elementary outline of exchange and markets and their
operation in society, is only a beginning of the analysis of market-oriented
societies.

Persuasion and
Preceptoral Systems

Persuasion as a Control System

Not the gun but the word is the
symbol of authority. The most frequent governmental activities are talking, writing, listening, and reading. Persons in authority find themselves
barraged with persuasive communications—fact, analysis, entreaty, exhortation, and lies—and they reply in kind. They can also hunger for
information. An official who has to take a position on monetary policy,
for example, comes to depend on persons who can explain to him the
complexities of flows of money and credit. In endless hours of talk,
persuasion also carries much of the work load of mutual adjustment of
authorities to each other. Fact, analysis, idea, and misinformation achieve
their effects even when influence is unintended, simply because all of us
constantly react to our perceptions of the world around us.

Because man is a knowing animal, and culture an accumulation of
knowledge, persuasion touches not only authority systems but also every
aspect of man's behavior. While some scholars have described the political
system as a cybernetic system of communication and feedback,[1] others
have tried to characterize all human interaction as communication, or
persuasion broadly conceived.[2] Yet as a method of social control, per-

suasion does not appear to play the defining role in any complex system that exchange plays in market system or authority in government.

Later we shall examine its role in democratic government. Some interpreters of democracy—Lord Bryce, among them—have gone so far as to define democracy as "government by discussion," which might be taken as synonymous with government by persuasion. We shall also later take account of persuasion's great role in market systems in the form of commercial advertising.

Advertising, however, has arisen as only the first of two comprehensive programs of persuasion never seen until the twentieth century—both incessant, broadly targeted, and vast in the resources poured into them. The second is massive, centrally managed, and saturating political indoctrination. Persuasion of the second kind is a principal instrument of totalitarianism or—to avoid the controversies that have sprung up around the term—of systems characterized by extraordinary attempts of elites to establish authority so broad, so deep, so unconstrained as to require the emasculation of the authority of church, labor union, fraternal association, school—even family.[3] In this guise, persuasion comes closer to becoming the defining element of a whole system.

Almost 150 years ago Tocqueville predicted just such a system, not as a wild guess but by his reading of social mechanisms then at work in democratic society. That he could do so suggests that German and Italian fascism, far from being "accidents" unlikely to be repeated, are variants of a predictable pattern, of which communism is another. Along with communist states, the fascist systems may be forerunners of monolithic authoritarian systems yet to be spread over the globe. "An immense and tutelary power" will "extend its arm over the whole community." It "compresses, enervates, extinguishes, and stupefies a people."[4]

German and Italian fascism employed all the coercive forms of authority, including terror, against various ethnic and political minorities. But its control over the great masses is better described in Tocqueville's words, as "minute, regular, provident, and mild." It employed indoctrination to capture men's minds so that they would "willingly" do what harsher controls did not therefore need to compel. Nazism tried to suppress all alternative sources of persuasion and then through broadcasting and pageantry set out to mold the minds of its subjects. By virtue of number of radio sets and frequency of political broadcasts, Germany probably achieved more thorough radio coverage of its population than any other country of the time. In his first year in office, Hitler himself made as many as fifty broadcasts.[5] Small facts, but possibly the beginning of a new age yet to be unfolded.

Fascism is a form of authoritarian control suited to the age of democracy. Where citizens are educated, informed, and ambitious enough to press for democracy, as they were in Germany and Italy, it becomes necessary for authoritarian rulers to persuade them that they do not want it.[6] Old-fashioned methods that simply deny political demands no longer succeed. Not simply an alternative to democracy, fascism emerges as democracy's child. Had democratic demands and capacities never been aroused, fascism would never have been born. The central message of the fascist indoctrination against democracy is simple: obedience to unilateral authority, specifically obedience to one free will—that of the Leader.[7] In the Italian fascist motto, "Everything for the state, nothing against the state, no one outside the state."

As we shall see, the indoctrination programs of communist states also thwart popular aspiration, maintaining unilateral authority through the control of minds that would otherwise upset it. Yet communist persuasion differs from fascist. It does not unambiguously exalt unilateral authority. Instead it promises a democratic future. Nor does it exalt elitism. Instead it actively practices a reduction of inequalities on some fronts and promises it on some others. And it appeals, we shall see, far more than does fascist persuasion, to the rational in man. It does not exhort him, as in the phrase attributed to Hitler: to "Think with your blood!" Neither Lenin, Mao, Castro, nor the early Stalin was a Hitler. All spoke for egalitarian—and sometimes democratic—aspiration, as Hitler did not; and we have little ground for alleging more hypocrisy in their words than in those of a Churchill, a de Gaulle, or a Roosevelt.

We need therefore consider the possibility that a certain pattern of communist persuasion or indoctrination is genuinely different from fascist and is indicative of a fundamentally different view of man. Because persuasion has been singled out by Maoists as the major form of social control to be practiced in China, we need to examine it carefully and—for ease of further reference to it—give it a name. We shall call it, for lack of any existing name for it, a preceptoral system, from the word "preceptor," meaning teacher.*

The Preceptoral System

In idealized form, a preceptoral system is, in brief, massive highly unilateral persuasion in which a small enlightened governmental elite instructs the masses in much the same way that Rousseau advised teacher

* Following Tocqueville, we might have called it a tutelary system.

to educate child and imagined a "superior intelligence" transforming each individual.[8]

No highly developed preceptoral system is to be found in the world. It is only an imperfectly realized element of communist systems. It is more an aspiration than an accomplishment, more often a disguise for coercion—even terror—than an independent system of control. It was, however, the most distinctive and ideologically central element of Chinese communism under Mao, one that excited many people who had dismissed European communism as bureaucratic and repressive. Yet in such models of a new social order as communists have formulated, preceptoral and conventional authority systems are always mixed. The two models have been in conflict in China. If the Cultural Revolution was Mao's attempt to assert the first at the expense of the second, it appears that since the Cultural Revolution China has been moving back to conventional authority.

To illuminate the possibilities of a method of organization based to an extreme on highly unilateral persuasion, we need to create a simplified picture or model of it. It should be as spare as possible and beg as few questions as possible. We shall postulate that the elite is enlightened in the sense that it is informed no less well than leadership in a democratic system, and it is no less respectful of fact and reasoned argument. We shall also assume that it does not deliberately and broadly exploit the masses, although it may rationalize exploitation and sometimes blunder into it. We shall not assume that it is wholly competent to know what is best for them, nor that there is no conflict between elite and mass.

The preceptoral model turns out to be somewhat more intricate than at first might be supposed. One does not get to it simply by removing conventional authority from, and inserting persuasion into, the conventional model of a hierarchical authority system. As one begins to make such a substitution, other changes follow.

In outlining them, we shall draw on examples taken disproportionately from China, where the preceptoral element is most conspicuous. We do not intend in this chapter, however, to describe the Chinese or any other politico-economic system. We intend only to concretize the concept of a preceptoral system. Like authority and market system, it is an abstraction; the model selects a group of closely related elements from real-world mixed systems.

Education, the New Man, and Voluntarism

A preceptoral system is a system of social control through highly unilateral governmental persuasion addressed not to an elite or to a bureaucracy alone but to an entire population. It is also a system for

55

elitist

moving toward centrally desired aspirations, not a system for widespread participation in the establishment of social goals.

"Persuasion," though technically the appropriate word, hardly does justice to the variety of persuasive communications employed in the preceptoral system. Persuasion, information, indoctrination, instruction, propaganda, counseling, advice, exhortation, education, and thought control constitute the range of methods used to induce the desired responses. The word "education" is closer to declared communist intention than any other single word, but we shall have to leave it in quotation marks to keep in mind that it is an umbrella.

Persuasion or "education" is aimed first—but perhaps only transitionally—at a transformation of personality, at the creation of the "new man," as he is often referred to in communist discourse. Mao speaks of the need to "remold people to their very souls." "We must fight 'self.' "[9] The "fundamental task," Castro declares, is "the formation of the new man, a man with a profound consciousness of his role in society and of his duties and social responsibilities. . . ."[10]

For the U.S.S.R., Cuba, and China alike, the template for the new man has been fashioned from socialist thought, George Orwell's *1984*, and Victorian England. Selflessness, cooperation, egalitarianism, and service to society mix as themes with duty, hard work, self-discipline, patriotism, and moral conservatism in dress, the arts, and sexual behavior.[11] Two features of the new personality are indispensable. "Education" tries to create men who will "autonomously" serve collective interests, that is, who will do on their own initiative what in other societies they must be commanded or induced to do. It must also create men who will voluntarily respond to state and party when either asks for specific performance.

To explain, justify, and win agreement on all tasks takes too much time; such persuasive efforts have to be reserved for inducing personality transformation and for motivating major tasks. Hence citizens must be persuaded simply to accept the authority of their leaders on the assignment of most tasks.[12] How then does such a system differ on this point from a conventional authority system? It differs in that the new man will *ordinarily* need no external direction. When he does, authority is a residual tool to be used only in cases in which persuasion is not feasible because too costly in time and effort. In addition, such authority as is needed rests on its prior establishment by persuasion alone. If these requirements seem difficult to satisfy, they help explain why a preceptoral system remains largely aspiration rather than fact. In communist systems today, persuasion on particular tasks, such as a campaign to induce Chinese city dwellers to volunteer for work assignments in farming, often disguises an underlying command backed by the coercive powers of state and party.[13]

Hostility to Bureaucracy

A preceptoral system inevitably requires a hierarchical-bureaucratic system for organizing the preceptors, that is, for organizing the cadres, as Lenin put it, of "teacher, guide and leader" engaged in "educating" the citizenry.[14] One might suppose that on this point a conventional authority system and a preceptoral system differ only in that in the former a bureaucracy authoritatively commands the population while in the latter the same kind of bureaucracy "educates" the population. The difference is, however, greater. Within the preceptoral system, members of governmental and party bureaucracies are themselves "educated" rather than authoritatively commanded by top authority.* Seeking by thorough-going "education" of the cadres to reduce bureaucratic influences, a preceptoral system shows ideological hostility to bureaucracy, such hostility being a conspicuous element, for example, in Maoist thought.[15]

Mobilization and Revolution

Control of communications to induce the passive obedience of a population is an old story in politics. "Education" in a preceptoral system goes far beyond that. It elicits active responses from everyone, such as harder work on the job, delivery of agricultural product to the cities, work on irrigation projects, street sweeping, neighborhood espionage, participation in small group mutual criticism, and teaching the illiterate how to read.

"Education," its advocates would argue, cannot be persuasive against the resistance of men hardened by a capitalist milieu in habits of personal gain and antagonism to their fellows. Moreover, if men are to be made responsive to "education" at the hands of the state, they have to be made less responsive to the appeals of family, union, church, employer, landlord, and other associations. A man will not listen to his preceptor if he is still listening to the village elders. Hence, even if "education" were not designed to achieve a revolution, it is a possible method of social organization only in a society that has eliminated pluralistic association and

---

* Most bureaucracies rest on some degree of indoctrination of officials, but much less so than in preceptoral systems (Benjamin Ward, *The Socialist Economy* [Berkeley: University of California Press, 1967], pp. 110–13).

attachment, which is to say only in a society that has undergone a revolutionary transformation.*

Intense and Pervasive Education

Only intense and all-pervasive education can accomplish social transformation. All the ordinary methods of communication must be deployed: press, radio, public announcements by officials, wall newspapers, public assemblies, classes, public celebrations and ceremonies. In addition, party cadres work in continuing sessions with small groups in workplaces and homes and through individual visits to homes for study of ideology, for self-criticism, and for formulating public responsibilities of the citizens. A neighborhood pact in Peking indicates how far "education" goes—or went at the height of preceptoral education in China. The residents agreed, however implausible it may seem:

> To strengthen unity and mutual assistance, help neighbors who are busy or sick, criticize others for their shortcomings, and accept criticism in return; to prevent fires, restrain "bad people" from inciting incidents, and observe regulations requiring the reporting of the arrival and departure of visitors; to accept responsibility for cleaning streets, ditches, and toilets and for killing all flies and mosquitoes; to maintain personal health and hygiene by bathing, changing clothes, washing hands before eating, washing all food, and dressing children carefully with an eye to the weather; to be "diligent and frugal" in managing the household, thinking up ways to economize on food, clothing, coal, water, and electricity; to participate in study for the elimination of illiteracy and to read the newspaper regularly; to respect all policies and decrees of the government, respond to every call of the government, participate in all activities and pass on information to those who cannot attend meetings.[16]

The most intense experience is normally reserved, at least as practiced in China, largely for members of the party and for government officials.

> Every individual who aspires to become a member of the Party must go through the process of thought reform. First, the Party collects as complete a dossier (*tangan*) as possible on his background. . . . Then, in Party small group sessions, he must recite, day after day, every detail of his personal life, both public and private. . . . As the recital goes on, the group begins

---

* A political system in which a centralized leadership mobilizes positive responses for some great effort like economic development or social revolution has been called a mobilization system in some circles in recent years, thus being contrasted both with traditional authoritarian systems and with market-oriented societies in which energies are largely given over to pursuit of individual aspirations. Some authority systems and all preceptoral systems are mobilization systems. See David Apter, *The Politics of Modernization* (Chicago: University of Chicago Press, 1965), chapter 10, for his more precise concept.

to criticize him intensely. . . . All the while, the individual is forced to use the categories and language of the ideology to analyze himself. Criticisms from the group are stated in similar ways. When he has completed his recital, he has made public every shred of what was earlier private. Moreover, he faces a hostile group that attacks every fault of his. This is the point of juxtaposition of opposites, when the contradictions have become most acute. At this time, the attitude of the group changes, and they begin to "help" him develop a correct standpoint.[17]

Yet ordinary citizens will be put through extraordinarily intense experiences from time to time.

. . . each individual peasant had to be raised to a level of consciousness so that he would personally step forward and denounce his landlord. . . . For this it was crucial to make the landlord express his true thoughts, and to give the peasants consciousness to "speak out their bitterness" in full. When the individual peasant pointed the finger of accusation against the landlord, he finally had vanquished his traditional awe before the embodied authority of the old ruling class.[18]

Rationalism

While fascist indoctrination appealed to unconscious, irrational motives, a preceptoral system appeals to the conscious and rational; this is so fundamental a difference as itself to justify conceptualizing "education" as different from the kind of indoctrination once practiced in Germany and Italy.[19]

In a preceptoral system rationality rests on an ideology which once taught to the individual gives him both a "correct" understanding of the social world and guidelines for his own decisions. Although a preceptoral system depends on simple moral and emotional appeals to supplement the rational, the core element in the creation of the new man is his ideological education, a genuine attempt to raise the level of his conscious, thoughtful, deliberated understanding.[20] For members of the party, a high level of consciousness is all the more demanded. They must speak, write, and publish.[21] All this is possible because "education" is usually intended to help men discover many of their true or objective interests, not typically to hoodwink or exploit them.

Mao has written: "You may ban expression of wrong ideas, but the ideas will still be there. . . . it is only by employing the method of discussion, criticism, and reasoning that we can really foster correct ideas and overcome wrong ones." Mao coerced when it suited him to do so; yet his rationalistic aspiration seems genuine, as in his demonstrated preference for changing a mind rather than destroying it.[22]

A New Formula for Efficiency and Creativity

The stress on "education" and the intensity of "education" of cadres, coupled with hostility to bureaucracy, support one of the most fundamental characteristics of a preceptoral system, perhaps its most definitive aspiration. It is to rely on individual energy and resourcefulness rather than on social coordination—far more than in conventional authority or market systems.

In social organization great feats can be accomplished in either of two ways. By a finely tuned coordination of individual efforts, which is an accomplishment prized both in market theory and administrative theory. Or by somehow inducing each only loosely coordinated participating individual to rise to unusual levels of individual accomplishment and innovation. Although all social systems embrace mechanisms for both, in the vision of the preceptoral system the second dominates. The assumption is that all other existing systems are grossly wasteful, because they fail to tap individual energies and resourcefulness. To "unleash a huge reservoir of enthusiasm, energy, and creativeness," "education" will provide the masses with "the knowledge to channel their energy most productively."[23] The big problem to be overcome is individual and organizational slack, for most people have never been challenged.

In a preceptoral system, consequently, the conventional bureaucratic concern for coordinated assignment of tasks gives way to less precise assignments. Such assignments leave each participant with options for defining his own responsibilities and with corresponding obligations to bring his full energies, resourcefulness, and inventiveness to his work. The change in emphasis holds both for cadres and for ordinary citizens in work and civic activities. Looser coordination also implies substantial decentralization of decision making relative to conventional bureaucracy. It further implies a great deal of mutual adjustment—not, however, among top authorities, but among ordinary citizens and cadres.

A preceptoral system goes even further. Technical competence yields to correct (because "educated") attitudes. Resourceful and innovative energy exceeds the efficiency of technical proficiency. The rivalry between th two paths to efficiency shows up in the continuing Red-versus-expert controversy in Chinese administration.[24]

The shift in emphasis from technical competence to right attitudes further implies that a preceptoral manager or cadre is more the generalist and less the specialist. He develops less of the dogged narrowness of the ordinary bureaucrat, understands more of the larger common effort of which he is a part. Because of his breadth, he becomes more generally resourceful. In any case, specialism is seen as breeding inequality and undercutting social cohesion.[25] Although Durkheim may be correct in holding that organic solidarity deriving from interdependence of specialists is superior to mechanical solidarity resting on the sameness of individuals, specialization of function is seen as going to excess, isolating men from each other in rank, patterns of deference, mutual distrust, callousness, and countless failures of understanding.[26]

The preceptoral emphasis on decentralization, initiative, resourcefulness, and generalized competences has a counterpart in market-oriented systems. It appears in recent experiments in work organization in which management stops the assembly line, teams of workers decide on their own individual work assignments, and workers change assignments from time to time rather than steadily pursue any single task. Innovations of this kind may become widespread only with reeducated workers and citizens. Such a supposition underlies "education" in a preceptoral system.

A great distance separates Adam Smith's belief in efficiency through division of labor from the preceptoral faith in the productivity of "educated" new men. Yet neither Smith nor his followers in market ideology ever wholly neglected individual incentives. Indeed, much of the conventional argument for the market system hinges on the persistence, specificity, and strength of individual pecuniary incentives. In recent times, both the "human relations in industry" movement and a resurgence of interest among professional economists in sources of economic efficiency and innovation have given new emphasis to individual resourcefulness and creativity.[27] Not, therefore, foreign to the rest of the world, the preceptoral vision of "educated" energy and resourcefulness cannot be dismissed as fanciful. It aims at a revolutionary reorganization of human energies by making much of what other systems underplay.

A Humane System?

At least from time to time, real-world systems that make room for the preceptoral vision also practice ferocious oppression. In the mid-1970s, the new communist rulers of Cambodia, for example, practiced compulsory mass transfers of population, forced labor, assassination, and massacre of entire families and villages. The U.S.S.R. and China may or may not have left the worst of these practices behind. In any case, all of them continue to practice a ubiquitous intimidation of the population.

In its monopoly of communications and its saturation of the citizenry with messages, a preceptoral system promises a foundation for tyranny that neither a Stalin, a Hitler, nor a Mao has yet fully exploited.

One can be cynical about the preceptoral aspiration itself, for all over the world men who want authority look for improved ways to disguise it. A scholarly comment on tendencies toward participatory democracy in the Western business enterprise, for example, appears to rejoice in its revolutionary implications:

> The widespread development of . . . initiative on production problems from the ranks of workers and union officers amounts to a veritable revolution in organization. It requires that the manager think and act in terms of leadership instead of simply in terms of power and control.

But the conclusion reveals the fraud:

> This does not mean that he [the manager] has less control of the organization than he had before.[28]

If authority hides in a rhetoric of participation and initiative in the liberal constitutional West, it would be no surprise to find it disguised in a preceptoral ideology.

Yet some credence has to be granted to some conspicuously humane elements of the preceptoral vision of social organization. Despite earlier mass executions, the later Maoist practice was to reeducate rather than execute fallen leaders, and Maoist thought puts its emphasis on human spontaneity and consciousness rather than on technology.[29] It is difficult to dismiss Mao's "Of all things in the world, people are the most precious,"[30] as mere rhetoric. On some counts as humane as any other great vision of man in the history of human aspiration, the vision of an "educated" citizenry is appealing on many counts—on some points more so than the vision of market man—even if it is already declining in China.

Taken as a set of aspirations, the preceptoral system needs to be compared with liberal democratic aspirations for government by persuasion, for liberal democrats prize their cloudy vision of noncoercive government for individual self-development. As we shall see, they postulate a "new man" too, one not exclusively molded by the state but one who instead emerges from a competition of ideas.

II

INCOMPETENCES OF AUTHORITY AND MARKET SYSTEMS

Authority Systems:
Strong Thumbs, No Fingers

THE organization of a politico-economic system through authority rather than market is on certain points clumsy. That is not meant as an evaluation, for authority on many other counts can be made highly effective when markets cannot. But the particular features of authority that can be called clumsy need to be understood. Those who understand them dispense with much arm waving and emotional discharge about capitalism and socialism. As a by-product of an examination of them, we shall also have a preliminary look at communist systems. These particular features—thumbs where one would want fingers—are conspicuous in communist systems. Comparable though different incompetences of market systems will then be examined in the following chapter. The two chapters constitute a kind of primer on familiar disabilities of authority and market systems; through the understanding of these chapters both systems will become much clearer in main outline.*

We begin with a simple but broad and abstract characterization of two fundamental problems of politico-economic organization. Specifically,

---

* Most of these two chapters will be familiar to economists. Perhaps the setting of the problems of economic choice in a larger context of rational choice will not be entirely familiar. Parts of the incentives discussion, as well as a recasting of the conventional analysis of "market failure," may also not be wholly familiar.

in all societies people face both a general problem of achieving rational choices and a special problem of achieving economic choice. Let us give that statement some specific content.

The General Problem of Rational Choice

The human condition is small brain, big problems.[1] People therefore need help—devices, processes, and institutions—to simplify problem solving: among others, paper and pencil, a written language, science, specialized devices like double-entry bookkeeping, and institutions like bureaucracies, legislative representation, and markets.

At one level social problems seem simple. No great feat of problem solving is required to put food in a hungry child's mouth. But people complicate problem solving. Some do not want to feed the hungry. And those who do usually want to do so with a minimum of coercion (and of taxes to pay for what needs to be done). Or they do not want to act if doing so will increase the power of government or give rise to any other of many possible inconveniences. Hence in every kind of politico-economic system countless objections are raised against any possible solution of a problem. In fancier language, all solutions have to satisfy a multiplicity of criteria. That is inordinately difficult.

To cope with complexity, we have seen that hierarchy and bureaucracy divide problems up, apply specialized skills to each subproblem, and routinize decisions to apply standard solutions to categories of problems. New and rapidly emerging mathematical and computational aids to rational decision making have vastly expanded the capacities of hierarchy-bureaucracy to solve problems.

Hierarchy and bureaucracy nevertheless fall short. The brain is still too small. Even with skill specialization, specialized decision makers will not be able to produce or find much of the information they need. They will still fall short of the ability required to devise appropriate policies. They will still stumble over the complexities of evaluation of alternatives. The U.S. Interstate Commerce Commission, for example, limited in its task to the regulation of rates and services for interstate transport, cannot predict the consequences for the United States of alternative possible rate structures. It has been unable to grasp the interconnectedness of the economy well enough to recommend to Congress a significantly more rational transport system. It only imperfectly copes with the staggering question of what array and interconnection of values ought to govern transport policy.

Moreover, hierarchy and bureaucracy themselves pose obstacles to rational decision that weigh against some of their advantages. Dividing up problems requires that someone be given authority to coordinate the interdependent solutions reached by each subdivision. So difficult does coordination become that no politico-economic system in the world attempts more than a loose central coordination of the economy as a whole, reserving its intense efforts for a few key or critical sectors of the economy. Central allocation of resources in the United States in World War II had to be organized around only three commodities: aluminum, copper, and steel. In the U.S.S.R., we shall see, central planning for the economy has always been selective.

Among familiar failures in central authoritative coordination, one is communication failure. For example, low-level members of the hierarchy misrepresent to their superiors what their capacities are for fear that the truth might lead their superiors to ask for too much from them. It is, for example, a chronic issue in communist economic planning.[2] A Soviet writer says:

> The basic flaw in planning and management was that every detail was supposed to be decided from the center and, since it was impossible to know the circumstances at each enterprise, the center proceeded from average conditions that did not exist in reality in any one enterprise.[3]

Another familiar failure is information overload. A recent environmental impact study on breeder reactors prepared by the Energy Research and Development Administration ran to 5,000 pages in ten volumes. The total flow of paper to any one decision maker is always more than he can digest. Yet another commonplace problem is failure of internal control. Subordinate agencies pursuing their own special interests escape the authority of their superiors or become engaged in battles with other subordinate agencies, a problem so familiar to the Soviets and the Chinese that each has a name for it: *vedomstvennost* and *pen-wei chu-yi*.[4]

We have seen that, overlaid on the formal pattern of unilateral pyramidal control, informal controls run in all directions in ostensible hierarchies. Participants trade favors with each other, exchange current favors for future obligations, and "cash in" on older obligations. Through these transactions, mutual adjustment takes on many of the characteristics of a market. But markets, we have already seen, work well only with money, posted prices to indicate the terms on which exchanges can be made, and built-in protections against monopolistic exploitation of one exchanger by another. As an instrument of rational choice, a bureaucracy is therefore often a kind of clumsy market, an unexpected

67

outcome for those who seek in the rationalism of formal organization an escape from the "chaos" of the market.

In these respects the specifics of markets illuminate—by contrast—certain characteristic points of clumsiness of hierarchy-bureaucracy. In a well-organized market system there are specific ways of coping—fingers instead of thumbs—with both the core difficulty imposed by complex problems and with deficiencies in hierarchy-bureaucracy. Market systems transform complex decision problems into drastically simplified ones. In the absence of a market system, someone has to face complex problems such as what goods and services are to be produced, how much of the gross national product should be consumed instead of invested, what sections of the country should specialize in what kinds of economic activity, and whether the society should encourage farming or import agricultural commodities from abroad. In a market system responsive to individual consumer demands, no such questions have to be faced as decision problems by anyone. To "solve" problems like these, each of many persons grapples with a much reduced problem: whether it will be to his advantage to buy or sell.

As for problems of central coordination, no central coordinator at all is required in a market system, for coordination—even global cooperation—is achieved through exchange. Market systems also permit the factors that have to be weighed in a decision to be expressed quantitatively in a common denominator (prices) for comparison with each other. All these aids to rational choice are lacking in authority systems.

The Problem of Economic Choice

Problems of rational choice in an authority system take on a special character when costs become an issue, when choosing any one alternative requires, because of scarce resources, that the benefits of another alternative be sacrificed. More guns, less butter.

The Illogic of Priorities

One might think that authorities could rank—the current ugly terminological fad is to "prioritize"—various alternative possible uses of the nation's resources in order of priority of outputs or end products. But it makes no sense to rank, say, housing as against health services, or growing grain as against fabricating eyeglasses. Because people need all of them, the problem is of proportions, not rank.

Moreover, whether doctors are generally more important than lawyers, or bicycles more than eggs, is irrelevant to any practical decision. The relevant question is whether, given the existing flow of each of these various services and commodities, an expansion in the flow of one is more important than in the flow of the other. If priorities make sense, they would have to be transitory priorities or marginal changes in priorities that shift as demands and supplies change. Marginal priorities would bear no relation to any such notion as the intrinsic merit of a good or service. From a German wartime planning document:

> To fix an order of priority for important production in accordance simply with the nature of the product must lead to serious mistakes and misdirection. . . . The provision of single screws, which may be all that is needed to complete some agricultural machinery, may be much more important than supplying the same screws to a tank factory, which has a much higher priority, but which will need the screws only some months ahead.[5]

In the simplest terms, what needs to be produced depends on what else is being produced. Production planning is a matter of deciding on mixes or combinations of flows of production, not of estimating priorities of each line of production as though characteristics of the commodity or service can make clear its priority rating. Even so elementary a point can be missed when authorities set targets or investment plans. In an extraordinary statement, Mao acknowledged a failure to calculate transportation requirements for coal and iron outputs: "Coal and iron will not walk by themselves. . . . I did not anticipate this point."[6] On another occasion, Chou En-lai wrote: "We failed to strike a proper balance between capital construction and the capacity for supplying materials. . . . As a result . . . there occurred a serious shortage of building materials such as steel products, cement, and timber."[7]

If rational authorities are to decide whether to expand any one line of production, they will also ask in particular about its costs—what cutbacks in other lines would free sufficient resources for the required expansion. But they cannot know this unless decisions have already been made about what resources are assigned to other goods and services. Yet decisions on required resources for each of such other goods and services could not have been made rationally without decision makers knowing *their* costs. But—and here the argument repeats and becomes circular—their costs could not be known unless resources have been assigned to other lines of production, including the first line contemplated. In short, in order to set production targets decision makers need to know costs. But to know what the costs will be, they need to know what the production targets will be. Any one decision depends on all others in a process of mutual determination.

A way out? Find trade-off ratios. Find rates at the margin at which any one good or service can be substituted for the most valuable alternative production possibilities. Although efficiency prices express just such ratios, authority systems lack them.[8]

Difficulties of Input Allocations

Priorities on outputs aside, consider the problem of deciding, for any given resource, to which of its many already planned uses it should be put. Suppose, for example, that both truck and aircraft companies need more engineers. To whom should the authority assign available engineers? Perhaps a few to each. But how many to each—should one get more than the other?

Should he allocate all the engineers to the industry with the largest production target? No, since even the secondary target needs a few. Should he assign them proportionately to size of target? No, for aircraft may be more dependent on the engineers than trucks, regardless of differences in targeted output. Or one industry may already have a more liberal allocation of them than the other.

He looks for another criterion. He finds that the output of one industry is lagging further behind target than the other. A good reason for assigning the engineers to the lagging industry? Not at all, since the lag may be a consequence of factors that will not respond favorably to increase in inputs. On U.S. experience with authoritative direction of the economy in World War II:

> Many people in WPB [War Production Board] thought that the Board was in the best position to determine labor requirements and priorities, and that the role of WMC [War Manpower Commissioner] should be restricted to recruiting and supplying workers in the numbers and at the places specified by WPB. . . . WMC officials, on the other hand, insisted that the fact that a plant is making an important product or even that it is behind schedule does not necessarily indicate that it needs labor.[9]

Suppose now that the authority decides that the shortage has obstructed aircraft manufacture more seriously than truck manufacture and that aircraft production will greatly respond to more engineers. Does he now have a case for allocating to aircraft? Again, no. He would first have to know about alternative remedies—for example, whether the shortage of engineers could be remedied by giving each of the engineers a staff of assistants or some new labor-saving equipment.

70

Suppose he finds that aircraft manufacture, though lagging more seriously than truck manufacture, would probably respond fairly quickly to substitute remedies while truck manufacture would not. Would he then do best to assign the engineers to trucks and ask aircraft to solve its problem through the substitute arrangements? Again, no. For whether the aircraft manufacturers would be well advised to use substitute measures would depend upon the costliness of these substitute measures. But the authority has no way of knowing, nor does the industry, the actual cost of substitutes.

Controlling the Enterprise

A further fundamental difficulty in an authority system arises out of the many choices that have to be made by or for each enterprise. When should an enterprise try to enlarge output? When, instead, should it raise quality? Or turn saved inputs back? Should an enterprise strive to meet its prescribed output target if, as is commonplace, it receives information from product users that the product is unsatisfactory—that it needs redesign? Or should it alter its product to suit users, and thus fail to achieve its target? If the enterprise produces more than one product—most enterprises produce hundreds of shapes, grades, or sizes of a multiplicity of products—then these and other choices are enlarged. For at any time, any one production target can be pursued by neglecting any one or more alternative targets.

Authority systems have not been able to find a satisfactory way to instruct and control the enterprise with respect to these and other similar choices. This is the problem of "success indicators" that torments all communist regimes. Khrushchev complained: "It has become the tradition to produce not beautiful chandeliers to adorn homes, but the heaviest chandeliers possible. This is because the heavier the chandeliers produced, the more a factory gets since its output is calculated in tons." [10] Whatever the indicator chosen, a comparable distortion occurs. The same problem persists in China and Cuba.[11]

> If the target is merely for "tons of nails shorter than 2 inches" the factory will try to produce all 1 9/10″ nails, because this is easiest. If it is for "numbers of nails," the factory will try to produce all ½″ nails. But if the plan is set in terms of ½″, 1″, 1½″, and 1 9/10″ nails, there will be overcentralization. If the target is set in terms of gross value of output, the factory will maximize its use of materials and semi-fabs and minimize the net value it adds to each product.[12]

Lacking a common-denominator indicator, any instruction to the enterprise leads it to overplay certain values and neglect others. By contrast, a profit-seeking private enterprise in a market system has a relatively clear criterion for governing any of its choices: maximize profits.

Implications of the success-indicator problem spread out in more directions than we can take time to trace. For example, in order to meet targeted obligations managers are compelled to break the laws. They see no alternative but to do so. They have to find other managers willing to break the law with whom they can exchange favors. Thus, networks of mutual obligation develop, forming mutually protective cliques which then constitute quiet but significant challenges to party and governmental control.[13]

How Market Systems Facilitate Economic Choice

The clumsiness of authority systems in these respects becomes clearer again if we take note that certain features of the market system permit it to solve, although imperfectly, each of the problems just outlined. In a market system, no authority needs to set priorities or come to any other judgment about what is most important to produce. People—consumers, suppliers, businessmen—simply decide whether to buy more or less of any given commodity or service.* And the decision question is always one of marginal choice. Does the decision maker want, at this point, more bread, or more milk—or more educational services or more medical —or a little of both, given the supplies of each that are already available to him? No decision maker makes any choice without knowing its cost. All buyers, both private individuals and public officials, find that choices bear price tags, the prices representing—though, again, imperfectly— the value of what has to be given up.

How does a market system solve the specific problem of whether truck or plane production should have the engineers? All the considerations that frustrated a systematic allocation of the scarce engineers in a system of authoritative assignment enter into market system allocations in a manageable way. All the considerations are quantified in terms of money; and calculations are made by plane and truck manufacturers that integrate at least roughly a consideration of (1) the value of output relative to other possible outputs (represented in output price), (2) the productivity of the engineers in achieving that output, (3) the potential productivity of substitutes for engineers, and (4) the value of both

---

* For each participant, the valuations he can make effective in the market reflect, it should never be forgotten, how much productive capacity and how much income he has at his disposal. The preferences of the poor are therefore not of much account; their small spending has little effect on prices and production. For market systems, consequently, the correct claim is not actual performance but only a potential—to be realized only if and when the distribution of income is greatly improved.

engineers and substitutes to other lines of production (represented in their wage rates and prices).

As an example of the capacity of prices in highly organized markets to measure, weigh, and combine in a common denominator all factors bearing on rational economic decision, as an authority system cannot, consider a melon shipper in California who knows that consumer demand for his melons in eastern markets will depend on many factors, including the quality of his melons, their conditions on arrival, the availability to consumers of melons from other shippers, the seasonal availability of fruits as alternatives to melons, and weather as a factor affecting menu. Bearing all these in mind, should he ship to Boston, New York, or Philadelphia? What he does, in fact, is to start a railroad carload of melons on the way to the East without specifying destination beyond Chicago. He then nervously watches telegraphic reports on market prices as they vary from hour to hour in eastern cities. If in the last hours of the run to Chicago, a glut of melons in the New York market or any other adverse influence reduces demand there for his melons, a late price quotation will signal him to divert his carload to Boston or any other market in which the price is higher.

All the considerations bearing on where his melons should go are represented in one common denominator of price. He need not know which of several factors are unfavorable to delivering his melons to the New York market. All he needs to know is that on the balance the favorable and unfavorable factors add up to a single signal to divert to another city. And no one masterminds the process as a whole, no one needs to grasp it as an intellectual problem and solve it. The necessary calculations are largely acted out by many buyers and sellers. Again, these various devices for economic choice are not to be found in authority system.

Incentives

To know enough to choose wisely—to know costs, for example—is not enough. People have to be stirred to act. The incentives of authority systems are often crude. And, again, the specific incentives of market systems offer an informative contrast.

In a market system, the consumer does not merely *know* his choices, he is *motivated* to choose rationally because he can obtain services and commodities only by surrendering money claims on other resources. Similarly, a businessman does not merely know the relevant values to be compared; he is placed in a cost-price squeeze that motivates him to act appropriately. Market incentives also tie strength of motivation to the value of the goal. An increase in demand for a product, for example, sets in motion a chain of transactions that leads to more job offers to workers who can help satisfy the increased demand, but only to the degree warranted by the demand.

No comparable structure of incentives operates in an authority system. In such a system, an enterprise is instructed to produce some specified quantity of each of a list of commodities or services. Some quantities of resources to be used are provided. The manager then finds himself in a position such that, even if he knows (which neither he nor his superiors do) that the value of a particular input in some alternative employment is greater than in his line of production, he is under no specialized incentive to stop using it. More than that, he is motivated to achieve a certain output quota regardless of the possibility that the output is not worth the total of inputs necessary to meet it.[14] In communist systems, these are commonplace complaints.

Conflicts of Incentives

Once authority is established, it works through incentives other than simple self-interest. To establish authority systems, people are given an incentive—fear, expectation of future advantage, and the like—to accept authority; and authority thereafter instructs them to do things that they often do not want to do. Even when people voluntarily set up, say, a rationing system, they may want to outwit it. Or the personal incentives of an official—for fame, an easy life, or easy money, for example—may be at war with the assignments authoritatively given him. Thus, a common flaw in authority systems is a conflict of incentives. And the punishments of authority systems are sometimes more effective in teaching respondents how to escape them than in motivating them to do what they are authoritatively instructed to do, a phenomenon made much of by B. F. Skinner.[15] No such conflict exists in market systems.

A counterpart phenomenon in market systems is illuminating, however. Because market incentives are not in conflict, they are powerful—so powerful indeed that they induce businessmen to break the law when the law interferes with profits and to violate a number of moral conventions respected outside the world of the market. It has become increasingly clear that in the United States, for example, barely disguised forms of corporate bribery of government officials, product adulteration, misrepresentation, environmental abuse, and a relatively unconstrained assault through television advertising on the sensibilities of the young are common business practices.

Resourcefulness versus Coordination

To Adam Smith, the market system was both a coordinating mechanism and a form of decentralized incentive to encourage a multitude of individual initiatives that authority systems could not tap. It may turn out to be that societies make a fundamental choice: either coordination over resourcefulness or the reverse. Coordination, we shall see, is the emphasis in much planning theory and in Soviet communism, as well as in some market theory. Resourcefulness is the emphasis in other interpretations of the market system,* and in the preceptoral system.

* * *

If the absence from authority systems of specialized devices for rational calculation and economic choice, as well as for fine-tuned incentives, makes the hand of authority look like all thumbs, no fingers, the thumbs are nevertheless powerful. They are strong enough, we shall see, to account for the high growth rates of communist systems and for Soviet achievements in space technology. They are strong enough too to account for such diverse accomplishments as, on one hand, China's health-care system and, on the other hand, massive feats of American worldwide military organization in World War II. The argument of this chapter is not that authority systems do not work or that on balance they are less efficient than market systems. It is only that they are without certain efficiency and incentive mechanisms that can be found in market systems. We can best understand authority systems only by taking careful note of these particular points of difference between the two systems.

---

* Richard R. Nelson has suggested that economists share an oral tradition in which the market as a force for initiative, resourcefulness, and energizing is more fully appreciated than in their written work. ("The Economic Problem and the Role of Competition," [mimeo] paper presented to the Society of Government Economists, Atlantic City, N.J., September 17, 1976.)

The Limited Competence

of Markets

A MARKET is like a tool: designed to do certain jobs but unsuited for others. Not wholly familiar with what it can do, people often leave it lying in the drawer when they could use it. But then they also use it when they should not, like an amateur craftsmen who carelessly uses his chisel as a screwdriver.

What is it that markets do badly or not at all? The answer is not to be found in high-flying critiques of "capitalism." The grand critiques are imprecise. They also hurry us on to evaluation, which is not our purpose, and skimp the clarification of just how market systems work.

Take three grand critiques as examples: those of Karl Polanyi, Erich Fromm, and Marx. Polanyi's most sustained critique draws on English economic history as his case in point. But he does not disentangle the effects of market from those of private property or from the effects of a new distribution of property brought about by enclosures of land. The market system came to England in an unusually bruising way.[1]

Fromm uses psychoanalysis to argue that life in market societies compels people to bear an intolerable burden of decision making; hence his title, *Escape from Freedom*.[2] However sophisticated the psychoanalysis, the economic analysis displays a naive faith that an undefined institutional reform called "planning" brings an end to the psychic strain of market life.

Marx's comprehensive analysis of an entire social system and culture is a synthesis that no other social scientist has ever rivaled. But the very ambition of the synthesis interlaces market, private property, private enterprise, the historical distribution of property rights, historically established class inequalities, and political structures so tightly as to obscure the separable effects of market. Aside from a few insights (on the "cash nexus," for example), one cannot take directly from Marx a set of defining characteristics of market systems or of characteristic incapacities.

Before we proceed to our own list of incapacities, however, let us take note that the incentives discussed in the preceding chapter are part of the machinery of rapid change and growth in market systems, no matter how defective markets may be on many counts. Like authority systems that can organize millions of people in great tasks of social cooperation despite the characteristic flaws of such systems, market systems accomplish great tasks despite their misallocations and inefficiencies. Market systems encourage thousands and millions of initiatives. They are turbulent, open-ended systems that can change or grow at any of innumerable points. They allow great room for invention and improvisation, individual and local resourcefulness, a multitude of challenges and potential responses—all of which we shall see in greater detail in subsequent chapters.

However, some of the characteristics of market systems that account for change, growth, and affluence are, from another point of view, their defects. For example, it is a kind of defect or irrationality in market systems that innovators can throw the costs or hardships of innovation onto other persons. Innovations throw people out of work during transition; they also make equipment, skills, sometimes whole communities obsolete. But a profit-calculating businessman can ignore these hardships; they do not fall on him. It is to this irrationality that we owe much of the surge in productivity that in the nineteenth and twentieth centuries brought Western Europe and North America to relative affluence. The innovative irrationality of market systems made them a force for change such as the world had never before seen. It was not rivaled until after the Bolshevik revolution. Then it became clear that another powerful mechanism for innovation—forced savings—was available.

The Conventional List of Market Defects

To identify market defects or failures, theoretical economists imagine a perfect market, even if no perfect market has ever existed and cannot. To imagine one, however, permits economists to say that markets fail for all the reasons that deny perfection. Thus, their conventional list of defects includes both impossibilities and difficulties. It identifies some feats of social organization that cannot be accomplished through exchange and markets. It also identifies those that can be accomplished though only imperfectly. Since all social organization is imperfect, the second category of defects has to be understood in the light of comparable imperfections of alternative forms of organization.*

Pareto Optimality

In any case, with the help of the concept of a Pareto optimum for defining perfection, economists construct a list of "market failures," that is, circumstances in which their concept of perfection is unattainable. They do so by assuming a private-property society of free men. Since in such a society any one individual can often increase his want satisfaction through exchange and his doing so does not decrease anyone else's want satisfaction, it would appear that under appropriate circumstances an optimum could be reached in which all possible mutually advantageous noninjurious exchanges are accomplished. The list of defects, which can be formulated abstractly or concretely, then specifies those circumstances in which for one reason or another such a no-loss-to-anyone optimum cannot be reached.† Such a list is the following:

* The concept of a perfect market sometimes also leads an economist to confuse the perfect with real-world markets. Many of the propositions subsequently developed about markets in this book will often trigger a "not true!" response from an economist because he is accustomed to generalizing about idealized markets while this book discusses those in the real world.

† In economic theory, the pursuit of theoretical simplification leads to attempts to subsume all market defects under what may be excessively abstract concepts like "externalities" or "transaction costs." At best these concepts are a preface to analysis. See, for example, E. J. Mishan, "The Postwar Literature on Externalities," *Journal of Economic Literature* 9 (March 1971); Kenneth J. Arrow, "The Organization of Economic Activity," in *Public Expenditures and Policy Analysis,* eds. Robert Haveman and Julius Margolis (Chicago: Markham, 1970). Other economists have tied the analysis of market defects to comparison of specific organizational alternatives; for example: Oliver E. Williamson, *Markets and Hierarchies* (New York: Free Press, 1975). For an excellent summary of various attempts to organize the analysis of market defects, see Jesse Burkhead and Jerry Miner, eds., *Public Expenditure* (Chicago: Aldine Atherton, 1971), chapter 4.

Individual incompetence.   Obviously an optimum is impossible when persons are ignorant of their own preferences or of the qualities of the goods and services they buy. In actual fact, no consumer is competent across the range of his purchases: insurance, medical care, mechanical and electronic equipment of many kinds, and foods treated with additives. This is of course a problem in all forms of organization: decision makers are never wholly competent in any form of politico-economic organization.

Uncounted costs.   When a factory pollutes the air, it uses up resources not counted in its costs of production. Some of what the factory produces is therefore not worth its costs and is profitable to produce only because not all costs are counted. The factory sells at arbitrary rather than efficiency prices. Uncounted costs are borne both by parties to the transaction—customers of an enterprise—and by innocent bystanders. A rising incidence of cancer hints that all of us may be bearing the costs of air pollution. As man has learned to harness increasing amounts of mechanical energy and organize it in ever larger ventures, his organized capacity to blight the earth, sicken himself, and malform his offspring is —in the old meaning of the word—terrible.

Again, markets are only one of several forms of social organization that permit him the exercise of these heroic new competences; all other forms do also. Environmental degradation is one of the products of Soviet planning, made conspicuous by the impact of industrialization around Lake Baikal.* China has its hands full of environmental problems, some inherited from the old agricultural system, some a consequence of the methods of development employed since the Liberation.[3]

The difference between market and other systems with respect to uncounted costs is that market systems, unless supplemented by governmental authority, cannot count certain costs, while other systems can, even though they commonly fail to do so. With governmental authority in market-oriented systems, uncounted costs can be counted: by imposing taxes, for example, as some governments now do, to charge enterprises for the value of the air or waterways they pollute. These solutions will be far from ideal; but they have to be compared with nonideal solutions in alternative systems.[4] And note it is just this feature of markets—the possibility that decision makers do not count the costs (that fall on others) of what they do—that, we have seen, accounts for much of change and growth.

---

* And a problem throughout the Soviet system. "There is not one river in the Ukraine whose natural state has been preserved." Air pollution, coast erosion, salinization of the soil appear in the U.S.S.R. in roughly the same form as in the market systems. Marshall I. Goldman, "The Convergence of Environmental Disruption," *Science* 170 (October 2, 1970). See also Cynthia H. Enloe, *The Politics of Pollution in a Comparative Perspective* (New York: David McKay, 1975).

Uncounted benefits. Uncounted benefits might seem to promise a bonus—an extra efficiency in market systems. Not so. They represent another systematic inevitable miscalculation in market systems and another departure from efficiency prices. If the training program of a corporation is a benefit to all other employers to which the trainees drift over the years, the apparent benefit hides a failure to achieve an optimum. The parties to the exchange—corporation and trainee—will arrive at transactions that underproduce. Because of failure to count benefits to other corporations, the training program will be carried only as far as is rewarding to the originating corporation. More training would be optimal. Again, this is a problem common to all organizations in that decision makers *may* fail to seize benefits. The problem is distinctive to market systems in that decision makers are certain to fail to seize all benefits.

Costly transactions. In the United States as many as one out of five employed civilians works in wholesaling and retailing. Although much of their work goes into storing, moving, packaging, and other services, much of it goes to nothing more than buying and selling—that is, making exchanges and keeping records of them. Transactions themselves are costly. Again, however, the administrative and other processes necessary to any alternative system are costly.

Negotiation of an exchange is sometimes more costly than it is worth. That is one reason that business enterprises exist and grow large—to create a working group within which continual exchange is unnecessary. It is cheaper to pay a group of employees once a week to obey commands all week than to negotiate contracts with independent workers for the thousands of services required.[5] In other circumstances, it is the costs of authority or of persuasion that will be too high.

Monopoly. When, in any one market, there are only a few buyers or sellers, one person or a collaborating group can restrict production purchases, or sales in an arbitrary way. Again, they can restrict production in arbitrary ways in all alternative forms of organization.

Of this list of market "defects," none are to be denied. Identifying them helps us to understand markets. But they do not constitute a list of breakdowns or impossibilities for markets—only a list of defects that markets share with all other forms of social organization. They are not even the most important shortcomings of markets; the list is derived not from an appraisal of what is most important about markets but from an attempt to specify the conditions in which markets will and will not achieve the impossible perfection of a Pareto optimum.

Public goods and the free rider. Another failure to achieve a Pareto optimum stands on a different footing. For certain products like national defense, some kinds of education, and traffic control, benefits spill over to other parties in such a way as to undercut the incentive of any one buyer to buy. A lighthouse will shine for anyone at sea. But since ordinarily anyone can use its services without paying, everyone wants to be a free rider. For such "public" goods, authority is required to impose a charge on users; otherwise they will not be produced. In this "defect" we have identified an impossibility—a feat of social organization which exchange in markets cannot accomplish and which an alternative method of social organization can.

A Greater Incapacity

The above list is, however, not long enough. The idea that markets are perfect when they can achieve a Pareto no-loss-to-anyone optimum and imperfect when they cannot is itself arbitrary, and its rejection points to additional market incapacities. For many tasks of social organization, it is necessary to impose a loss on some people—for example, a redistribution of land to stimulate economic development in Mexico under Cardenas or in Japan after World War II. Or it may be important to train the young whether they want the training or not. Insofar as markets can organize only voluntary, mutually advantageous, acts of coordination, it will be necessary to find nonmarket alternatives. On this very point, the conventional virtues of markets are often disadvantages.

Failure of Market Incentives

The point can be put in terms of incentives. In the conventional argument market incentives are perfect; they draw willing responses, and only willing responses. They never require a response that coerces, damages, or imposes a loss on the respondent. Yet just such a response is often needed, as we have just seen.

In other cases, market incentives will work, but only at prohibitive cost. Unlike control through authority, control through exchange, we have seen, is costly on each occasion when it is employed. Something of value has to be given up by the controller.* Sometimes neither an individual nor a government official can afford to offer a benefit of the size necessary to induce the desired response. Acknowledging their short-

---

* Even in the absence of already established authority, when control is exercised through a threat which is costly to implement, the threat never needs to be made good for those respondents who obey. In control through exchange, the controller has to pay every time.

ages of consumer goods, China and Cuba have therefore been trying to motivate workers as much as possible without reliance on pay. Many other less developed countries have millions of unemployed and millions of tasks left undone—in common sense, a monumental and tragic irrationality. But governments often see putting the unemployed to work as too costly and leave them unemployed.

Declining Power of Market Incentives?

Market incentives are powerful. Indian peasants, for example, whose social isolation might be expected to render them impervious to market incentives, have repeatedly demonstrated their sensitivity to them by shifting from one crop to another as relative prices change. Yet in wealthy societies we increasingly hear such opinions as this: "What is happening around us is that the incentives of the old order have run down, that the habit of work is deteriorating and that the incentives of the new society have not yet been created."[6]

Some of Castro's difficulties in getting the sugar crop harvested find a cause in the unwillingness of the Cuban worker, who now is better assured than before of a livelihood, to put in the back-breaking hours in the fields to which the threat of hunger used to hold him.[7] Britain's low productivity is sometimes attributed to a welfare state in which workers are not now "afraid enough."[8] On the other hand, we have seen, even more fully developed welfare programs in Sweden seem consistent with high productivity. Unusual job security in Japan, unmatched by any other market system, does not seem to undermine the incentives of a highly productive labor force.[9] It may be that concern about the decline of the work ethic confuses market incentives with the incentives of authority systems. What is commonly called worker alienation, as we shall see in a later chapter, seems more probably a consequence of the way in which authority is organized in the workplace than a consequence of market incentives. Hour by hour in modern industrial societies workers are motivated—or fail to be motivated—by the devices of authority.

Insecurity and Instability

A further common and pertinent objection to markets is that they foist insecurities on the population. Because exchange is usually abruptly terminable, what one wins in exchange is at risk. Termination, we have seen, is all the more a problem when livelihood is at stake. Short of termination, every participant in exchange knows that the price of what he sells can decline relative to other prices, or that prices he pays may climb when prices paid him do not.

A person suffers job or income loss for any of many reasons, all of which reduce to the simple phenomenon that other people no longer can or want to keep on paying for what he is able to offer. Technological change, shifts of consumer preferences, or a depression in one industry or sector of the economy will wipe out their demand for what he can offer. Before World War II market-oriented systems regularly brought catastrophe to large sections of the population through wild inflation from too much spending and gross unemployment from too little. Looking back, it is hard to believe that civilized people tolerated such degradation as in the Great Depression of the 1930s, when unemployment in the United States rose to one-fourth of the labor force and remained severe for almost ten years. Since then Keynesian innovations in economic theory—coupled with national income accounting—have transformed these systems, a transformation that may represent man's greatest accomplishment so far in the direct application of social science to social problem solving. Since World War II, only rarely has recession hit hard enough to reduce gross national product; now it usually only slows growth. Even so, the problem of unemployment is hardly solved. Nor the problem of inflation, on which the industrialized nations are backsliding rather than advancing.

Production itself, some studies now show, fluctuates more in communist systems than in the market-oriented systems of Europe and North America.[10] But in communist systems unemployment does not fluctuate correspondingly.* It is a proud claim of many communist leaders that in their systems there is no unemployment. In fact there is, as is inevitable in any system in which people move from time to time from one job to another. But it is held to very low levels by making a job a "right," which means greatly restricting the employer's authority to fire. The result is excess payrolls in many firms, waste of labor, and in some circumstances restrictions on the worker's freedom to move when he wants to.[11] But unquestionably communist systems provide a degree of employment security that existing market-oriented systems do not, although unemployment compensation is a long step toward job security and market systems could provide even greater security of employment.

A new instability in market systems is revealed in simultaneous unemployment and inflation.[12] One explanation is price and wage manipula-

---

* And inflation is suppressed through government price setting, income control, and other policies difficult in market systems.

tion by corporate monopoly and unions. Another is just such a decline in incentives as we have acknowledged may be occurring. At any given time, there presumably exists some rate of reward for management that will induce the volume of entrepreneurial activity required for full employment. At the same time, there presumably exists some structure of wages attractive enough to maintain a level of employee productivity acceptable to management, forestall a wave of expensive wage demands, and avoid a widespread strike threat. Although it has always been assumed that the sum of the required returns to management and employees is not larger than national income, the assumption may now be mistaken. If an excess of claims is met by monetary expansion, the result is inflation; if it is not met, the result is retarded business activity and consequent unemployment. If partially met, the result is both inflation and unemployment, such as characterize the market system of the world today.

Market-oriented systems may have prospered historically only because subtly working social mechanisms—we shall look into some in later chapters—have restrained the total demands put upon them. If these constraints are eroding, we may have to look forward to decades of growing economic disorder in market systems. The United Kingdom may be the shape of the future for the market-oriented systems: declining ability to compete in international trade, falling productivity, and a gradual slide in the standard of living.

Other Limitations on Markets

Corporate Discretion

One requirement for a Pareto optimum is that businessmen, like all other market participants, be competent to make the right choices. Just what that means is not wholly clear. But it at least means that entrepreneurs can find and recognize the least-cost method of producing any given output and that they can find and recognize the level of output that brings marginal cost equal to price. For complex productive processes, we can be certain that they cannot. A practical question is whether in their discretion corporate executives and other businessmen can approximate the two requirements well enough—though opinions will differ on what "well enough" means—and whether market controls drive them toward an acceptable approximation.

Consequently, we are listing corporate discretion as a major possible limit on the use of market systems. In an age of technologically complex giant enterprises, the range of discretion open to corporate management may have become inconsistent with the claims conventionally made for the usefulness of market systems. It is a point to which we return in later chapters.

Inappropriateness of Individual Preferences

Looking about at affluent market-oriented systems in which the production of trivialities often takes precedence over the provision, say, of basic medical care to millions of children, critics call into question a system in which individual preferences, no matter how unreflectively considered, set production targets for the system. They believe that collectively deliberated production targets would almost certainly be better. It is a fact that most market systems are in large part tied to individual preferences, which may be inadequate guides to production. In the next chapter, however, we shall see possibilities for organizing market systems to respond either to individual or collective targets.

Moral Objections

Some people register not merely practical but moral objections to the dominance of individual preferences in market systems. Other moral objections are also raised, each challenging some aspect of exchange left unquestioned in the conventional economic justification of it. Almost everyone will say that in some circumstances exchange is itself immoral. Selling oneself is an example, and it is legally prohibited almost everywhere. Moral and aesthetic judgment sometimes combine in the opinion that in "getting and spending we lay waste our powers." Moreover, an exchange or market system implies private property. If private property is itself immoral, as some people believe, then on that count exchange and markets are again immoral. Many people will also raise a moral objection to exchanges that seem unfair because, even if both parties gain, one party gains much more than the other. They also object to what they consider harsh bargains.

Some Dubious Inferences

Personality Disorder

Other critical allegations about the market system are not very illuminating. Some allege distortions in personality and culture. For example, it is alleged that life in an industrial milieu is damaging to personality as life in an agricultural milieu is not. Here it is clear that criticism ought to be aimed at industrialization, a worldwide phenomenon not limited to market systems. Or market systems put some men in the position of controlling others, a relation harmful to both. But that is an obvious feature of all organized social life; in all systems men control other men. Or the market system puts men in competition with each other. But so also does competition for jobs, power, and advancement in an authority system. Or exchange relations turn people away from co-operative ventures to their own individual concerns. In fact, the exchange relationship achieves a cooperative international division of labor to a degree that no alternative mechanism has ever achieved.

Although Aristotle thought exchange a suitable human activity if limited to serving man's moderate needs, he thought it corrupting as a major preoccupation or instrument for unbridled gain. More than 2,000 years later, John Ruskin wrote:

> . . . in the community regulated only by laws of demands and supply, but protected from open violence, the persons who became rich are, generally speaking, industrious, resolute, proud, covetous, prompt, methodical, sensible, unimaginative, insensitive, and ignorant. The persons who remain poor are the entirely foolish, the entirely wise, the idle, the reckless, the humble, the thoughtful, the dull, the imaginative, the sensitive, the well-informed, the improvident, the irregularly and impulsively wicked, the clumsy knave, the open thief, and the entirely merciful, just, and Godly person.[13]

Throughout the history of thought flows a powerful undercurrent of antagonism to exchange, breaking to the surface from time to time, as in Montesquieu among many others, and of course in Marx, and manifested in long-standing moral and legal rules like those against usury. Even if the antagonism often fails to point to specific characteristics of market systems such as those we have been trying to identify, it, like the emerging revulsion to bureaucracy, has to be acknowledged.

Neglect of Future

It is also alleged that market systems neglect the future. Granted. In all systems, men probably do not take a long enough view. But market systems are not necessarily less future oriented than alternative systems; one can buy a piece of the future. If, in a market system, an owner of a natural resource comes to believe that the resource will become scarcer in the future, he will be motivated to withhold some of it from the current market in order to take advantage of the higher price in the future. If he is not yet an owner, he will be motivated to buy the resource and hold it for the future. This both enriches him and conserves the resource.

The Contemporary Radical Economics Critique

Finally, a new school of radical economists claim that capitalism is the root of crime, racism, sexism, and military expansion.[14] Taking "capitalism" to denote a private enterprise market system, a connection between these problems and such a system is not apparent. For these problems are as old as history; they long antedate market as well as private enterprise systems. In the contemporary world, they are all also to be found in the communist world and in the world of the developing countries. We lack evidence that the problems are more severe in one kind of system than in another. Nor can particular features of market institutions be closely tied to these problems. Private enterprise market systems can be argued to incorporate exploitative features, and exploitation might be argued to be the root of all these problems. But all alternatives to private enterprise market systems also incorporate exploitation.

It may someday become clear that private enterprise market systems persist in such characteristics as racism or sexism while other kinds of politico-economic systems gradually shed them. China shows, for example, that under an authoritarian system, extraordinarily rapid progress can be made toward sexual equality. Yet so far the evidence is that differences in culture or historical circumstance, rather than differences in economic structure, account for such variation in these traits as can be observed among nations. Communist China would probably be judged less sexist than the Soviet Union, for example, but more so than Sweden.

To some of these problems—alienation, for one—we shall return in later chapters. For none of them should we discount the subtle indirect ways, even if they are still beyond our understanding, in which politico-economic institutions might affect such attributes of a society as its crime rates or patterns of sexual or ethnic discrimination. No doubt some solid connections between such phenomena and the institutions of private enterprise and market system can be established, and similar connections for other politico-economic systems. For in none of them do these phenomena simply vanish; they are somehow perpetuated in various degrees in all.

87

Implications for Government and Politics

In their pursuit of a definitive list of market shortcomings, economists do not include adverse effects of market system on government and politics. It is a blind spot in their analysis. Economists are correct in believing that on some counts the use of a market system simplifies government and politics by accomplishing, through exchange among private parties, tasks of social organization that would otherwise be a burden on government. They are also correct in believing that market systems help support liberal democracy; and, indeed, we will look into the character of that support in a later chapter. They miss, however, the ways in which, because major decisions are made in the market rather than in government, the tasks of government are complicated and the powers of government in some ways crippled. In particular, they miss certain threats to democracy that follow from power in the market. These complications and threats all have to be counted as limitations on market systems. The analysis of them will be pursued in many of the following chapters.

Scope of Market System

Let me say once more that our list of limitations on markets is intended to clarify characteristics of market system, not to accomplish an evaluation or to come to a judgment like Aristotle's, Ruskin's, or Marx's. And to identify in summary form not market weaknesses, which are too many and too complex to simplify, but market impossibilities, a final question is useful: What can an organization succeed in doing through exchange and market if permitted, and what can it be permitted to do?

It can organize thousands or millions of people to produce a variety of ordinary marketable goods and services, we all know. Beyond that it can do many things that some of us mistakenly assume that it cannot. It can build and operate a highway, for example, as is illustrated by privately maintained toll roads. It can build and operate educational and research institutions that survive by selling services for a fee. It can provide the services of a judiciary through organizations like the American Arbitration Association that offer adjudication at a price. It can provide military and police services, as illustrated by mercenaries in Angola in the 1970s and by Pinkerton and other private police forces on hire. It can provide postal services, as illustrated by growing private postal services in the United States.

It can also build, maintain, and govern an entire city on the proceeds of sales of land and houses to occupants. Indeed, a number of corporations are doing just that, establishing retirement towns such as the Leisure Worlds built and governed by the Rossmoor Corporation. Citizens, if they can be called that, pay the corporation for roughly the whole range of services ordinarily provided by municipal government; and they also pay the corporation to make most of the governmental decisions that citizens usually have to make themselves or through their elected and appointed officials.

For all that, a market system is a limited-use institution. Some tasks no market system can attempt or achieve. In simplest and very rough form, the distinction between what markets can and cannot do is this: For organized social life, people need the help of others. In one set of circumstances, what they need from others they induce by benefits offered. In other circumstances, what they need will not willingly be provided and must be compelled. A market system can operate in the first set of circumstances, but not in the second. Its limitation is conspicuous when compared with an authority system. Although authority is not required in the first set of circumstances, it can be used for both.*

---

* As the first circumstance is described, it might seem as though it would be uncommon. Yet the ubiquitous use of markets suggests that it is commonplace. Governments vastly expand the frequency of the first circumstance by conferring a fund of important resources on most adults in the form of physical assets or money (through the law of property). Hence, most people have something important—highly persuasive—to offer in order to induce cooperation. Most of us take private property for granted, but it is illuminating to see it as a man-made device that makes the first circumstance common rather than a rarity.

PART III

THE VARIETY OF

MARKET SYSTEMS

Alternative Market Systems

DOWN through the centuries, markets and private enterprise developed side by side. As a result, neither Adam Smith nor Karl Marx, for all their monumental intellectual accomplishments, managed to disentangle them. In our age we can. Market systems, we now know, are not always private enterprise systems. Yugoslavia is a socialist market system of one type; other types not yet in existence can be imagined. We also know that any one of the world's actual private enterprise systems is a mix of several types of market system.

Smith and Marx missed another possibility: the market as an instrument of central planning. We now know that in principle—and in emerging practice—central planning divides into two distinctive methods: administrative or authoritative planning, and market planning. It is just possible that the world is on the brink of realizing a great new potential for planning, although it is probably no higher a probability than is nuclear self-destruction.

Private Enterprise

The private enterprise system gives us a familiar point against which other possibilities can be located in an overview.* Every industrialized market-oriented system in the world today combines two pervasive forms of market system, the first of which is the market system of the individual or family enterprise. In the United States, individual and family owners operate more than 4 million small enterprises; Japan, for another example, has almost 3 million in small manufacturing alone. The second is the market system of bureaucratized corporate enterprise. In the industrialized systems most market production is in their hands. In the United States, roughly 60 percent of production is corporate; and at least 80 percent of employment is in establishments of 20 or more employees.[1]

After the Department of Defense with its more than 1 million civilian employees, the largest organizations in the United States are not other branches of government but American Telephone and Telegraph and General Motors, each approaching a million employees, more than the industrial labor force of many nations. The Ford Motor Company, with only half that many employees, is nevertheless larger than any government department except Defense and the Postal Service. By amount of revenue, all of these, as well as Exxon and General Electric, are larger than the governments of California, New York State, and New York City, which are the giants among state and city governments. If industrial corporations are compared by output with state and municipal government, sixteen of the largest twenty organizations are corporations.[2] General Motors' sales alone are larger than the gross national product of most nations.

In other nations, corporations are smaller but still very large both absolutely and relative to the size of their economies. In number of large industrial corporations, after the United States comes the United Kingdom,

---

* A common term for private enterprise market-oriented systems is "competitive." I use the term "private enterprise" because it denotes the characteristic institution that separates these systems from other real and hypothetical market systems. Moreover, "competitive" is a misleading term. No less than in a market system, people in authority systems compete for good jobs and other advantages. Democratic politics is also competitive. Socialist emulation in Cuba and China is competitive. Finally, many forms of market behavior called "competitive" in market systems are not competitive in the psychological sense. Wheat farmers, for example, are said to be competitive in a market system. But they do not rival each other, do not seek to displace each other. Each of them is largely indifferent to thousands of other wheat farmers, and to those in his own neighborhood he is tied by common interests and sociability rather than separated by rivalry. On the relation between rivalry and competition, see F. M. Scherer, *Industrial Market Structure and Economic Performance* (Chicago: Rand McNally, 1971), pp. 9–11.

Japan, Germany, France, and Canada in that order.[3] And multinational corporations have proliferated. Sixty-two of the largest hundred American corporations produce in six or more countries, and roughly one-third of their employees work in their overseas operations.[4]

The displacement, for most production, of individual and family by corporate enterprise constitutes a revolution—part of the bureaucratic revolution already noted. Never much agitated, never even much resisted, a revolution for which no flags were raised, it transformed our lives during those very decades in which, unmindful of what was happening, Americans and Europeans debated instead such issues as socialism, populism, free silver, clericalism, chartism, and colonialism. It now stands as a monument to discrepancy between what men think they are designing and the world they are in fact building.

In the industrialized private enterprise systems of the world most production is in the hands of salaried officials—corporate bureaucrats, strictly speaking—who own no more than a small fraction of the shares of the corporation. Authority mechanisms have had to be devised to induce them to act as though they were owner-managers. When this is done by varying the manager's income through bonuses and salary adjustments precisely as organizational income varies, then the manager remains motivated very much as he would be in ordinary individual exchange. But in large corporate enterprises, his income need not be tied so tightly to enterprise income. He may instead be authoritatively instructed to act as though the gains and losses of the enterprise were his, to play the game by that rule. In either case, he will usually take on corporate goals as his own. Although a private enterprise cannot ignore profits, for it cannot stay in business without them, beyond some level of profitability its officials can opt for growth, more sales, innovation, diversification, or a quiet stability instead of more profits. The options open to them make them look, again, like public officials.

Market Socialism

As an alternative to private enterprise, market socialism is, in principle at least, easy to establish. Merely remove top management from all existing corporations and put government officials in their places. Or put the same managers back in their jobs, but make them government officials. Instruct them to carry on as before: produce and sell whatever customers will buy, pay for whatever inputs are necessary, avoid losses, cover costs. An appropriate new rule might be: Make money but don't practice monopoly.* Since corporate managers are already salaried bureaucrats, they should find it easy to operate under the new rules, very imperfectly, of course, as in any system.†

All the market-oriented systems of the world practice market socialism for some industries: most often railroads and airlines, electric power, sometimes mining. They do so for a variety of reasons: socialist principle at one extreme and rescue of defunct private enterprises at the other. In these systems, we shall later see, market socialism is no revolution at all and is often a disappointment to its advocates. Indeed these touches of socialism make so little difference that customers and employees sometimes do not know whether the corporation from which they buy or for which they work is private or governmental. Even where socialized enterprises have been made a more effective instrument of the government's development policy, as has been the case in Western Europe since the late 1960s, they constitute one more arrow in a quiver rather than a major transformation of the system.[5]

As early as the 1890s, market socialism for an entire system began to be perceived as at least a hypothetical possibility by Barone and by Pareto, both nonsocialists interested only in theoretical clarification of the concept of the market system. From the 1920s on, the possibility was debated by economists, many of whom came to believe that no nation, for reasons of administrative practicality and political feasibility, was likely to inaugurate what seemed to be increasingly persuasive only as a hypothetical model.[6] And then, to the surprise of many who had thought that the concept appealed mostly to socialists in the liberal, individualistic, democratic tradition, market socialism was established in communist Yugoslavia, from which it appears to have begun to move to Hungary. Why and how we shall see in a later chapter.

---

* As in the case of private enterprises, some mechanism is required to prevent socialist enterprises from behaving monopolistically. One method is through government price setting, as in price setting for public utilities in private enterprise systems. That is the most familiar version of market socialism. Another is competition among socialist enterprises.

† F. A. Hayek is perhaps the leading expositor of the argument that in practice socialist market rules will not work. See his "Socialist Calculation," *Economica*, New Series, 7 (May 1940). In principle, they will. That is to say, one can outline a set of consistent, not self-contradictory pricing and production rules for government-owned market enterprises. In actual fact, the position of the manager, who is expected to follow the rules, is not so different from that of the contemporary salaried corporate executive as it is different from that of the owner-manager whom Hayek may have in mind. In actual fact too, Yugoslavia is now operating a version of market socialism. It works, though imperfectly.

Market socialism is of course not the general communist model. All communist systems, to be sure, make heavy use of the market system in distributing consumer goods and services and in allocating the labor force. Consumers go out and buy food, clothing, and other consumables; and members of the work force offer their labor in return for wages. But communist systems do not much use the market for determining what is to be produced and for allocating resources to the various chosen lines of production. In all communist systems except Yugoslavia and Hungary, managers of business enterprises produce not whatever they can sell, as in market socialism, but what they are instructed to produce by higher authorities. And resources and other inputs are administratively assigned to them; they are not bought at the discretion of the enterprise at whatever price is necessary to attract them. Even though prices are used in these systems, production is controlled directly by authority, not by exchange.

Until the great debate on market socialism began, economists appear to have believed that if private property in production were outlawed and a whole system were built around government-owned enterprises, the absence of private transactions in capital, land, and other natural resources would make a market system impossible. It now seems clear, however, that a government can create markets for them, even if it is sole owner. For petroleum, timber, and other natural resources, governmental authority needs to decide on the monthly or annual rate at which they are to be used up. Having decided, government can sell them to whichever enterprises will pay for them, allowing prices on them to rise and fall as necessary to clear the market. Land and capital can be similarly allocated not by administrative discretion but by making them available, at rents and interest rates that clear each market, to whichever enterprises wish to pay for them.

Because in both private enterprise and market socialism production is controlled by market demand, one is tempted to jump to the conclusion that both are what is commonly called a "consumer sovereignty" system. That term needs to be read as a technical term in economics rather than an accurately descriptive term, since it is possible to dissent from the implication that consumers are actually sovereign in such a system (as we shall see in later chapters). Without loading too much meaning into the word "sovereignty," however, we can indeed say of existing market systems and of all the market systems so far discussed that production is largely controlled by the market demands of millions of consumers. They are predominantly consumer sovereignty systems. Yet neither a private enterprise nor a socialist market system need be tied to consumer sovereignty.

97

Planner Sovereignty Market Systems

If it is not tied to consumer sovereignty, the market can be turned into an instrument of central planning—a revolutionary transformation of the market the possibilities of which are still not widely understood in any part of the world. Soviet planners, we shall later see, are much confused about it; Chinese planners have hardly given it a thought.

Some business enterprises sell to government as well as, or instead of, to individual consumers. Governments buy missiles and the services of soldiers, highways, parks and other recreational services, some medical care, and many other consumer goods, including public goods, which for one reason or another are not or cannot be produced directly or exclusively in response to consumer demands. Obviously, therefore, government purchases can direct production as surely as can consumer purchases. A planner sovereignty market system is one in which they do so. Government directs production by purchases *of final products* rather than by commands. Such a system is a possibility yet unrealized for the central planning of an entire economy.

In the fullest form of planner sovereignty, all production, consumer goods included, would be guided by the purchases of a government that has displaced the consumer as the "sovereign." All enterprises would sell either to government officials, who decide what consumers should have; or they would sell intermediate products to other firms that would in turn sell to government officials instead of individual consumers. Government authority would direct the allocation of resources and the productive processes by buying or not buying final products, or by buying more or less of them; it would not use authoritative assignments of targets and quotas.

Government planning would be limited to the desired assortment of final outputs. Through exchange all other production would be subordinated to those final outputs. Government would signal for shoe production, for example, by increasing its purchase of shoes; but how the shoes are produced, with what intermediate products, what machinery or buildings are used, what employees are hired—all that would be left to the enterprises to decide and arrange through markets.

Anyone not already familiar with the idea of a planner sovereignty system will be puzzled on one point: How in such a system will consumer goods be made available to consumers, who no longer direct the system with their purchases? Government can administratively allocate them goods, as in wartime rationing. Or government can sell consumer goods to the citizenry.

If the latter, why not simply let the shoe producers sell directly to consumers without the intervention of government at all? Because officials want outputs different from those which consumers would buy if left to themselves. So the planners buy the quantities of shoes and other consumer goods that they believe makes sense for the system. They might, for example, buy fewer automobiles and many more highly nutritious foods than consumers would buy if left to themselves. Such a system operates simultaneously two separate sets of market systems—one for controlling production, and the other for distributing to consumers neither more nor less than the planners want them to have. Prices in the two systems will be quite independent of each other.*

All market-oriented systems are in part planner sovereignty systems simply because government is a buyer of many final outputs. Governments buy highways, medical services, and education, for example, and then distribute them free or at subsidized prices. Another commonplace method of accomplishing a degree of planner sovereignty is through subsidies to the enterprise that change the effective price received by the enterprise or through taxes that change the effective price that consumers must pay. A subsidy to an airline based on the volume of its services, for example, increases the effective price received by the airline, thus signaling them to produce more airline services than consumers had been demanding, in effect substituting to some degree government direction of final output for consumer direction.

In a planner sovereignty market system, government officials buy from either government-owned or private enterprises. Taking account of two forms of ultimate control over production (consumer preferences or governmental preferences) and two forms of ownership (private or

---

* In what is called a consumer sovereignty system, just as consumer preferences direct production, so also do the occupational preferences of workers to a degree. Workers are free to work wherever jobs are offered; they are not conscripted; and, moreover, if they prefer not to work, say, in coal mines, then the amount dug is restricted because workers will work in the mines only if they are paid a premium wage.

Like a consumer sovereignty system, a planner sovereignty system can accommodate worker sovereignty. But it is also possible to imagine a planner sovereignty system in which planners suppress worker as well as consumer sovereignty. In such a market system, just as the prices paid to producers for final outputs would reflect planner demands rather than individual consumer demands, so also wage rates charged to producers would reflect planner preferences with respect to workers' job assignments. Wage rates would have to be set accordingly, so that each enterprise would pay for labor a rate (a price for labor) that took no account of worker preferences.

The result would be that wage rates paid by enterprises might no longer be effective in attracting workers into undesired occupations. It would therefore be necessary to conscript labor, or it would be necessary to induce workers to go where planners wish by paying them bonuses not charged up as costs to the employing enterprise, hence not affecting production decisions. There would be two sets of prices on labor, just as there are two sets of prices on consumer goods in a planner sovereignty system. One set of prices guides enterprise decisions; the other does not.

TABLE 7.1

Four Types of Market System

	Consumer Sovereignty Systems (production responds to consumer preferences in the market)	Planner Sovereignty Systems (production responds to planner preferences in the market)
Private Enterprise	1. Conventional private enterprise systems, as in Western Europe and North America.	2. Occurs in industries in private enterprise systems from which government buys or which government taxes or subsidizes to control demand.
Public Enterprise	3. Yugoslavia and, to a degree, Hungary.	4. Advocated by certain reformers in U.S.S.R. and Eastern Europe.

governmental) we can now see that we have so far uncovered four kinds of market system, as in Table 7.1. All of them, it should never be forgotten, look simpler and more efficient on paper than in practice.

A Mathematically Computed Market System

Still other kinds of market system are possible. Both theoretically and as a practical issue in European communist systems since World War II, the issue is raised whether mathematics and electronic computation can greatly improve planning. That issue opens up several possibilities. To sort them out quickly we begin with the question: Can mathematics and electronic computation improve on existing market systems by computing efficiency prices instead of leaving them to be determined by actual buying and selling in imperfect markets? There is nothing internally inconsistent, nothing illogical, in such a proposal. The necessary mathematical techniques are gradually being developed—on the foundation of linear programming developed in the Soviet Union by Leonid V. Kantorovich and in the United States by George B. Dantzig and Tjalling C. Koopmans. (In 1975, Kantorovich and Koopmans won Nobel prizes for these efforts.) Most economists would, however, say that for a consumer sovereignty system the task would be both in fact impossible and of little use. Impossible because efficiency prices must reflect many millions of consumer preferences, more than can be observed and estimated. Impossible again because the only way to discover the preferences of the consumer is to leave him free to make such purchases in actual markets as test and reveal his preferences. Not useful because actual buying and selling does the task much more cheaply that if it were attempted through computation.

A Planner Sovereignty Market System through Computation?

For a planner sovereignty market system, the task of computing prices would be simpler. Only planner preferences need be observed and taken account of. But it is also widely agreed that even these simpler computations cannot in actual practice be accomplished, and some economists say they could never be.[7]

Prices can be assigned centrally: the Soviet government assigns by one estimate, 8 million prices.[8] The question, however, is on the practicality of assigning efficiency prices. To compute such prices requires an enormous volume of technological information on how variations in inputs of all kinds affect variations in outputs of all kinds. To get it would presumably require an inordinate share of a society's total labor force.[9] It would also need constant revision. Technological innovation renders this year's data inaccurate next year. Moreover, changes in planner preferences call for alterations of the technological relations. If over the years demands for steel, for example, rise so high as to compel the use of lower grade ores, the relations between ore and steel output will change.

If the data were in fact available, there are not enough computers and not enough trained operators in any nation for the required price computations. For certain simplified calculations to be discussed below— calculations that do not approach in complexity those here in question—a Soviet estimate is that 14,000 computers would be required for the U.S.S.R. instead of the several hundreds now available and that it would take a hundred years to train the required technicians at present already rapid rates of training.[10] Estimates of this kind are not in the least precise, but they indicate something of the possible magnitude of the computation problem.

Computing difficulties are not all. Although in principle the required mathematical techniques are available, the task of drawing up the necessary equations or a model of the economy is large, subject to error, and in actual practice probably beyond any profession's competence. Competence aside, manpower requirements are again formidable, though impossible to estimate. But adding together the tasks of data collection, mathematical model building (and fitting to data), and computation, the total required labor force for computerized pricing might leave only a few workers available to produce anything.

Computation of Input Allocations for a Noncomputed Set of Outputs?

Mathematics and computation may be more useful for authority systems than for market systems. We can digress a moment to note the possibilities. One is that, to escape from difficulties in computing efficiency prices, planners might choose, without the aid of any prices or markets, the outputs they want and then employ computation only to determine an efficient planned allocation of inputs to achieve that desired set of outputs. No markets or prices; computation alone. To compute efficient inputs would require, however, the same data on changing technological relations as are needed for a computed market system. The same techniques of mathematical programming are also required. All the basic difficulties of the first alternative remain.

Moreover, if the planners want to achieve an efficient use of resources, they will not be satisfied to know the best allocation of inputs through which a predetermined set of outputs can be produced. They will want to know what other possible sets of outputs are possible with the same resources. As a practical matter, then, they need information on what they would have to give up of current outputs in order to achieve some new set of outputs. Their problem is the same old economic problem again: What has to be given in order to get? In short, planners need to know the cost of each output. But if so, they need—after all—prices.

Consistent Planning through Computation?

The actual use of mathematics and electronic computation in economic planning—in the U.S.S.R., for example—has been neither to support a computed market system nor to attempt optimal nonmarket planning. Instead these techniques have been proposed to try to achieve a "balanced" plan, one in which, although misallocated, all available resources are employed but none overallocated. Such a plan wastes resources, but it "works" in the elementary sense that it is internally consistent.

The procedure proposed is input-output analysis, through which for any product those input-output ratios are calculated that indicate its necessary inputs. For any targeted set of outputs, then, the input requirements can be added; and it can be determined whether the inputs are under- or overcommitted. In either case, a series of adjusted recalculations of targets can be undertaken—as many iterations as needed—until the requirements on each input are made equal to its available supplies for the period in question.

Since in this process planners try to find only one consistent set of relationships, they do not need to know about all the possible input-output relationships among which some are more efficient than others. Yet even this much smaller amount of data is costly to gather. The direct steel input required, say, for one automobile body is not difficult to determine; but the manufacture of steel itself requires an input of electric power, which in turn requires some input of automobiles (for the use of electric power companies) and hence some further input of steel. These indirect and circular effects—secondary, tertiary, and so on —become laborious to compute.

Input-output tables have been calculated in no system for more than roughly 250 items, a figure that should be set beside the estimate of 8 million prices in the U.S.S.R. Research groups, both in the United States and in the Soviet Union, as well as in other countries of the world, have labored for years to produce tables for one single year; it has not been practical to attempt a continuing updated revision.[11] Mathematical and computational techniques can improve the consistency and efficiency of selected decisions.[12] So far, however, neither the U.S.S.R. nor China has actually put input-output analysis or any more ambitious form of mathematical planning to work on its larger planning process.[13]

Computing versus Acting Out

Among the difficulties that bar central planners from collecting necessary computations, one to which we have so far given only glancing attention is that consumer and planner preferences are not empirical phenomena to be observed and measured, like rainfall or frequency of alcoholism. They are "not facts to be gathered, but choices to be made." Not even the chooser himself knows his preferences until he is confronted with an actual choice, and his understanding of his own preferences is to be doubted unless he is in a real choice situation in which he chooses not hypothetically but actually. Hence the acting out of choices in market systems may be indispensable, and computation of preferences no substitute.

The distinction between computing and acting out is a special case of a fundamental phenomenon to be explored more fully in later chapters: In various ways, all societies combine two methods of achieving desired social organization—problem-solving analysis and problem-solving social interaction. People both think their way and act their way to solutions.

103

Alternative Forms of Private Enterprise and Property

Let us turn back to more conventional market systems. The familiar proprietorships and corporations of private enterprise are not the only forms that private ownership can take in a market system. Other forms include producer cooperatives, consumer cooperatives, and nonprofit organizations like hospitals, colleges, and foundations. Nonprofit market business enterprises of various kinds, including cooperatives, account in the United States for less than 1 percent of gross national product.[14] Some other market systems make a larger place for them. Consumer and producer cooperatives account for only 1 percent of the gainfully employed in France, but 10 percent in Finland and 30 percent in Israel.[15]

A great surprise that may be in store for the world is employee management of private enterprise. The kettle is simmering in worldwide dissatisfaction with the conventional authority relations of the business enterprise. New work groups in industry challenge the traditional right of unions to speak for workers. Yugoslavia has taken the extraordinary step of establishing self-management throughout industry. The movement is spreading in Western Europe.

If ownership of both capital and of the enterprise itself were in the hands of employees of an enterprise, the "tools" of production would no longer be in the hands of one group, labor power in another. The distribution of income from the enterprise could be transformed. So also might authority relations within the enterprise.*

Another possibility is an enterprise owned by workers who do not own the capital supplied to it. Workers, not owners of capital, are recognized as the managers of the enterprise. They establish and maintain the firm. They decide on what to produce, where, how, with what technologies, and with what complement of workers. They "hire" not employees but capital. They pay investors for the use of their funds, and they as workers take their income from the enterprise not as wages but as profits.

Organizations like that are rare, but they are not illegal or known to be impossible in practice or in any way inconsistent with the maintenance

---

* In Israel, Histadrut, sometimes called a trade union and sometimes "a state within a state" because of its multifold activities preceding the establishment of the state of Israel and continuation in these activities since, owns and operates dozens of enterprises accounting for roughly a fifth of Israeli production. Repeated attempts to introduce new forms of industrial democracy in Histadrut have largely though not wholly failed. (Milton Derber, "Histadrut and Industrial Democracy," in *Israel,* eds. Michael Curtis and Mordecai Chertoff [New Brunswick, N.J.: Transaction, 1973].)

of a market system. They do not exist simply because, as Marx saw more clearly than the classical economists, the historically given distribution of wealth is such that, when potential suppliers of capital and potential suppliers of labor contemplate joining with each other in an enterprise, the suppliers of capital have the necessary exchange or bargaining power to insist that authority be in their hands rather than in the hands of the workers. Not by logic but by history, owners of capital have become the owners of the enterprise.

Many of the characteristics of familiar private enterprise systems are not attributable to private enterprise and property as such but to this particular historical form of private enterprise and property in which owners of capital rather than workers own the enterprise. It is a form full of consequence for the distribution of wealth and authority, for job rights, for alienation, and for patterns of social conflict.

Many other characteristics attributed to private enterprise market systems—insecurity, income inequality, class conflict, educational disadvantage, inequality in political access, and political influence, among others—are more correctly attributable, as will increasingly become clear, not to private enterprise itself but to a historical inequality in the distribution of wealth. The market-oriented systems of the world are all inheritors of this inequality. None have gone very far in experimenting with a private property market system from which the effects of marked inequality in wealth are eliminated. Yet market systems that do so can be imagined. They would be drastically different from any existing market system.

Nonmarket and Market Systems

All the market systems above can be seen more distinctly in a recapitulation that lists them alongside certain nonmarket forms, real and hypothetical.[16]

1. *Authority without prices.* At this extreme is central authority without money, prices, and markets. Pure authoritative organization. No economy in the world is so organized, although Lenin attempted such a system between 1918 and 1921.[17]
2. *Authoritatively computed prices and production plans with no money or actual markets.* Near the extreme, government computes "markets"

105

rather than organizes actual markets. It calculates synthetic or shadow prices and other magnitudes to attempt an optimal set of physical input allocations and output assignments. No such system actually exists.

3. *Central authoritative planning with subsidiary use of prices.* Next is authoritative specification of output targets both for end and intermediate products, along with authoritative allocations of inputs, all facilitated, however, through money payments and prices. This, we shall see, is the method of Soviet, Eastern European, Cuban, and Chinese communism. Prices by no means play the signaling and allocating role they play in market systems; direction of the economy is through central authority. But consumer goods and services are sold in markets, and labor is hired in markets.

4. *Planner sovereignty market system.* Central governmental authority is limited to purchasing final outputs, with market coordination of all intermediate production. Such systems so far exist only as segments of all market systems in the real world.

5. *Consumer sovereignty market system.* No central governmental authority directs production; production responds to consumer demand in markets. This is the main component of the existing market-oriented systems of the world.

6. *Communes.* Neither central governmental authority nor a market system organizes production. Instead decentralized highly self-sufficient small production units look after themselves in loose association with each other. It is an aspiration partially realized on a small scale in the kibbutzim of Israel.

Each of the market systems (the fourth and fifth on the list) divides into systems of:

A. Governmental ownership and management
B. Private ownership and management, which in turn divides into
    (1) The familiar forms: owner management and corporate management
    (2) Worker control
    (3) Cooperatives and nonprofit enterprises

If this appears to be a handy classification of alternatives, it needs to be remembered that it is only a set of blueprints. Not only are real-world systems mixed, as will be apparent in the following chapter, but in addition there are differences in systems that the blueprints do not at all capture: cultural differences, for example, that will make one private enterprise system thrive while another one stagnates; a pace of technological innovation that gradually transforms the quality of life in one but is so retarded as to leave another in squalor; or, as later chapters will make much of, a passion for symmetry and order in some societies and an open-ended and untidy opportunism in others.

The Market-oriented Private Enterprise System

Looking back, it appears that Western Europe became a market-oriented society in the late eighteenth and early nineteenth centuries, North America in the nineteenth, Australasia and southern Africa later in the nineteenth, and Japan in the twentieth. In Asia, Latin America, and Africa, other market-oriented societies are still on the way. Yugoslavia aside, they all bear the private enterprise label, yet all mix the alternative systems of the preceding chapter. Beyond their familiar characteristics are a few other traits that are less well understood. With the concepts and clarification of the preceding chapters we can now characterize this set of systems with relatively few words.

1. *They are not in fact predominantly market systems (and no real-world system is).* This has always been so with these systems; it is no recent result of new governmental activities. In these systems life and work go on in family, business enterprise, and government agency. Within each, *internal* coordination is necessary, but not by market systems. Parental authority and various informal mutual adjustments organize the family. In countries largely given to subsistence agriculture, production is largely

organized within the family. But even in industrialized systems, family production is a large part of economic activity, though not counted in calculations of national product and income. In the United States, for example, nonmarket family production, if counted, would total, by rough estimates, close to a fourth of gross national product.[1]

Within the enterprise and government agency, countless tasks of organization are achieved through bureaucratic authority, as in all modern systems, although large firms use internal markets too. Only in *external* coordination, the coordination of groups with each other—families with business enterprises, enterprises with each other, government agencies with enterprises, unions with enterprises—does the market play a predominant role.

Even there, however it shares its task with a government that both authoritatively coordinates some aspects of economy and society and plays a larger role by far in the marketplace than does any other participant in the market. In these systems, government is typically the largest spender, lender, borrower, employer, property owner, tenant, and insurer. And in its role in the economy it grows ever larger. In the United States, government expenditures as a percentage of gross national product tripled from 10 percent before the Great Depression of the 1930s to over 30 percent in the 1970s. Paradoxically, therefore, one of the best ways to draw the outline of these market-oriented systems is to specify the great role governmental authority plays in them.[2]

The role of governmental authority in this kind of politico-economic system is illustrated in the configuration of the American landscape. Property taxes have driven residents and businesses out of decaying central urban areas. Subsidies to homeownership have sprawled housing developments over vast suburban areas. Both an older federal roads program that first made automobiles feasible and a newer interstate highway system that speeds them on their way have increased people's mobility enough to destroy in many areas the distinction between city and country. Highway and overpass construction has altered the contour of hill and valley. Industrial enterprises have been scattered over the countryside as local governments compete for tax-paying businesses. All this—often blamed on market chaos—we owe in some large part to active and powerful governments in market systems. Some of the prized accomplishments of these systems are also in large part those of government: among many others, the near eradication of the plague, typhoid, and malaria; literacy and public education; a modest level of income security for the aged; and a landing on the moon.

As an estimated percentage of gross national product, total government expenditures are as follows:[3]

Sweden	53%
United Kingdom	45
Austria[4]	44
Japan	42
France	40
Italy	40
West Germany[5]	39
Canada	37
United States	28
Brazil	19
India	18

Simply as an income redistributor, government operates as a major economic coordinator—for example, in financing free public education and welfare payments. Welfare payments, pensions, and subsidies alone (not including education) as a percentage of gross national product are roughly as follows.[6]

France	20%
Austria	16
Italy	16
Sweden	15
West Germany	15
Chile	12
Canada	11
United Kingdom	11
United States	6
Japan	5
India	2
Nigeria	2
South Korea	2
Venezuela	2

A great amount of government economic activity is often referred to as "government regulation of business." It is indeed a vast set of activities. But the term is a misnomer. It actually refers to government promotion of business, which takes an endless variety of forms. The promotional role of government is, however, so crucial to other major features of these systems that it deserves its own chapter; and we shall therefore leave the proposition standing for the moment only as a hypothesis yet to be explored.

2. *Each of these systems mixes nonmarket governmental authoritative control over production (independently of the business enterprise) with three forms of control over the enterprise: "direct" authoritative control, "indirect" manipulation of their markets, and (as a special form of "indirect" control) planner sovereignty.*

The *nonmarket authoritative control* that operates independently of the business enterprise is represented by governmental administration of production by government employees. Habits of thought obscure our understanding that all government agencies are producing organizations. Judges produce adjudication. Agricultural extension agents produce technical advice. Congressmen produce both rules and investigatory services. Armies and navies produce a variety of services: conquest, demolition, terror, national defense, and sometimes peace. That all are productive services is indicated by the willingness of citizens to pay for them through taxes. Yet for all these productive services there is no market; production has to be administratively organized—much as all output is organized in a Soviet-style system.

Exclusive of the military, the size of this sector is often roughly estimated by counting civilian government employees, exclusive of employees of publicly owned enterprises, as a percentage of all gainfully employed:[7]

United States	14%
France	8
West Germany	7.5
Japan	6
United Kingdom	6
India	4

For government control over enterprises, *direct controls* take the form of authoritative prohibitions, permissions or commands: import prohibitions, for example, or import licensing, requirements that enterprises hire quotas of disabled workers, specification of procedures for floating new securities issues, prohibitions on discharging union activists, specification of forms of financial accounting and reporting, or prohibition of mergers. The list is endless.

In order to cope with large corporations whose decisions are increasingly pivotal for the whole economy, government officials have increasingly learned to extend authority granted to them in other areas in order to achieve control over the corporation. Thus, American presidents extend their authority to investigate, publicize, tax, and contract in order to threaten corporate executives, with the result that some corporations now clear proposed price increases with the White House before announcing them.

Indirect controls operate through setting minimum or maximum prices—for example, minimum wage laws—or through governmental buying and selling—for example, buying farm products to maintain farm prices—or through any other form that affects the profitability of an enterprise's activity.

110

Of the many forms of indirect control, one is the practice of *planner sovereignty,* that is, control through governmental purchases of final products. Governments contract to buy weapons and highways, for example. It is an old practice, familiar even if not under the name of planner sovereignty. Yet until about 1950, wages and salary payments constituted the biggest item in the U.S. budget. Only since then have contract disbursements been larger. The change marks a shift from government reliance on authority or administrative direction (over its own employees) to market direction through purchases of final products from enterprises.[8]

Government purchases from business enterprises, excluding new capital investment, as a percentage of gross domestic product are roughly the following. The figures exclude purchases of inputs by socialized enterprises.[9]

United States	7.3%
West Germany	7.2
Sweden	6.7
United Kingdom	6.7
Canada	6.2
India	3.0
Australia	1.7

The appearance of planner sovereignty sometimes disguises, however, direct administrative authority over the enterprise. In the United States, planner sovereignty in defense production is mixed with direct administrative control, in a form that Seymour Melman calls Pentagon capitalism.[10] Twenty thousand civilian and military personnel in the Defense Contract Administration Services exercise detailed authority over the contracting enterprises. Their authority goes far, for example, as to supervise the enterprise's insurance policies, packaging and packing, safety requirements, production schedules and reporting, procurement from its own subcontractors, inventories, tests, and engineering studies.[11] It is a major new form of politico-economic organization in a large sector of the American system which is larger in output than the gross national product of many nations, larger than India, almost as large as Canada.

3. *Since World War II the governments of these systems have been steering the market system through certain policies that go by the name of national economic planning.* What they do is far removed from planning as practiced in communist systems, where "planning" means authoritative nonmarket controls over production. Planning is one of government's major methods of promoting business—a prestigious new one since World War II. As we shall later see, planners do not seriously contemplate other objectives like constraining business enterprises, planning production, or

111

changing the fundamental character of an economy, of a countryside, or of a culture.

4. *All these systems practice some degree of market socialism.* Public corporations in these systems do not differ greatly, however, from private corporations; they operate through roughly the same kind of bureaucratic corporate structure to be found in private enterprise under the authority of a salaried top management instructed to avoid losses and make profits, a management in no conspicuous way different from private management.

Once the central institution of the socialist model of society and still central in communist thought, public ownership lost the enthusiasm of democratic socialists in the years after World War II. Other policies and institutions began to look more promising, especially redistributive income taxation coupled with social welfare programs and Keynesian techniques for maintaining high levels of employment. Socialists also saw that the orderly acquisition by government of business enterprises through purchase rather than confiscation does not much change the distribution of wealth. (Purchase is typically thought necessary in democratic systems.) And for democratic socialists living in nondemocratic systems, they find little virtue in turning an enterprise over to the state. Even in democratic systems, turning it over to a public instead of private bureaucracy has become an increasingly dubious gain, especially since the main controls over the enterprise are market controls in either case.

As a result, after a socialist flurry at the end of World War II the socialization of enterprises has again fallen into nonsocialist hands. I say "again" because both the very early and the most recent ventures in public enterprise were not principled or ideological ventures in socialism. The Mercantilists established state monopolies of tobacco, salt, matches, and alcohol, for example, as easy revenue sources for the state. In the nineteenth century, socialization of public utilities, like railroads, telephone and telegraph, and electric power were pragmatic responses to the difficulties of controlling the "natural monopolies" spawned by new technologies. Then at the end of World War II, although a socialist wave of nationalizations rose in the United Kingdom, some of the French nationalizations—Renault, for example—were undertaken to punish Nazi collaborators; and the Italian government was left with a large number of public enterprises on its hands as a legacy of fascism. The most recent nationalizations in Western Europe in the 1960s and 1970s have been advocated as useful for economic growth; and on that score they have been more appealing to planners, bureaucrats, and businessmen than to socialists.

Whether public enterprise becomes a practical instrument for economic growth remains to be seen. Such planning as the market-oriented systems practice, largely through indirect market controls, can be brought to bear on private as well as public enterprises. Because these public enterprises are operated under a regime of consumer sovereignty instead of planner sovereignty or direct authoritative control, they are not designed to be especially receptive to state directives. In the past, it has often been questioned whether central government achieves any more significant effective control over these enterprises than over private corporations. In France, for example, the conduct of the private "iron and steel industry was as much dependent on government policies as the conduct of nationalized deposit banks or of the nationally owned Renault Company." And "in Italy the wholly nationalized petroleum industry was no less independent of State discretion than the wholly private chemical industry."[12] It has been argued that the nationalizations of the central banks of the United Kingdom and France have produced no gain in public control over them.[13]

Market socialism has not challenged the conventional authority structure of the business enterprise; moves toward reform of workplace organization and corporate governance are as lively in private as in public enterprises. Nor has public enterprise in these systems been marked by a new set of managerial attitudes toward profit and public interest. In France, executives of public corporations are members of employer associations; and "a common managerial spirit" obliterates differences that might be expected between the two kinds of enterprise.[14] Executives of private corporations have, in many countries, been appointed managers of public corporations.

Public enterprises also approximate private enterprises in policy. In France, the publicly owned Renault Company has conspired with its private competitors to hold up prices. In Italy, public corporations do the same. In the United Kingdom the chairman of the publicly owned steel corporation revealed how little had changed when he declared his opposition to competition among subordinate plants: "that would be giving the profits to the consumer."[15] To join the management fraternity, managers of public enterprises apparently must assimilate themselves to their more numerous private enterprise colleagues. For reasons that we shall subsequently explore, a predominantly public enterprise system in which public managers are dominant might, however, turn out quite differently.

In the United States, market enterprises owned and operated by governments play only a small role, accounting, roughly, for less than 2 percent of national income and of employment.[16] Electric power is partially socialized. Many municipalities—almost all large ones—run their own water supply enterprises. Some railroad services and much urban transit are socialized. A large part of the insurance industry is socialized through compulsory old-age and unemployment insurance. Both federal and local governments own and rent housing; many states have socialized liquor wholesaling and retailing; irrigation water is sold largely by the federal government; state governments operate toll highways; and a variety of governmental units own and operate warehouses, docks, conveyors, grain elevators, and other transport terminal facilities, selling their services on the market.[17] Military commissaries—the PX's—are socialized retail establishments with aggregate sales larger than Woolworth's, J. C. Penney, or Montgomery Ward.[18] One estimate puts the total number of public enterprises in the United States at 18,000.

In other market-oriented systems, publicly operated market enterprises usually play a larger role, accounting for the following percentages of total employment:[19]

Austria	13%
Ireland	13
France	12
United Kingdom	12
Italy	11.5
Sweden	10.5
Finland	10
West Germany	9
Belgium	8
Netherlands	8
Norway	6
Luxembourg	5.5
Canada	5
Denmark	5
New Zealand	5
Australia	4
United States	3

5. *In all these systems, labor unions remain in certain ways a major unintegrated element.* Unions appear in all of them in various strengths. The estimated percentage of the work force in labor unions is as follows:[20]

Sweden	more than	55%
Austria		50
Belgium		50
United Kingdom		40
Argentina		35
Netherlands		35
Italy		35
West Germany		30
Japan		30
Canada		25
Chile		25
United States		25
France		20
Mexico		20
India	less than	5

Most people do not see the union as a productive organization like family, enterprise, and government agency.[21] Nor is it seen as discharging a necessary "public" function but instead a factional task, the protection of the particular interests of its members. Indeed, its own leadership usually makes no greater claim, unlike business leadership, which never doubts that it performs a public function even if it is profit motivated. Aside from strikes, both the work restrictions and higher wage costs that the union can sometimes win often cast it in the role of a disruptive rather than a constructive social institution. As for employers, even those who have committed themselves to the principle of collective bargaining typically continue to look upon the union as subversive of the traditional structure of corporate authority.

Union members themselves are often hostile to their union. A major trend in European unionism in recent decades has been a shift of decision making on job assignments and job rights from established union procedures to shop-floor procedures of spontaneous origin.[22] In some unions, the relationship between much of the membership and union officialdom is no closer than between employee and employer. In the United States, union membership has, for some years, actually been declining in relation to size of work force.[23] Unionism has also come under increasing attack as itself exploitative on the ground that its wage gains are at the expense of the unorganized.[24]

Nevertheless, unionism is often the foundation of a system of industrial jurisprudence. And it transforms the process through which wages are established in the market. It substitutes elaborate discussion, negotiation, and exercise of discretion for either of two earlier forms of wage setting: competitive supply and demand, and employer monopoly power.[25] In Sweden, at an extreme, wages are negotiated for the nation as a whole by a single employee organization meeting with a single employer organization. In the United States, by contrast, negotiations are at enterprise or industry levels. Whatever the level, the effect of collective bargaining is to throw wage determination into the hands of two countervailing groups, each of which exercises some discretionary power over wages.

A result is that wage rates, the price of labor, may depart far from efficiency prices. If so, possible consequences include resource misallocation and—more seriously—inflation and unemployment. While economists differ as to whether in fact collective bargaining is or is not a major source of contemporary inflation and unemployment, governments seem to be in no doubt. They try to persuade unions to soften their wage demands, experiment with government participation in wage bargaining, or lay down guidelines for wage negotiation.[26] Britain's economic decline is often attributed—the evidence is inconclusive—to union demands that raise costs beyond what the system can afford.

Conflict between market system and unionism is a major fact about politico-economic organization. Only a fact, however, not a judgment. It leaves wide open the question of how the conflict is to be resolved.

6. *No government skillfully employs the market as an instrument of democratic public policy.* This proposition too we can leave as a hypothesis until later chapters. But consider: Historically, the market system has been tied, as we have seen it need not be, to private enterprise and private ownership of productive assets. Until recently, supporting governments have employed it in ways that protect these associated institutions. It has also been associated with a simplified ideology. As a result of these circumstances and others, private enterprise systems are better characterized as having been permitted to dominate other institutions, including government, than as having been skillfully employed by governmental policy makers for democratic purposes.[27]

7. *However poorly the market is harnessed to democratic purposes, only within market-oriented systems does political democracy arise.** Not all market-oriented systems are democratic, but every democratic system is also a market-oriented system. Apparently, for reasons not wholly understood, political democracy has been unable to exist except when coupled with the market. An extraordinary proposition, it has so far held without exception.

Part IV will examine the fundamental processes of popular control and will lead to a partial explanation of the tie between democracy and market.

* Unless one is willing to call communism a form of democracy (see chapter 20 on alternative meanings).

IV

POPULAR CONTROL
OF POLITICAL-ECONOMIC
SYSTEMS

Politics: The Struggle over Authority

I N an untidy process called politics, people who want authority struggle to get it while others try to control those who hold it.

Hobbes thought the fundamental struggle was over "men's persons, wives, children, and cattle." But the great struggles recorded in history do not tell a story of cattle thieves, kidnappers, and wife stealers. We have long ago learned that the Greeks did not sail to Troy simply to recapture Helen. Men fight over authority, for the control over men and wealth that authority achieves, for control over formal organizations and especially over the state's administrators and the military. It is only through organizations that men can raid, tax, irrigate the land, build roads or pyramids, keep the peace, and fight off invaders. Alexander, Xerxes, Caesar, Genghis Khan, and Napoleon struggled over authority, not over wives and cattle. So did Philip II, Cromwell, Bismarck, and de Gaulle. And so did Lincoln and Ho Chi Minh, and, for that matter, so did or does Richard Nixon, Richard Daley, Patrice Lumumba, Ian Smith, Mujibur Rahman, Stokely Carmichael, Yasir Arafat, and Harold Stassen.

In Stalin's purges and the turmoil of the Great Cultural Revolution in China, the struggle was violent; in the writing of the Mayflower Compact, it was made peaceful. The struggle takes innumerable forms. Along with exchange and persuasion, authority itself is thrown into the struggle for authority.

Control over Top Authority

However the struggle goes, it always brings authority under some degree of control. Authority consequently never accomplishes wholly unilateral control. Even when the struggle seems won and settled—a Stalin without rivals cows his subjects into docility—top authority is brought under at least weak control. For even exploitative politics requires social cooperation—of an army, or a police force, or tax collectors and other petty officials. To play a supervisory role, top authority must consequently respond at least minimally to their wishes. Inevitably too, those on whom top authority confers subordinate bureaucratic authority will extend the use of their authority to reach upward and gain power over top authority itself, a phenomenon that Mao conspicuously long struggled to resist.

In particular, because every person in high authority needs information, he comes to be in some degree the captive of knowledge specialists— experts, analysts, intelligence agents, statisticians, and the like. President Kennedy was their captive when he acquiesced in the Bay of Pigs invasion, and so was Krushchev in his defeat on educational reforms in 1958. Top authority's need for information, analysis, and advice will give rise to specialized governmental institutions like the sultan's vizier, a kitchen cabinet or the Indian Planning Commission. More than 3,000 years ago, when great folk movements brought the Aryans into India, the Persians into Persia, the Latins into Italy, and the Greeks into the Aegean Basin, all their governments had councils and assemblies to advise and constrain the kings.[1] The exercise of influence through discussion and persuasion will be dispersed beyond persons in government itself to anyone who can get the ruler's ear or the ears of people close to him—a crony or friend of a friend, a petitioner, or a newspaper columnist, among others.

The Supporting Organization

So great a prize as control over the state motivates unending contention. And the struggle drives every contender to seek help. No one alone can seize or hold top authority in a large social system. He needs organization: a private army, like Hitler's bully boys; or an informal group such as supported Stalin in his later years; or a political party, like the Soviet or Chinese communist party; or a faction within a party or bureaucracy, like Nixon's Committee to Re-Elect the President; or guerrillas, like those who brought Castro to power. Whatever the form, the supporting organization fastens controls on top authority. Often it can depose top leadership; for example, the Polish communist party swiftly eliminated Wladyslaw Gomulka in December 1970.

Mutual adjustment in the supporting organization constrains top leadership—probably more than it does in government proper. To induce members to grant him authority in the supporting organization, top authority offers benefits to them: policies they favor, loot, a share of his own authority, promotion within the organization, or protection against their enemies.

Although top authority in government can use police and army to coerce grants of authority from the bureaucracy and the population, it cannot coerce grants of authority within the supporting organization— unless it can create within that organization a smaller group capable of coercing members of the larger organization. But in that case it must offer benefits to members of the smaller group to induce grants of authority from them. At some point in every system, top authority inevitably comes to be dependent on a supportive organization built on multilateral exchange and persuasion rather than on unilateral authority. That is one of the most fundamental facts of politics. Despite his once great authority in Egypt, "at every stage, Nasser had to evaluate the risks involved in discarding one of his companion's [*sic*] advice: viz. whether or not he would become an open opponent, and whether this opposition could become dangerous."[2] Examples like that are found everywhere in the history of authority.

When Stalin died, a major supporting organization available to a new leader was the Politburo. But for a time the Politburo chose otherwise. It collectively exercised top authority rather than pledge its obedience to a successor to Stalin, even though for ceremonial purposes it briefly cast Georgi Malenkov in the role of top authority. A common phenomenon in politics, the supporting organization collectively takes authority away from top leadership and exercises it through whatever arrangements it can maintain: elections within the group or informal mutual adjustment, including exchanges of benefits, internal alliances, mutual threats, even assassinations.

But every major player in such a game depends on the help of other persons who accept his authority. Hence each major player engaged in controlling the others is in turn controlled by his own supporters. Sometimes, rival supporting groups share and contend for top authority. After the Cultural Revolution in China, "three kingdoms" shared authority: the army under Lin Piao's military committee; the Cultural Revolution group under Chen Po-ta and Chiang Ching; and the government machine under Chou En-lai's State Council.[3]

Some supporting organizations do not try to play a decisive role in deciding who rises to the top. They do no more than influence persons who hold or might soon hold authority. They therefore exist by sufferance of government and other stronger supporting groups.

In most countries, top authority tries to make use of such organizations—interest groups—by using them as sources of information and often too as a channel of communication *to* the population. The resulting intimacy between interest group and government official gives each influence over the other, even in highly authoritarian systems. Although communist and fascist systems prohibit interest groups, we shall see that they nevertheless appear in these systems as informal followings attached to various leaders.

The Elements of Politics

Government and politics thus come to embrace at least the following:

Government in our original sense, carrying out various tasks through an ostensibly hierarchical structure of authority.

Top authority engaged both in directing the hierarchy and in a struggle to maintain itself.

Advisors to top authority who gain controls other than authority over top authority.

Supporting organizations, including interest groups.

The army, or other military organization, which may or may not supplant all other large supporting organizations.

In addition, politics, though varying from country to country, comes to be in large part not a pyramidal exercise of authority but a vast and complex set of mutual interactions:

Looting, raiding, extorting, borrowing, or taxing by supporting groups and government in order to obtain the wherewithal to pay and equip the army and gratify other supporting groups, including those persons induced to defect from rival supporting groups.

In a general exchange of benefits, offers by top authority, potential rivals, and others to induce the cooperation of others in their struggle for top authority, or in a struggle to constrain top authority. Benefits include not only loot and money but position, status, shares of authority, and the like.

Threats of many kinds (death, exile, prison, and disgrace), especially threats by persons in authority to terminate benefits to followers and allies, and threats by supporters and allies to withdraw grants of authority and other cooperation.

Use of leadership's authority, directly, obliquely, and extended, to compel support in the struggle for power and, for leaders already on top, to suppress the struggle.

Construction (by leaders of government and of supporting organizations) of coalitions and alliances through mutual adjustment, especially stable alliances heavily based on reciprocity, so that any rival for top authority can count in a predictable way on a stable structure of supporters.

Unceasing mutual persuasion by all participants.

When benefits, threats, entreaties and authority are not enough, then assassinations, incarcerations, massacres, and war.

In such a crude struggle for authority, it would seem that top authority would always go to military leaders, for they hold the guns. In fact, they do not hold the guns; their subordinates, the ordinary soldiers, do. Whether, then, military leaders can capture top authority positions depends on their authority over their own men. Top military authority engages in the political struggle very much as other leaders do.

It is probably truer to say that top authority goes to the persons who have the money, which is a more immediately controllable instrument of influence than guns in the hands of the ordinary policeman or soldier. But that is also too simple a proposition. Yet money not only talks in politics; it whispers conspiratorially and, at the other extreme, sometimes shouts so loud that no other messages are heard. Every supporting organization is expensive. Money, whether from private wealth or from public funds subject to authoritative disbursement in patronage and public contracts, is a universally effective instrument for hiring supporters and for equipping them with either weapons or printing presses. Contestants for authority can sometimes simply also buy out the opposition.

What we have just described is the fundamental struggle for authority that underlies all government. On top of it, we shall see in later chapters, certain other key struggles over authority are also fought, struggles that vary depending on the form of politico-economic system.

Popular Control and Welfare

If that is politics, the prospects for popular control look poor. Although top authority is constrained in many ways, it is clear that the struggle neither promises any significant degree of popular control over top authority nor imposes a concern for the populace on those in authority. Indeed, we shall see, the variety of mutual controls in politics bodes ill for the possibility of ever establishing adequate democratic control.

Yet some influences over top authority short of democratic procedures do accomplish a degree of popular control and motivate some top authorities to pursue a general welfare as diligently as some democratic leaders. So energetically do they pursue it that some people hold that neither freedom nor democracy is any longer necessary for the general welfare.*

Democratic and communist systems do not differ greatly with respect to public expenditures on health and welfare as a percentage of gross national product.[4] Without any of the instruments of democratic control, communist China has given more attention to food, housing, health, and education for its population than has democratic India; perhaps no nation in the world can match its energy in controlling schistosomiasis, typhoid, cholera, malaria, and venereal disease. The Soviet Union gives advanced training to more of its young people than does democratic Britain.[5] The characteristic American neglect of the nutrition, health and training of low-income groups (justified in the American ethic on the ground that every individual is responsible for himself) is perhaps becoming as obsolete as the traditional oligarch, despot, or military chief all now widely discredited unless energetically reformist. The Haile Selassies, Ibn Sauds, and Batistas have largely given way to Sadats, Castros, and Nyereres.

What are the mechanisms that account for this state of affairs? For some systems, ideology may be the largest part of the answer. Putting that aside for the moment, we must ask what the specific social mechanisms are.

---

* And presumably governments may in some circumstances and in some degree attend to the welfare of the population even without any elements of popular control over leadership. The idea is at least as old as Plato's philosopher-king. The possibility is everywhere recognized in frequent reference to the benevolent despot. Hegel saw even larger possibilities in the rise of the rationalized national state; and it seems clear that professionalism in public administration introduces at least a weak element of autonomously benevolent authority. On the latter, see Hugh Heclo, *Modern Social Politics in Britain and Sweden* (New Haven, Conn.: Yale University Press, 1974), chapter 6, esp. pp. 301–4.

New National Aspirations

One reason for leadership's concern for popular will is to be found in new national aspirations. In the less developed systems, a new breed of national leaders now want growth, industrialization, and modernization. Almost all of them also want the international standing that makes them appear fit to receive economic aid. Some national leaders also compete for regional or world economic leadership, as the U.S.S.R. does with the United States or as Pakistan once did with India. Or, like Nasser, Sadat, Nehru, Peron, or Ulbricht, they want their nations to play more than trivial roles in international politics. As a result, the new fashion is to regard subjects as resources to be developed and therefore to be treated well.

This constraint on ambitious leaders is tighter than might be thought. A modernizing ruler cannot simply dole out food, health services, and training to develop his nation's human resources. He must first organize production to make these benefits available. The whims of politics as "bread and circuses" consequently give way to a demanding politics of organizing a productive society. At this point, many of the ruler's options are closed. He has to do whatever is called for by whichever development strategy he decides on. Many of his options are surrendered to experts, members of the bureaucracy, economists, engineers, lawyers, agronomists, and scientists. And when they advise him on many points they will give him the same advice they would give to a democratic ruler. What is required to stimulate agricultural production is the same for India whether democratic institutions are preserved or not. Top authority is imprisoned in the necessities of economic development.

The emerging international standards of regard for human life and welfare which were ceremonialized in the Universal Declaration of Human Rights voted in the United Nations in 1948 are another constraint on top authority. International scrutiny has been powerful enough to push nations toward health, social security, and educational programs, all hastily inaugurated by rulers who fear they will look obsolete without them. These are the same rulers who fear that they cannot claim modernity without their own national airlines.

Voluntary Authority

A possibility for popular control also lies in the desire of rulers to induce voluntary rather than coerced grants of authority from their subjects. The ever present possibility that subjects will riot or will obey clumsily when intelligent responses are required—the fear, for example, of a slowdown or subtle sabotage if not of a strike—curbs top authority. In the Soviet Union, these controls have won, among other gains, the benefits of religious toleration, increased supplies of consumer goods, and social security. Their effects have been noted in particular decisions. Krushchev's housing policy after 1957 appears to have owed something to these pressures; his later removal from office was probably hastened by popular unrest because of the bread shortage after the harvest of 1963.[6] Fear of unrest, strikes, or violence accounts in part for elite "consultation" with the masses through the cadres in China.[7] It is a force even in the democracy. It was probably that same fear more than democratic politics that brought unemployment compensation to Britain in the 1920s.[8]

The same emerging international moral standard that induces rulers to provide various benefits for their subjects is also at least a weak force undermining coerced authority. Massive coercion against a population now threatens a ruler with a kind of ostracism from the family of nations, as Yahya Khan found when in 1971 he turned his army loose on the citizens of East Pakistan to maintain his eroding authority. Soviet military intervention in Czechoslovakia in 1968 brought down on the U.S.S.R. a near universal condemnation, some of it from communist parties themselves.

In addition to all these mechanisms is the steady influence of rules on the responsiveness of top authorities, especially the influence of constitutionalism, which is a historical development that predates democracy.

Rules, Laws, and Constitutionalism

In folklore and fairy tale, authority is arbitrary in the extreme. Solomon proposes to cut a baby in half to settle conflicting claims to it. Kings offer half their realms, as well as their daughters, to enterprising young men who can succeed in ridiculous tasks. But in actual fact, we have seen, top authority is constrained by rules. And those who participate in controlling top authority—advisory councils, assemblies, electors—do so according to rules.

Some of the constraining rules, only some of which are enacted as law, are ordinary rules of social life: ethical rules, for example, that condemn violence. Among top authorities some rules appear to be largely tacit agreements, like those in the U.S.S.R. and Communist China that have in recent years prohibited the killing of top leaders who have lost their share of top authority. Some rules represent explicit agreements among members of small formal organizations, like decision making by majority vote among top leaders in the Bolshevik Party during the Russian Revolution.

Although a ruler who uses police or military forces to coerce a population into conceding him authority need not be bound by rules that fix his obligations to that population, he cannot maintain a police or army without voluntary grants of authority from members of his supporting organization. They will enforce rules on him as a condition of their grants, doing so through their capacity to withdraw their grants of authority and to use their own authority over their subordinates to bring him down. Or, in simplest terms, because a ruler needs cooperation, he has to obey rules to get it.

Rules to regulate the struggle for authority sometimes have origins in explicit agreement and tacit understandings that curb its ferocity. When men struggle for so great a prize as authority over the machinery of the state, they must fear impoverishment, imprisonment, mutilation, or death if they lose. Little wonder then that they try to soften the struggle by agreeing on rules that reduce their risks. Losers are to be treated with honor; they keep not only their swords but their freedom and property as well. The same caution today constrains nations from germ warfare, poison gas, and use of nuclear weapons. Insofar as the rules curb violence and rapaciousness, however, they protect not only rival claimants to authority but the entire population.

Four major constraints by rule preceded later democratic constraints on authority. The most fundamental was the age-old establishment of those prohibitions that are known as the rights of private property. Indeed, for good or bad, the law of property is perhaps the most fundamental of all political rules, reserving as it does a set of decisions for each individual and prohibiting interference by others, the ruler included. Even in communist societies, property rights in consumer goods are widely established, together with consequent prohibitions on top authority. Property rights carve out for each citizen a domain of free choice that the state does not easily invade.

A second constraint was the whittling down of unspecified broad authority. Thus there emerges in most systems a general rule that declares that top authority has only those powers explicitly granted (by others powerful enough to impose such a rule). The contemporary common rule that authority be specific—that A exercise authority over B only in specified circumstances for a specified category of responses—man can claim as one of his great inventions. Although its origins are lost in a distant past, its restatement and refinement is recorded from time to time, as in the Magna Carta. However commonplace today, the rule is a historical development of the first order of importance.

A third was the separation of powers: assigning by rule some top authority to one office and some to another. Hence the familiar division of top authority among executive, legislature and judiciary, each granted certain authority not granted to the others. The principle does not require any particular separation. Top authority in the Roman Empire was at times divided among tribunes rather than between executive and legislative officers. In seventeenth- and eighteenth-century England, it was divided between king and Parliament long before Parliament became a democratic institution. In the U.S.S.R., after Krushchev's removal, the two top offices of party secretary and chairman of the Council of Ministers were separated. That and other separations introduced a form of "oligarchic parliamentarianism."[9] Whatever the division, it often curbs the tyranny of any one authority. For separation of powers is to a degree paralytic. For exploitative governments, it therefore cripples their ability to exploit.

The fourth was checks and balances. When top authority is divided, rules sometimes provide for a further limit on authority by giving each official some explicit positive authority over others, like the presidential veto of acts of Congress, which is a predemocratic constitutional feature of the American system.

Constitutionalism

It is under the same name of constitutionalism that the development of a variety of such rules constraining top authority in government became an overwhelming historical force. The term sometimes denotes the development of a set of fundamental and stable rules that allocates top authority and specifies organization of government. Sometimes it means government by law or rule rather than by personal discretion. Or the development of a body of rules that specify a separation of powers. Or the development of rules that protect subjects from their rulers in specific ways, as in the American Bill of Rights. Each of these meanings captures an aspect of it.[10]

At one extreme in politics is the constitutional aspiration toward a "government of laws, not of men." At the other extreme is, say, Saudi Arabia, from which constitutionalism is almost wholly absent, or Cuba, when Castro declares that "Revolutionary Justice is based not on legal precepts, but on moral conviction. . . ." Among the major nations, China may be the least constitutional. China has gone further than the Soviet Union in giving nonjudicial organizations broad powers to punish individuals.[11] Generally, who holds just what authority is not well specified in

Chinese law, nor do the rules in China provide for a separation of powers, early forms of which now appear on the Soviet Union. Nor do laws much curb arbitrary discretion of those in authority. Of the party, "No laws, not even those which it itself has dictated, are binding on it if 'objective circumstances' seem to warrant a change."[12] Even Chinese government, however, rests on a minimum of constraining rules.

In many countries of the world, constitutionalism is weak; and the disposition to continue a violent struggle for authority remains strong, despite protestations to the contrary by rulers eager to be accepted into the roster of modern nations.[13] A study by the International Commission of Jurists reports that, under the personal control of the shah of Iran, political suspects are subjected to psychological and physical torture.[14] In Spain after the death of Franco, despite the new regime's claims to enlarge constitutional protection of citizens' liberties, political suspects were subjected to torture.[15] And the new Khmer Rouge regime in Cambodia was reported to practice assassination of whole families and villages, mass deportations, torture, compulsory labor in the fields, forced evacuations from homes and hospitals, and other hardships imposed by a punitive government, giving rise to estimates of deaths as of mid-1976 as high as one-tenth or one-fifth of the population.[16] Yet constitutionalism remains a persistent and growing influence for curbing authority and for introducing some forms of popular control, as in India in 1977.

Constitutionalism and the Basic Struggle for Authority

People struggle ferociously, we have noted, first over who will win authority and then over attempts to control those who have won it. However the struggle goes, the pattern of authority always remains to some significant degree uncontrollable because of ever present possibilities, open to anyone who holds authority, to give it what we have called extended use. However much the exercise of authority is hedged about with constraining rules, people with authority can always find some loophole to make possible its extended use, including the creation of new informal authority structures, say, in a party, army, or political machine.

In Western history, the liberal constitutional movement has to be seen as a multiple response to this state of affairs. It was—perhaps first—a movement to convert an often deadly struggle for authority into peaceful procedures so that noncontestants could escape the pillage common to armed contests for authority and losers could go on living and enjoying their property. It was secondly an attempt to achieve some predictability in the struggle over the use of authority—that is, to move at least modestly toward making the machinery of government systematically controllable in a purposive way (not yet controllable by the masses but by a nobility, merchant group, or middle class). In this attempt, the movement sought to curb the extended use of authority by laying down constitutional restrictions on how rulers might use their authority—to forbid, for example, a ruler's making extended use of his taxing authority to persecute a political adversary. This attempt to limit the extended use of authority will perhaps never run its course. The ease with which authority can be given extended use was revealed once more in the history of the Nixon administration and will repeatedly be revealed again.

A third response of the liberal constitutional movement is the audacious attempt to institutionalize through detailed rules a high degree of mass or popular control over top authority. Since, as we have just said, government is in large part simply uncontrollable, because everybody controls it in complex, unpredictable, and ever changing ways, this third aspiration will always be frustrated. But it persists. The democratic faith is that any significant accomplishment in this direction is greatly to be prized. In the next chapter, we look at this audacious attempt at popular control. Democratic designs amend, though they never replace, the underlying struggle for authority described in this chapter.

Polyarchy

IN roughly 30 of the 144 nations of
the world, the struggle over authority is regulated by rules in a distinctive
way. To these systems tradition gives the name liberal democracy or, in
the Marxian tradition, bourgeois democracy. As of the 1970s, no more
than the following countries would be admitted to the list, and some on
the list are questionable, or were or will be, since in many countries
democracy is fragile:[1]

Australia	Italy
Austria	Jamaica
Belgium	Japan
Canada	Luxembourg
Costa Rica	Netherlands
Denmark	New Zealand
Federal Republic of Germany	Norway
Finland	Philippines
France	Sweden
Greece	Switzerland
Iceland	Trinidad and Tobago
India	United Kingdom
Ireland	United States
Israel	Venezuela

These systems, as well as the more ideal forms which they approximate,
have stimulated a wide variety of democratic theory that confuses hope
with fact. For Lord Lindsay and others, democracy is "government by dis-

cussion."[2] To Lincoln, it is government of, by, and for the people. Bentham sees it as a process for protecting the "numerous classes."[3] Many think of it as the collective pursuit of the common good. Or "democracy consists in the fact that the individual members of any group recognize themselves and each other as a group, which faces group problems, and that they consciously act as a group in solving these problems."[4]

A key element of much democratic theory is the informed, active, rational participant, a point on which democratic theory can be suspected of being a form of wishful thinking.[5] To John Stuart Mill, the first merit of ideal representative government is its contribution to the citizen's "advancement in intellect, in virtue, and in practical activity and efficiency." The second is that it ideally organized "the moral, intellectual, and active worth already existing, so as to operate with the greatest effect on public affairs."[6]

Whether democracy, real or imaginable, has all or any of these virtues is problematic. Whether in any real-world instance popular control is in fact made highly effective is also problematic. All that we know about these systems to begin with is that their social machinery for the control of authority is of a particular and distinctive kind. To analyze this family of systems without begging the question by calling them what they may not be, we had better make use of another name for them and keep our wits about us. Following recent precedent, we shall call the controls "polyarchic," meaning rule by many,[7] and a system that incorporates them a polyarchy rather than a democracy.*

control of leaders by followers

Polyarchy as an Authority System

The core of polyarchy is a specific new pattern of behavior called for by a particular complex set of authoritative rules. Polyarchy is not a social system. Nor, strictly speaking, is it a political system. It is only part of a political system: a set of authoritative rules, together with certain patterns of political behavior that follow directly and indirectly from the existence of the rules.

* For convenience we will call the United States, the nations of Western Europe, and certain others polyarchies, just as many people call them democracies. Strictly speaking, however, poyarchy is no more than one system of social controls embedded in these nations. Strictly speaking, therefore, they contain polyarchy; they are not polyarchies.

Just what are the core authoritative rules of polyarchy? They are rules that limit the struggle for authority, specifying a particular orderly and peaceful process to replace armed conflict, threat of force, and other crude contests. But, in that respect, they are like the rules of any other constitutional system, however undemocratic it may be. What is distinctive about a contest for authority designed by polyarchal rules is that top authority is assigned in response to a routinized indication of citizens' wishes—that is, an election—an indication, moreover, in which any one citizen's vote is by some formula counted as equal to any other's. It is hard to imagine how the struggle for authority could be made simpler, more peaceful, or more egalitarian.

In all polyarchies citizens are authorized not only to choose their top leaders in government, but also to inform and misinform themselves, express themselves wisely or foolishly, and organize into political groups in order to decide how best to cast their votes and to influence others. They are also authorized to communicate their wishes to political leaders and in other ways influence them. In all polyarchies, these authorizations are to a significant degree effective. They are worth a great deal more than the paper they are written on. They are, however, not effective for all, nor equally effective, nor always effective.

In summary outline, the rules guarantee the following familiar rights and prerogatives:[8]

> Freedom to form and join organizations
> Freedom of expression
> Right to vote
> Eligibility for public office
> Right of political leaders to compete for support
> Right of political leaders to compete for votes
> Alternative sources of information
> Free and fair elections (open, honestly conducted, one man–one vote), which decide who is to hold top authority
> Institutions for making government policies depend on votes and other expressions of preference.

All polyarchal authority systems include by rule each of these guarantees, though all imperfectly.[9] Some of the guarantees are surprisingly recent, only as late as 1929 did the United Kingdom sanction universal adult suffrage; France not until 1945; and Switzerland not until 1971.

Citizen Volitions

A number of contemporary democratic theories have borrowed the concept of preference from economic theory.* Just as people have preferences for goods and services, they are considered to have preferences for leaders or for particular public policies. It then follows that the "key characteristic of a democracy is the continuing responsiveness of the government to the preferences of its citizens considered as political equals." This requires that citizens must have opportunities to formulate their preferences, to signify their preferences, and to have their preferences weighed equally.[10] Yet the concept of preference distorts the picture of polyarchy (and democracy). Let us see how in the following paragraphs.

Types of Choice

An individual can choose in at least four ways. First, he may merely respond to taste and simple preference. "I'll take vanilla" is a good example. There is no need for calculated thought or for finding reasons. *Des gustibu non est disputandum.*

Second, he may make a complex judgment, hastily or after considerable analysis, about a variety of considerations. "When I think about how much we are spending for weapons even though the Cold War is over and I see the shape our cities are in, I think we ought to spend more money on public housing." A critical feature of these choices is that they are dependent on facts, probability estimates, and analysis, not merely preferences.

Third, he may choose according to a moral or ethical rule. "Abortion is wicked." "I don't think it's right to pay farmers not to grow things." More often, moral or ethical considerations are mixed into his complex judgments, as when one consideration on whether "we ought to spend more money on public housing" is that "it isn't right that we neglect the poor."

---

* And also the concept of utility maximization. Among many borrowings by many scholars, an especially fruitful one, in which utility maximization in democratic politics is throughout seen as parallel to utility maximization in the market, is Anthony Downs, *An Economic Theory of Democracy* (New York: Harper & Brothers, 1957). Not all contemporary models of democracy rest so explicitly on preferences. See, for example, Felix E. Oppenheim's model ("Democracy—Characteristics Included and Excluded," *Monist* 55 [January 1971]). Yet in many theories, political choice as expression of preference (or utility maximization) is so often taken for granted that it is not even made explicit.

Fourth, he may treat as simple preferences—irrationally or nonrationally, most of us would say—what other people would call complex judgments. "No, I don't believe in foreign aid, but don't ask me why."

In economic theory, consumer choice in the market is treated as simple preference, either of the first or fourth type. In the theory of perfect competition, every buyer and seller is assumed to know all the technical properties of each commodity. Hence no complex analysis and judgment are required, and choices reduce to preference.

For voter choice, however, the reduction of all four categories of choice to simple preference is not possible. Voter choices are almost never simple preference. Typically they contain large elements requiring analysis and moral judgment. Even irrational or nonrational preferences are, when challenged, transformed into complex judgments. Voter choices are complex choices on which deliberation is both possible and practiced. Moreover, when voters face certain choices, they see themselves as called on to do what morally "ought" to be done, not simply what will maximize their own well-being or utility.*

Nor can the complexities of voter choice be dismissed on the ground that the choice is private and of no concern to others in the society. A voter's choice is always a choice about interdependencies. Who is to represent not only me but us in parliament? Should we, not I alone, go to war? What rule should apply, and who should adjudicate, when I find myself in conflict with another person? For all such questions, a voter is tied to others both by bonds of sympathy, which are narrow or wide depending on the individual, and by strategy. It is a matter of strategy, for example, when one cannot vote taxes on others without voting them on himself.

Volitions Not Preferences

For political choice, therefore, preference is too simple a concept. Preferences are facts. They are "there" to be discovered. A chooser does not decide on a preference. He finds, discovers, or knows it. But there are only a few bedrock preferences to be discovered as fact or data: to eat rather than be hungry, for example. In contrast, what we *choose* to eat is to be decided not discovered. Choices are volitions.[11] For understanding political choices we need a concept that will identify not a datum but an emergent act of will. Only after political choices are made can they be referred to as data.

* One can of course broaden the concept of utility maximization so that doing what one ought, however much one would rather not, is in fact a method of maximizing one's utility. But the concept is then of little use.

I do not discover the fact that I approve of euthanasia; I decide that I do. I do not discover that I approve of one candidate over another; I decide that I do. The process of voting is therefore not simply a voyage of discovery, although one may make some discoveries about one's preferences. It is instead a mixing of preference, analysis, and moral judgment to arrive at a state of mind and will that did not before exist. It could not have been observed as a datum because it only now has come into existence.

Volitions Formed by Polyarchy

Preferences as data we might conceive of as exogenous to polyarchy. But not volitions. When we substitute volitions for preferences, we consequently realize that polyarchy is a process that forms volitions as well as a process for making policy respond to them. To form volitions, citizens need information, consultation, stimulation, and advice from the political system itself. We can then admit back into the contemporary model of polyarchy (and of democracy as well) elements from earlier democratic theory. Democracy as "government by discussion" refers to the activities of analysis, discussion, persuasion, and consultation that lead to volitions of category 2, complex judgments. Democracy as a moral pursuit or as a search for the common good is reflected in category 3 volitions, moral judgments, and as a search for truth in policy making in category 2 again. Democracy as a molder of character or developer of human capacities is reflected in both categories 2 and 3. We can also acknowledge the existence of rational, irrational, and nonrational elements in voting and other citizen choices in politics, without sweeping all three under the rug of preferences, where their distinctive differences are lost sight of.

Moreover, democratic systems are impossible without some significant degree of harmonization of individual demands on the system.[12] On some issues, most citizens have to think alike—at least some of the people most of the time or most of the people some of the time—on the main outline of the politico-economic system itself, among other things. On other issues, however, they must not think alike. It is no help to a peaceful moral order if everyone wishes to be mayor or live in California or if all men want the same wife. Polyarchy—and all government to less degree—requires, therefore, some intricate mixture of like and different demands.

If what one votes is simply a matter of preference, the possibility of achieving the required harmony or intricacy of adjustment is slight—perhaps an impossibility. On the other hand, if choices are volitions, turning on questions of fact, moral rules, and acts of will, the possibilities are large. Mere preferences, of either type 1 or type 4, can of course be compromised. But compromise may provide insufficient harmonization for voluntary acceptance of polyarchal rules. What is required over many areas of potential conflict is the construction of "integrated" rather than compromised solutions. These can be reached by reconsidered volitions that reduce conflict because they are re-formed in the light of political conflict and seek to avoid it.[13]

Leader-Citizen Interchange

If volitions rather than preferences are at the core of polyarchy, it is constant and varied interaction between leadership and citizenry that enables citizens to form volitions and guides leadership's response to them. Much of contemporary democratic theory has forgotten the older emphasis on the centrality of two-way interchange to polyarchy, as it appeared, for example, in the thought of John Stuart Mill and Lord Bryce.[14] The key process is persuasion. Where competition for authority in nonelectoral systems calls largely for a potential leader to coerce or otherwise manipulate his rivals and their coteries, competition for office in an electoral system requires that he persuade masses of voters.

Persuasion plays many parts in polyarchy, since in every human situation at least one person seems to believe that talking will help. But reciprocal persuasion between leaders and citizenry plays a special role. It becomes the immediate and primary process through which many citizens arrive at type 2 and type 3 volitions, that is, at prudential calculations and moral judgments.

The process is not a simple one connecting top leaders with a homogeneous mass of ordinary citizens. Rivals for the highest positions—the presidency of the United States, for example—do not make their appeals only to, and listen to communications only from, ordinary citizens. They also enter into persuasive interchange with intermediate leaders, who have followings. They in turn enter into interchange with lesser leaders, who have followings at yet lower levels. Or a member of Parliament and potential prime minister builds his campaign and his continuing interchange with citizens on a ladder of interchanges with parliamentary, party, and other leaders. They and he both interchange with ordinary MP's and party functionaries, and so on down. It is not, however, an unmixed or even predominantly hierarchical set of relations. Reciprocal persuasions runs out in all directions. Included in it are noncandidates, such as columnists, religious leaders, and union officials. At the "bottom" are more the informed and active citizens whose fellows turn to them for advice and information.[15]

The structure of persuasive interaction in competitive polyarchal politics can be represented in part by a ladder. Interchanges occur between persons on different rungs, often but not always adjacent rungs as well as between persons on the same rung. For the United States, the ladder would look roughly like the following:[16]

President

Congressional and other Top Party Leaders, Congressional Committee Chairmen, Top Administrators, and Supreme Court Justices

Other Legislative Leaders, Policy-Making Judges, and High Level Administrators

Ordinary Legislators and Some Administrators

Lower-Level Party Leaders, Interest-Group Leaders, and Major Public-Opinion Leaders

Politically Active Citizens

Ordinary Voters

Nonvoters

Up the ladder moves information and persuasion to express voter volitions. Down the ladder moves information and persuasion on what is possible or most feasible, as well as what leaders propose. A good deal of misinformation moves up and down too. Volitions are endlessly reconsidered in the light of what is thought possible or most feasible. What is possible and feasible is constantly reconsidered—and the possibilities themselves reconstructed—in the light of citizen and leader volitions.

At every step of the ladder, it is usually the more active and informed participants in policy making who pass information on what is possible, feasible, and in their opinion desirable downward to less active and less informed participants. At every level, a participant who wants information and advice can choose among competing (and mutually criticizing) sources of information (and misinformation) and advice. Because many of the sources of information and advice (for example, interest-group leaders and candidates for office) compete for followings, they are highly motivated to outperform their rivals in offering pertinent information and advice to those who are looking for it. They compete in other less helpful ways as well.

If we could imagine a "beginning" of such a process of persuasive interchange, the communications moving upward on the ladder would be no more than expressions of general discontent and vague aspiration. But the upward flow of opinion becomes a good deal more than that. It is a more specific statement of discontent, aspiration, and policy volition profiting from the downward flow and undergoing increasing refinement as it moves upward.

The process of two-way influence is fundamental and comprehensive in polyarchic systems. Proximate policy makers are engaged in it for most of their waking hours. Citizens participate in it in forming all their political volitions—whenever they read editorial comments in their newspapers, whenever they give their attention to any low- or high-level public opinion leader. Even some apathetic citizens will occasionally rise to a vote or other expression of discontent, or by their inactivity signal upward that politics is working well enough not to trigger their active participation in it.[17]

The process should not be idealized. In the United States, politics is ordinarily pursued explicitly and actively by only a small percentage of the adult population, as can be seen in Table 10.1, representing U.S. participation rates in the late 1960s.[18] Except for their higher voting rates, Western Europeans are even less active.[19]

Mutual Adjustment among Leaders

Mutual adjustment among leaders, we saw in an earlier chapter, is inevitable even in a highly authoritarian system. It is enlarged, we have seen, by constitutional innovations like private property, separation of powers, checks and balances and sometimes federalism. In polyarchy additional forms of mutual adjustment further complicate the political process. Authority is further divided. Ordinary citizens now share authority—to choose and remove officials through voting. Elected officials now share authority with bureaucratic officials. The former do not simply

TABLE 10.1

Political Participation in the United States

Type of participation	Percentage of a sample of American adults
1. Report regularly voting in presidential elections	72
2. Report always voting in local elections	47
3. Active in at least one organization involved in community problems	32
4. Have worked with others in trying to solve some community problems	30
5. Have attempted to persuade others to vote as they did	28
6. Have ever actively worked for a party or candidates during an election	26
7. Have ever contacted a local government official about some issue or problem	20
8. Have attended at least one political meeting or rally in last three years	19
9. Have ever contacted a state or national government official about some issue or problem	18
10. Have ever formed a group or organization to attempt to solve some local community problem	14
11. Have ever given money to a party or candidate during an election campaign	13
12. Presently a member of a political club or organization	8

supervise the latter in hierarchical symmetry but develop specialized intermittent controls, like the congressional or parliamentary investigation of the administrative agency.

Leader-citizen interchange stimulates on its own account a growth of mutual adjustment. Leaders of various kinds are constantly engaged in the formation of alliances for winning legislative or electoral votes. Interest-group leaders seek common cause among themselves and with additional parties. Alliances are formed between interest-group, congressional, administrative, and executive leaders. It is a vast process of mutual accommodation to win votes, to assemble the votes of smaller groups in ever larger blocs and, for some leaders, to achieve influence by delivering votes to others.[20]

Despite the egalitarian norms of polyarchy, the pluralism of these systems remains grossly inegalitarian. Two already noted characteristics of the struggle for authority can be singled out as conspicuously, though not exclusively, responsible. The first is the inevitability that authority, no matter how precisely assigned by constitutional tradition and contemporary redesign, is always given extended use. The result is that the actual distribution of authority and other power never corresponds to whatever egalitarianism may have been envisaged in its design. An incumbent congressman, for example, can use his authority to assemble campaign staff and funds unavailable to his challenger. The second characteristic is that participants in polyarchal politics, remain grossly unequal in wealth. Some can hire a supporting organization; others cannot. Some can hire public relations consultants, broadcast time, newspaper space, and other public platforms; others cannot. "The flaw in the pluralist heaven is that the heavenly chorus sings with a strong upperclass accent."[21] The two inequalities reinforce each other when a public official can extend his authority, through control over patronage, public contracts, or other budgets, to put public wealth at the disposal of his political purposes. There is no more common phenomenon in polyarchal politics than that.

Other defects in pluralistic mutual adjustment are widely acknowledged.[22] While a proliferation of public and private groups engaging in mutual adjustment brings a remarkably wide range of interests and considerations to bear on public policy, the same process tends also to take gains for the organized at the expense of the unorganized: gains for union labor at the expense of nonunion, gains for organized agriculture at the expense of smaller unorganized farmers, or gains for producer groups at the expense of consumers. Every organized interest will take at least some of its gains at the expense of "unrepresented millions at the bottom of each natural economic grouping."[23]

It is also a weakness of pluralism that the clienteles for whom leaders speak and act are often inactive within their organizations. Business organizations, unions automobile associations, conservation groups, veterans organizations, and the like often lack effective internal polyarchal controls. Their leaders often use rather than serve the membership.[24] Perhaps even more obstructive to polyarchal control is the widespread confusion between group and individual in the rules and norms that regulate polyarchal politics. Equality among groups is taken as a standard: for example, equal representation for management, employees, and public on a wage-setting board or "balance" between business and consumer in food and drug regulation. The groups are vastly different in number of members, and equal rights for groups implies the grossest inequality of rights for individuals.[25] Several of these defects will be discussed in later chapters.

Finally, the mutual adjustment characteristic of polyarchy only amends, it does not replace, the harsher mutual adjustment of the struggle over authority described in the preceding chapter. Because such mutual adjustment persists, with frequent recourse to intimidation, coercion, violence, and even occasional assassination, its refinement by the rules of poly-archy still leaves government far from any ideal.

Grand and Secondary Majorities

One final major point about polyarchy remains. Polyarchy is not unambiguously a system of majority rule. Certain kinds of majorities can be said to rule, but not others.

The formation of majorities is most visible in a hypothetical simpli-fied two-party system that captures certain main features of actual systems. In such a system, a political party becomes an alliance of political leaders —loose in some polyarchies, tighter and more stable in others—for cooperation to win elections. To achieve that purpose, leaders of both parties will be motivated to pledge the party's candidates to those policies that are favored by an overwhelming massive majority of voters. (In the United States, for example, both parties and almost all candidates are committed to private enterprise, peace in most circumstances, high levels of employment, and public education.)

Although the two parties usually are both committed to this, the grand majority, they will nevertheless divide on issues on which a massive unmistakable majority is not clearly perceived: issues like income tax reform, regulation of unions, foreign aid, gun control, energy policy, the defense budget, and abortion. Being in doubt on what will best appeal to voters, each party and its candidates will tend to espouse the traditional positions and ideology of the party greatly modified by an estimate of what will appeal to voters. (Yet they may sometimes hold to tradition and ideology even in the face of an unmistakable contrary majority voli-tion as conservative Republicans often do in the United States.) Each party will also try to differentiate itself from the other and then try to persuade undecided voters to move their volitions in the direction of what the party proposes. The result is that on these secondary issues the two parties will differ. And neither may succeed in discovering what the majority wants.

Because, moreover, each party and associated candidates approach the election with a platform embracing a variety of secondary issues, any one voter will endorse some and reject some of each party's platform. Inevitably, therefore, any vote he casts is for a candidate or party whose stand on many issues is not his.

The outcome for majority rule is that the majority volition normally prevails only on issues on which there is an unmistakable massive and long-standing majority opinion—a grand majority—to which both parties commit themselves. Secondary majorities—that is to say, majorities favoring a position on a secondary volition that is at issue do not necessarily prevail.*

* In addition, if parties build their platforms on each secondary question so as to appeal to those voters whose volitions are strongest and if those who feel most intensely are, as seems likely, a minority, parties will build up their secondary platforms around appeals to one minority after another. On secondary issues, polyarchy consequently often proceeds through minority rule—not majority rule at all (Dahl, *Democratic Theory,* chapter 5).

Through various other complications of voting, popular control is sometimes implemented, sometimes confused or obstructed. On the way in which different electoral rules affect outcomes, see Douglas W. Rae, *The Political Consequences of Electoral Laws* (New Haven, Conn.: Yale University, 1967). On failures of electoral voting to achieve a Pareto optimum, see Gerald Sirkin, "The Anatomy of Public Choice Failure," in *Economics of Public Choice,* eds. Robert D. Leiter and Gerald Sirkin (New York: Cyrco Press, 1975). On voting and market defects in a larger perspective, see Duncan MacRae, Jr., "Normative Assumptions in the Study of Public Choice," *Public Choice* 15 (Fall 1973).

Polyarchal
and Market Controls

WHEN the market system is tied to individual consumer preferences, as for the most part it is in all historical and existing market systems, it is itself a system of popular control. People "vote" with their dollars, francs, or rupees. Thus, a nation's railroads can be subjected to polyarchal control or market control—or, as in actual fact in many systems, to a combination of the two. In many countries, popular control over public schools is attempted almost entirely through polyarchy, leaving only private schools to be market controlled. Medical services are mixed: some sold, and thereby controlled by consumer demand; others, like medical care for veterans in the United States, made available through polyarchically controlled programs without sale on the market.

To see polyarchy and market clearly as alternative systems of popular control, we have to penetrate two smokescreens. One is thrown up by contemporary lore. It is an obscure body of belief that corporations can do pretty much what they want and that, theory aside, market controls in the hands of consumers are really of little effect. People who hold these beliefs often do so with serene confidence. They seem untroubled by the evident fact that corporations have to sell what they produce, that consumers pick and choose—between a new car and house improvements, between two or more kinds of cars, between more pairs of shoes and better food, between tobacco and liquor. All sellers, including corporations, can survive only by responding at least well enough to make sales. Rather than deny the existence of popular control, one ought to ask whether "well enough" is good enough.

The other smokescreen is thrown up by people who misuse economic theory. Their mistake is one of oversimplification. Every corporation has to sell its products. As they see it, that is all that needs to be said. Obviously it is then under the control of its customers. These enthusiasts do not stop to ask any questions at all about the possibilities that customers may be incompetent to choose, may even be hoodwinked, or that markets may be rigged. They simply rest their faith in a model to which they assume the real world conforms.

Specific Comparisons

Some specific comparisons of popular control in the two systems throws light on both. We restrict the comparisons to functions or activities in which market and polyarchy can be thought of as feasible alternatives, because markets are inoperable for many functions.

Withdrawal versus Reform

One comparison runs like this: If a potential Olivetti customer does not like its typewriters, he can simply make his purchase elsewhere. That possibility keeps those in charge of Olivetti on their toes. In contrast, if the "customer" or client of a municipal public works department does not like its performance, he has nowhere to go. He has to try to persuade its officials to change their ways, and in some circumstances he can threaten to join with other voters in removing them. But his prospects for getting satisfaction are often poor.[1] Withdrawal, so the argument goes, is more effective than the dubious attempt at internal reform.

For popular control over decisions on what goods and services are to be produced, threat of withdrawal is indeed often a simple, fast-working mechanism. It often achieves simplicity and precision of control far superior to the laborious and only approximate control citizens would have over production if they voted for officials who in turn appointed economic administrators.

145

Precise Voting

The analogy with voting throws a different light on the same phenomenon. If people want more or less of something they simply "vote" for more or less by spending more or less on it. Unlike political voting, market voting is easy, so easy that the consumer can cast a vote dozens of times a day, day after day. Unlike the political vote for candidates of unpredictable intention, market voting is precise. A consumer votes for exactly what he wants: for example, a 100-millimeter low-tar mentholated filter cigarette in a red and white package. He can also change his vote at any time; and over some range of choice, what he gets will then also immediately change. In electoral voting, the connection between vote and results is loose and uncertain.

Private Gain versus Public Spirit

As some people see the two systems of popular control, the difference is a simple one. The market system puts decision making into the hands of a group of leaders—businessmen—motivated to make money with no responsibility to pursue any kind of public interest. Polyarchy puts decision making into the hands of a group of leaders—elected officials —who do carry just such a responsibility. On a naive view of the choice, the latter is obviously to be preferred.

Seals are easily trained because they have an appetite for fish. It ought to be fairly clear by now that a money-pursuing leadership might be more precisely controllable than a public-interest leadership if the populace can systematically vary leadership's opportunities to satisfy its appetite for money. A market system is a mechanism for doing just that, for harnessing a strong incentive in a precise system of social control that manipulates money making in order to steer businessmen in just those directions called for by consumer spending. And, on the other hand, it is a characteristic of polyarchal control that, although leaders may be devoted to the public interest, that in itself contains no promise of popular control. For the public interest may be undefined, or defined only by leadership itself in ways not responsive to popular volitions.

A striking characteristic of polyarchy is that in democratic theory and practice alike the responsibilities of elected leadership are left largely indeterminate. The issues eloquently raised in Edmund Burke's classic speech to the electors of Bristol in 1774 are still unresolved. Some elected representatives still choose to follow their own best judgment on policy issues. Others choose to follow the wishes of their constituents. Elected officials also choose, we have seen, between satisfying each of a variety of intense minority interests among constituents or satisfying interests shared by all or by a majority of them. Voter control is attenuated because these choices are not theirs to make.

In the U.S. system and some other systems, a congressman can choose to make a reputation by leadership on national issues; or by focus on issues of particular concern to his own constituency; or by favors and services, including patronage for members of his constituency; or by service to his political party and to political colleagues, who can help him at election time and advance him to other elected or appointed office. These are all his options, not the voter's.[2]

Control by Results or Control by Process

The difference between the two systems of control is sometimes put as a difference between controlling outputs or results and controlling inputs or processes. Enterprises are controlled by outputs. Either they produce, or they go out of business. But polyarchy cannot achieve that kind of control over governmental organizations. "No demonstration has been made," a typical complaint reads, "that the federal expenditure of $5–10 billion dollars has had any result whatever in improving the education of the students whom it was to aid."[3] Polyarchal controls specify budget, personnel practices, table of organization and other specific inputs and processes; but output or results may escape control.

Yet it is easy to misperceive the significance of this distinction. When people face a problem beyond any known competence to solve, a business enterprise, knowing it cannot promise results, will not attempt to do the job. The impossible assignment can nevertheless be assigned to a government agency. If, for example, it is feared that heroin use is growing out of control, government agencies can be instructed to try to do something about it, little matter that no one knows what or how. It is then actually the nature of the task, not the form of organization, that makes popular control ineffective.

Direct and Delegated Decisions

A more fundamental difference is that, although both polyarchal and market controls give the populace direct control over no more than a small proportion of necessary decisions, they differ greatly in what that proportion consists of.

In all large popular control systems a vastly larger number of decisions have to be made than can possibly be made or directly controlled by the populace. To achieve popular control it is necessary to find some way,

147

first, to permit direct popular control over some feasible small number of decisions and, second, to subordinate all the other delegated decisions to that small number. Both polyarchy and market system accomplish just such a solution. In both, a tail has been found to wag the dog.

Occasional referenda aside, in polyarchy the direct decisions of the population are those that choose the occupants of the top positions of leadership. Choosing and removing top leadership is a way of controlling indirectly all delegated decisions: decisions on policies and on choice of other leaders who are appointed by top leaders.

In market systems, the population makes no choice at all of leaders. The direct decisions of the population are instead those that say yes or no to final outputs of consumer goods and services. To these direct decisions on end products all delegated decisions—so the argument would go—are then subordinated: decisions, for example, on what manpower and other resources are to be used, what methods are to be followed, where the activity is to take place, and how and by whom it is to be supervised.*

Choice of end products seems, at least under the best circumstances, more effective for popular control than choice of leaders. Consumers enjoy a direct tight, precise, and quick control over what they want. Scarcity or efficiency prices serve up cost information. Businessmen are consequently informed precisely about the amount of each output consumers want intensely enough to pay for.

The subordination of the delegated decisions to the direct decisions— so the argument goes—is tight. Because each firm is pressured by many competing firms, each has to find the most profitable technology, the most profitable location, and the most profitable personnel or otherwise go out of business. For each of the many delegated decision problems of the businessman, there is only one correct answer that permits the firm to survive and many wrong answers that do not. The subordination of all delegated decisions to those choices made directly by consumers is therefore complete, exact, unqualified. That is of course an idealized version of market control. But significantly, no one has imagined a comparable model of polyarchy in which direct choices tightly control all the delegated decisions that elected officials make. Even idealized polyarchy does not promise a comparable linkage of delegated to direct decisions.

---

* Strictly speaking—but it is a complication not essential at this point—the populace expresses two sets of key preferences: those on final outputs (through consumer purchases) and those on occupational choice (through choosing among alternative jobs available), to both of which sets all other decisions are subordinated.

Monopoly

Idealized markets aside, it is often argued that monopoly, about which we have said hardly a word so far, in fact vitiates popular control through the market. Monopoly indeed creeps into almost all markets. Corporations typically exercise some degree of monopoly control over price and output. So do farmers through producer cooperatives. And organized workers through unions. And doctors and lawyers through professional associations. And various trades and crafts, like barbers, liquor retailers and dry cleaners, through licensing laws that restrict entrance into the trade. Even the corner drugstore or the neighborhood service station enjoys monopoly power because of a locational advantage over less conveniently placed competitors.*

For big companies in national markets, a common pattern is oligopoly, as in the American automobile industry where four companies account for 99 percent of output or the farm machinery industry where four firms account for over half the output. Perhaps as much as 60 percent of manufactured goods in the United States are produced by enterprises that make their production plans and set their prices in light of their interaction with two or three other dominant firms in their industry.[4]

Although monopoly is unquestionably a serious problem in market systems (economists dispute its magnitude and character), it constitutes a minor defect in popular control when compared with the defects of polyarchy. That perhaps surprising allegation can be made for a particular and specific reason. Monopoly weakens responses to popular control, but it neither eliminates a response or leads to a perverse one, as is commonplace in polyarchy. Rare, even bizarre, circumstances aside, it never profits a monopolist to do more when customers are signaling for less, or less when they are signaling for more, as frequently in polyarchy.

Oligopoly, monopolistic competition, monopsony—all the forms of

---

* Because monopoly power is a source of security for the enterprise, it has long been argued that some degree of monopoly power of certain kinds encourages enterprises to take risks they would otherwise be unwilling to take. Monopoly consequently contributes to innovation and growth, so the argument goes. (Joseph A. Schumpeter, *Capitalism, Socialism, and Democracy,* 3rd ed. [New York: Harper & Brothers, 1950]. See also J. K. Galbraith, *The New Industrial State,* 2d ed., rev. [Boston: Houghton Mifflin, 1971].) The significance of this argument is an issue of continuing debate among economists, many of whom believe that monopoly permits management to relax. The broader implication of the controversy is that depending on circumstances, enterprises will perform either with maximum efficiency or with minimum daring when freed to some degree from popular control, which is a hypothesis that may also hold for government officials subject to polyarchal control.

monopoly—are market situations in which a buyer or seller can restrict purchases or sales in order to win a more favorable price, or can somehow directly set prices to his own advantage. Hence some increases in demand will induce a monopolist to respond with a combination of higher price and increased production in contrast to a rigorously competitive enterprise that would respond wholly through an increase in production. In many circumstances, the effect of monopoly is thus to impose a kind of tax, in the form of a monopoly price, on the monopolized commodities. In all the various possible manifestations of monopoly, responses to consumer controls are made conditional on a kind of tax, or are slowed, or are reduced; but—to repeat—response is neither stultified nor made perverse.*

By contrast, the imperfections of polyarchal controls are gross, all the more so perhaps in the largest polyarchies. There are innumerable possibilities for policy to move either not at all or to move opposite to the direction called for by a majority of voters. It is commonplace, for example, for candidates to be elected to office over a majority volition against them simply because the majority is divided between opposing candidates. Allende won the Chilean election of 1970 with only 36 percent of the vote. Nixon won in 1968 with only 43 percent. Or party and governmental leadership, for ideological or other reasons, may refuse to respond to popular demands, in the expectation that its intransigence will be forgotten by the time the next election rolls around. Or citizens may have no effective way to communicate their volitions since, in any one contest, the candidates differ on many issues, and the winner can thereafter interpret his victory to be a mandate on any one or a few of the issues he chooses to make prominent. After World War II the British Labour Party's nationalizations of industry were carried out with a claim of a mandate from voters. Subsequent election studies have shown that voters chose Labour for quite other reasons.[5]

All the imperfections in polyarchy arising out of the underlying struggle for authority, or out of the impossibility of achieving a precise control over the bureaucracy, or out of its inadequate mechanisms for rational choice, especially economic choice, will frequently prevent a response of

---

* Moreover, because to the extent that monopoly, by restricting production in one field, makes unused resources available for use in other areas, its net effect is not output restriction but resource misallocation. Consumers get less of monopolized commodities and more of others than would be the case in the absence of monopoly. The new mix of commodities and services is less to their liking than it would be in the absence of monopoly, but that is the extent of the loss. Various statistical estimates put the misallocation loss from monopoly anywhere from less than 1 percent up to 9 percent of gross national product (William G. Shepherd, *Market Power and Economic Welfare* [New York: Random House, 1970], pp. 196–97; and Scherer, *Industrial Market and Economic Performance* [Chicago: Rand McNally, 1970], pp. 400–409).

government to popular volitions or cause government policy to move in directions opposed to popular volition.

Moreover, to vote for candidates rather than directly on policy is to place winning candidates in complex organization like parliaments, legislatures, and cabinets. Because each such organization has its own internal operating procedures, like seniority rules in the U.S. House of Representatives, the decision of these organizations will not predictably respond to the direct choices or votes of the electorate.

Polyarchal governments, it needs to be remembered, have been designed not simply to achieve popular control but to curb the power of top authorities. Separation of powers between legislature and executive, for example, sets each of two groups of top authorities as watchdog on the other. Polyarchal government is thus a collection of bodies all intentionally crippled because of their otherwise fearful strength. As a consequence, all are to a degree perverse or impotent when the citizenry asks that something be done.

In a market system, moreover, an individual or corporate seller wants market voting to continue. By contrast, many political leaders try to destroy the polyarchal control. Many succeed in doing so: for example, Lon Nol in Cambodia and Yahya Khan in Pakistan. Short of outright suppression of elections, there are corruptions of the process, as under Mrs. Gandhi, in miscounting ballots in Chicago style.

The fundamental reason why a monopolist dampens but does not paralyze or reverse the effect of popular control is that the "voter" always has many opportunities open to him to substitute another supplier for any supplier who does not satisfy him. The substitution is at some cost to the "voter"—if it were not, monopoly would be no problem at all. But there are always many possibilities for substitution, even if fewer than the consumer would like.

In this light, monopoly is, one should note, not the opposite of competition but only a dampening of competition. Competitive alternatives always continue to exist in multiplicity. "Monopoly" typically refers to weakened or absent competition among firms selling the same products. Whatever weakness marks interfirm competition, substitution among products from different industries always keeps interproduct competition alive. Interproduct competition is a good deal more powerful than most people have taken the trouble to see. Technological substitution or competition is one of its forms: people can heat their living spaces with gas, oil, or coal. Organizational substitution is another form: people can "buy" custodial services for their funds through banks, savings and loan associations, the post office (in many countries), insurance companies, or investment counselors. Household services compete with commercial services. For durables like refrigerators, radios, beds, or clothing, used

151

products compete with new ones; customers will replace old products earlier when new prices are low. Nonessential purchases, like theater tickets, vacation trips, fancy foods, and home improvements, compete with each other as possible amenities. For amenities, market demand is highly elastic and hence gives less scope to a potential monopolist than does the demand for basic foodstuffs or minimum housing. In a wealthy country like the United States, most consumer spending is on amenities. In fact all products compete to a degree with all others.

Not surprisingly, conservative economists are tempted to deprecate the significance of monopoly. But at the other end of the spectrum, Paul A. Baran and Paul M. Sweezy, authors of a leading Marxist critique of modern capitalism, agree that competition persists as a powerful popular control, inducing producers to give customers what they think they want. One test of the strength of competitive controls is downward pressure on costs of production. On that, they believe that in monopoly capitalism the pressure "is no less severe" than before the rise of the giant corporation. Corporations are endlessly engaged in a "struggle for larger market shares."*

Corporate Discretion

If monopoly were the main obstruction to popular control in markets we could, in light of the above comparison of it with defective polyarchal control, now conclude that, where the market system is possible to use, polyarchy is much inferior to it as an instrument of popular control. Yet there is a further defect in market control of the greatest consequence. In ways not ordinarily embraced in the concept of monopoly, corporate executives exercise discretionary authority and other controls that permit them to escape to a significant degree from popular control through the market system.

Let us go back and reconsider the precision of consumer controls in the

* They attach great significance, as do most non-Marxist economists, to the corporations' fear of competitive price cutting. Despite the strong tendency they see for corporations to compete instead through product design and quality and accompanying services, "the abandonment of price competition does not mean the end of all competition: it takes new forms and rages on with ever increasing intensity." And "sellers must be forever seeking to put something new on the market." *Monopoly Capital* (New York: Monthly Review Press, 1966), pp. 67, 70, 71, 64.

market system. Can a consumer vote effectively for insurance or medical services that fit his preferences? Or a kitchen range? Or a headache remedy? Not, we saw, if he is incompetent to judge on technical grounds the characteristics of the services offered. In fact he is not very competent. To the degree of his incompetence, corporate officials make many of his decisions for him. He controls them only imperfectly.

If, in addition, corporations deliberately misrepresent their products to him, he is even more crippled in his ability to control them. An obvious point should not be overlooked. The rules and incentives of market systems encourage sellers to resolve any doubts they have about the safety of their products in favor of profits rather than health of customer in all those circumstances in which injury to his health cannot be definitively tied to use of the product. The labeling of pharmaceuticals with obfuscating neologisms and the continued resistance of the food industry to adequate indication of additives on packaged foods drown us in evidence both of consumer incompetence and of corporate energy to preserve so splendid a source of earnings. The magnitude of the phenomenon is indicated by the possibility, now that new chemical food additives are developed every day without much testing of long-term consequences, that the major diseases of the affluent peoples of the world will from now on be man-made epidemics. There will be more on misrepresentation of products in chapter 16.

Can even a highly competent informed consumer vote for precisely the product he wants? Only if the corporation has taken the initiative to put the product on the market. Although the consumer wields a powerful veto, the initiative is largely in corporate hands. For twenty-five years after World War II, the automobile industry in the United States demonstrated that industry response to consumer wishes can be extremely slow. Until the last few years the entire auto industry was so fixed in its opposition to small cars as to leave the market for them to foreign firms. Clearly corporations exercise substantial discretionary controls over the timing and fullness of their responses to consumer demands, including the possibility that for a decade or more they may ignore them. This is a possibility much more damaging to consumer control than is monopoly. How can it happen?

For any large, heavily capitalized, technologically sophisticated enterprise facing an only partly predictable future, there is no one obvious production and sales strategy that will avoid loss and maximize profits, sales, or whatever other desideratum the corporate leadership pursues. Even simple profit maximization would be complicated. Should the enterprise take all the profits it can in the immediate future? Should it moderate its ambitions now in order to build a clientele that in a longer future

153

might make higher profits possible? The tightest of possible consumer controls cannot shortcut these and other complex decisions. They remain at the discretion not of the consumer but of the corporate executive.

Discretion on Delegated Decisions

Corporate discretion is especially broad on what we have called delegated decisions. In a market system, direct consumer decisions are limited to saying yes or no on what is to be produced and in what quantities. The delegated decisions are all the other decisions instrumental to production: among others, on technology, organization of the work force, plant location, and executive prerogatives. Even in an idealized market system, consumer control over them ranges from weak to nonexistent, except to impose least-cost decisions. Almost nothing we have said about the sometime ease, directness, and precision of consumer control applies to this broad category. The ten major coal mining companies run by coal companies showed a record, for one period, of over 40 injuries and deaths to their employees per million man hours worked compared with less than 8 for mines operated by the steel companies.[6] That kind of differences in the human cost of mining turns on executive discretion; obviously consumer control is not a significant influence on it.

Corporate executives exercise their discretion, for example, in decisions on whether production of any one good or service will be scattered about in small firms or whether it will be concentrated in a few larger ones. The conglomerates of recent years are the consequences of discretionary corporate decisions not much linked to consumer volitions. Discretionary corporate decisions of that kind, not popularly controlled decisions, decide much of the main outline of the industrial structure of an economy.

On their own broad discretion, corporation executives also decide whether their workers should be displaced by automation and when technological innovation should be brought into use. Corporate discretion accounted for the persistence of open hearth furnaces in steel for more than ten years after the superior basic oxygen process had been introduced in Europe.[7] And decisions on technology throw into the hands of corporations major decisions on how air, water, and earth are to be polluted, as no one can now escape knowing.

Corporation executives decide on how to finance new investments. By their discretionary decisions to reinvest rather than distribute portions of their profits, they have in fact accomplished a fundamental restructuring of the social mechanism through which the politico-economic system decides on how to divide its energies between consumption and savings. Corporation savings in the United States now constitute 40 percent of all net savings.

In the 1970s a number of corporations like Volvo in Sweden began experimenting with alternatives to assembly lines. Whether to tie workers to an often stultifying technology or try to organize them in possibly more humane processes is a discretionary corporate decision not popularly controlled.

Corporation executives also decide on the magnitude and character of the massive attempt at public information and thought control that goes by the name of public relations and commercial advertising. They also decide on who will reach their own top positions in the management of the economy. The executives of Unilever, Royal Dutch Shell, Courtaulds, or Southern Pacific reach their positions of authority not by popular election or governmental appointment but by self-selection. Corporation executives also decide whether, and in what amount, to assign corporate funds to the support of education and research. Through assignment of funds, and sometimes of personnel, they breathe life into or leave moribund a variety of community projects: libraries, recreational centers, redevelopment, and the like. And on their own discretion they decide whether, when, and on what sides of what issues their energies and funds will be thrown into political activities like lobbying or party organization.

Corporate discretion poses an increasingly serious threat to popular control as the business enterprise grows in size. The discretionary decision of a single large corporation (to move in or out) can create or destroy a town, pollute the air for an entire city, upset the balance of payments between countries, and wipe out the livelihoods of thousands of employees.

A textbook "theoretical" dismissal of the importance of the phenomenon of corporate discretion on delegated decisions takes roughly this form. Consumer control will drive each firm to find the one correct maximum profit decisions on all delegated issues. If consumer control fails to do so, it is because of monopoly; and at that point the discussion turns back again to the familiar problems of monopoly. The fact is, however, that even under highly competitive conditions, corporate executives cannot, as we have just seen, unerringly find one correct solution to their complex problems. Since they cannot, they have to exercise discretion. Even in principle there is no one least-cost solution to a complex problem. A least-cost location for a new plant, for example, depends on the range of products that might be produced, the flexibility built into the plant, and the period over which costs and revenues are estimated. Inescapably, corporate executives find delegated decisions to be in their hands with no guidance from popular control, not even pressure toward least cost.*

---

* A frequent view is that corporation management has developed a sense of social responsibility toward customers, stockholders, employees, suppliers, and government. A number of corporate executives make such a claim; and some independent observers do also—for example, A. A. Berle in *The American Economic Republic* (New York:

Hybrid Popular Control in a Range of Discretion

Reflecting on all the foregoing, it is hard to miss seeing the hypothetical possibility of a hybrid form of popular control that combines market control over outputs with polyarchal control, weak as it is, over the delegated decisions on which market control is weak. Zoning and land-use legislation are examples. Other instances are governmental control over some aspects of labor relations, the securities markets, environmental protection, and emerging forms of economic planning in the polyarchies. But the hybrid is so far only an embryo. None of the polyarchies has wholly acknowledged the lacuna in popular control represented by grossly defective market controls over certain categories of major decisions only ostensibly subordinated to consumer preferences.

Historically, enterprises have fought off any massive invasion by polyarchal controls into these great areas of corporate discretion. They have argued in effect that the rules of the market system require that enterprises keep control over their costs, which they can do only if they maintain control over all the subordinate decisions and are free to reach least-cost outcomes. Yet if enterprises cannot unerringly find least-cost decisions and if in any case there are alternative least-cost decisions depending on corporate strategy, it follows that polyarchal regulation need not necessarily result in higher costs.

Some economists would see the threat of government regulation somewhat differently. They would fear that the substitution of polyarchal for

---

Harcourt, Brace & World, 1963). Without even arguing whether corporate management does assume such diffused responsibilities—it seems quite clear that many executives believe that they do—we are not giving this view any further attention here. For the socially responsible corporate executive, like a socially responsible civil servant, has great discretion in his hands and thus escapes popular control. To say that he expresses that discretion in what he considers to be a socially responsible way does not deny that he has it. See Christopher D. Stone, *Where the Law Ends* (New York: Harper & Row, 1975).

The related lively argument among economists on whether corporations do or do not maximize their profits (see Robin Marris and Adrian Woods, eds., *The Corporate Economy* [Cambridge, Mass.: Harvard University Press, 1971] is also a secondary issue, not necessary to resolve for a comparison of market and polyarchal controls. Clearly, as all the disputants agree, some level of profits is essential to corporate survival. Moreover, corporations are designed to be institutions for single-mindedly pursuing money (M. A. Adelman, "Some Aspects of Corporate Enterprise," in *Postwar Economic Trends in the United States,* ed. Ralph Freeman [New York: Harper & Brothers, 1960], pp. 292–93). Whether, in pursuing money, they push for growth, or maximum sales, or immediate profit maximization may be an important question to resolve if one wants to predict corporate behavior precisely, but it is less critical to a comparison of market and polyarchal controls than is the clarification of the whole range of corporate discretion and various aspects of it.

market controls would, by imposing "arbitrary" costs on enterprises, subvert a system of efficiency prices. Indeed polyarchal controls may do so. In principle, however, there is a range of discretion in corporate decision making, we now see; and within that range polyarchal impositions on the enterprise need do no more damage to efficiency pricing than will corporate discretion itself. Moreover, polyarchal decisions within that range of discretion can in principle systematically turn corporate decision making in any direction government desires—toward growth, toward energy conservation, toward environmental protection, or any other national objective—rather than leave corporate decisions within a range to be determined by the accidents of corporate policy or the private proclivities of corporate leadership.

On the possibility of hybrid controls, we are discussing, however, nothing more than blueprints, since there are, as we shall shortly see, formidable obstacles to the actual establishment of such a hybrid set of controls as has just been imagined. For the moment, we simply take note of what on some counts seems an obvious possibility for combining politico-economic controls in new ways. Subsequently we can examine actual possibilities and difficulties.

THE CLOSE BUT UNEASY RELATION BETWEEN PRIVATE ENTERPRISE AND DEMOCRACY

Market and Democracy

O F many ways to classify politico-economic systems, one is through a two-by-two table distinguishing market-oriented from other systems, and polyarchal from authoritarian (see Table 12.1).

TABLE 12.1
Politico-Economic Systems

	Polyarchic	Authoritarian
Market-oriented systems (not exclusive of authority)	All polyarchal systems: North American, Western European, and others.	Most of the world's systems, including Yugoslavia, Spain, Portugal, most of Latin America, new African nations, the Middle East except Israel, and all of noncommunist Asia except Japan.
Centralized authority and preceptoral "systems" (not exclusive of market)		Communist systems except Yugoslavia and perhaps Hungary. Also Nazi-Germany.

Remarkably, all polyarchies go into the same box; all are market oriented. One box consequently remains empty, although the temporary arrangements for wartime economic mobilization made by the United Kingdom, the United States, and other polyarchies in World War II might be placed in the otherwise empty box.

Why All Existing Polyarchies
Are Private Enterprise, Market Oriented

The polyarchies are not only without exception market systems but specifically are private enterprise systems. What explains this great historical fact—the dependence of polyarchies on market and private enterprise?

Because both private enterprise market systems and polyarchy are methods for popular control over "public" decisions, one might guess that societies in which popular control is prized would employ both. But they do not. Most market-oriented systems are not polyarchies. Nevertheless, one might ask whether any society prizing popular control so highly as to maintain polyarchy would not also want to strengthen popular control by using the market. An obvious answer is that such a society might believe polyarchy to be superior to market for achieving popular control and hence might displace the market.

Conceiving of polyarchy and market as systems of popular control, we will not therefore find any compelling reason for the two to be tied together. Perhaps, then, they share some other characteristic that accounts for the existence of polyarchy only when tied to market system. That is a clue: a common origin. The two are historically tied together because in the forms in which they have arisen, we shall see that both are manifestations of constitutional liberalism. And it is therefore not polyarchy as a general phenomenon that is tied to market. It is only polyarchy under liberal constitutional auspices, presumably only one of several alternative possibilities of polyarchy.

The history of democracy is largely an account of the pursuit of liberty. Logically, people can enjoy a great deal of liberty even if they do not live under a democratic regime, or be unfree on many counts although under a democratic regime. And historically man appears to recognize the difference between liberty and democracy. One way he has tried to insure his liberties, however, is by instituting the more or less democratic regimes we call polyarchies, polyarchy being a means, liberty the end. Democracy is "vowed to the cause of liberty."[1] "The fight for democracy is historically a fight for political freedom."[2]

In the early development of constitutional liberalism, from the Magna Carta through the Puritan and Glorious revolutions of the seventeenth cenutry, the liberal constitutional movement was not associated with democracy or polyarchy. It was a movement to enlarge and protect the liberties first of nobles and then of a merchant middle class, incorporating as a means of so doing constitutional restrictions on the prerogatives of government. As the movement came gradually to be associated with ideas of popular rule in the late eighteenth century, it maintained its preoccupation with liberty, to which popular rule was, however, never more than a means, and a disputed means at that.

Equality is another end for which democracy has often been viewed as a means.[3] But because during the nineteenth-century egalitarian and libertarian aspirations were widely perceived to be in conflict, they parted company. Marx and the socialists became the spokesmen for equality, liberals the spokesmen for liberty. Since then the egalitarian tradition in democracy has been subordinated to the libertarian.

The great "democratic" revolutions, American and French, set as their goal the enlargement of the "rights of man." The French "Liberty, Equality, and Fraternity" does not elevate democratic popular control to the status of a revolutionary objective. Nor in fact was popular control valued by France's new leaders during the revolution. It gradually became established in postrevolutionary France as no more than a means to liberty and to a rectification of the grossest political inequalities. In America, the revolutionists declared their commitment not to popular control but to "certain Unalienable Rights, that among these are Life, Liberty, and the Pursuit of Happiness." They wanted their rulers to leave them free but differed on what degree of popular rule would accomplish such an objective. The Constitutional Founders were fervent liberals but no more than timid democrats, some not democrats at all.

Not a single one of the great figures in political thought in the modern era speaks for the value of popular control through democracy—except for those who see it as a means to liberty or equality. They are all liberals first and democrats second, if at all: Locke, Montesquieu, Burke, Bentham, Hegel, the Mills, and Spencer. Rousseau, the greatest figure missing from this list, is neither a liberal nor a democrat unless we give these words meanings that depart from the usages of the others.

If in its actual historical origins polyarchy is an institution for introducing that amount and those forms of popular control that serve liberty, then it is not at all surprising that men who create polyarchies will also preserve market systems. For much of the fuller development of personal liberty

liberty vs democracy

freedom vs popular control

that men have sought is freedom to engage in trade and to establish enterprises to pursue the gains of trade, freedom also to move about, to keep one's earnings and assets, and to be secure against arbitrary exactions. In Halifax's phrase, "trade is the creature of liberty."

The tie between market and liberalism is tightly knotted in Locke, the principal source of American revolutionary thought. For Locke, the foundation of the liberal constitutional state was property. The function of the state was protection of property, including property rights in one's own body, a set of rights that consequently subsumes liberty under property. And property is one of the foundations of market exchange, since people cannot exchange assets or money for assets or services if they do not "own" the assets and money.

A market system requires certain minimum liberties for ordinary workers as well. Marx wrote:

> The immediate producer, the laborer, could only dispose of his own person after he had ceased to be attached to the soil and ceased to be the slave, serf, or bondman of another. To become a free seller of labor-power, who carries his commodity wherever he finds a market, he must further have escaped from the regime of the guilds, their rules for apprentices and journeymen, and the impediments of their labor regulations.[4]

The association between liberal constitutional polyarchy and market is clearly no historical accident. Polyarchies were established to win and protect certain liberties: private property, free enterprise, free contract, and occupational choice. Polyarchy also served the more diffuse aspirations of those elites that established it—"the end is always individual self-help."[5] For both the specific liberties and for the exercise of self-help, markets in which the options can be exercised are required.

> The job of the liberal state was, and was seen to be, to provide the conditions for a capitalist market society. The essence both of the liberal state and the market society was competition, competition between individuals who were free to choose what they would do with their own energies and skills.[6]

In our time the connection between the market and the particular liberties prized in the liberal tradition is still intimate. If you and I as ordinary citizens are to be free to choose our own occupations, we need a labor market, rather than an authoritative system of conscription. If we are to be free to travel, and do not want to ask a government official's permission, we must be able to buy tickets on the market. If we are to be free to read, we must be able to buy books. The liberal notion of freedom was freedom from government's many interventions, and for that kind of freedom markets are indeed indispensable.

164

If we understand that polyarchy is a component of a highly developed form of constitutional liberalism and that constitutional liberalism in turn is a set of institutions assuring individuals of their liberty to enter into trade in order to develop their own life opportunities, we would not expect a polyarchy without a market. But we would expect markets without polyarchy. For short of polyarchy, some nations would be expected to develop a form of constitutional liberalism sufficient to guarantee the rights of an elite or middle class to try to enrich itself. Such a set of guarantees might be protected by agreement within an elite or by constitutional tradition short of polyarchy.

That is indeed the situation in most noncommunist systems of the world. There markets operate under at least weak constitutional limitations on state interference, hence there is some individual liberty to exploit market opportunities, all without polyarchal control over government. Mexico illustrates the degree to which, short of polyarchy, a set of rules can enlarge the liberties open to a middle class for exploiting market opportunities. But almost all nonpolyarchal noncommunist systems are members of this large and in some eyes disreputable family.

Although one can imagine polyarchical governments of a different stripe, all historical and contemporary examples are, in their anxiety over the conventional liberties, marked by a separation of powers and other devices to prevent a great mobilization of authority in one person or organization, even for what might be thought to be legitimate national purposes. Polyarchies are systems of rules for constraining rather than mobilizing authority. They grow out of a struggle to control authority rather than to create it or make it more effective. They are therefore political systems that are, again, like markets. They practice decentralization, diffusion of influence and power, and mutual adjustment so that individuals and small groups rather than national collectivities can strive for whatever they wish. Existing polyarchies and market systems, we have seen, both encourage extremes of pluralism.

Two questions are now forced on us. The first is: Can we conceive of a polyarchy arranged to achieve popular control over a government bent on collective purposes, one much less committed to the traditional individualistic liberties? Yes, it is not difficult. Logically, therefore polyarchy and market are independent. That is an important conclusion.

Many liberals, however, will believe a nonmarket polyarchy to be a practical impossibility. They will, for example, fear that people will fight rather than agree on collective goals and will suggest that polyarchies have been able to keep domestic peace only because in the main they facilitate a diversity of individual goal seeking. Yet we know that polyarchies have pursued collective purposes like war, public education, and control of communicable diseases. In any case, in a new era of collective problems like energy shortage, environmental degradation, and potential atomic holocaust, increasing numbers of thoughtful people may be reaching the conclusion that only a new form of polyarchy can survive: either there will be a less liberal, more collectivist polyarchy, or there will be no polyarchy at all. It is an issue on which we shall have more to say later.

The second question is: Why have no polyarchies, notwithstanding their liberal and constitutional origins, made a significant attempt at a centrally directed authoritative system? Would one not expect that as origins become obscured with the passage of time the citizens of at least one polyarchy would make the attempt? Somewhere in the history of the last two centuries at least one polyarchy should have marched or blundered into an attempt at polyarchal central planning. Curiously not a single one has, except sometimes in war.

Polyarchal Planning in War

Neither a small war nor a nuclear war—say, a generous exchange of hydrogen bombs—calls for wartime economic planning. For quick wars, whatever planning is not done before the outbreak has to be done after the war—and then to reconstruct rather than to fight. World War II, however, like World War I, did require central authority over production.[7]

To move the labor force quickly and massively into new assignments, the most conspicuous mechanism in the United States, the United Kingdom, and some of the other systems was authoritative assignment to military occupations through conscription. The threat of the draft was also used to induce workers to move into essential civilian occupations. For moving productive capacity into war needs, like other nations the United States prohibited certain kinds of production—private automobiles, for example. It also forbade enterprises to buy certain inputs except by administrative authorization of government.

The U.S. government did not, however, simply command enterprises to produce. Although by late 1945, 60 percent of all manufactured output was for the armed services, military requirements were consistently bought through contracts rather than requisitioned by command.[8] Granted that under wartime circumstances the distinction between purchase and command evaporates to a degree, it is still of some significance. Simply to command a corporation to produce would leave it unable to respond unless either it or the government acting on its behalf could command all necessary suppliers, including workers, to make themselves available to the enterprise. This the U.S. government chose not to do. By negotiating contracts with its direct suppliers, it assured them funds they then could use to procure inputs and labor on the market. The market was by no means wholly replaced.

In industrial supply, however, the market was greatly supplemented and regulated. A long list of essential inputs was subject to direct government administrative control. In the Controlled Materials Plan, three key metals—steel, copper, and aluminum—were administratively controlled in detail on the assumption that a sufficient direction of many other inputs would be achieved as a by-product of the control of these three.[9]

Wartime experience does not by any means demonstrate that such a system would be feasible in peacetime. It shows, however, that a polyarchal government can at least in some circumstances go much further in displacing the market than any of them now do, yet maintain simultaneously a highly organized economy, polyarchy, and a wide range of personal liberties. Clearly, such a system shifts national energies to a significant degree from "private" to national goals.

Why Polyarchies Do Not Practice Central Planning

Why, then, has no polyarchy tried to plan production centrally in peacetime? These days almost everyone believes in town planning, energy planning, fiscal planning, and planning on national security, health conservation, population, investment, development, transportation, and housing. Socialists do. So also do liberals, progressives, conservatives, Tories, Labourites, Republicans, and Democrats. Yet in the polyarchies almost none of them advocate the central planning of production and of resource allocation, except when war requires.

A superficial explanation is that historical and contemporary problems call for solutions more specific than central production planning. Inflation and unemployment, for example, call for the management of money and credit. The U.S.S.R., as well as market-oriented systems, must cope with unemployment and inflation; its central planning does not simply wipe away these problems. Similarly, problems of income inadequacy and insecurity seem to call not for central planning but for income transfers. And specific production shortages—medical care or housing, for example— call for subsidies or other specifics.

This line of explanation has to be rejected as too convenient. For in periods in which the polyarchies had every reason to doubt the efficacy of regulatory devices and to give sympathetic hearing to central production planning, they did not. When in the Great Depression of the 1930's, one-fourth of the American labor force was unemployed—pushed out of the market economy and left destitute—central planning even then had only a few advocates and perhaps none among leading political figures.

Can we explain the refusal of polyarchies to experiment with central planning of production on the assumption that polyarchal citizens and their leaders simply know, for all the superficial appeal of central planning, that it is in fact not a better solution to their problems than the market system? They could not possibly know that to be true. No one knows it to be true—or false. It is a matter of dispute. One would think that at least one polyarchy would experiment, even if for the worst of reasons. But they do not dispute, let alone experiment. It is a deeply puzzling phenomenon.

We do know that central production planning is anathema to some people in polyarchies because, as no one since Marx has been permitted to forget, it abrogates the rights of private property. Not private property as the individual householder knows it, but the rights that go by the name of private property in the production process: rights to control enterprises, rights to organize and dispose of productive assets, and rights to income from them. Central production planning is no mere technical alteration of national economic organization. It is subversive of the existing system, specifically of the prerogatives, privileges, and rights of the business and property-owning groups.

Is it possible that the polyarchies are actually under their control? We must at this point consider the possibility that existing polyarchies are not very democratic, that political debate in them is not very free, and that policy making in them is actually in the hands of persons who want to protect the privileges of business and property.

Only if the wealthy (or persons allied with them) exercise at all times in all polyarchies an extraordinarily disproportionate influence on governmental policy can the challenge of central planning to the privileges of property explain the remarkable uniformity of polyarchal hostility to central planning. If we can find no other explanation for the hostility, that in itself suggests that perhaps they do exercise such an influence. There is of course a long established and documented Marxian argument to that effect. Yet circumstantial evidence is weaker than direct evidence, and the Marxian argument is insufficiently persuasive. We shall therefore want to look into other kinds of evidence; and that we shall do in the chapters that follow.

The mere possibility that business and property dominate polyarchy opens up the paradoxical possibility that polyarchy is tied to the market

argument

system not because it is democratic but because it is not. If all past and existing polyarchies are dominated by business and property, it is to the dominating minority that we may owe its ties to the market system. That is to say, it is possible that genuine democracy would not be dependent on the market system. Only existing polyarchies are, and that only because, although they are libertarian, they are controlled undemocratically by business and property.*

* For a different but supplementary analysis of the polyarchy-market connection, see chapter 19, "Two Models."

The Privileged Position
of Business

[handwritten marginalia: weird reasoning / has more to do in popular perceptions & people. People pushed for it. Doesn't even try confort]

ONE might have expected that central planning of production, whatever its merits, would have been attempted under democratic pressure in at least a few polyarchies. The universal hostility to it, however, opens our eyes to the possibility that genuinely popular control in the polyarchies is even weaker than described in earlier chapters. We shall examine that possibility not only to explain the hostility of polyarchy to central planning and its universal dependence on markets but because we have now raised a major question about polyarchy: Is polyarchy not very democratic at all? Are the polyarchies controlled by business and property?

We begin the analysis by exploring in this chapter the political role of businessmen in all private enterprise market-oriented societies. This role is different from what it is usually perceived to be. It is not, we shall see, merely an interest-group role.

The Business Executive as Public Official in the Market System

If we can imagine a politico-economic system without money and markets, decisions on the distribution of income would obviously be political or governmental decisions. Lacking markets and wages, income shares would have to be administered by some kind of public authority, perhaps through rationing. Decisions on what is to be produced in the system would also have to be made by political or governmental authority. So also decisions on the allocation of resources to different lines of production, on the allocation of the labor force to different occupations and workplaces, on plant location, the technologies to be used in production, the quality of goods and services, innovation of new products—in short, on every major aspect of production and distribution. All these decisions would be recognized as public policy decisions.

In all societies, these matters have to be decided. They are of momentous consequences for the welfare of any society. But in a private enterprise market system, they are in larger part decided not by government officials but by businessmen. The delegation of these decisions to the businessman does not diminish their importance or, considering their consequences, their public aspect. In communist and socialist systems, heads of enterprises are government officials; it is taken for granted that their functions are governmental. In private enterprise systems, whether polyarchal or not, their functions are no less of public consequence. On all these matters, moreover, not only do business executives make consequential decisions; but, as we have seen in Chapter 11, corporate executives exercise broad discretion in making them.

For example, for a twelve-year period, while European steel companies held outputs and employment relatively stable by permitting prices of steel to fluctuate, American steel companies held prices steady with the result that output and employment fluctuated. It was a discretionary choice full of consequences for jobs, economic growth, prices, and the balance of payments.[1] But it was steel industry executives, not governmental officials, who made the decision.

We hardly need, however, further illustration of the public consequences of discretionary corporate decisions in the market. The major decisions that rest in corporate hands have been outlined in Chapter 11. Corporate executives in all private enterprise systems, polyarchic or not, decide a nation's industrial technology, the pattern of work organization, location of industry, market structure, resource allocation, and, of course, executive compensation and status. They also are the immediate or proximate and discretionary decision makers, though subject to significant consumer control, on what is to be produced and in what quantities.

In short, in any private enterprise system, a large category of major decisions is turned over to businessmen, both small and larger. They are taken off the agenda of government. Businessmen thus become a kind of public official and exercise what, on a broad view of their role, are public functions. The significant logical consequence of this for polyarchy is that a broad area of public decision making is removed from polyarchal control. Polyarchal decision making may of course ratify such an arrangement or amend it through governmental regulation of business decision making. In all real-world polyarchies, a substantial category of decisions is removed from polyarchal control.

The Businessman as Public Official in Government and Politics

What we have just said, however, only begins to describe the public role of businessmen in all private enterprise market-oriented societies. As a result of the "public" responsibilities of businessmen in the market, a great deal more is implied. Businessmen generally and corporate executives in particular take on a privileged role in government that is, it seems reasonable to say, unmatched by any leadership group other than government officials themselves.* Let us see, step by step, how this comes about. Every step in the analysis will refer to a familiar aspect of these systems, the implications of which, taken together, have been overlooked by most of us.

Because public functions in the market system rest in the hands of businessmen, it follows that jobs, prices, production, growth, the standard of living, and the economic security of everyone all rest in their hands. Consequently, government officials cannot be indifferent to how well business performs its functions. Depression, inflation, or other economic

* In contemporary thought, especially democratic thought, "privilege" often connotes something improper. That is not my intention in using the term. Webster says privilege is "a right or immunity granted as a peculiar benefit, advantage, or favor; *esp.*: one attached specif. to a position or an office," and something that is privileged is "not subject to the usual rules and penalties because of some special circumstance" (*Webster's Seventh New Collegiate Dictionary* [Springfield, Mass.: G. & C. Merriam]).

distress can bring down a government. A major function of government, therefore, is to see to it that businessmen perform their tasks.

Every day about us we see abundant evidence of governmental concern with business performance. In the polyarchies, government responsibility for avoiding inflation and unemployment is a common issue in elections. In all market-oriented systems, a major concern of tax and monetary policy is their effects on business activity. In subsidies and other help to water, rail, highway, and air transport; in patent protection; in fair trade regulation; in tariff policy; in overseas trade promotion through foreign ministries; in subsidized research and development (recently conspicuous, the Concorde in the United Kingdom and France, the aerospace industry in the United States)—in countless ways governments in these systems recognize that businessmen need to be encouraged to perform.

But take particular note of another familiar feature of these systems. Constitutional rules—especially the law of private property—specify that, although governments can forbid certain kinds of activity, they cannot command business to perform. They must induce rather than command.* They must therefore offer benefits to businessmen in order to stimulate the required performance. The examples above are all examples of benefits offered, not of commands issued.

On of the great misconceptions of conventional economic theory is that businessmen are induced to perform their functions by purchases of their goods and services, as though the vast productive tasks performed in market-oriented systems could be motivated solely by exchange relations between buyers and sellers. On so slender a foundation no great productive system can be established. What is required in addition is a set of governmentally provided inducements in the form of market and political benefits. And because market demands themselves do not spontaneously spring up, they too have to be nurtured by government. Governments in market-oriented systems have always been busy with these necessary activities. In the eighteenth century, for example, England established almost a thousand local road improvement authorities. When railroads became feasible, special legislation—more than 600 parliamentary acts between 1844 and 1847—granted attractive benefits to railway companies. In late eighteenth and early nineteenth century England, Parliament passed almost 4,000 enclosure acts, both creating a commercial agriculture to replace subsistence farming and driving a labor force off the land into industrial employment.

* But private property is not the key to the process being described. For any market system, whether private or public enterprise is the rule, enterprises must have autonomy or "rights" to respond to market cues rather than be obliged to obey governmental commands. See chapter 22.

173

In the United States, Alexander Hamilton's *Report on Manufactures* put government in an active supportive role for business. So also did early federal policy on banks, canals, and roads; governmental profligacy in indulgences to western railroads; the judicial interpretation of anti-monopoly legislation to restrict unions rather than business enterprises; the deployment of Marines to protect American enterprise in Latin America; the use of public utility regulation to protect business earnings; and the diversion of fair trade laws from their ostensible public purposes to the protection of monopolistic privilege.[2]

In the United States, as in all other market systems, the modern corporation could develop only with the assistance of new corporate law in the mid-nineteenth century that limited stockholders liability and in other ways conferred new authority on organizers of large enterprises. In the United States the courts transformed the Fourteenth Amendment, ostensibly written to safeguard the rights of former slaves, into an instrument for the protection of the corporation in its new role as a legal person.

Even more so than in England and America, continental European governments explicitly accepted a responsibility for the development of private enterprise, Germany most conspicuously. Perhaps learning from Europe, Japan went even further with loans, subsidies, and legal privileges for business enterprise.

What, then, is the list of necessary inducements? They are whatever businessmen need as a condition for performing the tasks that fall to them in a market system: income and wealth, deference, prestige, influence, power, and authority, among others. Every government in these systems accepts a responsibility to do what is necessary to assure profits high enough to maintain as a minimum employment and growth. If businessmen say, as they do, that they need tax offsets to induce investment, governments in all these systems seriously weigh the request, acknowledging that the tax concessions may indeed be necessary. In these systems such concessions are in fact granted. If corporation executives say that the chemical industries need help for research and development, governments will again acknowledge the probability that indeed they do and will commonly provide it. If corporate executives want to consult with government officials, including president or prime minister, they will be accommodated. Given the responsibilities of businessmen in these societies, it would be a foolish chief executive who would deny them consultation. If corporate executives ask, as they frequently do, for veto power over government appointments to regulatory positions, it will again be acknowledged that such a concession may be necessary to induce business performance. All this is familiar. And we shall see below that governments sometimes offer to share their formal authority with corporate officials as a benefit offered to induce business performance.

174

In the eyes of government officials, therefore, businessmen do not appear simply as the representatives of a special interest, as representatives of interest groups do. They appear as functionaries performing functions that government officials regard as indispensable. When a government official asks himself whether business needs a tax reduction, he knows he is asking a question about the welfare of the whole society and not simply about a favor to a segment of the population, which is what is typically at stake when he asks himself whether he should respond to an interest group.

Any government official who understands the requirements of his position and the responsibilities that market-oriented systems throw on businessmen will therefore grant them a privileged position. He does not have to be bribed, duped, or pressured to do so. Nor does he have to be an uncritical admirer of businessmen to do so. He simply understands, as is plain to see, that public affairs in market-oriented systems are in the hands of two groups of leaders, government and business, who must collaborate and that, to make the system work government leadership must often defer to business leadership. Collaboration and deference between the two are at the heart of politics in such systems. Businessmen cannot be left knocking at the doors of the political systems, they must be invited in.

A leader of a West German business association comments on the world of politics, "This is not an alien world to the entrepreneur; it is his own. At stake for him is the leadership of the state."[3] Drawing on his experience in Du Pont, an American writes, "the strength of the position of business and the weakness of the position of government is that government needs a strong economy just as much as business does, and the people need it and demand it even more."[4] The duality of leadership is reminiscent of the medieval dualism between church and state, and the relations between business and government are no less intricate than in the medieval duality.

Thus politics in market-oriented systems takes a peculiar turn, one largely ignored in conventional political science. To understand the peculiar character of politics in market-oriented systems requires, however, no conspiracy theory of politics, no theory of common social origins uniting government and business officials, no crude allegation of a power elite established by clandestine forces. Business simply needs inducements, hence a privileged position in government and politics, if it is to do its job.

Other Privileged Positions?

How might the thesis that businessmen occupy a privileged position—that they constitute a second set of major leaders in government and politics—be challenged? It can hardly be denied that business performance is required in market-oriented systems. Nor that it has to be induced rather than commanded. Nor that, consequently, government officials have to be solicitous in finding and offering appropriate inducements. Perhaps, however, other groups enjoy similar privilege for similar reason? It seems reasonable to suggest that labor leaders, who might be thought the most likely occupants of a similar privileged position, do not occupy one. They and their unions do not provide, we have already noted, essential services. Their function is instead to advance the segmental interests of workers. But workers themselves provide essential services, it might be replied. If they do not work, the whole productive system halts.

The plain fact, however, is that workers do work—without special inducement from government. Their livelihoods depend on it. Their position is quite different from that of the businessman, who has a dimension of choice. He will not risk capital, reputation, or the solvency of an enterprise in order to undertake an entrepreneurial venture unless the conditions are favorable. The test of the difference is an obvious one. All over the world men work at ordinary jobs because they have no choice but to do so. But in many parts of the world the conditions that call forth entrepreneurial energy and venturesomeness are still lacking, and the energy and venturesomeness are therefore not forthcoming. The particular roles that businessmen are required to play in market-oriented systems they play well only when sufficiently indulged.

But a sufficient degree of union organization and ambition, it would seem, could at least in some circumstances put workers or their union leaders in a privileged position in government. It could happen if unions could successfully stop production, not simply in one firm or industry, but broadly as in a general strike. Ordinarily, however, a general strike—except as a demonstration for a few days—is impossible because it provokes the government, even in the polyarchies, to break the strike, as in the aborted British general strike of 1926. In short, the rules of market-oriented systems, while granting a privileged position to business, so far appear to prohibit the organizational moves that would win a comparable position for labor. Hence a privileged position for union leaders and their unions is approximated only in special circumstances. A noteworthy example is the use of the strike threat among municipal employees in New York City. Their privileged position in New York City government seems unquestionable.

From time to time other groups achieve a limited privileged position. Physicians in the United States enjoy privileges in policy making on health because government officials fear that their performance will be adversely affected if they do not. In many of the developing nations, the internal security forces hold a privileged position because higher government officials know that if unsatisfied these forces can turn on their ostensible masters. Farmers are another case. Many of them are businessmen and share in the privileged position of business. But many very small farm operators have no more choice about performing than do ordinary workers.

Changing Privileges

The level and character of privilege that businessmen require as a condition of their satisfactory performance vary from time to time and place to place. All about us is conspicuous evidence that some older privileges have been withdrawn, even to the point of nationalizing some firms and industries. In many of the market-oriented systems, business enterprise is more heavily taxed than before. It is also subjected to increasing regulation on some scores—for example, regulation of industrial relations, monopoly, and now environmental pollution. Clearly businessmen have commonly demanded of government more indulgences than are actually necessary to motivate their required performances. As some of these indulgences have been taken away, their performance has not faltered.[5]

On the other hand, the removal of some privileges appears to require the institution of offsetting new ones—for example, tax credits. Forty percent of net investments in manufacturing equipment in the United States in 1963 was estimated to be attributable to the investment tax credit of 1962.[6] In the market-oriented systems, governments underwrite much of the cost of research and development for business. They also provide security to business enterprises through a variety of protections for monopoly, like fair trade legislation. In some industries, government shares or bears the risk of new plant construction by renting facilities to firms that do not want to construct their own. Half of the plant facilities of U.S. defense plants are provided by government. Governments also bail out failing enterprises with loans. And in much of recent capital planning in Western Europe, businessmen are brought into a new intimacy of consultation with government officials.

Many of the new privileges, which offset some taken away, are not widely recognized to be such. Urban renewal, for example, comes to the aid of retailers, banks, theaters, public utilities, brokers, a id builders. Highway development promotes a long list of industries including cement, automobiles, construction, petroleum, construction equipment, and trucking.[7] But the ostensible purpose of urban renewal and highway development is not aid to business.

Conflicts among Businessmen

On some demands—those pertaining to enterprise autonomy, private property, limited business taxation, and tax incentives, for example—business volitions are relatively homogeneous. On other demands, some businessmen want one kind of benefit; others want another. That businessmen disagree on such demands is not usually a barrier to their occupying a privileged position, for to give one kind of business a benefit is not necessarily to deprive another. On some issues, of course, privilege granted to one segment of the business community represents the withdrawal of a privilege from another. Large meat packers, for example, may press for inspection laws that, by raising the costs of small packers, give the large ones a competitive advantage. But it is possible for government officials to find an offsetting benefit to the small packers to compensate for the injury, if officials understand that redress is necessary.

Mutual Adjustment between the Two Groups

So far we have stressed controls by businessmen over government. But of course controls go in both directions. In briefest outline the reciprocal controls look like the following:

Government exercises broad authority over business activities.

But the exercise of that authority is curbed and shaped by the concern of government officials for its possible adverse effects of business, since adverse effects can cause unemployment and other consequences that government officials are unwilling to accept.

In other areas of public policy, the authority of government is again curbed and shaped by concern for possible adverse effects on business.

Hence even the unspoken possibility of adversity for business operates as an all-pervasive constraint on government authority.

Mindful of government concern for business performance, businessmen, especially corporate executives, actively voice and negotiate demands on government, with both implicit threat of poor performance if their demands are not met.

For all these reasons, business officials are privileged not only with respect to the care with which government satisfies business needs in general but also in privileged roles as participants in policy deliberations in government.

178

At least hypothetically, government always has the option, if dissatisfied with business performance, of refusing further privilege and simply terminating private enterprise in a firm, industry or the entire system. Short of taking that course, however, government has to meet business needs as a condition of inducing business performance.

Market and private enterprise thus introduce an extreme degree of mutual adjustment and political pluralism, even in the absence of poly-archy. The mutual adjustment is not always explicit through meetings and actual negotiation. Nor does government usually enter into an explicit exchange with businessmen. Mutual adjustment is often impersonal and distant. It operates through an unspoken deference of administrations, legislatures, and courts to the needs of business. And it relies on a multi-tude of common tacit understandings shared by the two groups of leaders, business and governmental, with respect to the conditions under which enterprises can or cannot profitably operate.

In addition, business executives come to be admitted to circles of explicit negotiation, bargaining, and reciprocal persuasion, from which ordinary citizens are excluded. Other leaders are admitted—union and farm leaders and other interest-group representatives. In these consulta-tions, however, corporate executives occupy a privileged position, since they and not the interest-group leaders are there mainly in their capacity as "public" officials.

It follows that evidence, which is abundant, of conflict between business and government—and of business defeats—is not evidence of lack of privilege. Knowing that they must have some privileges and knowing that government officials fully understand that simple fact, businessmen ask for a great deal. They also routinely protest any proposal to reduce any of their privileges. They are not highly motivated to try to understand their own needs. It might weaken them in governmental negotiations to do so. Hence they often predict dire consequences when a new regula-tion is imposed on them, yet thereafter quickly find ways to perform under it.

It appears that disputes between government and business are intense because of—not in spite of—their sharing the major leadership roles in the politico-economic order. Inevitably two separate yet cooperating groups of leaders will show hostility to each other. They will also invest some of their energies in outwitting each other, each trying to gain the upper hand. Conflict will always lie, however, within a range of dispute constrained by their understanding that they together constitute the neces-sary leadership for the system. They do not wish to destroy or seriously undermine the function of each other.

They therefore do not dispute the fundamentals of their symbiotic

179

relationship—private enterprise itself, private property in productive assets, and a large measure of enterprise autonomy, for example. They dispute over an ever-shifting category of secondary issues—such as tax rates and particulars of regulation and promotion of business. Imagine a continuum of possible combinations of business and governmental control over politico-economic life, ranging at far left from extraordinary autonomy for the business enterprise—some extreme form of laissez-faire —to a terminus at the extreme right at which the autonomous business enterprise vanishes in favor of production in the hands of government agencies. Extreme positions on such a continuum are not disputed by government and businessmen. Some narrow range of disagreement is, however, constantly disputed.

It appears also that the range slowly shifts, decade by decade, in the direction of less privilege for business and more authority for government. But at any time there is, even allowing for businessmen's gradually learning to perform in a less privileged position in government, some minimum of privilege short of which inducements will fail to motivate business performance. An illustration is the demand for privilege that giant multinational corporations can impose on small nations. Either the demands are met, or the corporation goes elsewhere.

Dimensions of the Privileged Position

Everything we have now outlined on the privileged position of business and on the duality of leadership in all private enterprise systems rests on familiar observable aspects of these systems. Some further brief detail, however will illuminate the phenomena.

Government officials, we have seen, routinely and explicitly acknowledge the necessity of adapting public policy to the needs of business whenever, say, they talk about using tax or monetary policy to stimulate business. The explicitness and precision of their acknowledgement, however, often goes further and clarifies the full dimensions of the privileged position of business. For example, in a suit brought against the Richardson-Merrell pharmaceutical company because its product MER/29 produced a variety of symptoms including cataracts, it was established to the judge's satisfaction that over a ten-year testing period the company had repeatedly suppressed evidence of the drug's dangers, filing falsified reports to the

Food and Drug Administration. Yet the judge refused to award punitive damages, fearing that if he did,

> A sufficient egregious error as to one product can end the business life of a concern that has wrought much good in the past.[8]

It is an elegantly simple example of acknowledged need to accommodate public policy to the needs of business, if business is to do its tasks.

For another example, Peter Peterson, then the chairman of the President's Council on International Economic Policy, declared: "The government has to foster in a planned and targeted way" those industries—he was speaking of American enterprise abroad—that are most promising.[9] Or, commenting on a $250 million loan to save Lockheed, U.S. Secretary of Commerce John Connally said: "We feel that the impact that the demise of this company would have would be of such proportions that it ought not to be permitted in the interest of the economic revival of the nation."[10] An Italian civil servant says: "The bureaucrat then is in a very weak position if he seeks to oppose Confindustria, particularly when the latter says, 'you must do the following regarding this industrial sector or you will cause crisis, bankruptcy, and unemployment.' "[11]

Businessmen sometimes acknowledge their privileged position in both word and deed. In the United Kingdom, for example, the Federation of British Industries (now merged in the Confederation of British Industry) routinely maintained both formal and day-to-day informal communication with the Treasury, Board of Trade, Home Office, and the ministries of Housing, Education, Local Government, Power, Transport, and Aviation, in addition to frequent communication with other ministries and offices. In so constant and broad an exercise of influence, the Federation "acted as if it were the industrial counterpart of the Civil Service, and avoided as far as possible actions which made it look like a pressure group." "It looked and acted like a government department."[12]

In Japanese politics an intimacy of connection between businessmen, civil service, and legislators goes beyond that of the United States or the Western European polyarchies. It is a connection that government officials do not establish with labor or any other groups. It is achieved by devices including family connection, old-school ties, and movement of personnel from government to business. "Business becomes the major concern of government," business and the bureaucracy achieve a "symbiosis." A prime minister describes the big business community as the "compass" of the ship of state.[13]

A former public relations officer in an American corporation advises businessmen: "Let it be publicly known that business climate is a very important factor in determining the selection of states and communities in which to locate new plants. The importance of this is that it places on the defensive the people who are beating upon, overtaxing, and harassing business.[14] He is speaking of a commonplace phenomenon that most people take for granted: extracting privileges from state and local government. Many other responses to business demands are also routinized without controversy.

But if government accommodation of business demands is often routine and familiar, it sometimes takes a twist that refreshes our understanding of the strength of corporation executives in their privileged portion. For example:

> Unless the British government agreed to provide massive aid for Chrysler's troubled British subsidiary, Riccardo [chairman of Chrysler] said, the company would be forced to shut down its five major plants in Britain and cashier its 25,000 employees there. . . . Wilson denounced the Riccardo ultimatum, angrily protesting that Chrysler had left the government "with a pistol at its head." But last week in a startling, if characteristically Wilsonian, about-face, the Prime Minister agreed to help out Chrysler after all.[15]

Governmental responsiveness to business demands shows up in other unexpected ways. An oddity in American law, for example, permits corporations whose officials have been convicted of crimes to continue to use their services while they are on probation or after their sentences have expired, while union officials are prohibited from returning to office for five years after conviction.[16] For another example, a subcommittee of the Senate Armed Services Committee found that stockpiling of materials ostensibly needed for national defense was actually undertaken without respect to national security needs, the "primary purpose" being the subsidization of mining companies.[17] A French businessman says of French planning:

> I would disagree . . . that the primary purpose of the plan is "to bring economic power under political control." It is rather to help the businessman to expand his economic activity.[18]

And from a study of French planning:

> . . . there is no doubt that the activity of planning, as it is practised in France, has reinforced the systematic influence exerted by large-scale business on economic policy. Sometimes this influence is open and apparent, as when the Fourth Plan's investment policy for steel was modified in 1963 in deference to the wishes of the steel industry, despite the barely concealed objections of certain government officials. Subsequently, when the industry was offered a sufficient financial inducement by the Government—in the form of a reduction in the tariffs on imported US coking coal and a rebate

on their social security payments—they agreed to an increase in the steel manufacturing capacity to be laid down in the Fifth Plan.[19]

French planning is thus in some part even an explicit exchange of favors: industry offers performance—expansion, relocation, technological innovation, and the like—in exchange for governmental favors like tax rebates, subsidies, or credit advantages. Similarly in the National Economic Development Council in the United Kingdom "each party offers something which is conditional on certain actions by others."[20]

In Germany earlier corporate decentralization measures left business unwilling to undertake the vast tasks of postwar reconstruction. The measures had to be abandoned. Demands from business accomplished the same erosion of controls on business size in postwar Japan.[21] In Italy for Institute for Industrial Reconstruction is a focal point for business demands and governmental responses necessary to induce business to mobilize the large amounts of capital needed for modern industry.[22]

Obviously in no system do businessmen get all they ask for. The task of government is to find responses to the demands of businessmen sufficient to motivate them to perform the tasks delegated to them, but without simply turning policy making over to them lock, stock, and barrel. It is a task that requires great skill if it is to be done well enough to maintain both economic stability and growth. French planning has in recent years been applauded as a demonstration of skill in the design of indulgences to business, and sluggishness in the American economy held up as an example of its absence.

Sometimes governments fail to respond to business demands even though the penalties, which come in the form of slowed growth and unemployment, are severe. In the less developed parts of the world, the growth of markets and enterprise is repeatedly hindered by the failure of governments to provide necessary infrastructure and other supports. In India a principled hostility to private enterprise has for more than a decade constrained the Indian government not to provide the supports that business wants. The result has been retarded industrial and commercial development. The possibility arises also in the developed nations. After World War II, French business was under heavy attack for its collaborationist tendencies during the war. It was consequently not disposed to invest. Some businessmen prepared to emigrate, so great was hostility to them. The government of France had to find new inducements for French business in order to induce it to take up its responsibilities again.[23,] *

* When in his inaugural address in 1953 President Eisenhower declared that "we need markets in the world for the surpluses of our farms and our factories," he was acknowledging that businessmen make demands on government in foreign policy as well as domestic policy, just as the chairman of the President's Council on International Economic Policy, we saw, understands that government has to foster business activity

Yet ordinarily as new conditions or problems arise—for example, public demands for restriction on air pollution—businessmen know that government officials will understand their wishes—in this case their unwillingness or incapacity to bear without help the costs of stopping industrial discharges into the air. Businessmen will find the government official ready to acknowledge their special competence and interest, eager to welcome them into negotiation, anxious about the possible adverse effects of costly antipollution measures on prices and production. Thus, as environmental concerns mounted, President Nixon established in 1970 the National Industrial Pollution Control Council to allow businessmen communication with the president "to help chart the route by [sic] which our cooperative ventures will follow." Similarly, out of concern that widespread new consumer offices in various federal agencies might be damaging to business, he established in 1971 the National Business Council for Consumer Affairs, again to allow businessmen to communicate regularly with him.[24]

---

overseas. We would go astray if we tried to incorporate into the analysis the complexities of business in international markets and politics, but it is essential to note that the duality of leadership in market-oriented systems extends to foreign policy.

Whether business demands on government in market-oriented systems drive governments inevitably into a new form of imperialism is a somewhat different question, again beyond our inquiry. The smaller market-oriented systems are not imperialist, and France and the United Kingdom appear to be retiring from earlier imperialist roles. The charge of imperialism is an interesting allegation only when brought against the United States as a superpower—and against the U.S.S.R. as another. Yet unquestionably the superior resources and capacity to mobilize authority and other power in international relations give all the industrialized market-oriented systems, large and small, great advantages in international negotiation and commercial dealings with the less developed countries, which they typically use to their own perceived advantage. See Benjamin J. Cohen, *The Question of Imperialism* (New York: Basic Books, 1973).

It is also alleged that business demands on government drive market-oriented systems into heavy defense expenditure and into war, and indeed that these systems cannot grow without heavy defense expenditure. Again, the exploration of the many facets of these allegations is beyond us. But some points are quickly established. Military expenditure is not correlated with type of politico-economic system. The big spenders are both the United States and the Soviet Union. Most industrialized market-oriented systems spend less than the communist nations of Eastern Europe. As for whether defense spending helps the economy, among market-oriented systems those with the largest defense spending are the slowest growers. Heavy defense spending is possibly an obstacle to growth and may help explain slow American growth in recent decades, just as its absence helps explain high Japanese and Mexican growth. For a summary of evidence, see Harold J. Wilensky, *The Welfare State and Equality* (Berkeley: University of California Press, 1975), pp. 82–84.

Similarly, the military-industrial complex, called to the nation's attention by President Eisenhower at the end of his term, is, again, largely an American and Soviet phenomenon, hence presumably attributable, at least in part, to their superpower roles. In amount of military spending, intimacy and frequency of association between defense corporations and government officials, and development of a special sector of the American politico-economy, a distinctive phenomenon has developed, to which Eisenhower's term is appropriately applied. But not in the market-oriented systems as a category.

Businessmen only rarely threaten any collective action such as a concerted restriction of function. Ordinarily, they need only point to the costs of doing business, the state of the economy, the dependence of the economy's stability and growth on their profits or sales prospects—and simply predict, not threaten, that adverse consequences will follow on a refusal of their demands.

Ostensibly businessmen do nothing more than persuade. They simply acquaint government officials with the facts. But prophecies of some kinds tend to be self-fulfilling. If spokesmen for businessmen predict that new investment will lag without tax relief, it is only one short step to corporate decisions that put off investment until tax relief is granted.

Business Authority in Government

The far edge of the privileged position of business is represented by actual grants of government authority to businessmen. Decades ago in the United States the right of eminent domain was granted to private utility corporations, conferring on them compulsory authority to acquire land for their operations. In this and other ways governments respond to demands with a formal or informal grant of authority to businessmen, cementing their privileged position in government.

Business groups that become established as clients of specific U.S. government agencies often win grants of informal authority. Examples are the civil contractors dealing with the Army Corps of Engineers, the Rural Electrification Administration, and the Small Business Administration, respectively. Their collaborations have been characterized as "joint government by public and private bodies."[25]

Some of these grants are relatively explicit. The president of the United States grants authority to executives of regulated industries to veto appointments to regulatory agencies.[26] Some are formal. Since 1933, the president, Cabinet members, and other high officials have met with the Business Council, composed of leading corporate executives.[27] The federal government has also established between 1,000 and 2,000 business councils to consult with agencies on common policies—this in addition to about 4,000 particular to the Department of Agriculture.[28] In addition, it invites corporation executives, while still active in and salaried by their own corporations, to serve as unpaid government officials.

In 1953, that practice was given a more permanent peacetime basis when the Business and Defense Services Administration was established. Of it, a congressional committee said:

> In operation, the organization arrangements of BDSA have effected a virtual abdication of administrative responsibility on the part of the Government officials in charge of the Department of Commerce in that their actions in many instances are but the automatic approval of decisions already made outside the Government in business and industry.[29]

For less formal grants, the line between granting a rule of obedience, thus establishing an acceptance of authority, and yielding to the offers or threats of exchange is often a thin one. This point is made by a report on consultations on New York city and state finance:

> One stumbling block to the [absorption of] $3 billion of New York City's short-term debt was resolved yesterday. . . . The one agreement reached . . . was on a demand from the investment community that the city sales tax be converted to a state sales tax.[30]

In France business committees are also commonplace.[31] An industry and its associated ministry commonly develop a sharing of authority in making and implementing policy for the industry. It is intended that authority be shifted to the industry, and the shift is made even more definitive by moving much of the work of the ministry to the industry, whose cooperating staff often greatly outnumbers that of the ministry. The result is that decisions reached by the industry are ordinarily given ministerial approval.[32] In French planning, ostensibly a cooperation among government officials and business and union representatives, authority denied the latter is granted to the former: businessmen but not labor leaders can chair the *commissions*.[33]

In the United Kingdom hundreds of business advisory committees confer authority on corporate executives. In addition are special departmental committees and royal commissions, in which what begins as an advisory role for businessmen and other participants "becomes active participation in administration, as if the administrators were no longer able to bear alone the burden of the administrative State and had to pass it along to private individuals."[34]

In West Germany, representatives of national industry associations confer on new legislation with civil servants who refuse similar rights of participation to members of parliament.[35] And government agrees to membership on a special body on cartel legislation "even though to do so had the rather unorthodox effect of putting the BDI (Federation of German Industry) on an equal level with itself in the formulation of policy."[36] In Japan, the *genkyoku* offices, each responsible for certain industries, are paralleled by industry associations, and for each industry the two organizations negotiate and collaborate on policy for the industry.[37]

*　*　*

Under these circumstances, the "For years I thought what was good for our country was good for General Motors, and vice versa," spoken by a president of GM is easy to understand. However partisan they may be in fact, however uncritical about the coincidence of their own interests with broader public interests, businessmen do understand that they carry a public responsibility for discharging necessary public functions that other nongovernmental leaders do not carry. If they are, on the one hand, capable of gross abuse of that responsibility, they are, on the other hand, at least dimly aware of their special role as one of two groups that constitute a dual leadership in the market-oriented systems.

In a passage that could be taken as a summary comment on the line of analysis so far, Woodrow Wilson once wrote:

> The government of the United States at present is a foster-child of the special interests. It is not allowed to have a will of its own. It is told at every move: "Don't do that; you will interfere with our prosperity."[38]

In these comments, Wilson is angry. He sees these characteristics of government as inexcusable. On that, opinions will differ. My point has been only to explain the fundamental mechanism by which a great degree of business control, unmatched by similar control exercised by any other group of citizens, comes to be exercised over government and to indicate why this is inevitable in all private enterprise systems if they are to be viable.*

Again; businessmen do not get everything they want. But they get a great deal. And when they do not get enough, recession or stagnation is a consequence.

We have not wholly specified the policies or objectives that corporation executives use their privileged position to pursue. Some of their pursuits

---

* The proposition does not deny that persons who have scientific, technical, and other specialized information grow in influence in a society that is increasingly dependent on that information. They do not demand influence; they simply achieve it by reason of what they know. See Daniel Bell, *The Coming of Post-Industrial Society* (New York: Basic Books, 1973), pp. 358–67, and R. E. Lane," "The Decline of Politics and Ideology in a Knowledgeable Society," *American Sociological Review* 31 (October 1966). However pervasive their influence, it is ordinarily indirect, affecting outcomes through its impact on government officials, businessmen, and others who employ the producers of knowledge.

have been made clear: among many others, autonomy for the enterprise, tax favors and subsidies, restrictions on unions, a great variety of monopolistic privileges (tariffs, patents, retail price maintenance, weak antitrust enforcement, encouragement of mergers, fair trade restrictions on competition, occupational licensing, permissive regulation of public utilities, among others). All represent pursuits on which business prevails, though never without limit and with even occasional sharp defeat. We have also seen that the entire industrial structure is largely the result of business decisions on the whole sanctioned and sometimes implemented by responsive government officials. These decisions determine the size of plants and firms, the location of industry, the organization of markets and transport— hence the configuration of cities, on one hand, and the bureaucratization of the workplace, on the other.

It might therefore be argued that some of the most fundamental and pervasive features of industrial society are what they are because of the privileged position of business in government and politics. The possibility also has to be entertained that a remarkable historical stability in the distribution of wealth and income—despite all the policies of the welfare state, and even in egalitarian Scandinavia—owes much to the privileged position of business. So also the survival of the private enterprise system itself. All these possibilities will be explored further in later chapters. We begin by examining now the particular relations between business privilege and polyarchy.

The Consequences for Polyarchy

THE preceding chapter brings us to a question: What are the implications for polyarchy of the privileged position of business? An answer does not seem hard to find. The systems we call polyarchies are in fact complex systems in which two forms of control operate on government officials: those of polyarchy and those exercised by businessmen through their privileged position. Or, to put it another way, the systems we call polyarchies operate under two groups of leaders. But only one of them is systematically subject to polyarchal control.

A New York Times political columnist noted at the time: "Two months before he takes the oath of office as President, Jimmy Carter already is face to face with one of the major questions that will determine the course of his Administration. Will he seek at the outset to gain the confidence of the business and financial community, or will he risk their disfavor by moving rapidly and perhaps radically to attack the economic and social ills he campaigned against?" At the same time Carter's advisor on appointments declared that the new president wants a secretary of the treasury "who can verbalize the concerns of the financial community and anticipate the financial community's reaction to economic decisions he might take."[1] Such comments occasion no surprise. That officials are torn between two control systems is widely acknowledged.

Polyarchal rules and procedures, we saw earlier, are in any case already compromised by an underlying struggle for authority that persists in every political system and that polyarchy only reshapes. The rivalry between polyarchal and privileged business controls thus constitutes one more—a third—great element in the struggle over authority. One of the effects of the rivalry between business and polyarchal controls is to restrict polyarchal rules and procedures to no more than a part of government and politics, and to challenge them even there.

Rival Controls

For all the reasons of the preceding chapter, privileged business controls are largely independent of the electoral controls of polyarchy. To be sure, the electorate in a polyarchy wants a high level of employment and other satisfying performance from businessmen. Its frequent passivity might be taken to imply an approval for many of the privileges of businessmen so long as business goes on producing. But the particular demands that businessmen make on government are communicated to government officials in ways other than through the electoral process and are largely independent of and often in conflict with the demands that the electorate makes. Many business demands represent a condition of business performance whether the electorate knows it or not, whether it cares or not, whether it approves or not. In their voting citizens may or may not give careful consideration to business demands. Nothing in the polyarchal process requires that they do.

In recent years in the United States, businessmen have successfully protested against many new proposals for government regulation that arise from the public and its polyarchal representatives. The federal government has often deferred, for example, to requests from industrial corporations to postpone or soften proposed antipollution legislation. In West Germany, civil servants grant to businessmen rights of consultation that they refuse to members of parliament. In Italy, polyarchal controls ask for expansion of industry in ways that will increase employment. But businessmen ask instead for expansion that will raise productivity.[2] French planning in the 1960s has been described as relying on

> the close contacts established between a number of like-minded men in the civil service and big business. . . . Most of the time, the ministers of the government of the day were largely passed by.

Similarly, development planning in the United Kingdom slides out from under parliamentary or other polyarchal control.[3]

There are countless other examples of rivalry between business and polyarchal control. For example, like many government officials who wish to restrain polyarchal discussion, both President Johnson and President Nixon suppressed the reports of their own committees on antitrust. They did not want to permit polyarchal processes to operate in an area in which they were, as inevitably they must be, subject to controls from businessmen. For another example, when in 1976 the U.S. government asked pharmaceutical companies to undertake emergency production of swine flu vaccine, the companies successfully required, as a condition of their cooperation, new legislation making the government rather than the companies the defendant in any suits arising from the vaccinations.

Another kind of evidence now appears to be emerging from the history of American reform efforts. A new group of historians believe they are finding evidence of a common pattern. Policy is changed in response to business controls and is then paraded as democratic reform. Meat inspection legislation, once thought the consequence of popular revulsion against the conditions revealed in Upton Sinclair's *The Jungle*, is now found in large part to be a consequence of the packing industry's desire for universally enforced standards to improve the quality reputation of American meat exports. Food and drug regulation was sought by pharmaceutical companies to limit the excesses of some manufacturers whose products and claims damaged the pharmaceutical industry as a whole. Forest conservation was sought by processors of lumber who wished to engage the U.S. government in the expenses of reforestation. Municipal reform was pushed by businessmen who required improved municipal services. The Clayton Act and the Federal Trade Commission Act were urged on Congress by big businesses wishing to regulate their smaller competitors. Insurance of bank deposits, a reform of the depression of the 1930s, was inaugurated to draw deposits into the banks in order to make funds more easily available to business. To none of these reforms was popular demand an important contributor.[4]

Whatever the sources of such reforms as these, there is for the United States an impressive record of reforms being turned sharply away from their ostensible polyarchically chosen purposes. The Fourteenth Amendment to the Constitution, intended for the protection of freed slaves, was for that purpose rendered ineffective for many years by judicial interpretation. Simultaneously it was made the foundation for corporate autonomy, based on the doctrine that the corporation is a "fictitious person" and therefore entitled to the protection specified in the amendment. The Sherman Act, ostensibly enacted to regulate industrial monopoly, was used to constrain unions rather than enterprises. It continued to be so used

191

even after the Clayton Act explicitly exempted unions from its provisions. Regulatory policies generally are diverted from their ostensible purposes in order to meet many of the demands that businessmen can place upon government.[5]

An oft-quoted statement from an earlier U.S. attorney general shows how business controls can work even when reforms are popularly demanded. Commenting on the new Interstate Commerce Commission, he said in a nice demonstration of his understanding of the political system:

> It satisfies the popular clamor for a governmental supervision of railroads, at the same time that that supervision is almost entirely nominal. Further, the older such a Commission gets to be, the more inclined it will be found to take the business and railroad view of things. It thus becomes a sort of barrier between the railroad corporations and the people and a sort of protection against hasty and crude legislation hostile to railroad interests. . . . The part of wisdom is not to destroy the Commission but to utilize it.[6]

As acknowledged in the preceding chapter, businessmen do not win all they ask for. The point here is that business and polyarchal controls are largely independent of each other and are in conflict. The scope of polyarchy is consequently restricted.

Coordination of the Rival Controls

The implications for polyarchy of this rivalry go much further. Conflict between electoral and privileged business controls seems much less apparent than would be expected if the two controls were wholly independent. Why do we not see more frequent electoral demands for, say, corporate reform, curbs on monopoly, income redistribution, or even central planning? The answer must be that the two controls are not genuinely independent of each other. They are coordinated in large degree.

I suggest that the coordination is accomplished largely by controls that bend polyarchy to accommodate business controls. The controls are exercised through interest-group, party, and electoral activity of businessmen, about which we have so far said almost nothing. We recognize these activities now not as the chief instruments of business influence over government but as processes for adapting polyarchal controls to privileged controls by businessmen. The proposition puts business interest-group and electoral activity in a new light.

192

One of the conventional insensitivities of contemporary social science is revealed in scholarly works on interest groups. By some unthinking habit, many such works treat all interest groups as though on the same plane, and, in particular, they treat labor, business and farm groups as though operating at some parity with each other. Business interest-group activity, along with its other electoral activity, is only a supplement to its privileged position. And it is, we shall see, greatly more effective than any other interest-group and electoral activity of its ostensible rivals. It is a special case. That is not to say, however, that businessmen always win or even that they are unified in electoral and interest-group activity.

It is difficult to offer such propositions as we have been developing without appearing to allege conspiracy or subversion. I mean to do neither. Both the privileged controls in the hands of business and the additional controls businessmen exercise through their energetic participation in polyarchal politics are established, stable, and fundamental parts of government and politics in the systems called market-oriented polyarchy. Although these controls challenge and limit the effectiveness of popular control, they cannot on that account be deprecated as peripheral or as aberrations. Only in the light of democratic aspiration are these controls subversive; but these systems never have been highly democratic; and their polyarchal processes, which approximate democracy, are only a part of these systems.

Business Participation in Polyarchy

It is not necessary to detail business activity in electoral politics: the frequency and intimacy of business consultation with government officials from prime minister or president down to lesser officials, the organization of business interest groups, business financing of political parties, and business public relations and propaganda. All of this is familiar and has often been described.[7] Let us instead look for certain key phenomena.

The activities that businessmen undertake to capture polyarchal politics cannot always be distinguished from their privileged activities which are not dependent on polyarchal channels. But an analytic distinction is possible, and an empirically observable distinction is often easy. Corporate financing of political parties is clearly part of businessmen's participation in polyarchal processes. So, for example is the participation of business interest groups in legislative hearings.

No other group of citizens can compare with businessmen, even roughly, in effectiveness in the polyarchal process. How so? Because, unlike any other group of citizens, they can draw on the resources they command as public "officials" to support their activities in polyarchal politics.

To some degree, every public official inevitably uses his public position to advance his private or his partisan objectives in politics. Yet the law draws a distinction between a public official in his governmental role and the same man as candidate, interest-group activist, or citizen. In the United States the president is expected to raise his campaign funds from private contributions and not from the government's treasury. Neither he nor other government officials freely use government funds and personnel for partisan objectives, even though they often find ways to evade constraints.

Not so with corporation executives. The funds that pass through their hands in their official capacities—that is, the proceeds from corporate sales—can, with little constraint, be thrown into party, interest-group, and electoral activity in pursuit of whatever objectives the corporate executives themselves choose. The ease with which executives can bring corporate assets to the support of these activities is a remarkable feature of politics in market-oriented polyarchies. It has no rationale in democratic theory.

Not until the following chapter, however, will we consider the possibility that businessmen indoctrinate citizens so that they think they want what businessmen want. Here we are considering only the possibility that, *given conflicting volitions*, businessmen win—disproportionately—in political competition in polyarchy.

All citizen groups compete in politics with the use of their members' own incomes and energies. Except for businessmen. They enjoy a triple advantage: extraordinary sources of funds, organizations at the ready, and special access to government. Let us look at each.

Funds for Businessmen in Polyarchal Politics

Corporate funds go to political campaigns and to parties, to lobbying and other forms of corporate communication with governmental officials, to entertainment and other factors for government officials, to political and institutional advertising in the mass media, to educational materials for the public schools, and to litigation designed to influence governmental policy or its enforcement.[8]

We have no adequate figures on how much of their funds they allocate for these political activities, all of which overwhelm those of ordinary citizens. But there are a million corporations in the United States, 40,000 with at least 100 employees. Each of the largest of them takes in more receipts than most national governments. We also know that American businesses allocate roughly $60 billion per year to sales promotion, a large part of which is institutional advertising with a political content, like Exxon's "Energy for a strong America." On top of that are additional amounts available explicitly for politics. Hence the scale of corporate spending dwarfs political spending by all other groups. Something of the discrepancy is suggested by the fact that all campaign expenditures in 1972, a presidential election year, totaled only a half billion dollars.[9]

In the 1972 presidential election, unions spent $8.5 million on activities on which organizations are required by law to report. In addition, they spent $4 million or $5 million on nonpartisan "get out the vote" activities. Thus, the total was roughly $13 million. Business groups reported spending only about $6 million. But since corporate contributions of most kinds were illegal, business contributions took the form of legal and illegal expenditures, often routed personally through corporate executives. One can only guess at their total. But we have to account for a grand total of campaign expenditures that year of nearly $500 million, of which the union contribution was only about $13.5 million. We have other clues. Some members of the President's Business Council are known to have contributed jointly over $1 million, officers and directors of five oil companies $1.5 million, officers and directors of the 25 largest defense contractors over $2 million, and NASA contractors over $1 million.[10] On hundreds of other major business contributors, we have no record.

In 1964 union committees made contributions of less than $4 million, while a total of no more than 10,000 individuals, mostly from business, contributed $13.5 million. And in 1956, a year for which direct union-business comparisons are possible, it took the contributions of only 742 businessmen to match in amount the contribution of unions representing 17 million workers.[11] If these figures begin to scratch the surface, they are enough to indicate the enormous discrepancy between business spending in politics and that of any other group, including labor.

Some years ago a House of Representatives committee estimated expenses of various interest groups to influence legislation. They queried a sample of 173 corporations, the principal national farmers organizations, the AFL-CIO, and the major independent national unions (but not the national unions affiliated with AFL-CIO). These organizations reported expenditures for a three-year period in the following gross disproportions:[12]

173 corporations	$32.1 million
Farm organizations	0.9 million
Labor unions	0.55 million

For the United Kingdom, some figures from the election campaign of 1964 show that press and poster expenditure came from the following leading sources. The disproportions are again extremely large.[13]

Conservative Party (itself financed) largely through corporate contributions)	£950,000
Aims of Industry (an industrial association)	270,000
Steel Federation (an industrial association)	621,000
Stewards and Lloyds (a single corporation)	306,000
Labour Party	267,000

Notice that corporation expenditures are the overwhelming source of funds. Notice too that expenditures of one corporation alone are larger than those of the Labour Party.[14]

To compare political contributions from the personal incomes of ordinary citizens and allocations from business receipts is to compare mouse and mountain. Perhaps the most effective organizer of funds from personal income is indeed the labor movement. Yet we have seen that union expenditures of all kinds are tiny when compared with political expenditures of business. Another indicator is assets. Total union assets in the United States, exclusive of welfare and pension funds usually administered by employers, are roughly $3 billion. Corporate assets total roughly $3 trillion.[15]

Business Organization for Polyarchal Politics

In politics organization counts. Single individuals acting alone, with some exceptions like Ralph Nader (and even he long ago organized), are ineffective in influencing elected and appointed officials. Citizens can organize themselves—if they are willing to pay the price in time, energy, and money. But the corporation is already there as an organization. Organized for other purposes, it is at hand, ready to be used by its executives for political activity ranging from discussions with civil servants to financial support of political parties. Its personnel are available. Political action does not require tedious or frenzied energies of organizers. And the political workers in a corporation are not volunteers of dubious reliability but paid employees.

Consider the roughly 40,000 American corporations large enough to have at least 100 employees. Each of them is concerned with public policy and acts toward government like a small or large interest group. There is nothing else like it in politics, no other category of organization so massively engaged in seeking to influence local, state and national government. In addition to corporations themselves are their associations. The *Encyclopedia of Organizations in the United States* gives 256 pages to the listing of national business associations. By comparison, 17 pages is sufficient for labor organizations; 60 for public affairs organizations; and 71 for scientific, engineering, and technical organizations. In a total of roughly 4,000 national associations in the United States, one classification shows a distribution as follows:[16]

Business	1,800
Professional	500
Labor unions	200
Women's	100
Veterans and military	60
Commodity exchanges	60
Farmers	55
Blacks	50
Public officials	50
Fraternal	25
Sports and recreation	100
Other	1,000

A count of organizations is, however, largely irrelevant. For every separate business enterprise is a financed organization that can, and typically does, act as an interest group, which an individual citizen or worker cannot do. The practice by businessmen of using their own enterprise rather than a trade association for political influences has been widely noted in studies of business interest-group activity in the polyarchies.[17]

Information, Open Doors, and Sympathetic Hearings

The third great advantage of businessmen in polyarchal activity is their ease of access to government officials. Because of their privileged position in government and politics, they are already known to government officials, already attentively listened to, already engaged in negotiation. When they reappear in the role of ordinary citizens engaging in polyarchal politics, neither they nor government officials will ordinarily note the difference. They will enjoy all the advantage of their privileged role, an advantage not available to their citizen competitors in interest-group activity.

Japan, we have seen represents an extreme in case of business access to government. We have already also noted in some detail how intimate the relations are in French planning. Another indicator is the reliance of committees of the National Assembly and of individual members of the assembly on staff work, documentation, and research provided by businesses and business associations, as is also common in business-legislative relation in the United States.[18] In many of the polyarchies a common practice that makes the business-government relation congenial is the movement of government personnel into corporate positions.[19]

The Inferior Position of Labor Unions

By way of recapitulation, we take note once again that labor unions do not appear to enjoy in government and politics a privileged position like that of business, on whom government is dependent for production, growth, and jobs. It has also been noted that unions can command in polyarchal competition far fewer resources than businesses. In other subtle ways, unions suffer a relative disadvantage. On the relative strength of business and labor in West German politics, for example, a German scholar finds elements common to the polyarchies.

> Employers', businessmen [sic] and artisans' associations have quite a different standing in the community than the unions. First of all, they are rarely forced to work in the open, but can operate behind the scenes. Thus, people are far less conscious of their very existence than of that of the unions. But even if wider circles were informed about them, they would be more popular than labor because they seem more respectable and because their members have a higher social status. The values they hold—private property, authority, etc.—are those of the majority. Especially when they speak about the defense of the middle classes, they can be sure of broad sympathy. Always in calm times, things are easier for the defenders of the established order than for those who want changes. But even if all this were not true, the prestige of organized business in public opinion would be bolstered by the good contacts it has with the press through ownership and advertising.[20]

In addition, potential union initiatives to challenge business and corporate influence have been increasingly undercut by collaboration between union and management to avoid conflict and instead to raise wages and improve working conditions at the expense of the consumer and the unorganized. A similar disincentive to a union challenge has been union-management cooperation in interest-group activity on behalf of the enterprise or industry.

The influence of unions in electoral and interest-group politics is, in the judgment of most observers, greater in the United Kingdom than in most polyarchies. So great an influence is it that some observers hold union demands in collective bargaining, reinforced by labor's political influence and supplemented by welfare demands also made through electoral politics, to be the root cause of the "English sickness"—the decline of British productivity and economic stagnation. Whether that is the correct explanation can be neither asserted nor denied conclusively. But even if it is correct, it would not seem to deny the disproportionate influence of businessmen in electoral and interest-group politics.

The explanation, if true would instead suggest that even moderately successful union demands—far short of those demands that would be pressed successfully if union political influence were stronger—can undercut the entrepreneurial energies on which market-oriented systems depend. To put the point in another way, a market-oriented system may require for its success so great a disproportion of business influence, both through the privileged position of business and through business disproportion in electoral and interest-group activity, that even modest challenges to it are disruptive to economic stability and growth. Union power may be "too much" for the survival of private enterprise long before it is great enough to match the privileged position of business. Similarly welfare state demands may be "too much" long before they manifest a political equality in electoral and interest-group activity.

It seems reasonable to regard British labor demands as still modest, despite their success relative to some other countries. For all their demands, union members have not won any great alteration in distribution of income and wealth, or in participation in management, or in recent decades any substantial equalization of educational opportunity for their children. It is difficult to reconcile these timidities or defeats with the hypothesis that unions have either disproportionately large political influence or the more modest hypothesis that they have influence equal to that of businessmen.

Lacking objective criteria for equality or disproportion in polyarchal politics, no one can confidently speak with precision on allegations of disproportion. And our insights are obscured by long-standing ideological obstructions to clarity of perception. Most of us fall into the habit of taking many features of the status quo as suitable standards or benchmarks. Thus, we take the customary privilege and influence of businessmen as an acceptable standard of equality. Doing so prevents our recognizing privilege and disproportion when we see it.

*   *   *

In highly simplified summary, polyarchal politics and government in market-oriented systems take on a distinctive structure. There exists a basic governmental mechanism, given by inheritance to each generation of citizens. At any time, that existing mechanism provides a system of controls for controlling authority. The system is a combination of market, privileged business controls in government, and polyarchal politics. Who are the main leaders in the market? Businessmen. Who are the main leaders in the exercise of privileged business controls? Businessmen, of course. Who are the main leaders in polyarchal politics? Businessmen are influential in enormous disproportion.

Thus, in these systems, the struggle over authority is composed of:

1. The basic struggle over authority that is common to all systems (described in chapter 9).
2. Polyarchal politics, which reshapes the basic struggle (described in chapter 10).
3. Rivalry between privileged business controls and polyarchal controls (described above in the first part of this chapter, pp. 189–192).
4. The struggle of businessmen to dominate polyarchal politics, in which they win greatly disproportionate influence (described above in the latter part of this chapter, pp. 192–199).

These are the four fundamental aspects of the struggle over authority in what we call the market-oriented polyarchies. That is our main conclusion. To put it in another light, what we call polyarchies are complex systems of which polyarchy is actually only one contested part.

Of the four components of these systems, we may add that it is the third and fourth that account in some large part for an earlier remarked consistency in polyarchal policy: it never pursues central planning of production and is always tied to market systems.

Circularity in Polyarchy

C. WRIGHT MILLS says that on key decisions American government is in the hands of three cooperating elites: governmental, business, and military.[1] Ferdinand Lundberg, with great detail, says that the United States is governed by its most wealthy families.[2] John Kenneth Galbraith tells us that a corporate "technostructure" is the dominant group in economic affairs.[3] Gabriel Kolko asks the question that is on many minds:

> Do a small group of very wealthy men have the power to guide industry, and thereby much of the total economy, towards ends that they decide upon as compatible with their own interests?[4]

"The answer," he says, "must inevitably be affirmative." Why? Because the leading corporations are in the hands of a small group of managers who enjoy substantial ownership shares in their firms. By his estimates, the largest 200 industrial firms are controlled by not more than 2,500 men. "These men, in both direct ownership of economic assets and control over the corporate structure, are the most important single group in the American economic elite."[5]

Good question, but poor answer. In the first place, 2,500 is hardly a small number of leaders. If we add roughly the corresponding number of managers for the largest 100 nonindustrial and financial corporations, as well as the number of managers of, say, the top four corporations in each industry which are not already included in the top 200 firms, the total rises to at least 4,000. It is neither surprising nor especially illuminating to read that 2,500 or 4,000 men occupy critical leadership positions in the economy, no more so than to read that 2,500 or 4,000 men occupy critical leadership positions in government. One might even be surprised that the number is as large as it is: in any one polyarchy there is only one president or prime minister; and a parliament or legislature numbers only in the hundreds.

A more important defect in Kolko's answer turns on the fact that inevitably in any large-scale system the immediate or proximate decision makers are only a tiny fraction of all participants, a point clarified at the turn of the century by Mosca, Michels, and Pareto.[6] The significant question is whether such a decision-making elite, whose existence can be taken for granted, is popularly controlled. On that question Kolko, as well as Mill, Lundberg, Galbraith, and others like them, has little to say.[7]

We have, however, been pursuing just that question for the last several chapters. We have found major breaches in popular control. We do not yet, however, have all of the answers. In addition to the general obstructions to popular control already specified is the ominous specific possibility that popular control in both market and government is in any case circular. It may be that people are indoctrinated to demand—to buy and to vote for—nothing other than what a decision-making elite is already disposed to grant them. The volitions that are supposed to guide leaders are formed by the same leaders.

To be specific: One obstruction to polyarchy is the privileged position of businessmen. It is a rival, we have seen, to polyarchal control of government. Another obstruction is the disproportionate influence of businessmen in interest-group, party, and electoral politics. It permits businessmen to win, we have seen, disproportionately in their many polyarchal struggles. Both possibilities we have examined. But now suppose that the business influence strikes even deeper in a particular way. Consider the possibility that businessmen achieve an indoctrination of citizens so that citizens' volitions serve not their own interests but the interests of businessmen. Citizens then become allies of businessmen. The privileged position of business comes to be widely accepted. In electoral politics, no great struggle need to be fought. Circularity of this kind is a particular, a specific, possibility in polyarchy which we have not yet sufficiently examined.

And so we must further examine persuasion as a method of control, not the mutual persuasion of liberal democratic aspiration but a lopsided, sometimes nearly unilateral persuasion by business, governmental, and political leadership directed at ordinary citizens who do not themselves easily command, as leaders do, the services of printing and broadcasting. Persuasion, we shall see, takes on at least a few characteristics of preceptoral persuasion or "education." And in particular "every general medium of mass communication carries a heavy freight of business ideology."[8]

Leadership's Molding of Citizen Volitions

Businessmen participate in polyarchal politics disproportionately, we have seen, to bend polyarchal decision making so that it coordinates with privileged business controls. It is that disproportion, already documented, that is the chief evidence of indoctrination. In the variety of their disproportionate participations, we can discern, however, three patterns important for understanding indoctrination and consequent possibilities for circularity of control.

Influencing Policy on Secondary Issues

The least circular of the three is their engagement in polyarchal politics on what we have called secondary issues. In contrast to the grand issues, these are disputed rather than agreed on in polyarchal politics. Businessmen are themselves in disagreement on many of them. A long-standing conflict, for example, separates small from big business in the United States; thus, the National Association of Manufacturers stands apart from organizations that attract the giant corporations. To the degree that businessmen are not agreed, they subject the citizen to competitive messages rather than an indoctrination.

Legitimizing the Privileged Position of Business

In a second form of participation, businessmen try to legitimize the controls they exercise through their privileged position by persuading citizens that the controls are part of polyarchal politics. In this form of control, they make no demands on government, nor do they ask citizens to join with them in any demands. They simply try to indoctrinate citizens to overlook their privileged position. On this businessmen are in agreement.

As is obvious from their messages in the media, they try to associate private enterprise with political democracy and identify attacks on the former as attacks on the latter. Nation, democracy, liberty, and private enterprise are all intertwined, for example, in a statement of purpose of a British industrial association, which declares that "the preservation of personal freedom is essential to national well-being," and that it will actively oppose all "subversive" forces that undermine the "security of Britain in general and British industry in particular."[9] In the United States they send business representatives to participate in or lead those many voluntary organizations, like the United Fund or the Red Cross, that in some versions of democratic theory are said to characterize a vital democracy. They also provide a wealth of teaching materials to the public schools, not to argue any partisan policy position but to indoctrinate children with a private enterprise version of democracy.

These and other attempts to legitimize their privileged participation are all high-minded in appearance rather than conspicuously self-serving. They are often widely accepted as educational, the messages seen as in the public interest. Government officials in large part cooperate in sending the same messages to the citizenry, sometimes enthusiastically, as when U.S. Secretary of the Interior Thomas S. Kleppe, in 1976, declared: "This is the year to wave the flag and wave the free enterprise flag."[10]

In legitimizing their privileged participation, businessmen take advantage of the looseness of polyarchal control over secondary issues. Governmental decisions on secondary issues that in fact respond to the privileged demands of businessmen are relatively easy to publicize as though they are the outcome of polyarchal processes. All that is required is that businessmen go through such polyarchal routines as appearing in legislative hearings and other interest-group forums, and all this they do conspicuously. In France the Planning Commission sometimes submits its plans to the National Assembly well after the plan is in operation, and parliamentary consideration has been largely formal and symbolic.[11]

How far they succeed in legitimizing their privileged position is both a matter of dispute and a point of difference from country to country: less in France and the United Kingdom than in Germany and Belgium, for example; and very much so in the United States. A self-congratulatory tone is evident in a statement from a Sears, Roebuck vice-president.

> Business in America occupies a place of unique prestige and power. Collectively, businessmen represent one of the leadership groups of our society. Here there is no landed gentry, ancient nobility, or party elite to compete with, and high social position itself is usually based on means and status acquired in business pursuits. . . . Their control of economic resources vests them with great power, in the use of which they are permitted wide discretion.
>
> Nor is their power confined to economic affairs. They are consulted on all matters involving the welfare of the community, and their advice carries weight.[12]

Removing Issues from Politics

In a third form of participation, businessmen use their disproportionate influence to try to create a dominant opinion that will remove grand issues from politics.* They do not press for agreement on the grand issues but

* The legitimization of privileged controls removes business privilege as an issue.

for political silence on them. It is here that their participation in polyarchy, even though not always successful, goes furthest toward indoctrination. It short-circuits popular control—that is, renders it circular in significent degree.

In this activity, as in legitimizing its privileged position, business tends to speak in one voice. It is not much challenged by any other voice. Medium-sized and large corporations in all the polyarchies approach a consensus on what we have called the grand issues of politico-economic organization: private enterprise, a high degree of corporate autonomy, protection of the status quo on distribution of income and wealth, close consultation between business and government, and restriction of union demands to those consistent with business profitability, among others. They try, through indoctrination, to keep all these issues from coming to the agenda of government.

On the grand issues, corporate voice is joined by the voice of many government officials, and for several reasons. One is that they are caught in a potential crossfire between privileged controls and polyarchal controls. Hence they would like to remove from politics those highly divisive issues on which businessmen would be loath to yield. Since theirs is the task of seeing to it that business performs, they do not want the fundamentals of private enterprise to become lively political issues.

In Britain, the problem of molding volitions to protect the fundamentals was posed explicitly by the Second Reform Bill of 1867, which enfranchised a large proportion of the working class. The working classes, a British member of Parliament perceived, now "have in their hands the power, if they know how to use it, of becoming masters of the situation, all the other classes being, of necessity, powerless in their hands."[13] As a result, in the very year the bill was passed, British conservatives established the National Union of Conservative and Constitutional Associations to begin the publication of a large and steady stream of tracts addressed to the working population.[14] The effort has been sustained ever since. Among its other objectives, Conservative communication carries two messages: workingmen have every reason to prize the fundamental political and economic institutions of their society, and conservative leadership should be trusted to protect those institutions.[15]

Schools and colleges have been particular targets of corporate opinion formation on the grand issues. For example, in the United States:

> The electric companies, organized in the National Electric Light Association, had not only directly influenced Congressmen and Senators on a large scale, but had also conducted a massive campaign to control the substance of teaching in the nation's schools. Teachers in high schools and grammar schools were inundated with materials purporting to be aids to learning on such topics as the wonders of electricity and the romance of the kilo-

watt. Each pamphlet included carefully planted disparagement of public ownership of utilities. The Association took very active, if inconspicuous, measures to insure that textbooks that were doctrinally impure on this issue were withdrawn from use and that more favorable substitutes were produced and used. College professors, notoriously a needy lot, were given supplemental incomes by the Association and, in return, not infrequently taught about the utility industry with greater sympathy than before. Public libraries, ministers, and civic leaders of all kinds were subjected to the propagandistic efforts of the electric companies.[16]

Effectiveness of Business Molding of Volitions

What people read and hear influences them. That is how we learn to speak, read, write, and think. Yet it is sometimes suggested that despite the torrent of corporate communication addressed to the citizen on grand issues and not effectively challenged by any comparable contending communication, the citizen somehow fails to succumb to the indoctrination.

If such an argument is correct, it is because the citizen somehow rejects business communications while accepting others. It is an interesting idea, but without a shred of evidence. Corporations employ all possible methods, overt and covert. The source of their communications is usually obscure. The message usually reaches the citizens indirectly in a news story or broadcast, a magazine article, a film, an editorial, a political speech, or a conversation. Only a small part of it comes explicitly from a business source.

The skeptic may believe, however, that most of the corporate message on the grand issues is transmitted through the mass media, which, he will claim, is relatively ineffective in changing volitions. Some research evidence refutes him. A media campaign, for example, was measured as achieving within one week a net change from con to pro in attitudes toward the oil industry of 4 percent of respondents. A presidential campaign lasting five months, in which conflicting propaganda from the two parties cross-pressured the voters, was measured as achieving a switch of parties for 5 percent of those studied.[17] If that is so, the cumulative effect of propaganda can be great indeed if it is only infrequently challenged by counter-propaganda and persists not for five months but for the lifetime of the citizen. Nothing in the research literature on the mass media establishes any ground for doubting its effectiveness.

Moreover, corporate molding of volitions on grand issues is usually to confirm rather than to change volitions, since it extols the status quo. On that, media campaigns are even more effective.[18] The point has sometimes been made that advertising of products and services can effect responses because the means lie easily at hand to do what the message urges (one simply goes out to make a purchase). Corporate political persuasion on the grand issues asks for even easier responses. It ordinarily asks that the citizen do nothing, that he not stir himself.*

Moreover, it usually asks no more than that the citizen continue to believe what he has already since childhood been taught to believe. Early, persuasive, unconscious conditioning—we shall see evidence of it in a later chapter on social class—to believe in the fundamental politico-economic institutions of one's society is ubiquitous in every society. These institutions come to be taken for granted. Many people grow up to regard them not as institutions to be tested but as standards against which the correctness of new policies and institutions can be tested. When that happens, as is common, processes of critical judgment are short-circuited. In some societies a Protestant ethic comes to the support of private property, private enterprise, and corporate autonomy. So also child-rearing practices that stress individualistic autonomy. The competitiveness of sports often comes to be identified with market life, or vice versa, so that some people think of constraints on corporate autonomy as in some vague sense similar to imposing an arbitrary handicap on a player. In their attempts to influence the volitions of the citizenry, businessmen often need do little more than evoke deeply embedded sentiments.

The influence of the mass media has also been deprecated on the ground that personal influence, rather than press and broadcasting, is the primary molder of the political volitions of the overwhelming majority of persons. It is true that they do not pay close attention to political writing and broadcasting. But they are, we have also seen, influenced by face-to-face relations with other people who do read and listen to the mass media. And the influencers are in turn influenced, both in the media and in face-to-face communication, by others who read and listen even more attentively.[19] As Elmo Roper has put it with perhaps more terminological grandeur than is called for, there are great thinkers, great disciples, great disseminators, lesser disseminators, participating citizens, and the politically inert.[20] The effect of the mass media on personal influence is thus part of the interchange on the ladder of public opinion formation.

---

* In communications with government officials too, the request is usually not to act rather than to act. In one study, 85 percent of corporate communications to government officials were in opposition to proposed legislation. Edwin M. Epstein, *The Corporation in American Politics* (Englewood Cliffs, N.J.: Prentice-Hall, 1969), p. 99.

Constrained Volitions

If the business message is getting through as a result of the disproportionate participation of businessmen in electoral politics, we should expect a somewhat narrowly constrained set of volitions that does not much question business enterprise, the corporation, private property, and other fundamentals. Just so. Although volitions are less narrowly constrained in European polyarchies than in the United States, they are everywhere constrained. Public opinion hugs central tendencies, and only a few people entertain nonconformist political opinion. Conformity is a familiar phenomenon in politics.

Generations of leaders and observers have applauded what they take to be an accomplishment, perhaps without quite understanding what they were applauding. After Britain's first experience with a socialist party in office—an experience that might have been expected to transform the British system—Lord Balfour could say complacently:

> Our alternating Cabinets, though belonging to different Parties, have never differed about the foundations of society. And it is evident that our whole political machinery pre-supposes a people so much at one that they can safely afford to bicker.[21]

The removal from politics of the issue of central planning we have already noted in the preceding chapter. A later chapter will confirm that, despite universal suffrage, income distribution in the polyarchies has not changed greatly, though it has changed more in some than in others. In few of the polyarchies is there serious discussion, even among the politically active, of major alterations in the distribution of wealth and income.[22] And citizens are extraordinarily ignorant on the issue. In the face of ample objective evidence of inequality of opportunity, Robert E. Lane's intensively interviewed men believe that opportunities are roughly equal. They also seem blind to real-world factors that account for income differences. There is "little reference to the overpowering forces of circumstance, only rare mention of sickness, death of a breadwinner, senility, factories moving out of town, and so forth."[23]

In Great Britain a recent survey offered sampled voters a hypothetical choice on incomes policy. Did they favor rewarding special skills? Or would they prefer to guarantee a reasonable wage to the lowest paid? Or should income distribution be made more equal? Only 10 percent chose more equality.[24] Two recent studies of British working-class attitudes and opinions agree in finding both a narrow range of opinion and widespread deference of working class to upper class[25]—this in a society many of whose nineteenth-century leaders feared that universal suffrage would bring about demands for a more equal sharing of income and wealth, so obviously advantageous did they see such policies for the mass of voters.* It is one of the world's most extraordinary social phenomena that masses of voters vote very much like their elites. They demand very little for themselves.

Other evidence is suggestive. In his work on white-collar crime in the United States, Sutherland was able to show in variety of detail that crimes committed by corporate executives, although on important points legally indistinguishable from the ordinary crimes of the citizen, are viewed by courts, lawmakers, and citizens as belonging to a different category, for which penalties are small, mitigating circumstances easy to plead, methods of prosecution different.[26] That in itself testifies to the position of the corporation in society. But that the discrepancy between the two kinds of crime is little remarked, that his studies did not stimulate a substantial exploration of issues he raised, that citizens do not seriously consider reducing the discrepancy, even if occasionally revealing spasms of irritation with it—all this is again evidence of volitions systematically constrained so that certain issues are left quiescent

An additional fragment of evidence is the continued stability of volitions on the fundamentals of politico-economic organization in the face of remarkable recent instability of opinion on such once deep-seated beliefs as sexual behavior, marriage, dress, and polite speech. Clearly in some circumstances people break out of old patterns of thought, even abruptly. Yet neither war, nor weapons rivalry among nations, nor inflation, nor unemployment, nor threat of nuclear destruction has opened up a greatly broader range of volitions on the grand issues of politico-economic organization.†

Yet volitions are by no means wholly constrained. In systems with four or five political parties, one is often a communist party, as in France and Italy; and another may be an extreme right or another left party. On the other hand, most of the effective political competition will even so continue to fall within a narrow range of secondary policies. The communist party itself will often, as a practical matter, endorse not a distinc-

---

* Many reasons other than indoctrination can be offered to explain why governments do not actually inaugurate and voters do not actually vote for more equality. We are trying to explain why the issue is not even seriously discussed by any large number of leaders or citizens.

† To all of this evidence of constrained public opinion, the counter position may again be asserted: the opinions to which the citizenry appear to be constrained are simply those and only those that can intelligently be defended. Even if that were true, it is no explanation or denial of constraint. People do foolish things in politics. It remains puzzling that no polyarchal citizenry even discusses, let alone attempts, an unintelligent major policy alternative on certain fundamentals. They remain outside politics.

tive grand alternative but policies within the narrow spectrum of alternatives. A communist party often has to pay that price for admission to parliamentary politics.

Constraint on Dissident Volitions

Even dissenting or reformist volitions on grand issues display a characteristic constraint. Robert Heilbroner has pointed out that "all seek to accommodate their proposals for social change to the limits of adaptability of the prevailing business order."[27] Thus, among many examples that might be offered, the coal miners' union in the United States for many decades did not press for enforcement of mine-safety legislation. The miners were not irrational to oppose enforced mine safety. They simply feared for their jobs if the companies were to be forced to practice safety and bear the high costs of doing so. Their constrained minds could not seriously entertain an alternative—for safety procedures to be paid for by government funds, by subsidies to mining companies, or by subsidies to their own union. They could not break out of their customary view that the corporations were responsible for mine safety and that asking them to do any more than profitability permitted would have adverse effects. Similarly it is not seriously debated in any of the polyarchies that wages might, through offsetting subsidies to business firms, be broken free from their ties to productivity, so that business profitability need no longer be argued to pose a barrier to raising low incomes.

Dissident volitions are also constrained by what might be called the myth of "balance" in public debate. Many citizens take pride in their willingness to acknowledge that "there are two sides to every question," thus accepting without thought substantial insulation from the many other sides to whose appeals they remain either deaf or hard of hearing. "Equal time" broadcasting legislation in the United States ordinarily protects broadcast time for only two advocacies, Republican and Democratic. The two are positioned closely together on a continuum of possible policy positions. And the liberal columnists that some newspapers take pains to offer as counterpoint to conservative opinion offer dispute over no more than a narrow range. The "balance" of views thus presented to the citizen and the narrow competition of views do not much challenge the fundamentals of politico-economic organization in market-oriented systems.

Homogeneity of Opinion Not Required

To succeed in its purposes, which are perhaps only half understood by businessmen themselves, corporate molding of citizen volitions on grand issues does not need to accomplish tyranny over the mind, nor even a uniformity of opinion on the grand issues. Far short of either, we have already noted, it need only persuade citizens not to raise certain issues, not to make demands in politics on those issues. Hence on such an issue as the autonomy of the corporation, it succeeds if it persuades the citizen that the issue is not worth his energies, *or* that it is discouragingly complex, *or* that agitation on the issue is not likely to be successful, *or* that corporate autonomy is a good thing. Any one will do.

Thus, a canvass of roughly twenty-five empirical studies of value commitment in the United States and the United Kingdom, undertaken to ascertain whether value consensus is a characteristic of democratic politics, found "not a value-consensus which keeps the working-class compliant, but rather a *lack* of consensus in the crucial area where concrete experiences and vague populism might be translated into radical politics."[28] Values are more confused than conservative, and the confusion is sufficient to keep a range of grand issues quiescent.

Inevitability of Core Beliefs

Can we expect, however, any society to debate its own fundamentals? Has there ever been one that did? Can we not dismiss the evidence of constrained volitions on grand issues by acknowledging that all societies are marked by a core of common belief? They are indeed, and we shall not find in communist society or in the countries of the third world of developing nations any greater heterogeneity of volitions than in the polyarchies.

But our purpose is not to show that volitions on grand issues are constrained in the polyarchies and not in other systems. It is to show that they are constrained to a significant degree even in the polyarchies. The significance of the analysis is that the control mechanisms operating on volitions are as fundamental in these systems as polyarchal processes themselves. They therefore introduce, for good or bad, a significant circularity into popular control through polyarchy.

Constrained volitions are of special importance in polyarchal systems because of their aspirations to popular control. But what is critical, then, is not the existence of core beliefs but how the constraint is achieved—by whom or what, around what issues and why. This is what we have been trying to understand through the analysis of this chapter. On how these constraints are achieved, the analysis traces them back to the duality of leadership in these systems, to the consequent privileged position of business, and to the disporportionate influence of business in polyarchy. So that the significance of this connection is not missed, we should take note that at least hypothetically it is possible for a society to converge on a set of unifying volitions on grand issues that does not have its origins in a privileged position of any of that society's groups. To repeat, then, the significance of constrained volitions in the market-oriented polyarchies is that they are constrained in a particular way. The constraints are not consistent with the democratic theory or ideology often invoked to justify these systems. In the polyarchies, core beliefs are the product of a rigged, lopsided competition of ideas.

Limits on Manipulation of Volitions

What Americans do and do not read tells us that the United States may represent an extreme case of volition conformity. The United States is without the mass circulation of dissident journals like the communist party newspapers and magazines of Italy and France. In circulation per issue, mildly left publications in the United States like *The Nation* or *The New Republic* or a communist newspaper like *The Daily World* are midgets among giants.[29]

McCall's	8,000,000
Time	4,000,000
New York Times	846,000*
Harper's	379,000
Atlantic	326,000
New Republic	140,000
Nation	30,000
World	14,000

* Daily.

Perhaps the United States has no widely circulating radical newspaper because no wide audience wants it. But that is our very point.

In Western European polyarchies some citizens and major political leaders alike consider a broader range of alternatives on the grand issues than do Americans. Some of the leaders of the British Labour Party—Arthur Scargill, Norman Atkinson, Anthony Wedgewood Benn, among others—are reviving, and probably radicalizing to a degree, an earlier Labour radicalism that the party muffled over the years as it rose to and exercised governmental authority. More than Americans, Europeans debate central planning, major income and wealth redistribution, and private property in production. They debate a wider range of restrictions on corporate discretion. In France and Italy, they have been increasingly receptive to communist persuasion. If that is less significant than might first appear—because in these countries the communist parties are perceived as having disclaimed revolutionary objectives—it nevertheless demonstrates a receptivity unmatched in the United States. We shall later also see that reforms aiming at increased employee control within the corporation are more generously discussed abroad than in the United States.

Even in the United States, however, the fundamentals of the politico-economic system are being eroded by debate. Political reform on secondary issues implicitly raises aspects of grand issues for discussion. Corporations are increasingly regulated—more than in 1890, or 1932, or 1946. They are now being pushed again by demands for new restrictions arising out of ecological concerns. Income distribution is being altered, we shall see, even if at glacial pace. Corporate advantage in manipulation of volitions does not make popular control wholly circular.

In the polyarchies, constraints on citizen volitions fall far short—need it be said?—of the massive monolithic processes by which popular volitions are controlled in earlier fascist and contemporary communist systems. If in the polyarchies government, party, or corporate officials greatly outtalk dissidents, they do not come close to silencing them.

And the media are not quite monolithic. American television, for example, gives at least a small voice to radicals, protesters, and critics. Its marginal tolerance for the unorthodox, new, and offbeat is also proved by the women's liberationists, hippies, drug addicts, reformed convicts, and homosexuals, who bring their life histories, problems, and advocacies to millions of viewers. Granted that the juxtaposition of political radicalism with sexual deviation, crime, drugs, and eccentricity, as is common in both press and broadcasting, is one way to discredit the political message of radical groups, neither press nor broadcasting seal the population off wholly from contamination by opinions hostile to business, the corporation, and the status quo.[30]

Nor, for all the tendencies to orthodoxy in the universities are students greatly constrained in what they can take the initiative to read. More undergraduates read Marx than Adam Smith. Even in public high schools, it is not hard for a student to sample the whole political spectrum, though his curriculum may discourage him. Polyarchal politics is never quite a closed circle.

Constrained volitions are not an important phenomenon when set beside the control of public opinion in authoritarian systems. They become so only when examined in the light of democratic aspiration. In human history, the design of large national governments practicing a nonviolent competition for authority in such a way that men can be free, as liberals define freedom, is as great an accomplishment as man has ever achieved. It is difficult for citizens who enjoy that freedom to remind themselves of how unequal the competition of ideas is and of how far governments still fall short of achieving a larger liberation of man's minds to accomplish the degree of popular control that only then might be possible.

Circularity
in Market Systems

Is the same phenomenon of circularity that was discussed in the last chapter also to be found in the market system? Do people simply buy what they are persuaded to want by those who sell to them? It will throw additional light on polyarchal circularity to compare it with tendencies toward market circularity.

The manipulation of buyers' preferences by corporations is a big business. More precisely, it is a number of big businesses. In the United States, a calculation for the late 1960s showed that roughly $60 billion per year was spent on advertising and other sales promotion. The amount was about the same as the nation's expenditures on education or in health.[1] Advertising alone is about one-third of that total: For a sample of nations, advertising expenses run between less than 1 percent and almost 3 percent of national income. By very rough estimate:[2]

The United States spends 2.8 percent of national income.
Denmark, Canada, and Finland spend a little over 2 percent.
Britain spends roughly 2 percent.
Most other industrialized nations, including Japan, spend roughly 1.5 percent.
France and Belgium spend less than 1 percent.

Because sales promotion is itself big business, the market-oriented polyarchies are hampered in their efforts to study, even to debate thoughtfully, its effects in short-circuiting popular control. The various sales promotion industries and the corporations which use their services are not generous with information. With incredulity we hear the unbelievable about sales promotion: spokesmen for television, for example, declare that corporations can profitably spend millions on television advertising because it has been proved to be effective in influencing people, at the same time assuring us that it has no effect in sanctioning deviant behavior, even among impressionable children. Even granting the slim possibility that the two claims are not mutually contradictory, the audacity of the allegations and the apparent indifference of the industry to the possibility that a whole generation is being corrupted is testimony to the low state of public knowledge on the phenomena of sales promotion. As a result, this chapter will be thin rather than empirically rich.

Perhaps a first point to be made about possible circularity is that a substantial amount of sales promotion is genuinely informative—but we have no measure of it. A simple announcement of a useful new product or an announcement that a familiar product is now available at a lower price is helpful information not likely to make a consumer the dupe of a seller. Many people believe that announcements of that kind are too noisy and too frequent and that they consume too large a share of the nation's resources. But these complaints are different from the assertion that sales promotion short-circuits consumer control.

For sales promotion generally—informative and not—an appropriate elementary question to begin with is whether it has any effect. Casual observation is confirmed by meticulous statistical studies. Sales promotion affects—but how much it is again impossible to say—the kinds of goods and services that people buy, as well as the particular brands they choose.[3] Advertisers continue advertising because they find that it works. Yet limits are obvious. Millions of people do not drink beer, use genital deodorants, subscribe to life insurance, or take winter vacations in sunny climes, despite the best efforts of advertisers to induce them to do so. Nor do all of Hertz's customers desert to Avis, despite the persistence of Avis sales promotion, or vice versa despite the persistence of Hertz's. Nor do consumers buy all new items that advertisers urge on them. It has been estimated that 80 percent of new products introduced in American markets fail.[4]

Food and shelter in any case take up most of family income. And consumers spend as they do in some very large part because of class, income, socioeconomic status, ethnic identity, and the like. These factors largely dominate menu and style of house and furnishings. Major national, ethnic, and class differences in consumption are not well explained by sales promotion. American expenditure on automobiles, for example, is a consequence of American wealth, together with large markets that stimulated mass production of autos and large land areas that encouraged a bountiful construction of paved highways.

Many shifts in consumer spending are almost wholly free of any immediate influence of sales promotion. Beginning in the 1960s, several shifts in clothing styles—for example, to denim—caught on in the United States. Although now further encouraged by sales promotion, the shifts preceded the promotion. At about the same time, a new demand for bicycles also sprang up without benefit of sales promotion.

An aggregate effect of sales promotion may be to raise the amount that consumers spend and reduce the amount they save. Attempts meticulously to measure such an effect suggest so but are inconclusive.[5]

One must entertain a hypothesis that sales promotion may be a powerful, ubiquitous, relentless molder of the culture of those many nations in which it is a major activity. Inconclusive as our information is, sales promotion may succeed in pushing the populace toward the pursuit of marketed goods and services and, what may be more important, persuading the populace that buying is the way to popularity, honor, distinction, delight, and security. In early-twentieth-century America, at least some major business leaders believed that sales promotion should take on just such a task. They saw the emerging possibilities of mass production for great new markets. The possibilities, they thought, called for a new level and diversity of spending for which consumers needed to be prepared both through high wages and through campaigns to indoctrinate them to want what American industry was now able to provide.[6]

Making the Customer Stand Still

A specific point that can be made about sales promotion is that its practitioners do not unnecessarily fight the customer. There is obviously more money in selling him what he wants—or what can be passed off as something he wants—than in trying to sell him what he resists. Since businessmen aim to make money rather than to reform the world's choice of consumer goods, neither alone or in conspiracy with each other do they decide on what their customers ought to buy and then set out both to produce it and to induce them to buy. The nearest to that bizarre possibility is sales promotion by a corporation that lacks flexibility in its potential lines of production, has sunk its capital and skill in one or a few lines of production, and now finds that customers are moving away from it to new products. Since it is too old to change its ways, it may try hard to keep its old clientele.

But most sales promotion is not of this kind. Much of it sings the virtues of new products. And for new products—certainly for new enterprises and industries—sales promotion is harnessed to selling as much as possible of something that appears to be what potential customers think they want. Is there any reason that businessmen would do anything else? The strategy of sales promotion is most clear in the case of the versatile modern corporation capable of producing almost anything customers might want and using market research as a guide. If in some cases market research is only low cunning—a corporation asks researchers to determine how much it can shorten a cigarette without the customer's noticing it[7]—it is also an exploration of ways to please customers.

For a technical reason, however, even versatile corporations worry that customers will not buy what they produce for them. When complex new technologies or products require years of lead time for development, corporations cannot be sure that consumers will not change their minds during, say, the five-year developmental period. Corporations will consequently use sales promotion to hold customers to the pattern of preferences earlier predicted. Although Galbraith sees this form of sales promotion as evidence that control of what is to be produced is shifted from customers to corporations, by his own argument it would appear that in this kind of sales promotion the corporation is trying to respond to, not dictate, consumer preferences. In its attempt to induce the consumer to buy what was predicted, the corporation behaves like the old-style studio portrait photographer who fastens a brace to the back of his subject's head to hold it immobile long enough for him to take his picture. Is the subject then a prisoner of the photographer?

Some Comparisons

For perspective now, set sales promotion side by side with corporate and governmental attempts to manipulate volitions in the polyarchies. In politics, leaders hold press conferences and find other ready audiences for their messages. The media are full of their declarations, controversies with each other, and promises. What they say about what they want to "sell" is news. Not so for corporate officials with a new product. As sellers, what they have to say is of little sustained interest to the population, ordinarily of little interest to their own customers. They have to pay heavily for their audiences, and even so can capture their attention only in such spasms as 30-second commercials.

People also take political leaders more seriously than they do sellers. Just before President Nixon ordered the movement of ground troops from Vietnam into Cambodia in 1970, a Harris Poll reported that only 7 percent of respondents favored such a move. Once the president had actually made the move, 50 percent endorsed it.[8] That is a common phenomenon: citizen volitions changing quickly and substantially in response to leadership's acts or advice. There is nothing quite like it in market sales promotion. An actual new product may almost instantly create a new clientele, but customers do not take their opinions on products from corporate leadership in the way that citizens take their opinions from political leadership. If tomorrow a congressman or member of parliament declares that after much thought he has decided to endorse euthanasia, many of his constituents who trust his judgment and want his advice will accordingly change their minds. If tomorrow the head of Royal Dutch Shell announces that his company has developed an astonishing new product, almost none of the product's potential customers will do anything more than let his claim compete in their minds with many conflicting claims.

Another contrast is easily missed. It is extremely rare for a businessman to be so intent on selling what he thinks the public ought to have that he is willing to lose his business rather than sell the public what it wants. Only in politics is there place for the ideologue or the doctrinaire (or highly principled) leader who would rather lose a contest than change his mind. A Goldwater appears to enter presidential politics less to win than to persuade. He would apparently rather lead his party to defeat than to victory on the wrong terms. The same appears to have been true of Lincoln, de Gaulle, Churchill, Hitler, Wendell Wilkie, Robert Taft, and Ronald Reagan. As early as 1960, however, it was estimated that two-thirds of American senatorial and gubernatorial candidates used some form of market research.[9] Perhaps this difference between political leaders and businessman is disappearing.

Competition of Ideas

Perhaps the most fundamental comparison to be made—if we had the information that would permit it to be made with confidence—is on the character of the "competition of ideas" in the two arenas: politics and market. The competition of ideas in market systems is on some points far broader and more intense than in politics. Most of us cannot buy much more than our income permits, and none of us spends all his income on any one commodity. Hence, in considering any purchase, we are cross-pressured by the appeals of countless other possible purchases—either of a different commodity entirely or a different brand of the same commodity.

In very large part, therefore, any one advertiser's success is another's failure. Each competes against all others.

In a polyarchy, a voter is offered no more than a handful of candidates for an office and no more than a small array of policy alternatives on any one issue. It is true that proponents of hundreds or thousands of alternative potential policies compete for his attention: for example, advocates of capital punishment, low-cost housing, legalization of abortion, a hard line toward the Soviet Union, nuclear electric power, prohibition of vivisection, full employment, and urban redevelopment. But they do not compete in the way that every marketed consumer commodity or service competes for the consumer's spending. Most political appeals fall on deaf ears. On most issues the citizen delegates responsibility for decision making to officials, leaving himself to consider a few alternatives only. Sometimes the competition of ideas ranges no more broadly than to debate the merits of a few candidates, often only two, for each of a few elected positions on which he votes. And attempts of officials, candidates, and parties to influence citizen preferences are hardly competitive at all, we have seen, on grand issues.

Diffused Confusion

Although sales promotion and manipulation of political volitions alike obstruct popular control by creating some degree of circularity in it, they may obstruct it again—hence doubly—through a more diffuse disservice to the populace. The messages confuse and deceive the public. The result is that, although people do not always do what leadership wants, they are incapable of knowing and protecting their own interests.

Leading corporations succeed in persuading consumers to buy automobiles with risk of carbon monoxide discharges into the interior of the passenger compartment, pesticides harmful to those who use them, children's toys with lead paint, cosmetics and other drugstore products that do not perform as claimed, foodstuffs with dangerous additives, all kinds of goods with hidden or deliberately misstated credit charges, costly life insurance policies that do not provide savings that customers think they are arranging for, flammable rugs and fabrics, and development houses that quickly require expensive repairs.

In government and politics, persuasion equally disruptive to informed and thoughtful popular choice is everywhere apparent and has become increasingly conspicuous in American politics. President Kennedy tried to deceive the public on the Bay of Pigs and President Johnson on the Gulf of Tonkin. Today in the United States no official denial of any allegation on which an official might be vulnerable is given much credence. Credibility has, in the eyes of many citizens, become something of a stranger to government and politics.

Is there more deceit of consumers than citizens? Does it matter more? It is difficult to count instances of what is hidden, what is not known. We can take note, however, that polyarchal leaders make it their business to expose each other's misrepresentations on matters of policy and sometimes succeed. Kennedy was challenged on his version of the Bay of Pigs, and the true story came out. For his lies Nixon was compelled to resign. On the whole, however, market sales promotion follows a rule of avoiding explicit challenge of competitors' claims, as illustrated in pharmaceuticals. Thousands of claims are made year after year in newspaper and broadcast media without challenge.

Both polyarchal and business leaders try to dampen the competition of ideas by restricting disclosure and debate. In the United Kingdom a tradition of informal understandings and tighter legal control over news leaks than in the United States constrains criticism of government.[10] In the United States spasms of intolerance for dissenting opinion break out from time to time. Attorney General Alex Mitchell Palmer prosecuted radicals after World War I. In the 1950s, at Senator Joseph McCarthy's instigation, civil servants, college professors, and writers were intimidated and sometimes lost their jobs. In the 1960s Martin Luther King and other civil rights leaders were harassed by government officials. In 1973 the White House Office of Telecommunications Policy threatened broadcasters.[11] In the 1960s in France, government-owned television repeatedly violated traditional rules of neutrality in partisan politics, and protests continued into the 1970s.[12]

Businessmen have successfully made trade secrets a property right. The courts have held that certain disclosures need not be made even to government investigators. For many years, Consumers Union has been trying to compel the U.S. government to release the results of product tests carried out by U.S. purchasing agents in the course of buying products for government use. Its failure reveals the degree to which business rights to protect profitability—again, the privileged position of business—take precedence over consumers' rights to be informed about their market choices. Businessmen have also induced the press, sometimes through threat of suit, to be wary of disclosing names of specific corporations in news on corporate illegality and other questionable corporate conduct. In the United States, however, precisely identified corporate illegality is now increasingly published.

*   *   *

What to make, in summary, of the manipulation of market demands and of political volitions? We began the chapter by noting little evidence is available for comparative measurement. It appears—but judgments may differ—that the competition of ideas may be more rigorous in market system than in polyarchy. That is because corporations that rival each other in their attempts to capture the consumer's mind join with each other in indoctrination on the grand issues of politics.

The comparison between polyarchy and market is more difficult when considering diffused misinformation and consequent confusion in the mind of citizen and consumer, from which he suffers even if he is not successfully indoctrinated. In both polyarchy and market, the ordinary citizen and consumer is frequently—every day—assaulted with communications designed to deceive him.

Socioeconomic Class

To the foregoing analysis of circularity in popular control in the polyarchies, we must now add the effects of social class. It is a discouraging prospect. Furious controversies descend like swarming wasps on anyone who pokes the nest of class. Despite all learned papers and books written about class, the world of scholarship—like the larger world of informed thoughtful discussion—seems divided into two camps, both of which acknowledge existence of social classes, but one of which, the Marxist, makes class conflict the main mover in man's history[1] while the other, the conventional, reduces classes to parity with dozens or hundreds of other determinants of social organization, conflict, and change.[2]

An adequate analysis cannot be fitted within the covers of this book. Perhaps, then, each reader should supply his own chapter on how class affects the politico-economic structure of the polyarchies. We can do a little better than that, however. Let each reader write his own chapter, but let us preface each such chapter with a brief analysis, limited and cautious, that tries to specify certain connections between class and circularity of popular control in polyarchy. It will be a kind of primer on class. It will build up a few of the least controversial propositions about class, then from them draw a conclusion to which it is hard to refuse credence—though on the subject of class anything can gain credence in one camp and be denied it in others. That the propositions are elementary rather than advanced or original is their great merit for our purposes. Without rising into the rarified atmosphere of highly speculative thought about social class, we shall add some important elements to our analysis of identifiable mechanisms of politico-economic organization in the polyarchies.

For our limited purposes, it is not necessary to specify how many classes there are, whether their boundaries are well defined, whether members are conscious of their class position, or how much conflict exists among them. Nor do we need a precise definition. We do not in fact want what we say about class to hinge on one particular definition, thus to be false by any other.

A social class is a set of people.* It is a large set, numbering at least in the millions. It is distinguished by its members' sharing a common culture. In a national society, it is a subculture, for it does not include all those who are citizens or subjects of the nation-state. That larger national group may itself be a culture-sharing group. Seen globally rather than nationally, a class is a cross-national culture-sharing group. The subculture or culture is not organized around race, ethnicity, religion, language, or by political boundary. Instead the group, except for a few atypical members, is a "horizontal" socioeconomic stratum.[3]

It is a culture differentiated according to authority and wealth, hence also according to influence and power (whether in market, government, or elsewhere). To say that it is a culture is also to say that traits are packaged or interconnected and that they are passed from one generation on to another, though with unending gradual alteration.[4] Thus, connected with the authority, wealth, influence, and power of each class are other traits—for example, of language, forms of address and other standardized communication, and at least small differences in costume, ideology, habits of deference, and sexual behavior. Every class has its cluster of traits, but not all traits differ from class to class. Nor are trait differences always stable over time.

Because lower classes—or at least many members of them—take on many of the traits of upper classes, believing, for example, that their lower-class speech or dress is inferior, cultural differences between classes are on some points more subtle than obvious. And for our purposes we do not need to go so far as to assert—or to deny—such highly differentiated class cultures as are suggested by such concepts as the "culture of poverty."[5]

---

* Class can be defined as the interaction patterns connecting a set of people. For our purposes, either formulation will do.

Some Elementary Propositions

To begin with, classes exist in all the polyarchies.* We need pause over this proposition only long enough to dispose of the naive American allegation that classes exist everywhere except in the United States. The existence of classes in the United States is well documented. Dozens of investigators have found class differences among preschool and school children.[6] Kinsey and his many successors have found class differences in sexual behavior.[7] Social scientists find they cannot explain differences in voting behavior, political participation, or political attitudes without reference to social class.[8] Class differences permeate American society. Even the various Protestant denominations are differentiated by class. Many Americans, however, remain unaware of the pervasiveness of class distinctions in behavior, speech, and thought. For there has been no explicit challenge to these distinctions, nothing at all like the challenge of women's liberation to "sexist" habits of behavior, speech, and thought.

That classes exist does not deny that other cleavages exist or that the others may be more important from one perspective or another. Sex, ethnic, producer-consumer, and cosmopolitan-provincial cleavages command a great deal of attention, to say nothing of well-recognized divisions of race, region, religion, and national origin.[9]

The next proposition: One class contains most wealthy persons, many high-level political authorities (many top civil servants and legislators among them), many executives of medium to large corporations, some professionals and academics (depending on their income, their institutional affiliations, or their clientele), some journalists and other public figures, and some highly educated people who do not qualify under any of the other above categories.

These are the people among whom there is a sharing of a common package of traits: again, such varied traits as forms of speech, high income, authority, and a common relatively sophisticated folklore. The folklore is anchored in the American case by their drawing from such tacitly agreed sources of information as, among others, the New York *Times* and the weekly news magazines. The core traits of the class, as subsequent propositions will further clarify, are high income or authority in government, in the corporation, in some other organization. A perfect example of a class member would possess all of a group of core traits, but the group we are describing is a set of individuals each of whom is marked by a larger num-

---

* And in all other societies. But we do not need to take on that controversy.

ber of the traits or by a higher intensity of a few traits than others in the society whom we consider to be, therefore, members of a different class.

That there exists such a class as this most people will not dispute, although its exact composition will be debated. One evidence of its existence is the repeated testimony of social scientists that top corporate leadership, the upper levels of the bureaucracy, and most high-level elected officials are in many specific ways linked as a class. The literature of social science is full of reference to class homogeneity embracing these categories in all the polyarchies, as well as of explanations and evidences of it: socio-economic origin, old-school ties, intimacy of occupational and social interchange, clubs, intermarriage, and the like.[10]

The next proposition is that the class just described is favored in society in many ways. It is wealthy and influential to begin with. But that is only a beginning. Large and varied benefits follow from being a member of this class.

One study after another has documented the phenomenon that school-teachers are more helpful to students perceived to be of middle to upper rather than lower class, that school resources go more generously to upper classes, and that upper classes are presumed to need tracking into schools or curricula suited to their classes.[11] The same studies and others show that parental treatment of children encourages greater independence, imagination, self-confidence, and resourcefulness in middle- to upper-class children.* The many studies just cited on schooling and rearing of children show that habits of obedience to authority and of deference are instilled into children of the less favored classes. The judicial system is harsher in arrest, detention, and sentencing with lower class than with middle to upper. Sutherland's evidence, already referred to, is that corporate executives are treated with delicacy in the United States.[12] The history of language itself reflects the pervasiveness of differences in respect, prestige, and deference accorded to members of different classes. Many of our words that generally characterize good and bad people derive from differences in socioeconomic status: "noble," as a denotation of quality of

---

* What has just been said about schooling is no more than one single piece of evidence that people perceived to be members of different classes are treated differently, and that proposition in turn is only one small link in a chain designed to show class effects on the formation of volitions. Yet class effects on schooling, taken alone and without regard to their effect on volitions, themselves constitute a serious imperfection in popular control on other counts. Class-related educational disabilities reduce the probability that less favored students will rise to high positions in government or corporation. They also reduce somewhat the probabilities that certain students will develop the skills in writing, speaking, and social organization that make citizen participation in politics most effective. They create, in short, probabilities of political inequality that pose a barrier to meeting conditions of democratic popular control. Many other class phenomena have comparable effects.

person, from the same word that once denoted a class; "villain" from "villein," a low-ranking peasant; "mean" from an earlier word meaning common (as against elevated in class); and many others.

Those who actually enjoy unusual control or wealth are favored too in that control and wealth make it easier to win still more of each. Thus, members of this favored class are indeed broadly and ingeniously, in small things and large, in intangibles and material goods, given advantages by other members of their own class, by members of other classes, and by the impersonal rules and processes of society.

Distinguish now between being a member of a social class or being perceived to be a member. As class is sometimes defined, the distinction vanishes, but we can use it to sort out different strands in class phenomena. If a class shares a culture or subculture, it follows that there is some at least vague sense of belonging. Although persons in a class may never themselves use the concept of class in their own thinking, they will have some sense that "he is one of us" or "our kind." Or they will in fact feel more comfortable, open, or receptive to him than to members of other classes. But members of any class may make mistaken assignments of persons to their own class or to another. They and members of other classes may be led by dress and speech, for example, to treat another person as though he possessed many of the other traits associated with the favored class.

Our next elementary proposition, consequently, is this: Because it is rewarding to be perceived as a member of the favored class and thus to enjoy its benefits, powerful incentives exist in society to conform to visible characteristics of that class. Among these characteristics are the politico-economic beliefs, attitudes, and volitions of that class and, more particularly, of those members of that class who have the most benefits to offer. They are beliefs in private enterprise, private property, corporate autonomy, and opportunities for great wealth.*

For those who wish to acquire favored class status, the pressures of class toward an opinion conformity are of many kinds. They are perhaps most explicit when occupational or professional advancement is at issue. Many of the governments and corporations of the market-oriented polyarchies put candidates for important positions through security checks, which ask at least that candidates endorse the major politico-economic institutions of the society and often go much further in disqualifying candidates of

---

* The conspicuous phenomenon of upper-class radicalism might seem to weigh as evidence against these effects of class. Class influences do not, however, achieve a perfect conformity. And, if some people break out of them, certainly some of those who wonder if they can afford to do so will be reinforced in their daring by their great wealth. If radicalism is more frequent among the very rich than among middle-income to poor people, it is not surprising; it is a kind of freakish confirmation of the strength of class influences.

dissident opinion. In corporate and governmental organizations, the road to wealth, power, and influence along with the other benefits of class is smoothed for the traveler who accepts the opinions of the favored, despite what the law may say about his freedom to think and speak as he pleases. The dissident, the scoffer, the skeptic, the radical often finds the road rough or impassable.*

The Concluding Proposition

The result—our concluding proposition—is that governmental and corporate leaders, whose role in constraining volitions we have been examining, develop many allies in their own class and outside. They are persons in lesser roles in corporation and government, administrators and faculty in the universities, managers of the media, younger people who aspire to rise, and parents with ambitions for their children. They join in disseminating the beliefs, attitudes, and volitions of corporate and governmental leadership.

Early in a child's life, parents, school administrators, teachers, textbook writers, and the media join in a shared attempt, partly habitual, partly deliberate, to constrain his political opinions.[13] Or, for another example, leading members of an academic profession or of a single university department take up the beliefs of the favored class. The incentives then working on other, especially younger, members of the group are immediate and powerful, not because distant government or corporate leaders can grant or withhold benefits but because immediate colleagues do so by denying promotion to "rash" young scholars.†

Institutions like newspapers, broadcasting systems, research institutions, journals, foundations, and universities thus often become allies of the favored class. They are under strong incentive to do so because they need, even more than do aspiring young men and women, the funds that persons of wealth, power, and influence can provide. Many of these institutions need outright gifts to survive. Others need advertising revenue. Perhaps

* The unusually talented or distinguished radical or dissident can, however, make his distinction his path to success.

† Yet, as though protesting these constraints, many academic and other intellectual communities confer status on those members who are on the left, so long as they do not wholly break out of the broad consensus on politico-economic fundamentals. Thus, in some social science circles in American academic life, conservative Republicans are sometimes of low status.

the following statement from a recent president of Harvard University is not typical of institutional adaptation to the political opinions of the favored class. For so distinguished a university, one would like to dismiss it as an aberration. Yet its president did say, in defense of some of his faculty:

> Can anyone seriously charge that these men and the others in their depart- ment are subverting the American way of life? And can one seriously charge the same of the University as a whole, taking note of its program in history, government, public administration and social relations, and its far-reaching effort in business, which is almost completely directed toward making the private enterprise system continue to work effectively and beneficially in a very difficult world.[14]

Thus the phenomenon of social class reinforces tendencies toward circularity in popular control. Competing views are not silenced, but the disproportion in voice is great. The conclusion is an important one even if, as we shall later see, the effects of class on circularity may be declining.

Additional evidence on the conclusion just reached—and a point of importance in its own right—is that in all the polyarchies on which studies have been made, leading participants in polyarchal politics are dispropor- tionately from the favored class. Lower-class citizens participate less and do so less effectively.[15] So great is the difference in participation that leader- ship of the various interest groups—farmers, veterans, women's organiza- tions, and, to some extent, unions—falls disproportionately into the hands of people of the favored class. Thus, the very groups that might challenge class influences in the system are themselves class influenced.[16]

Again, nations differ somewhat. And the disproportion of favored class leadership in many nations is probably declining. If, for example, there are very few Marxists and other dissidents on the faculties of American and British universities, there are many in the social sciences and the humanities in some of the other polyarchies, including France, West Germany, Italy, and Japan.[17] American journalism—some circulation figures were given in an earlier chapter—gives small voice to dissident views. But socialist or communist journals enjoy large circulations abroad. Even in the United States such conventional journals as the New Yorker now and then voice far-reaching critiques of the politico-economic order. And a variety of small radical newspapers and magazines now proliferate throughout the United States. The major American newspapers and their many columnists, however, are committed to the fundamentals of the private enterprise system. And the public schools remain a major source of conventional indoctrination, near monolithic in the United States, hardly less so in the United Kingdom, but less so on the Continent.[18]

Class Indoctrination versus Class Conflict

Notice that this analysis of an effect of class does not allege class conflict. That class conflict exists, we have already acknowledged. But our point is a different one: one that the favored class to an important degree successfully indoctrinates much of the entire population in certain of its own favored attitudes, beliefs, and volitions. To Marx, class meant class conflict. But we are taking note of tendencies toward conformism that are an aspect of what some later Marxists and other social theorists sometimes identify as *embourgeoisement* of the working class, the acceptance of bourgeois values and volitions rather than hostility to them. Some of the very developments that Marx predicted—the breakup of old ties of kinship and community—have supported certain kinds of *embourgeoisement.* For, torn away from old roots, workers are vulnerable as never before to the mass media, to the appeals of business and governmental leadership, and to the appeals and pressures of members of a favored class and their allies, from which they were before insulated.[19] The widely reported decline of class in Western Europe and the United States often refers only to decline in class conflict.[20] It might in fact indicate a rise in a success with which one class and its allies wins all classes over to endorsing certain of its own attitudes, beliefs, and volitions, despite other evidence that it may be declining.*

Indoctrination of a population by the most favored class is, of course, never a complete success. An elaborate field study of affluent British workers shows the persistence, among occupational groups thought to be picking up middle-class life styles, values, and attitudes, of distinctive class differences, many of which are hostile to the upper classes. It is clear, if it could ever have been doubted, that the objective circumstances of their lives and a diversity of influences on their attitudes are a barrier to a complete indoctrination in those critical politico-economic beliefs, attitudes, and volitions that would maintain the advantages of the favored class.[21]

In the effects of the phenomenon of class-inspired indoctrination of politico-economic beliefs, attitudes, and values, it may be that the United States is the most class ridden of all of the polyarchies. That is because American workers have been more successfully drawn to the values and volitions of the favored class than have their counterparts abroad. They

* The consequent decline of obvious class differences has led some observers to suggest that status (differences in income, education, and occupation) replaces class as the source of social stratification. Status is, of course, connected with class; but, aside from that, status looms more conspicuously as obvious evidences of class differences decline, as they do to the extent that the attitudes, beliefs, and volitions of one class become those of all classes. (See Goldthorpe et al., *The Affluent Worker,* pp. 4–5.)

are conversely less self-conscious about their own distinctive inferior class position and less engaged in class conflict.[22] That is a reason why Americans choose to read and hear a more restricted range of politico-economic opinion than do Europeans and constrain their voting to a narrow range of political positions. By contrast Europeans, who know they are in conflict with members of other classes, more freely welcome acknowledgement of it. They seek the articulation of different class positions. They vote different class positions more than Americans do. Upper-class domination of taste, opinion, politics, and education is therefore less challenged in the United States and consequently more secure.

That being so, we would expect unions in the United States to be less active in politics than in Europe. In fact that has been the case. We would also expect demands for social security and other collective benefits to lag in the United States compared with Europe. And that again is the case. In social security, collective goods and services, and income redistribution, the United States lags behind the Western European polyarchies.

Other Explanations for Constrained Volitions

Marx alleged that, because of class domination, the masses suffer from false consciousness. The mechanisms he had in mind were a much richer and more complex set than those here outlined sparingly and cautiously. Our conclusion is not quite the same as his. To say that, because of class, bourgeois democracy is wholly a sham because the masses are mistaken about what they want, which is roughly what Marx said, is different from saying that because of class, popular control is crippled though not paralyzed by circularity. The latter is our conclusion.

It is crucial to be precise about the significance of our conclusion about class effects on circularity. A set of unifying beliefs that assert the virtues of the fundamentals of social organization will be found in any stable society. That has already been acknowledged. Our point in this chapter is not simply to confirm that fact. It is instead to clarify certain mechanisms that help explain how that unifying set of beliefs is established and to clarify their content. In the market-oriented polyarchies, the beliefs show a distinctive character. They are greatly influenced by inequality of wealth and by the existence of a dual set of leaders who enjoy a privileged position in politico-economic organization. Many of the unifying beliefs of the society are those beliefs communicated by a favored class to all other classes, with enormous advantage in a grossly unequal competition of ideas. For our purposes, it is enough to identify these mechanisms even if they do not entirely explain the existence of unifying politico-economic beliefs, attitudes, and volitions and even if some may be declining.

What other mechanisms help explain the unifying politico-economic beliefs that give broad social sanction to the advantages of the favored class in a society? Some of them bring us around once again to the influence of class. For example, deep-seated beliefs and attitudes that persist over time, some people will say, have to be understood as the product of random "spontaneous" social forces. What does that mean? It cannot mean that they arise without cause. Perhaps, then, it means that they arise without deliberate intent. No person or group or government plans them. They are unintended consequences of mutual influences of persons on each other.

Granted. Yet we know that, although people do indeed influence each other's attitudes in countless unintended ways, they also intend a great deal of control over attitudes, beliefs, and volitions. Parents and teachers, for example, teach children—explicitly and through their own behavior as example—the virtues of obedience to authority. In most societies they also teach children that improvement in their position in life will and ought to depend on their own personal qualities (rather than on an alteration in social structure). Moreover, many of the unintended influences of people on each other reinforce the intended indoctrinations, as when someone who repeatedly challenges authority makes his friends so uncomfortable that they gradually drop him. Much unintended mutual influence among persons is therefore patterned control rather than random, because it reflects a pattern in intended influence, which is itself not random.

Why the particular pattern of intentions that we perceive? Why the emphasis on such a theme as obedience to authority (rather than a skeptical, only conditional, and selective acceptance of it)? Why deference toward the wealthy (that does not even discriminate between earned and inherited wealth)? Why individual responsibility for improvement in the quality of life (rather than social cooperation to improve polity and economy)? Why generalized privilege for the wealthy and powerful (rather than offsetting constraints and responsibilities to balance their advantages in wealth or power)? Why so profound a respect for property as to lead many people to think it immoral to steal a load of bread to save one's family from hunger?

These are not random themes. They confer advantages on persons in the favored social class. How do they come to be "spontaneous"? How do they come to be near universally taught? They have been endlessly communicated to the population—explicitly and through behavior as example—through the church, the media, the schools, the family, and the pronouncements of business and governmental leaders. Since they have been in this way communicated for centuries, they have passed into folklore and common morality, with the result that almost everyone joins in the intended and unintended or "spontaneous" processes by which they are passed on to the young and reinforced for the old.

231

Too simple an explanation, it will be replied. For "spontaneity" points to a diversity of social controls over attitudes, beliefs, and volitions. Granted that the favored class uses its advantaged position to indoctrinate a population to perpetuate those advantages, innumerable other sources of indoctrination, both intended and unintended, compete in every society. Unquestionably they do. But as for the intended indoctrinations, we have shown in earlier chapters that the competition is lopsided, and greatly so. And the unintended influences, for reasons just indicated, are greatly influenced by the intended. The fact of diversity does not, consequently, challenge the proposition that class-inspired indoctrinations are of great and disproportionate effect. It would only challenge a more extreme allegation that they wholly override all other indoctrinations, which we do not hold to be the case.

Social theorists have long disputed on just how cultures or social systems are formed and endlessly reformed. Talcott Parsons sees normative elements—values, ethics, morality, mores, and meanings—more important than "material interests."[23] Others try to explain social structure by specific references to the control relationships that connect people with each other, and often by reference to the psychology of those relationships.[24] Others, like Kardiner, see social structure as arising out of complex interrelationships between culture and personality.[25] Any of these explanations can accommodate the particular and not unlimited influences on social structure and culture that we attribute to class. A disproportionate strength of influences from a favored class can be explained by reference to the values, morality, mores, and meanings these communications teach. It can also be explained by specific reference to control relations, as in this volume. The process is as complex as is suggested by those who see social structure as a product of interplay between culture and personality, for class influence helps form personalities as well as induces specific responses; and the formed personalities are instruments for cultural continuity.

Other Effects of Class

Effects of class on circularity of popular control are only a subset of the effects of class on politico-economic organization. These range widely and are not yet well researched and understood. In the history of American labor relations, for example, class allies—businessmen, heads of state and local government, judges, clergy, and newspapers—presented in many remarkable instances a solid front in sanctioning violence and other repression against activists in the union movement. A further effect that may be attributable to class is the ignorance of Americans about this very aspect of American history.

These other effects of class embrace one to which we shall attend in a later chapter: the possibility that polyarchies can survive only when conflict is dampened by class indoctrination. It is a possibility opened up by some evidences that the effects of class are declining in the polyarchies. If polyarchy—and the prospects of democracy—are crippled by class, it is nevertheless possible that such limited polyarchy as exists in the world could not survive without it.

*   *   *

One last point brings an end to the inquiry on popular control and private enterprise that we have been pursuing for six chapters. It returns us once more to the distinction between grand and secondary issues and between grand majorities and secondary majorities. The grand majorities usually prevail on the grand issues, but the secondary majorities may or may not form on secondary issues or may not be effective in controlling officials.

Corporations and the favored class indoctrinate, we have said, on the grand issues—the fundamentals of the politico-economic order. For secondary issues, indoctrination accounts for much less circularity. On secondary issues, corporations are in conflict and so are members of the favored class. Even if certain class solidarities show through, they will dispute among themselves over educational policy, tax reform, foreign policy, energy conservation, and space exploration, for example. But the mechanisms of popular control analyzed in earlier chapters showed, it will be remembered, a greater efficacy of popular control for grand majorities than for secondary. Secondary majorities are often dominated by a minority or a coalition of minorities. Or they are simply ignored by officials who are often not aware what the majority wishes on secondary issues. We now see, therefore, that circularity through corporate and class indoctrination obstructs what would otherwise be the most effective form of majority control in polyarchy, that achieved by the grand majority. Circularity has relatively less effect on the formation of secondary majorities. But secondary majorities do not achieve a very effective control in any case.

It is a less than happy ending to a long story. Clearly polyarchy is no more than an extremely rough approximation to any idealized models of liberal democracy or to any other kind of democracy.

233

PART

VI

COMMUNISM COMPARED

Communist Systems

A GREAT phenomenon of world history since World War I has been the spread of communist systems over the face of the globe. Russia turned communist, improbably in the light of Marxist theory, in 1917. Supplemented by an indigenous communism under Tito's leadership in Yugoslavia, communism was then carried by Soviet military power to Eastern Europe at the close of World War II. Prolonged disorder and civil war brought a new version of communism to China in 1949, from which it expanded to North Korea in only a few years. Still another style was established in Cuba in 1959. Colonial independence movements in Southeast Asia set in motion the turmoil out of which communism then arose in Vietnam, Laos, and Cambodia. Roughly one-fourth of the world's territory and a third of its inhabitants are now under communist regimes. China alone has a population variously estimated at from 750 million to almost a billion.[1]

So far, the movement seems not to have exhausted its energies. We should not be surprised to find communism established in the next quarter century in some of the now troubled nations of the world like Portugal, Italy, India, and Bangladesh, or somewhere in Latin America, Africa, or the Mideast.

Whether communism is polyarchy's future or whether communist and market-oriented polyarchal systems will remain in indefinite rivalry, we need to examine certain principal features of communist systems. Over the most familiar ones we shall not linger. Nor are we interested in what many Kremlinologists and China-watchers keep their eyes on: for example, the most recent shifts in foreign policy, evidence of a good or bad harvest, signs of thaw or heightened severity against dissidents, or clues to the rise or fall of a Brezhnev or Hua. Instead we want to grasp those characteristics of communism that will clarify why it is the great rival to market-oriented polyarchy.

At one time it looked as though fascism was to be polyarchy's great rival. And in many parts of the contemporary world neither polyarchy nor communism is existent. In those areas, rivalry is among alternative versions of traditional, conventional military, or oligarchic authority. But these forms are increasingly regarded as obsolete, not destined to last for many more decades except in the backwaters. The future, it is consequently argued, belongs to communism, to market-oriented polyarchy, or to some synthesis of the two.

In some senses, a communist system is simpler and therefore more easily described than a market-oriented polyarchy. It is, like all other political systems, an authority system. But it is without the additional complications of a highly developed market system. It also lacks the further complications of polyarchy. Its complications are the infinite complications of authority, but many of these are shared with all other systems. Indeed, in a very few words, we can go a long way to describe a communist system simply by identifying, with the concepts used in preceding chapters, the features that communist systems share with all other systems and those they do not.

Thus, a preliminary characterization of communist politico-economic systems would look like the following (for a summary listing we italicize the key characteristics): They display *great concentration of political authority* in the hands of one man or a ruling committee instead of the diffusion characteristic of polyarchies. Authority is much *less constrained by rules* than in polyarchy, and so also *less constrained by constitutionalism. Polyarchy is absent,* despite a *polyarchal facade,* including controlled elections, to support the claim to be democratic. Yet, on the other hand, communist systems *neither simply exploit their subjects nor neglect their welfare* as traditional authoritarian systems have.

In these systems, leadership is committed to *collective goals,* including, at least transitionally, social reconstruction, rather than to facilitating personal liberty and individualistic goal achievement, as in the market-oriented polyarchies. In the pursuit of them, the scope of *government is near all-encompassing*—wider than in any other politico-economic system. *Government owns most productive assets* of the society—private property in the means of production is not the general rule—and *government immediately and directly organizes the economy.* But it reaches as well into the control of religion, all education, family, labor unions, all organizations, and details of personal behavior usually outside the scope of government in other systems. Its scope also embraces the *full range of methods of control*, including terror and indoctrination to the saturation point. It seeks to control the mind, as far as possible, by *controlling all forms of communication* and suppressing much informal oral political communication. Consequently, *pluralism is extremely weak*—both as a norm that endorses loyalties other than to the state and as a structure that allows both public and private groups to organize autonomously.

In pursuing collective goals, top leadership and their cadres are guided by *an official ideology* that serves simultaneously both as a guide to "truth" and as a guide to practical political action to achieve the new society and the New Man that social reconstruction seeks. Ideology plays a role in communism different from its role in polyarchy.

Although all governments are authority systems, communist systems rely on *authority* far more than do the market-oriented polyarchies. They also use the *market*. But just as they use authority more than do the market-oriented polyarchies, they use the market less. They also employ, to a degree not even approximated by the polyarchies, what we have called the *preceptoral system*. They mount massive programs of "education" to induce their subjects to do what the rulers want them to do.

In order to maintain its authority, effectively control and manage the government, and "educate" the citizenry, top leadership employs *a privileged mobilizing organization* (which it leads) loyal to it and ideologically trained. The organization is typically a *political party* (the only political party permitted in the system).

In their reach into every aspect of life and in the weakness of major social constraints on their scope and ambition, rulers of these systems go far to substitute—deliberately—formal organization for the complex social structures found in noncommunist societies. *Formal organization supersedes a variety of other forms of social coordination*: ethnic solidarity, religious belief, market, family, and moral code.

> Though a social system may be re-forming, the story of Communist China to this day is still one of organization. Men spend most of their everyday life in organization. During the day, they work in factories, rural production teams, administrative offices, and schools. During the evening, they attend public meetings, rest in public parks, participate in public amusements. . . . In Communist China, man lives, works, and rests in organization.[2]

Despite perceptoral elements, especially in China, the form of organization is typically *bureaucracy*. The rise of bureaucracy is a worldwide movement, but communist systems push it further than in any other systems. The workplace, family life, recreation, neighborhood association, and education are all made the object of bureaucratic control to a degree unmatched in any other kind of politico-economic system.

In following chapters we shall explore some of these characteristics of communism but only those that require extended analysis. And we shall try to place communism in an illuminating comparative perspective. Here and now, however, we want to clarify two aspects of communism—party and bureaucracy. One is a great social innovation. The other is in some ways a reactionary feature of communism.

The Political Party in Communist Systems

The place in society that communists claim for the party is remarkable. In the U.S.S.R., party statutes describe the Communist Party to be "the leading and guiding force of Soviet society." According to a Chinese Communist Party document: "Every Party member must . . . discuss with the masses, listen to the opinions of the masses, concern himself with the sufferings of the masses."[3] When the first Soviet astronaut broadcast a message from space, he thanked the party, not his government, for the accomplishment.

In communist and certain other authoritarian systems, the party—not parties but *the* party—has emerged as an extraordinary new kind of institution, a distinctive product of the twentieth century. In some senses, it governs the country, governs the government. Sometimes it looks like a duplicate government. Why is so central an organization not part of government itself? Why separate? What are its functions?

The historical record is not clear on whether the party is actually an essential organization. In the Soviet Union, the party atrophied from 1917 to 1919. The possibility of dissolving the party was suggested, but perhaps only because of the utopian fever of the times.[4] Yet later under Stalin it declined again after he had employed his party and governmental authority alike in extended use in order to create a position of impregnable strength no longer greatly dependent on the party. After the Cultural Revolution in China, the People's Liberation Army for a time took over most party functions. In Castro's early years in power his guerrillas left little room for party; and party still may be of relatively little importance in Cuba.[5]

In the decline of party, Stalin did not dispense with what we have called a supporting organization. He used the secret police instead of party. He also built a "machine," a corps of government and party officials who granted him special authority.[6] For all his strength, even at the peak of his power, he needed specialized supporting organizations. For reasons earlier discussed, every ruler requires some kind of supporting organization.

Moreover, when for any of the reasons earlier indicated, authoritarian leadership—either fascist or communist—wishes to induce voluntary grants of authority from its citizens, the supporting organization, without losing its exclusive and privileged status, must be very large, large enough to reach millions of citizens. It can no longer be a clique or a faction of leadership, as would be sufficient if only a small fringe of the population had to be reached. And it must embrace many skills in order to reach the population in a broad variety of ways. An army might serve the purpose. But only by giving up its preoccupation with military skills, which leadership is loath to permit. Hence the necessary supportive organization becomes what we recognize as the political party: a supporting organization large and diverse enough to win and maintain support for top leadership. Although not by historical evidence indispensable, it is nearly so, is highly serviceable to leadership, and, once organized, can be put to a multiplicity of uses.

For a further and more particular reason, supporting organizations in recent and contemporary authoritarian regimes have been converted into large multiskilled organizations called parties. They are the most distinctive antidemocratic (not nondemocratic, but antidemocratic) institution of communism. In the twentieth century democratic agitation arises everywhere. An authoritarian leadership must counter it with mass campaigns. For that purpose, the old-style political clique or other traditional supporting organization is not enough. In this respect, communist regimes are cousins to fascist. Both need a larger, multiskilled supporting organization to carry the ideological campaign against democracy to those who are learning to demand it. That is a great mission of the party.

Why cannot the civil service itself take over these functions? Because leadership wants supporting workers to be bound by special authority and tight bonds of loyalty. To achieve these in any supporting organization, it will be remembered, leadership has to offer special benefits to its members. Hence, communist leadership offers the prestige of exclusive party membership, opportunities for advancement in positions of influence both in party and government, and a variety of other perquisites to a large but still select group. And it uses these benefits to draw them into indoctrination programs that further tighten their bonds to leadership and simultaneously instruct them in the messages and demands they should bring, in their party work, to government officials and citizens.

Party Tasks

The assignments of the party as a supporting organization are therefore basically twofold: to mold the behavior of citizens into patterns that support rather than obstruct the regime, and to maintain the obedience of government officials to top leadership. In both cases, the required party tasks include surveillance, indoctrination, and specific control.[7]

The public education and propaganda work of communist parties—carrying ideological instruction to the masses—we described in detail in Chapter 4, "Persuasion and Preceptoral Systems." It is strengthened by the "pastoral" work of the party cadres, who are available to help people with family and personal problems and to respond to permissible citizen complaints.[8] The scale of the operation is suggested by the numbers of party functionaries. In the U.S.S.R., for example, full-time party workers have been estimated at from 100,000 to 250,000, unpaid party workers at a million, and members elected to various party organs at 2 million.[9]

Party workers also have the task of keeping electoral politics under control. So great is the prestige of democratic forms that communist systems are full of them. Citizens elect members to the soviets, peasants elect chairmen for their agricultural collectives, the party central committee elects members of the Politburo, and so on throughout government. All these elections have to be controlled one way or another. In the Soviet Union, for example, the members of a kolkhoz elect their chairman only after the party has designated him.[10]

Of the party functionary's relation to the government official, a Soviet document declares:

> All these state and public organizations can only function successfully under the leadership of the Communist party, which works out the correct political line, and determines the direction of their practical activity. . . . Only the Party, expressing the interests of the entire nation, embodying its collective understanding, uniting in its ranks the finest individuals of the nation, is qualified and called to control the work of all organizations and organs of power.[11]

Party functionaries are attached to every unit of government and every productive enterprise. The picture is not clear in China and Cuba, but in the Soviet Union leadership has deliberately employed the party as a parallel bureaucracy in government and industry because it believes that a dual bureaucracy, though posing some problems of coordination, brings energies, information, and policy considerations to bear on administrative decisions more successfully than would a conventional monistic administrative structure.[12] The general rule is that, although government officials can act on their own authority on nonpolicy issues, they must consult with

party officials on policy issues.[13] The party leads. The government authoritatively issues orders. The distinction, however, is sometimes obliterated.

The party in the Soviet Union plays at least two other critical roles. It
supervises the selection of government personnel.[14] And its middle-level
organizations and functionaries serve as regional and local coordinators of
government officials. Each of them is vertically tied by a line of command
to a specialized central government superior authority but is in need of
horizontal coordination with other officials in the region or locality.[15]

In Soviet and Chinese communist parties, top leadership has been
formally designated as a presidium or politburo of the party. It is this tiny
component of the party—its top leadership but not the party as a whole—
that makes policy. Yet to implement policy in a particular region or
circumstance requires that subordinate leaders be authorized to decide
what appropriate policies, within the guidelines of the top policy makers,
should be pursued. Moreover, subordinate policy-making officials in any
organization will escape to some degree the control that their superiors try
to maintain over them. In either case, the subordinate party officials acquire some autonomous policy-making authority, as well as some small
influence over the policy decisions of their superiors.[16]

Party and Ideology

As some scholars see it, the party is also the instrument for ideological
control of the system. Others reverse the relation: ideology is the instrument of party control. To speak precisely, top leadership controls. It can
choose to subordinate ideology to party or party to ideology. Stalin appears
to have ruled by organization aided by ideology, Mao by ideology aided by
organization.[17] Because ideology is an extremely complex structure of
which some parts are less fundamental than others, some points of doctrine
can easily be rewritten by top leadership. They can then be used as an
instrument of control. Leadership dares not challenge other doctrines for
fear of discrediting itself.[18]

Despite Mao's repeated attempts at ideological renewal, ideology's
effects show tendencies to decline with the passage of time, except as
ideology becomes merely a set of rationalizations that support dominant
interests, as it is in the polyarchal systems. In the Soviet Union, ideology
has become "ambiguous and ill-defined."[19] The core of ideological doctrine has come to be "the basic demand for belief in the Party itself."[20]

Institutionalized Innovation through the Party

What has been said so far might imply that a communist party as a
supporting organization for the most part plays a defensive role for the

regime. In fact, once it has brought communist leadership to power (if that is its first great accomplishment, as in the U.S.S.R. and China), it becomes an instrument for a variety of positive or leadership functions. Perhaps on this score more than on any other communists should be credited with a great social invention: a specialized institution for innovation throughout the entire society. Communist leaders are intent on social transformation—at least in their early years in authority. They understand the difficulty of using so cumbersome and sluggish a machine as government for fundamental social change. In turning the party into an instrument for flogging, pacing, and driving the governmental bureaucracy, especially in preceptoral "education," they have invented a specialized institution not to be found in governments of other kinds.[21]

The weakness in this great social invention is that communist parties typically eventually lose their innovative zeal. In the Soviet Union, a continuing revolutionary rhetoric cannot disguise the degree to which top leadership and party apparatus fears further fundamental social change.[22] The resistance is revealed in controversy over economic reform that we shall examine in a later chapter.

The Bureaucratic Revolution

The formula for controlling the massive bureaucratic machinery of government in a communist system is to set the party on it—to watch it, indoctrinate it, stimulate it, and in other specific ways control it. But the party is itself a bureaucracy, and a more highly disciplined one than government itself. Indeed, communist systems have carried both bureaucracies to an extreme, well beyond bureaucracy in market-oriented systems. The greatest revolution of all—the bureaucratization of life—has submerged in large part the Bolshevik and other communist revolutions and given to communism a heavy flavor of archaic political orders. A great aspiration for a new society turns into the oldest of rigid forms. Not quite realizing what he was saying, Lenin joyously anticipated a future he should have feared: "The whole of society will have become a single office and a single factory"[23]

Communist systems have largely destroyed the thousands of small-scale enterprises that once provided a productive role in life outside of bureaucracy for their owner-operators and for a handful of employees, as is still the case in noncommunist systems. Even more of a transformation has been the conversion of family farming into bureaucratically organized state farms and collectives. Mao apparently wished to make the bureaucratically organized farm or industrial enterprise the key institution in a person's life, tying his housing, education, and recreation to this one key bureaucracy. China has gone far in doing so.[24] All communist systems have bureaucratized housing, sports, and other recreation, as well as associational and political activity. Even the young are collected and occupied in bureaucratic youth organizations.

The quintessence of bureaucracy is military organization. More than one observer has taken note of the military character of the Chinese commune, especially in the Great Leap Forward.[25] In Cuba, an unusually large army is regularly deployed as a work force, bringing military organization and discipline directly into the economy. And military organization has been repeatedly used to deploy, with varying mixtures of moral appeal and coercion, "volunteer" workers for weekend, vacation, and after hours tasks, for which other inducements to labor are not sufficient or are too costly.[26] In these forms, bureaucratization of everyday life goes further in China and Cuba than in European communism.

The ubiquity of bureaucracy in communist systems is an aspect of the extraordinary dependence of these systems on formal organization and authority. A distinction between social organization through "natural" or "spontaneous" structures like groups bound together by kinship or a common moral code or by barter or simple market relationships, on the one hand, and deliberately created purposeful structures like armies, bureaucracies, and corporations, on the other, has a long history in social thought. From the Greeks through Hobbes and in its elaboration in 1887 by Ferdinand Tönnies in his *Gemeinschaft und Gesellschaft*, this distinction divides communist from what one might call less organized societies. Communism attempts comprehensively to substitute "organization" for "society." Although "society" is never wholly obliterated and when extinguished frequently springs up again, the attempt to obliterate it is a major development in history.[27] Although some observers see that attempt as no more enlightened, progressive, or liberating than Orwell's society of *1984*, it is only fair to acknowledge that others see it as a potential victory of man's intelligence over blind tradition.

The Conservatism of European Communism

Having retained a market system for consumer goods and for labor and having developed an extraordinary dependence on bureaucracy and formal organization, we shall see that European communist systems—China may

245

turn out differently—have not yet accomplished more than what might be called a conservative revolution. For all their rhetoric of a new society, they remain prisoners of old and familiar forms of social organization.

Life in a European communist system is, for the great mass of people, much like life elsewhere, for the communists have not found—at least not so far—any great new life style for their citizens. Drop an ordinary man not trained to observe his surroundings with great care into communist Kiev or into "capitalist" Vienna. Language aside, he would be hard put to determine which was the communist city. In both he would see much the same sights: the streets busy with shoppers; men and women on business errands; people going to and from work in offices, factories, and shops. He would soon find that what was on their minds differed little in the two cities: the daily problems of earning a living, of work, of family and household. He would find bureaucracy ever present in both cities, for most people in both cities work in a bureaucracy and frequently encounter others: tax collectors, police, gas and electric companies, and schools. (He would probably not notice the broader scope of bureaucracy in Kiev.) He would see in both cities unmistakable marks of economic and social inequality, most obviously in forms of dress and housing. In a week's visit, he might never have any experience that loudly told him where he was. European communism, we shall later see, has changed the form of management of business enterprise, both in industry and agriculture. But the business enterprise remains—under new management. The social structure, individual motives, and life styles are left in surprising respects unaltered, except that bureaucracy is ubiquitous.

Two Models

IN unobscured view, no society looks defensible. In the U.S.S.R. the grossest offenses against the human spirit are commonplace: censorship and thought control, fraudulent trials on false charges, constant intimidation that demeans any citizen who would otherwise be capable of thinking for himself, a semisecret world of special privilege for the elite in a professed egalitarian system that does not even provide adequate medical care for its masses, and massive alcoholism coupled with widespread hooliganism. One can continue the list.

In the United States—though I am not pretending impartiality—great wealth still leaves a segment of the population in a demoralizing welfare system. Its streets and homes are increasingly unsafe. Its expensive legal system is open to the rich, inaccessible to the poor for civil law, and hostile to the poor in criminal law. Its factories, automobiles, and indifferent citizens degrade the environment in countless ways. And many of its business leaders—among them not only a fringe of irresponsibles but executives of leading corporations—practice bribery of government officials. They also routinely break the law on campaign contributions and elevate their incomes through expense accounts. They misrepresent their products and in various ways defraud their customers, whether individual consumers or corporate and governmental customers responsible for major projects like the Alaskan pipeline or space exploration. This list too can be extended.

We all know, however, that there is another side to both these societies and that we need to understand it. Market-oriented polyarchal societies are not all inequality and exploitation. Nor are communist societies simply traditional tyrannies or exploitative oligarchies. However tyrannical many communists leaders become when they gain power, in their earlier pursuit of power they are by all evidence emotionally and intellectually committed to transforming society for the benefit of the masses. Nor do successful communist revolutionaries at the height of their power necessarily betray their earlier revolutionary aspirations. Communist systems are, in the eyes of liberal democrats, peculiar in their mixture of elitist, tyrannical, progressive, egalitarian, and reformist traits.

In this chapter, we will develop a special perspective in order to understand communist systems. We will regard them as imperfect approximations to one of two highly sophisticated visions of a humanitarian society, two visions of how society might be organized to benefit "the people." The market-oriented polyarchies are imperfect approximations to the other vision. The two visions, or models, extract certain major characteristics from communism and liberal democracy, ignoring others, as well as ignoring inconsistencies in communist and liberal democratic thought. They thus capture a simplified and exaggerated central core in each of these two forms of social organization. But model and actual society should not be confused.[1]

The key difference between the two visions—and it is not a difference that one would at first expect or appreciate as fundamental—is in the role of intellect in social organization. Model 1 might be called an intellectually guided society. It derives from a buoyant or optimistic view of man's intellectual capacities. On a more pessimistic view of man's intellectual capacities, Model 2 postulates other forms of guidance for society.*

How societies weigh values and make calculated choices in various forms of politico-economic organization is a question we pursued in the analysis of problems of choice in hierarchy and market system and again in the analysis of how volitions are formed in the polyarchies. At this point in the book, we confront a watershed: on one side, a confident distinctive view of man using his intelligence in social organization; on the other side, a skeptical view of his capacity.†

---

* On some points, the distinction between the two visions or models is related to the distinction Talmon draws between what he sees as two models of democracy differing chiefly in their "different attitudes to politics" and in different concepts of liberty. Where his models play up these two differences, mine play up different concepts of how societies conceive of and organize problem solving. J. L. Talmon, *The Origins of Totalitarian Democracy* (New York: Praeger, 1960).

Model 1 is also on several points similar to Grossman's "solidary society" (Gregory Grossman, "The Solidary Society," in *Essays in Socialism and Planning in Honor of Carl Landauer*, ed. Gregory Grossman [Englewood Cliffs, N.J.: Prentice-Hall, 1970]).

† I am departing, I acknowledge, from a long-established tradition that makes liberty

The Efficacy of Analysis in Organizing Society

Let us set out the main elements of two contrasting sets, Models 1 and 2, of views on the efficacy of intelligence, thought, or analysis when applied to tasks of social organization.

Intellectual Competence

The model of the intellectually guided society, Model 1, specifies that some people in the society are wise and informed enough to ameliorate its problems and guide social change with a high degree of success. Thus, Marxian thought "postulates the absolute capacity of man to truly understand his reality as a point of departure for his active endeavors to shape it."[2] A Soviet author writes of development through "universal calculations" that are "scientifically based."[3] According to Model 2, however, "every one well knows himself to be fallible," as John Stuart Mill argued in *On Liberty*. Model 1 assumes a match between intellectual capacity and the complexity of the social world. Model 2 argues that it is a gross mismatch.[4]

Theory

As a consequence, in Model 1 the intellectual leaders of the society are envisioned as having been able to produce a comprehensive theory of social change that serves to guide the society. Marxist theory, as refined by Lenin (or Mao) and others, approximates such a theory. At times, Maoists have claimed that the thought of Mao contains all necessary social theory.[5] In Model 2, no such synoptic theory exists. Scholars produce only scattered partial theories—for example, on the causes of juvenile delinquency or on voting patterns. Even within their limited domains, they are tentative, inadequately tested, and consequently imperfect sources of guidance in practical affairs.[6]

---

the fundamental distinction between communism and market-oriented polyarchies. Although liberty may indeed be the key issue in evaluating the two, our task here is not evaluation but clarification of fundamental mechanisms (without which, it might be added, no one can competently proceed to evaluation). Moreover, communists typically claim that only an intellectually competent elite can lead a society to liberty. On that claim alone, it is necessary to begin with an examination of how the two different kinds of systems regard intelligence in its application to tasks of social organization.

The Correct versus the Broadly Willed

In Model 1, since some people *know* how to organize society, the test of an institution or policy is that it is correct. The 1969 Constitution of the Chinese Communist Party declares that the party is "great, glorious, and correct." Reflecting the official view in China, an editorial declares: "The correctness or incorrectness of the ideology and political line decides everything."[7] Since, in Model 2, people are not competent to know what is correct, they fall back on their own volitions, however imperfectly understood, as a test. As the point is often put, "The key characteristic of a democracy is the continuing responsiveness of the government to the preferences of its citizens. . . ."[8] We might therefore call Model 2 that of the preference-guided or volition-guided society.

Liberal democracy has sometimes been envisaged as a search for truth, and democratic values are indeed on some points—openness, free inquiry, criticism, and self-correction—paralleled by the values of the scientific community.[9] But where information, scientific inquiry, analysis, and theory are conclusive in Model 1 in discovering the correct form of organization for society, they remain insufficient both in Model 2 and in most democratic theory. At some point, issues cannot be scientifically decided. At that point the test of social institutions is whether they accord with what people think they want.

Criterion for Correctness

In the idea that solutions to problems are either correct or incorrect lies a crucial implication. Logically, it is not possible to say that one has the correct answer to a problem, a correct policy, or a correct set of social institutions unless one has a criterion of correctness. Only in Model 1 is it assumed that there always exists such a criterion. It is the correspondence of an institution or policy to man's true physical, psychological, and social needs, which can be known.

Ultimately both visions appeal to man's needs as, in principle, the test of institutions and policies. But since in Model 2 many needs cannot be known or known with sufficient confidence, institutions and policies cannot always be tested by reference to them. Instead the volitions of "the people" are taken as the best indicator of needs and wants.*

* If people preferred what in some more basic sense they need, then in both models the correct and the preferred would be the same. But people do not in fact understand their own needs, do not necessarily express preferences for what they need, are in fact misled about their preferences, and even often interchange what they think they prefer with what they actually prefer.

Discovery Not Choice

Thus, in Model 1 correct social organization is not chosen; it is discovered. In Model 1 the right method of social organization is not a matter of opinion or volition or of reconciliation of preferences or interests. It is a question of fact calling for diagnosis. There is a "single correct solution."[10] In Model 2, in which discovery is not possible, social organization has to be chosen. It is willed by many people. It is a consequence of their volitions.

Elites

Since it is knowledge rather than volition that guides society in Model 1, the intellectual elite is simultaneously a political elite. Hence, the political party has a special place, as noted in the preceding chapter. In the U.S.S.R., "the Party leadership lays claim to a monopoly over the interpretation and application of the sole scientific theory of social development."[11] In China, understanding society—specifically bringing Marxist theory and Maoist thought to bear on diagnosis—is the prerogative of a correct political leadership in the party.[12] In Model 2, there exists no such elite.

Harmony

In Model 1 is postulated an underlying harmony of men's needs that can be known to the guiding elite, "a preordained, harmonious and perfect scheme of things."[13] A publication of the planning commission in the U.S.S.R. argues: "Given a correct economic policy, in a socialist society there are, and can be, no groups of workers whose material interests lie in contradiction to the objectively necessary planned management of the economy. . . ."[14] Mao writes that "the realm of Great Harmony means communist society."[15] In Model 2, by contrast, it is assumed that harmony of needs is not only undiscoverable but nonexistent.

The assumption of harmony in Model 1 is necessary, given the assumption of a criterion for testing correct solutions. If the criterion is, as already noted, man's needs—if an institution or policy is correct if it serves man's needs and incorrect if it does not—the criterion can be applied only if an institution or policy that serves one man's needs does not obstruct meeting the needs of other men or if there exists some harmonizing resolution of superficially conflicting needs.

The two visions, one of harmony and one of conflict, manifest competing views of society that have divided men for at least two millennia:

ideal society as knit together by consensus, as in Plato, Rousseau, and Hegel; or conflict-ridden society, as in Aristotle, Hobbes and Kant.[16, *]

An Addendum on Democratic Theory

Arising in the Enlightenment, one great tradition in liberal democratic thought identified liberal democracy, which is an approximation to Model 2, with government by reason rather than by authority, or as "government by discussion."[17] A now parallel younger Western tradition identifies communism with force, authority, and the suppression of inquiry. Our characterization of the two models has just reversed the traditional identification of liberal democracy with reason and of communism with unreasoned authority.

However greatly actual communist societies constrain discussion and inquiry, communist doctrine displays a faith in elite intellectual capacity that is in sharp contrast to the troubled concern about fallibility that is characteristic of liberal democratic society as represented in Mill. The liberal democrat's faith in reason is historically impressive only in contrast to earlier traditionalism and authoritarianism in science, religion, and politics. Compared to the Marxian and communist faith in reason, it is puny. Marx's scientific socialism was meant to be scientific; the term is not just a slogan.

In the older vision of "government by discussion," democracy was less closely identified with Model 2, more reconcilable with Model 1. As, roughly coincident wth the eighteenth-century Enlightenment, the egalitarian democratic idea emerged in France, a democrat or egalitarian was typically also a rationalist, turning against traditionalism, authority, and superstition. He was likely to believe, as a result of his new faith in rationality and science, in the possibility that men could find the universe to be harmonious, man potentially no longer in conflict with his fellows, the intellect therefore capable of discovering "correct" solutions.[18]

This earlier faith, both in man's intellectual capacities and in harmony, has been eroded for numerous reasons, including, among intellectual influences, Freud's discoveries of man's irrationalities. Many thoughtful

---

* What is the relation of Model 1 to the earlier preceptoral model of politico-economic organization? The latter is a model of a process by which a leadership, not necessarily intellectually competent as in Model 1, undertakes to control a population through persuasion. It is not a model, as are 1 and 2, depicting how society is to be designed, but is only a model of how leadership can implement its design.

Yet the case for attempting a preceptoral system rests on the case for Model 1. No believer in Model 2 could make a defense for a preceptoral system.

There are, however, a few elements of Model 2 present, though not in strength, in a preceptoral system. For decision making at low levels, in factory and commune, for example, individual and small-group initiatives and interactions are more highly prized than a finely tuned coordination.

people also lost faith in contemplation of disturbing historical events like the Terror of the French Revolution and the later demands and counter-revolutionary bloodshed of the Paris Commune, a "pivotal event in European political thought."[19]

Thus, a once confident movement of thought that drew little distinction between democracy and socialism divided. Down one road, liberal democratic thought allied itself with classical economic thought and became increasingly skeptical of man's capacity to reshape his world. It therefore turned toward institutions that would hold fallible leaders responsible but would not grant them authority to create "correctly" an egalitarian world. Down the other road, the communist movement, armed with Marxian theory, pushed toward institutions that do not hold leaders responsible to an inhibiting electorate but do grant them authority to create by "correct" design an egalitarian world.[20]

Social Interaction in Model 2 as an Alternative to Analysis

If analysis cannot find correct solutions, how then are institutions and policies to be designed? Sometimes by guess, rule of thumb, and the like. The more important answer, however, is: by social processes or interactions that substitute for conclusive analysis.*

Suppose a small society of three people wants to decide which restaurant to go to for dinner. In the style of Model 1, it would study the question on the assumption that there exists one correct solution discoverable by diagnosis. In the style of Model 2, it would look for a process or interaction to make analysis unnecessary. It might take a vote. Or agree on some rule such as choosing the first restaurant they encounter as the three set out to walk. Or negotiate a decision, letting each of the three bring persuasion or other influence to bear on the others.

Now suppose a large society wants to decide how to allocate its resources. In the style of Model 1, an elite would study the question in an attempt to find correct decisions. Economic planning of the communist variety is the obvious example. In the style of Model 2, it would establish an interaction process that would make the diagnostic study unnecessary— the market system is the obvious example. Or suppose a society wants to

---

* Strictly speaking, social interaction other than purely intellectual interaction among a group searching for correct policies, for that too is a form of social interaction.

decide whether to encourage or constrain the further development of nuclear fuel for electric power development. In the style of Model 1, an elite can research the question in a search for the correct answer. Or the society can settle the question by an interactive process in which people express their volitions, however well- or ill-considered, as the people of the state of California did in a referendum in 1976. Suppose a group of officials want to control wage rates to head off inflation. In the style of Model 1, it can research the question in a quest for the correct solution. In the style of Model 2, it can set up a tripartite commission of representatives of workers, managers, and public and allow negotiation among them to settle the question, as the United States has done repeatedly to cope with wartime inflation. For all such problems, analyzing and "acting out" a solution are alternatives.

Insofar as interactions substitute for problem analysis within government, governmental problem solving is to that degree political rather than analytical, played out in the struggle over authority among conflicting interests rather than coolly studied, and capable on occasion, as in Model 1 too, of what most people would call gross irrationalities.*

In Model 1's reliance on analysis instead of interaction, its political system is simple. It is not much more than an administrative organization —the "administration of things" in Marxian doctrine. In a sense, there is no politics in Model 1. Marxist theory makes the point in the doctrine of the withering away of the state.[21]

Let us incorporate problem-solving politics, market systems, and all other substitutes for analytical problem solving in the term "interactions." We can then examine certain aspects of them that will bring out the problem-solving capacities of alternatives to analysis.

Interactions are a substitute for analysis in the specific sense that they constitute processes that produce decisions in circumstances in which a decision cannot be or is not, for any reason, reached exclusively through analysis. All the fundamental politico-economic institutions of market-oriented polyarchies are interactions that substitute for an exclusive use of analysis to reach decisions: private property, constitutionalism, polyarchy, and market system, as well as particular interaction processes like tripartite boards, committees, legislatures, and courts, and larger processes

* Problem solving by social interaction instead of analysis is represented by the international political order. International political order is achieved—when achieved at all—without an omniscient elite—indeed without any central authority. Every major participant in the construction of the international order is largely bent on his or its own private objectives, so that what order is achieved as a result of interaction among them rather than the product of an internationally minded designing mind or committee. On various models of an international Model 2 see Morton A. Kaplan, "Some Problems of International Systems Research," in *International Political Communities* (New York: Doubleday, 1966).

like interest-group and party politics. If from one point of view all of these are devices for social control, from another vantage point they also are all calculating devices for the society. They are procedures through which decisions are made without diagnostic studies in pursuit of the correct decisions of Model 1.

Obviously social interaction is to be found in all actual societies. In Model 1, however, interactions only implement elite decisions. They are not problem-solving processes that replace analysis. For example, negotiated collective agreements between management and employees in the U.S.S.R. are "solemn declarations of how the two will join forces to attain the tasks imposed on both from above."[22] In Model 1, problem-solving interactions are suppressed as a source of disorganization and trouble.

As we shall see in a later chapter, much of communist antagonism to market interactions, even under planner sovereignty, arises out of a fear that transactions among managers, ostensibly to implement planners' wishes, will gradually turn into policy-making interactions. Communist societies display a generalized fear that interactions, which of course abound in all systems, take on functions other than mere implementation.

In Model 2 it is not assumed that interactions produce perfect solutions to problems, only that they will often be superior to the solutions attempted directly by the intellect. Either can be a disaster. Looking at the "solution" to the problem of what should be the distribution of income in the United States (its distribution being a product of market interaction, as well as governmental interaction, rather than deliberate intellectual design), proponents of Model 2 would have to admit that in some people's eyes the "problem" has not yet been solved. But they would probably believe that it is "solved," however badly, better than it would be "solved" through a frontal intellectual attack on it, which they believe might be incompetent.*

Procedures Highly Valued

If a society depends heavily on social interaction rather than intellect for problem solving, it will highly value—as though ends in themselves—certain key interaction patterns. For example, that a decision be made by

---

* The contrast between the two models of the well-ordered society throws a little more light on a question pursued in an earlier chapter: why polyarchy develops only in market systems. On a view of man as a creature of limited cognitive capacity to organize his society and solve his social problems, the substitution of problem-solving interactions for impossible analytical tasks helps explain both the rise of the governmental interactive processes called democracy or polyarchy and the multifaceted profusion of interactions called market system. A sufficient faith in science and reason makes both unnecessary. Lacking that faith many people will think both are indispensable.

majority rule will be more important than that it be in any other way defensible. A fair trial will come to be valued more than that the fact of guilt or innocence be correctly established. A good defense for a bad policy will be that it is the result of a process in which everyone was heard.

Many interactions are seen in particular as protecting fallible men from their own errors in institution building and policy making. The civil liberties, for example, are prized less to permit men to design improved institutions and policies than to permit them to dissent, to question, to criticize. Another prized mechanism is checks and balances. It is a mechanism that prevents action by any one authority until others sanction the action.

In traditional liberal democratic theory, the emphasis on such mechanisms as these expresses a concern for personal liberty and popular control. Without contradicting the traditional view, our view adds that the emphasis on procedures in Model 2 also reflects a desire to safeguard problem-solving interactions as a substitute for analysis. By contrast, none of these mechanisms are necessary in Model 1, and indeed they are largely absent from communist societies.

Conflict Interaction

In Model 2 many interactions are designed to create (and then to cope with) conflict: separation of powers, tripartite boards, parliamentary removal of prime minister, and the like. Conflict is positively employed rather than suppressed as in Model 1 and in communist societies. "The clash of doctrines is not a disaster, it is an opportunity."[23] Conflict is harnessed to bring scrutiny to bear on possibly mistaken institutions and policies. It is also exploited to stimulate an always inadequate supply and quality of analysis. Courts, which might be designed as research institutions for disposing of cases before them, are not so designed. Instead, conflict is stimulated through an adversary system. The assumption is that the conflict will more fully bring out the facts. On larger questions of public policy, public hearings are sometimes designed to stimulate, for the same reason, partisan advocacy. Where conflict leads not to mere compromise but to a reconsideration of differences and a new "integration," it is especially valued.[24]

The Trip and the Arrival

Out of Model 2's emphasis on interaction, protected procedures, and useful conflict arises a disposition to value problem solving itself—the trip as well as the arrival. Hence the long-standing theme in much democratic theory: citizens are to be viewed as doers and achievers. We have already seen this element in democratic thought in Mill's argument that democracy contributes to the citizen's "advancement in intellect, in virtue, and in practical activity and efficiency."[25] This is different from a view of democracy as a system for want satisfaction, in which man is viewed solely as beneficiary.[26] Both are joined in Model 2 interactions.

Epiphenomenal "Solutions"*

Through the interaction processes of Model 2, societies routinely deal with problems not on the agenda of any participant in any interaction. Some of these problems are unrecognized. Compare, for example, voting and buying as interactive processes. Voting puts the selection of an official on every voter's agenda. The voter recognizes the problem and deals with it deliberately. Buying puts the allocation of resources into every buyer's hands. But he does not necessarily know it. He need not know that his purchases affect resource allocation, certainly need not feel any responsibility to deliberate on resource allocation before he decides what to buy. He participates in an interaction that solves the problem of resource allocation as a by-product or epiphenomenon of his own private problem solving.

So also the design of a city may be left to emerge as a by-product—that is, epiphenomenally—from individual decisions on land use. In Model 2, many people will sometimes shrink from proposals to solve certain problems through deliberate or intellectually guided choice. They will prefer a by-product solution. Sex distribution of newborn infants is an example. Some people want that "decision" to emerge only epiphenomenally. They might also shrink from analyzing directly a policy on euthanasia, preferring that death of invalids be decided as a by-product or epiphenomenon of customary medical practices. For another example, in Model 1, the hardships of social change have to be faced up to, weighed, and assigned. In Model 2, the delicate problem of who must bear the costs of change is often epiphenomenally decided through the interactions of a market system that permit, we have seen, innovators to throw the costs of change onto others—onto the workers whose skill is now obsolete or the town where a now outmoded factory is closed down.

* By epiphenomenon we mean here a by-product. In the philosophy of mind, the term has a special meaning: a phenomenon without causal efficacy. That meaning is not intended here.

In both models of society epiphenomena exist. The difference is that they are seen as trouble making or neutral with respect to problem solving in Model 1, but are often seen as problem solving in Model 2.

Mutual Adjustment and Pluralism

On several counts, a diversity of mutual adjustment—specifically that extreme degree that goes by the name of pluralism—is conspicuous in Model 2 societies. Logically, pluralism is not implied by the substitution of interaction for analysis. If, for example, all public decisions were decided by negotiation or voting among a half dozen oligarchs, we would not call the system pluralistic. But since in actual fact a principal instrument for substituting interaction for analysis is the market, Model 2 systems are on that point alone pluralistic to an extreme. Decisions are decentralized to thousands of corporate and other business leaders. In addition, governmental decision making is pluralistic.

These arrangements afford broad scope for participants in interactive processes to pursue their own individual or group goals rather than any one or a few overarching national goals. Although they do not compel a neglect of overarching collective goals, they permit it. If this is familiar in liberal democratic aspiration and polyarchal practice, it stands in sharp contrast to the assertion of centrally determined collective goals in Model 1. "As an orchestra conductor sees to it that all the instruments sound harmonious and in proportion, so in social and political life does the Party direct the efforts of all people toward achievement of a single goal."[27] That is Khrushchev. In Mao's words, communists "must grasp the principle of subordinating the needs of the part to the needs of the whole."[28]

Pluralism in Model 2 embraces a cultural diversity not acceptable in Model 1, in which an elite discovers and responds to the common needs and wants of all men taken as alike. Model 1 recognizes differences among individuals in age, sex, intelligence, strength, and certain special skills. Beyond that, however, it holds that racial, religious, ethnic, and other individual differences among men are only happenstances of cultural and personality variation from a past in which societies varied greatly because they were not intellectually guided. People are indistinguishable as "the masses," as in common communist parlance. Institutions and policies are adapted to what is universal in mankind. Group and individual differences tend to disappear. A "new man" will appear, as Cuba, the Soviet Union, and China have claimed for their own societies.[29]

In Model 2, group and individual diversity is positively valued. Liberal thought is emphatic on this point. There is some recognition in Model 2 that differences among individuals and groups are essential to order. People are bound together by Durkheim's organic solidarity, by differences that make them dependent on one another.[30] A society of likes is hardly imaginable. If all Frenchmen were alike, they would all want to live in Paris, or none of them would. In Model 2, differences in preferences make it possible for men to stay out of each other's way and also facilitate a division of labor.

Analysis in Interaction Processes

Adaptation of Analysis to Interaction

In Model 2 interaction never wholly replaces analysis. But analysis is adapted to problem-solving interactions. While the elite in a pure Model 1 will try to analyze so fundamental a question as "What is best for society?" a participant in interaction in Model 2 will try to analyze various simpler questions on which he needs answers in order to play his role in interaction. In simple cases, a buyer analyzes possible purchases. If the buyer is a business enterprise, it can afford to spend heavily on product analysis before making a purchase. Or a congressional committee, interest group, or party may establish research services to help it with its particular tasks in political interaction. In a later chapter on policy making and planning (chapter 23), the distinction between the two kinds of analysis will be further examined.

The Value of Analysis and of Initiative

Paradoxically, Model 2 values thought, intellect, or analysis more than does Model 1. It recognizes that analysis is difficult, in short supply, and of an inadequate level of competence. Although that undercuts a faith that men can solve social problems by the intellectual design of institutions and policies, it also leads people to prize highly what capacities for analysis society possesses, like a person in a desert who prizes the shade of any single tree he finds. Hence in Model 2, inquiry, thought and science are carefully protected. Problem-solving initiatives are also encouraged. In-centives to problem-solving are widely dispersed by holding participation in interaction open at all possible points. Especially in contemplation of social change, advocates of Model 2 will think it impossible to try to comprehend the future well enough to plan it. They will consequently encourage widespread dispositions to cope with emergent problems and to deal resourcefully with what can be grasped.

Confident of the adequacy of intellect and theory, Model 1 does not similarly protect scientific research, inquiry, public discussion, and dis-persed initiatives.

* * *

Both 1 and 2, it is to be remembered, are models of a humanitarian society. It is important, at risk of some repetition, to acknowledge fully that the vision of communist systems as an approximation to an ideal of a humanitarian society captures a fundamental aspect of communism, however imperfectly communist societies approximate the vision. It is difficult for a thoughtful liberal democrat to read Lenin or Mao without recognizing on some points a kinship of spirit. That they have given orders to imprison and to kill thousands, even millions, does not conclu-sively deny their humanitarianism any more conclusively than the massive civilian bombing of Germany in World War II, to say nothing of atomic bombing of Japan and the devastation of Vietnam, denies it for American political leaders. While we draw distinctions between the one and the other, and between one ethic and another, both groups of leaders claim to kill for humanitarian principles. Moreover, in buoyantly estimating their own capacities to understand society well enough to reconstruct it, com-munist leaders pay their respects to the heritage of the Enlightenment, even if they simultaneously suppress free speech and inquiry.

If the polyarchies are approximations to Model 2, in them we neverthe-less find ambitions for scientific problem solving in the style of Model 1. In the ranks of the most enthusiastic operations researchers, systems analysts, and planners are to be found, we shall later see, the cousins of Marx's scientific socialists, with an elitist faith in intellectual competence at the top. A former U.S. Defense Secretary says:

> . . . the real threat to democracy comes, not from overmanagement, but from undermanagement. To undermanage . . . is simply to let some force other than reason shape reality.' . . . Vital decision-making . . . must remain at the top.[31]

On a Model 1 view of the world, that is what the top it for.

Democracy, Freedom, and Equality

HAVE we gone wide of the mark in characterizing communist systems as imperfect approximations to a Model 1 vision of a humanitarian society? Clearly, many of their characteristics are not those of Model 1: terror, kangaroo courts, mass executions, innumerable forms of intimidation, and deliberately organized mob violence. They are a mixture of traits. Some further specific characteristics throw light on the degree to which they approximate the humane qualities of Model 1.

Democracy and Polyarchy

Humanitarian because democratic? It is sometimes suggested that communism has achieved a new kind of democracy. Even if government is not by the people, it is for the people.[1] There is good precedent, however, even in communist thought, for reserving the terms "democracy" for systems that achieve popular control. Lenin, Stalin, and many other communist leaders and theorists have recognized the distinctive character of a government subject to popular control. They have done so both in their doctrine that communist systems are at least not yet democratic and in their careful construction of polyarchal facades to give substance to claims that democracy is on the way.*

We have seen that in the celebrated Chinese "mass line" Maoists claim to have incorporated two-way communication, with elements of popular control, into what we have called a preceptoral system. Perhaps that is a form of democracy.

Mao's own exposition of two-way communication suggests that it is, in fact, structured to maintain top control.[2] A 1933 resolution of the Politburo, presumably written by Mao, asserts the principle of "from the masses, to the masses."

> This means summing up (i.e. coordinating and systematizing after careful study) the views of the masses (i.e. views scattered and unsystematic), then taking the resulting ideas back to the masses, explaining and popularizing them until the masses embrace the ideas as their own, stand up for them and translate them into action by way of testing their correctness. . . . And so on, over and over again, so that each time these ideas emerge with greater correctness.[3]

Pluralism and Interest Groups

Some small measure of popular control enters communist systems through interest groups that take on roles appropriate to Model 2. The Soviet Politburo is subject to some check by the Party Central Committee, by top authority in the army, by the bureaucracy, and by the party *apparat*.[4] In China, Mao's authority waxed and waned from period to period, as other leaders like Liu Shao-chi and Lin Piao were at times able to organize leadership groups against his faction.[5] Because their cooperation is essential, leaders of the military and of the government bureaucracy come to be informally recognized as spokesmen for legitimate interests or volitions in the system.[6] Ethnic groups may compel the attention of top

---

* It is significant, however, that Marxist and communist theorists, including Marx, Lenin, and Stalin, typically reserve the word "democracy" for government that is "by" the people. They do not think that what they dismiss as "bourgeois democracy" is genuine democracy. On the other hand, they do not claim that any existing communist system is democratic. Democratic communism is an aspiration for the future; democracy would be premature if introduced before citizens are sufficiently enlightened to operate it. The frequent rhetorical use of "democracy" by communists, as in the designation, "the people's democracies" is of course at variance with the more careful use of the term and is presumably justified by its propagandistic value. For documentation on this point see papers by J. P. Plamenatz, S. Ossowski, I. deS. Pool, R. Schlesinger, G. C. Field, A. D. Lindsay, R. McKeon, and J. H. A. Logemann in Richard McKeon, ed., *Democracy in a World of Tensions* (Chicago: University of Chicago Press, 1951).

leaders or actually come to play a legitimized role in policy making. This tendency has been especially marked in the U.S.S.R. To some extent the trade unions in communist systems play an interest-group role. For the most part, however, they are part of the apparatus for implementing top leadership's control over the system. The most publicly outspoken interest groups are those of students, artists, writers, and scientists. But in the U.S.S.R. they have only in recent years dared speak in general criticism of the system. Since 1969 various groups of intellectuals have gone so far as to circulate underground explicit statements of dissent, asking for specific major reforms in the direction of liberal democracy.[7] These groups in China and Cuba are still silent except for the brief "Hundred Flowers" episode in China in 1956.

In the Cultural Revolution, top Marxist leaders went so far in violating their loyalties to the Communist Party as to enlist popular support in efforts to unseat their opponents, as was most conspicuous in Mao's enlistment of the Red Guards to loot, smash, and obstruct, as well as mount pointed ideological attacks on Mao's adversaries.[8] Such an enlistment of the masses against leadership no Soviet leader has ever attempted.

The diversity of influences on top government officials and of groups within party and government leads some observers to hypothesize the rise of some degree of pluralism appropriate to Model 2 in the U.S.S.R. and China, as well as for the formation of interest groups. The interpretation has to be received with enormous caution. The principle of pluralism remains subversive. So also does the concept of interest groups, since doctrine is all on the side of Model 1. Nor in official pronouncements are interest groups recognized as in fact existing. It is also assumed that these groups, whatever they are called, are subject to hierarchal controls from the top, not, as in polyarchal societies, to controls from the bottom. Top leadership makes it its business to try to keep them from becoming loci of autonomous thought or action. Leaders use the groups; they do not represent them. The groups are more like personal followings than the interest groups of polyarchal politics.[9]

It is being seriously argued by observers that pluralism and interest groups are becoming significant influences in the communist systems, yet such debate suggests less that communism contains polyarchal elements than that forces foreign to the communist model and to Model 1 are emergent.[10] Some scholars see the U.S.S.R. as a "participatory bureaucracy," or, in reference to institutions like the bureaucracy, party, and military, as an "institutional pluralism."[11] The emergent pluralist forces are weak. Earlier Leninist aspirations toward popular control withered long ago. Yet in the U.S.S.R. since World War II political participation has been significantly on the rise.[12] It is not the same as participation in polyarchies. It is always closely controlled by party leadership. It by no means goes so far as to permit a Rachel Carson to write *Silent Spring* or a Ralph Nader to organize Public Citizen, Inc. Nevertheless, its growth may reveal at least a continuing pressure in the direction of pluralist polyarchy.

In Eastern Europe, in contrast to the U.S.S.R., a greater potential for polyarchy is still fermenting. In 1968, Czechoslovakia briefly loosened censorship, democratized the party, permitted a variety of groups to operate autonomously, and curbed the powers of the secret police in moves described, by some of their advocates, as putting Czechoslovakia on the road to becoming the first democratic socialist state.[13] In Poland, over the years, repeated demonstrations, strikes, and riots by workers have made it clear that elements of democratic pluralism there are stronger than in the U.S.S.R.[14]

It looks as though, if communist systems are to be called humanitarian because they display democratic or polyarchal elements, they are so only to the extent that they fail to approximate Model 1 and turn instead toward at least feeble elements of Model 2.

Liberty

Although not democratic or polyarchic, communist systems, nevertheless, claim to embrace Model 1's vision of a humanitarian society in their concept and practice of liberty.

Liberty as conceived of in polyarchal approximations to Model 2 is of course repressed. Communist systems, everyone knows, largely refuse to their citizens the civil liberties: freedom of thought, speech, religion, assembly, and movement, as well as privacy.[15] In liberal societies these are all highly valued liberties not only for themselves but also because they are specific requirements for polyarchy.*

Nor do communist systems maintain due process.† In any highly

---

* Yet polyarchal governments violate the civil liberties through wiretapping, intercepting mail, and harassment more commonly than we once thought, as, for example, exposure of FBI and CIA practices in the United States have disclosed.

† As, again, the polyarchies do broadly but not without exception. The U.S. Internal Security Act of 1950 established six standby concentration camps—I do not mean gas ovens, however—to be activated at the president's discretion in case of an internal security emergency and gave broad powers to hearings officers to incarcerate citizens without trial, a set of procedures much like those in India that Prime Minister Gandhi used to jail the opposition until she was removed in 1977.

authoritarian system a citizen, as in the case of Nazi Germany, may actually have no options. He is a Jew and he is put to death. Or he is a Chinese landlord or a Russian kulak and is put to death. No trial. No defense. No rights. Short of those extremes, he may be unprotected by "due process" rules. If he is charged with a crime, he may be punished without formal trial, specification of precise charges, and opportunity for defense. It can all be done, as in Communist China, in the absence of formal judicial action, even in the absence of a specific code of law pertinent to the charges.[16]

It was once a plausible hypothesis that all communist systems inevitably used terror as a major method of winning the broadest possible control over subjects' thought and action: middle of the night arrests, unspecified charges, imprisonment, torture, and execution, often on a large scale, as in Stalin's liquidation of the kulaks, Mao's mobilization of the poor peasants to eliminate their landlords, and Castro's executions of hundreds, perhaps thousands, of people he considered actually or potentially subversive.[17] But, although severe repression continues in all these systems, the extremes of terror have abated in all and were never widely practiced in Cuba.

A communist system may revert to terror at any time.[18] The Chinese have returned to it on several occasions, as in the ideological rectification campaign of 1957–1958.[19] It was a full decade after the Bolshevik Revolution that Soviet leadership, in the attempt to impose a new order on Soviet society in the 1930s, stepped terror up to a scale it had never earlier practiced. Estimates are of 1 million executions, 2 million more dead in concentration camps, and 3.5 million dead in the collectivization drive in agriculture in the 1930s alone.[20] For the whole Stalinist period, a common estimate is 30 million deaths in terror.

Yet Communists are not foolish in holding that their societies provide freedom of another kind—appropriate to Model 1. And they will observe —as a benchmark for comparison—that in the polyarchies men are not really free; they only think they are. A communist intellectual asks: "What are people free from in the Soviet Union?" "They are free from exploitation, from all moral oppression, and consequently their thinking and deeds are free from the age-old shackles created by the economic, political and moral rule of the exploiters.[21] It is not a ridiculous argument. In earlier discussion of polyarchal circularities we found many grounds for believing that in polyarchy not only are people indoctrinated—as inevitably in all societies—but they are heavily indoctrinated by leadership and a favored class.

The positive communist claim to a humanitarian concern for freedom —and I shall put the point in its most cautious and acceptable form—is that, since people are at least to some extent deceived in believing themselves to be free when they are in fact the victims of indoctrination, it is at least a possibility that they could be made more free by a reindoctrination that would permit them better to understand their own genuine needs and wants. I see no possible way to deny the truth of that proposition —stated as cautiously as it is. Granting its validity, it is then a possibility— at least a possibility—that communist censorship, indoctrination, and thought control, even in the extremes of their practice in a preceptoral system, might in time make men more free if they were ultimately abandoned. "In place of the old bourgeois society, with its classes and class antagonisms," Marx and Engels wrote in *The Communist Manifesto*, "we shall have an association, in which the free development of each is the condition for the free development of all."

Welfare and Equality

It is in communist provision of minimum standards of living and some degree of equality in the distribution of income and wealth that the communist claim to approximate the humanitarian vision of Model 1 seems undeniable. On these fronts communist systems have to be credited with great accomplishments, on the whole probably greater than those of the polyarchies. These have been communist aspirations since the nineteenth century, when the pursuit of liberty and economic equality, which had been taken up during the Enlightenment, went separate ways. Democrats went to the right, seeking liberty. Communists went to the left, seeking economic equality. More than in European communism, China and Cuba have in recent times refreshed egalitarian hopes throughout the world.

Communism, it has to be noted, has not aspired to political equality and has in fact disdained it in order to justify concentrating political authority in a ruling elite. Nor is its record on social equality distinctive. In the Soviet Union opportunities for higher education are biased toward children of the new upper classes.[22] Although women have been brought into the labor market and into some once male professions, their opportunities are limited in occupations, party, administration, and politics.[23] The age-old persecution of Jews continues, though diminished. In China, women are discriminated against in pay. In many committees and organizations in which they are ostensibly responsible participants, they remain

266

silent or pour tea.[24] In China and the U.S.S.R. rural people lag behind urban in privilege, opportunity, and amenities.

On social equality for minorities and peasants, however, China probably does better than the U.S.S.R., and Mao appeared to intend a complete equality.[25] Educational equality in China and Cuba, if it does not slide toward favoritism to children of officials as in the U.S.S.R., is another indicator of broad differences within the communist family. In the market-oriented family too, nations differ. In education, sex roles, job opportunity, and habits of deference from one class to another, Sweden, for example, is much more egalitarian than the United Kingdom. Social equality may vary more from nation to nation than from communism to market-oriented system, or from communism to polyarchy.

The main achievement is the equalization of income and wealth. Let us try to sort out what communism has done, beginning with welfare programs.

Collective Consumption

If we set China and Cuba against other developing countries of the third world—which seems a reasonable comparison—the two are remarkably egalitarian, as also in comparison with their own prerevolutionary history. China rations cotton cloth, edible oil, coal, and food grains at very low prices. Cuba rations an even greater number of consumer goods and services at low cost, perhaps, however, less for egalitarian principles than for expediency in a period of shortage. Both subsidize housing heavily. In Cuba urban housing costs account for only 10 percent or less of personal income, in China possibly less than 5 percent.[26] Both offer greatly expanded medical services to a large part of the population, some wholly free, some heavily subsidized and available therefore at low cost. And both have greatly expanded the training of medical personnel. Even if the now famous barefoot doctors of China are not doctors but social workers and nurses whose services do not in any case reach the whole population, these and other welfare innovations in China and Cuba set a new pattern for the less developed countries.[27] China's distribution of capital resources not to maximize the economy's growth but to bring some degree of equalization of opportunities among regions is also evidence of a commitment to equality not matched in any earlier communism.[28]

If we set China and Cuba alongside the industrialized polyarchies, both are again probably greatly more egalitarian. In the industrialized polyarchies, the egalitarian possibilities of welfare programs are only cautiously pursued. They continue to move tortoise-like toward more equality under the influence of the persistent forces of the ballot, labor unions in politics, party rivalry, and the egalitarian component of democratic ideology. In so doing, they fall behind the Cuban and Chinese accomplishments. They parallel Soviet communism instead. Yet even Soviet welfare and wage policy has taken a fresh egalitarian turn under Brezhnev.[29]

Comparing only industrialized nations (because level of development is itself a determinant of system characteristics), the market-oriented polyarchies and the industrialized communist systems alike allow a variety of collective goods to their citizens: child care, education, health, housing, transport, entertainment, and cultural activities. In one estimate, these account for 20 to 30 percent of consumption in European communist systems but only 5 to 15 percent in Western Europe.[30] But a more careful study by Pryor that attempts to correct for differences in per capita income and other variables indicates that governmental health and other welfare expenditures, when measured against national product, are roughly the same for European market-oriented and communist systems. Communist systems, however, spend proportionally more public funds on education.[31]

In Table 20.1—again, rough error-prone estimates—showing social security expenditures in 1966 as a percentage of gross nation product, the leaders are the small polyarchies.[32] The U.S.S.R. is well down the list (the United States even further, however).*

A pitfall in interpreting social security and public consumption figures alike is that many of the benefits go to middle and high income groups both in the market-oriented and in the communist nations. The figures tell us something about the government's disposition to begin to build a floor under income but very little about how effectively it is done for the poor.

Wealth

In the private enterprise systems, wealth is distributed in sharp inequality, in contrast to communist systems in which, aside from personal possessions, it is largely government owned. It is a major source of inequality both in the income it generates and in the authority over the nation's assets that it places in the hands of the property owner. By some estimates for the United Kingdom and the United States alike, the wealthiest 1 percent of the population owns roughly 25 percent of the nation's capital.[33] Because in the market-oriented polyarchies roughly a

---

* Affluent complacency in a wealthy country like the United States should not obscure the fact that at the low end of the income scale, where problems of income inadequacy are often exacerbated by ignorance, the circumstances of life are dismal. Inequality in the United States is severe in its effects. The indications of it are more numerous than we care to see. A U.S. Public Health Service study of a sample of 12,000 randomly selected low-income Americans disclosed a surprisingly high frequency of maltnutrition, comparable in severity to that in the poor nations of Africa, Asia, and Latin America, together with a high frequency of associated diseases (New York *Times*, 23 January 1969, pp. 1, 18).

TABLE 20.1
Social Security Expenditures as a Percentage of
Gross National Product, 1966

Nation	Percentage
Austria	21.0
West Germany	19.6
Belgium	18.5
Netherlands	18.3
France	18.3
Sweden	17.5
Italy	17.5
Czechoslovakia	17.2
East Germany	16.4
United Kingdom	14.4
Denmark	13.9
Finland	13.1
Norway	12.6
New Zealand	11.8
Ireland	11.1
U.S.S.R.	10.1
Canada	10.1
Switzerland	9.5
Australia	9.0
Israel	8.0
United States	7.9
Japan	6.2

quarter of national income goes to property, the effect on income of inequality in private property holdings is substantial. On this count alone, economic equality in communist systems is significantly greater than in the market-oriented polyarchies.

Earnings

Statistics on earnings from wages and salaries are grandly unreliable. Many are based on tax returns, on which there is widespread cheating. And different countries define income in different ways. For a large group of countries—less developed and industrialized countries—the best single though partial statistical estimate of wage and salary income is probably Lydall's (which omits greatly unequal incomes from capital).

Taking 100 to represent for each country the median per capita wage and salary income (before taxes) paid to nonfarm males, he estimates the corresponding figure for the 95th percentile, the 90th, and the 25th.

TABLE 20.2
Inequality of Income Expressed
as a Percentage of Median Income

	95th percentile	90th percentile	25th percentile
Czechoslovakia, 1964	165	145	85
New Zealand, 1960–61	178	150	83
Hungary, 1964	180	155	83
Australia, 1959–60	185	157	84
Denmark, 1956	200	160	82
United Kingdom, 1960–61	200	162	80
Sweden, 1959	200	165	78
Yugoslavia, 1963	200	166	80
Poland, 1960	200	170	76
West Germany, 1957	205	165	77
Canada, 1960–61	205	166	79
Belgium, 1964	206	164	82
United States	206	167	75
Austria, 1957	210	170	80
Netherlands, 1959	205	175	70
Argentina, 1961	215	175	75
Spain, 1964	220	180	75
U.S.S.R., 1959	245	195	69
Finland, 1960	250	200	73
France, 1963	280	205	73
Japan, 1955	270	211	64
Brazil, 1953	380	250	. .
India, 1958–59	400	300	65
Ceylon, 1963	400	300	. .
Chile, 1964	400	300	. .
Mexico, 1960	450	280	65

For Czechoslovakia, for example, the columns show that per capita the 95th percentile received 65 percent more than the median income, the 90th percentile 45 percent more, and the 25th percentile only 85 percent of the median. The countries are thus ranked according to increasing inequality. The increase in inequality is, as can be seen, large.[34]

In Table 20.2 it can be seen that the less developed market-oriented countries are the most unequal.* Of industrialized nations, U.S.S.R. wage

* As very poor countries begin to grow, as egalitarian squalor is replaced, as new jobs and incomes develop, a more inegalitarian distribution of income arises, although eventually (with high income) its distribution again begins to move in the direction of more equality (Irma Adelman and Cynthia Taft Morris, *Economic Growth and Social Equity in Developing Countries* [Stanford, Calif.: Stanford University Press, 1973], esp. p. 188).

TABLE 20.3

Inequality of Income Standardized for
Population and Per Capita Income

	95th percentile	90th percentile	25th percentile
European communist systems	202	169	77
Western Europe	238	189	71
Or, standardized for a higher level of gross national product per capita			
European communist systems	184	155	82
Western Europe	216	173	76

and salary income at that date was more unequal than the United States or Britain but less so than Japan and France. China is not included, but fragmentary evidence on its wage structure might put it somewhere between Denmark and the Soviet Union. Again, nations within a category differ more than do the categories themselves, and level of development is an important determinant of distribution. Since these calculations were made, the Soviet wage structure under Brezhnev has moved significantly toward more equality and is perhaps more equal than that of the United States.[35]

Because, as just noted, capital is governmentally owned in the communist countries but is an additional source of income inequality in market-oriented societies, Lydall's figures overstate the degree of equality in the market-oriented systems. On the other hand, if agricultural incomes which are low, were included for the U.S.S.R., it would appear as greatly more inegalitarian than in the table.[36]

Pryor has tried to correct the Lydall estimates to make comparisons between countries of equal size and stage of development. Standardized for population and per capita income, the results are as seen in Table 20.3.[37] Thus, even without the egalitarian effects of collective ownership of property, the communist systems are more egalitarian than their market-oriented counterparts.*

---

* A similar estimate by Peter Wiles of income of all kinds after taxes except capital gains but excluding farm income in the U.S.S.R. shows that the most egalitarian nations include both communist and noncommunist and that the United States is

For more information on Chinese wage structure we have to turn to reports from visitors and other scattered evidence. The reports vary, partly because the wage categories are not carefully specified. Some observers suggest that not unlike the United States upper-level industrial wages are five times the lowest rates. Almost all observers agree that wage differences have been greater than China's egalitarian rhetoric had led them to expect. If rural incomes are compared with urban, inequality has been even more pronounced.[38] Still, leaving agricultural-industrial inequality aside, the Chinese wage structure has probably been somewhat more egalitarian than either the American or the Soviet.

Because some necessities are rationed and high incomes can be spent only on additional goods and services available only at prices pegged at very high levels, a high wage does not imply a proportionately high real income as it would in a market-oriented systems. Moreover, China's declared wage policy is to hold industrial wages down as far as possible in order to reduce urban-rural inequality and to narrow wage differentials. Both are egalitarian policies.[39] Cuba's wage structure shows a substantial wage-rate inequality coupled again with only limited uses for high money income.[40] In both countries, conventional wage differentials mask a probable greater degree of equality than in the polyarchies or in European communism.*

Taxes and Transfers

Sometimes it is argued that taxes make money distribution in the polyarchies much more equal than so far indicated, hence more like China or Cuba. But taxes fall on everyone. The effect of taxes, consequently, is to achieve only a modest redistribution of income in the industrialized polyarchies. By one estimate, taxes reduce by about 20 percent the income share going to the upper 10 percent of income recipients in Australia and the United Kingdom, which are among the most egalitarian of the polyarchies. The reduction for West Germany and the United States is only about 7 percent.[41] If we take into account both taxes and transfer expenditures

---

considerably less egalitarian than the U.S.S.R. For each country a ratio is indicated between the income of a person at the 95th percentile line and one at the 5th. Thus, for Sweden, the former has three times the income of the latter. The results are as follows: Sweden, 3.0; Hungary, 4.0; Czechoslovakia, 4.3; United Kingdom, 5.0; U.S.S.R., 5.7; Denmark, 6.0; Canada, 12.0; United States, 12.7 (Wiles, *Distribution of Income,* pp. xiv, 48).

* We are all tempted to use numbers for measurement, even when they mismeasure, simply because they are available. But the point just made—that the magnitude of inequality associated with wage differentials depends on what can be bought, and at what price, with money income—makes clear that we cannot find any numbers that even roughly represent real income differentials as they vary from European communism to China, Cuba, and the market-oriented systems.

like social security, the results are only slightly changed: a small percentage shift from high money income receivers to low with a broad middle class neither gaining nor losing.[42] Social services and collective expenditures are paid for largely by those who receive them.

Some public expenditure increases rather than reduces income equality. In the United States, for example, the state university system subsidizes the education of students who, as it turns out, come disproportionately from the wealthiest families. A calculation of farm aid programs in 1969 estimated that $53 million was shared by 264 of the largest farmers, and an equal amount by 540,000 of the smallest.[43]

In the polyarchies, it is widely believed that the trend is in the direction of income equality. If so, it is a slow movement, so slow that it is now being debated whether the movement has quietly expired in the last few decades, while the U.S.S.R. by contrast moves significantly toward more equality.[44] In all the polyarchies a barrier to substantial equalization of income, if it were desired, is inequality in the distribution of wealth. Beyond some point wealth has to be collectivized or redistributed if more income equality is desired.[45] The possibilities of further income redistribution or redistribution of wealth then turn not on technical features of market system but on polyarchal politics, especially on the constraints on popular control discussed in earlier chapters. In private enterprise systems, moves toward equality are a threat to a large and disproportionately influential segment of the population. Political obstacles to equalization are often much reduced in some authoritarian systems.

A New Privileged Elite

If inequality in money income and wealth is a major barrier to economic equality, it does not follow that collective ownership of wealth removes the barrier. The wealthy enjoy authority over the nation's assets and special income derived from their property rights in them. To socialize the same assets does not eliminate the need for control over them. The transfer of control from a property-owning elite to a governmental elite not subject to popular control is no necessary gain. If the new managers of the nation's assets use their government positions to win new privileges, perquisites, and shares of income, there is no necessary change at all in the degree of income equality.

Elites have always feathered their nests, and communist elites do so to some degree. In the U.S.S.R. we noted some restriction of higher education to children of the elite. The U.S.S.R. also offers its elites automobiles, large apartments, country homes, servants, superior social clubs, medical care and privileged access to food, drink, and foreign travel.[46] That Cuba's elite is somewhat self-indulgent is becoming apparent, though the magnitude of the phenomenon is difficult to estimate.[47] For China, it is reported that influence will win "scarce goods, higher pay, and cushy assignments."[48] It is not clear how to compare these indulgences with those of the very rich in market-oriented systems, except to say that they are very much alike.

On Balance

A reasonable summary on income and wealth in communism and the polyarchies might be something like the following: Several of the industrialized polyarchies, not including the United States, have probably achieved more equality than any European communist system. As a family of systems, however, the polyarchies are almost certainly significantly less egalitarian than the communist family. The distribution of private wealth is greatly unequal in all private enterprise market-oriented systems. Authority over wealth, however, is unequally distributed in both kinds of systems—in the hands of the wealthy in the one kind of system, in the hands of the governmental elite in the other.

Communism in less developed countries like China and Cuba achieves greatly more equality than market systems achieve in comparable countries—India, Mexico, or any Latin American country. Compared with industrialized nations, China and Cuba stand out as special cases. In both, leadership has at one time or another committed itself to a degree of egalitarianism beyond anything attempted in European communism or in any polyarchy. "Some day," Castro has said, "we shall all have to receive the same."[49] And both countries have almost certainly achieved a degree of equality greater than in any other communist or market-oriented system, except for some of the smallest and most egalitarian polyarchies like Norway. One cannot, however, predict either the maintenance of such equality as has been achieved or its enlargement in the future. In Cuba leadership has already drawn back from its fullest commitment to equality —as we shall see in the next chapter. Mao's egalitarianism came under attack immediately after his death.

One egalitarian accomplishment of communist systems, already referred to in Chapter 6, is their great reduction of unemployment. Because communist systems do not acknowledge unemployment to be a problem, they do not report statistics on it. But observers agree that unemployment is not the problem it is in market-oriented systems. Employees are kept on the payroll in circumstances in which they would be let go in market-oriented systems. The result is, of course, some wasteful use of labor and some underemployment—probably a great amount of it in China. But almost every able-bodied adult male and a high proportion of females hold secure jobs. If they must be dismissed because no longer needed, their transfer to new jobs is relatively speedy. Communist policy in this respect is an alternative to unemployment compensation, which is not part of the social security system in communist countries. Rights to compensation expire, whereas the communist right to a job does not. Most thoughtful people perhaps believe there is a difference between, on one hand, keeping a worker in the status of a participating member of the community and, on the other hand, supporting him with a monetary benefit in periods in which he is exiled from it.

Preceptoral "Education" and Moral Incentives

THE enlightened ruling elite of Model 1 may choose to rule through "education" in what we have called a preceptoral system rather than through conventional authority. It is the preceptoral vision combined with the vision of Model 1 that suggests a major possibility of a revolutionary transformation of society such as communism has nowhere yet actually achieved—a profound revolution, whether nightmare or utopia. In Model 1 is the vision of an informed, theoretically enlightened elite. In the preceptoral model, from chapter 4, is an all-encompassing saturating "education" designed to reduce the system's dependence on bureaucratic and other authority by stimulating voluntary initiatives and wide-ranging resourcefulness in the discharge of energies that authoritative coordination cannot tap.

The Preceptoral Element in China

Less clearly now but conspicuously only a few years ago, China may have been developing a fundamentally new form of social organization through an unprecedented use of the many forms of persuasion and indoctrination that, in the preceptoral model, we labeled "education."[1] The Great Leap Forward of 1958 to 1960 was a massive—and heroic, it is perhaps fair to say—attempt to achieve through an outpouring of "educated" energy a greater advance than could be achieved through conventional coordinated planning. It was accompanied by decentralization of bureaucratic control over productive units, development of communes in agriculture, and an intensified ideological campaign.

The Cultural Revolution of 1965 to 1969 was a different kind of convulsion. It was a massive campaign for ideological rectification, again testifying to Mao's faith in persuasion and his extraordinary determination to transform society with it. It was mobilized not to increase production but to "educate" men and organizations that Mao believed were obstructing the continuing revolution in Chinese society. It was, consequently, a deeply divisive struggle for leadership of the revolution. Mao found himself increasingly on the attack against a bureaucratic party organization, increasingly in need therefore of some alternative source of organized support, which he found in hastily mobilized groups of youths, the Red Guards. They in turn were supported by the People's Liberation Army, for which they were sometimes only a front. The PLA finally not only put them down but also in large part for a time replaced the party in its functions. "Education" was in principle central to the Cultural Revolution. However, it was in fact accompanied by intimidation, coercion, outright violence, and military actions approaching civil war.[2]

The communist "new man" was to be achieved through preceptoral "education." He is to be a man "with no selfish interests, heart and soul for the people." Many visitors to China claim to have met these new men, however improbable that may seem. Chinese preoccupation with his creation has been more intense by far than the Soviet attempts. The Soviet Union has never attempted quite the massive ideological education represented for a time by the once universal circulation within China of the little red book, *Quotations from Chairman Mao*. It was studied, along with oral instruction in the thought of Mao, in countless meetings of adults and children in army, school, factory, shops, playgroups, communes, and the fields.

A difference is apparent again in Mao's and Lenin's attitudes toward mass "spontaneity." Lenin, like Mao, believed that the spontaneously expressed discontent of workers and peasants is often insufficiently revolutionary. It displays a cautious "trade union consciousness," easily dissipated in the pursuit of trivial gains. It is thus actually obstructive to revolutionary change. To Mao these very possibilities signal the need for "education" to redirect mass discontent, rather than Lenin's subordination of discontent groups to the authority of the communist party.[3]

In the Soviet Union, moreover, class struggle is structural, that is, a conflict between two classes. Mao sees it as a continuing struggle within each individual, between an older and corrupt man and the new man. That being so, it calls for "education" more than for new forms of authority to destroy vestiges of the old class.[4]

In a preceptoral system, we earlier saw, right attitudes are critical. Technical competence is downgraded. While the Soviet Union moved relatively quickly to a balance in industrial management in favor of the "expert" instead of the "Red," Chinese policy on the Red-expert issue went to an extreme of emphasis on right attitude over competence in the Great Leap Forward and again in the Cultural Revolution. Since 1971, China has, however, retreated again toward expertise.[5]

A corresponding feature of a preceptoral system, we saw, is an antagonism to specialization. In Chinese enterprises, unlike those of the U.S.S.R., managers, technicians, other experts, and skilled workers do a variety of jobs. And—at least for a time—managers often spent two days a week, sometimes more, doing ordinary work in the plant.[6] Energy, flexibility, resourcefulness, and varied initiatives are more valued than fine-tuned authoritative coordination.

In these innovations, Mao turned against both Adam Smith's now legendary specialized pin makers and the Soviet Union's highly specialized Stakhanovites. In these respects, preceptoral "education," we have seen, is part of a worldwide current of thought in which motivation is stressed at the expense of coordination. This new current is extraordinarily heterogeneous. It includes youth movements in the United States, some labor movements in Western Europe that seek participatory democracy, new forms of industrial engineering in which the assembly line is abandoned in favor of less specialized work assignments, and new developments in economic theory. Among economic theorists far removed from Maoist thought, a new interest in energetic resourcefulness in the business enterprise is illustrated by Leibenstein's seminal article on X-efficiency.[7] This aspect of a preceptoral system—resourcefulness rather than fine-tuned coordination—suggests an affinity of the system not with Model 1 but with Model 2. It accounts for much of China's appeal to many Westerners.

Mao, the Great Preceptor in Chinese communism, believed that "education" can make men capable of solving the whole range of human problems, from making bicycles "faster, better, and cheaper" to eliminating poverty or liberating the human spirit.[8] Yet the Chinese emphasis on "education" may not long outlive him.[9] China has already retreated to a degree from earlier decentralization of authority, foreshadowing a possible reemphasis on a conventional authority system over a preceptoral.[10]

A great deal of Chinese "education" is in any case only a pretense of a preceptoral system. It is in actual fact a device for surveillance, intimidation, invasion of privacy, brainwashing, and the other horrors of a would-be omniscient authoritarian regime. Authority rather than persuasion remains the main instrument of elite control in China. When, for example, China wants industrial workers to move out into the countryside, they go "voluntarily" under threat of reprisal.[11] And Chinese leaders themselves observe:

> Quite a number of party organizations and cadres fail to consult the masses before they make decisions and issue instructions. Moreover, in the process of carrying out these decisions and instructions, they do not try to persuade and educate the masses, but simply resort to issuing orders to get things done.[12]

In other ways, "education" is transformed into influence of different character, as in the "subtle transformation of the study of Mao's quotations from an act of creative learning to a new ritual of political control," from study to chanting and group rote recitation.[13]

Yet visitors, scholars, and persons who have interviewed refugees often comment on what could turn out to be a remarkable characteristic of a new Chinese society (the evidence is not at all strong, however):

> Refugees, both intellectual and nonintellectual, are articulate; and . . . they have the habit of analyzing (*fenhsi*) everything. Even peasants, dirty and clad in rags, will talk with eloquence about their experiences. . . . The Chinese communists have a habit of analyzing everything that happens in everyday life.[14]

The Preceptoral Element in Cuba

In the mid-1960s, in the face of obvious economic difficulties from inappropriate policies, Cuba turned away from institutions and policies imitative of the Soviet Union. Briefly, from 1966 to 1970, Cuban leadership was instead intensely committed to molding a new Cuban man through "education." "Society as a whole," Che Guevara declared, "must become a huge school."[15] In the Chinese mass campaign style, energies were also whipped up for vast collective efforts for a variety of specific tasks, like harvesting sugarcane or teaching illiterates to read.

As in China, Cuban preceptoral elements were often disguises for—or at least operated simultaneously with—the conventional repressive devices of authoritarianism. The Committees for the Defense of the Revolution announced as among their laudable purposes:

> It [each committee] will cooperate voluntarily in all operations and necessary steps of the productive process.
> It will organize discussion groups . . . to increase the political and civic capacity of all its members.
> . . . it will make sure that no one illiterate remains within its radius of action.

It will organize public audiences when the leaders of the revolution speak to the people.

But Castro's original announcement of the committees set another tone, and an ominous one:

> We're going to set up a system of collective vigilance. . . . Everybody will know everybody else in his block, what they do, what relationship they had with the tyranny, what they believe in, what people they meet, what activities they participate in.[16]

As we have also noted, Cuba like China relied in that period on the military to do what "education" often failed to do. As some observers saw it at the time, "The image of the army has become the image of society."[17]

Evidences of straightforward coercive authority rather than preceptoral "education" in Cuba have multiplied since about 1970. At that time Castro began to turn toward a more orthodox Soviet model of communism. On the one hand, various institutional reforms were introduced to separate army, party, and state administration. Similar reforms attempted to establish a variety of well-defined institutional responsibilities. They appeared in such diverse forms as integration of planning procedures, on one hand, and reintroduction of a scale of officers' ranks in the military. Cuban government became less personalistic and more bureaucratic. At the same time, farmers, workers, and youth were brought under more detailed authoritative control. Ideological conformity in education and cultural activities was enforced by new stringency in criminal law.[18] A once enthusiastic attempt at preceptoral "education" appeared to be coming to a close, though not without a legacy of doctrine that might bring the movement to life again, for good or bad, under less austere economic conditions.

Organization of the Labor Force

In addition to its diffused use throughout society, persuasion or "education" in a preceptoral system is, at least hypothetically, a specific way to organize the labor force. At least until Mao's death, China pursued such a course as a supplement to conventional authority, through substituting moral for market incentives. And for a few years, in the form of an extraordinary campaign to tap moral incentives, Cuba tried to pursue "education" to its limits. Their experiences are a preliminary test of moral incentives for a world that is almost certain to wish to test them further. They also provide more specific evidence of what "education" means in actual practice in economic organization.

For a time, what caught Western attention as the most conspicuous revolutionary feature of Chinese society was the commune. It was an extreme venture in preceptoral "education," no less than an attempt to transform, through a new form of social organization, the whole incentive structure surrounding workers in agriculture and in industry—to the degree communes were introduced in the cities. The commune was not a successful Chinese experiment with moral incentives, but its role in agriculture and the conventional communist alternatives to it are part of the story of moral incentives.

Agricultural Organization[19]

In the early heady years of Soviet communism, communal organization of agriculture was attempted in a small scale. It was abandoned after 1931. Then came forced collectivization and heavy compulsory deliveries of produce to the state, the latter a burden on agricultural enterprises not lightened until after Stalin's death.[20]

China's communal experiment was much broader. In the Great Leap Forward at the end of the 1950s, China established communes of several thousand families each as, among other things, a new method of cooperative production and consumption that would presumably tap moral incentives to replace market incentives. Capital, equipment, tasks and output were to be shared. Meals were distributed free in communal dining halls. Members were guaranteed—or were to be guaranteed—basic free supplies of clothing, medical care, housing, fuel, and services ranging from burials to haircuts. Free supply may have accounted, for a brief period in some communes, for as much as a half of peasant income.

The Chinese venture failed because of both management and incentive difficulties, some rooted in traditional family and clan cohesiveness. Communes quickly lost most of their economic functions, and production was then organized through smaller collectives—usually production teams of ten to twenty-five families. Free supply, as well as communal dining, was abandoned. The commune is now only the unit of local government charged with conventional functions, planning for local industry and agriculture, and operation of some local industry.*

---

* The brigade, a unit of perhaps 200 families on the average, oversees the work of the teams, nominates team leaders, and controls inputs of machinery, water, and electric power, as well as the allocations of educational and health services. The party at brigade level is responsible for ideological education of the teams.

The team consisting of perhaps thirty households typically, is the basic farming

Possibly communes were never viewed as more than an interim arrangement. The conventional long-term communist aspiration looks toward a quite different form of organization. Communists hold that socialist property is ideologically superior to private or cooperative property. For that and other reasons as well, the conventional long-term ambition is to organize the enormous agricultural sector bureaucratically like industry, specifically to establish large-scale, state-owned farms managed like factories.

But because communist systems have been discouraged in this ambition both by politically dangerous resistance from the peasants and by the inefficiencies—at least to this date—of state farms, none has yet forced all agriculture into that mold. Hence, communes having failed, communists today organize agriculture largely through combinations of authoritative and market direction, working through private, cooperative, and public enterprise.*

---

unit, the unit closest in function to the Soviet collective or the American farm. For ideological reasons there continues to be controversy among top leaders over the desirability of moving back to a larger unit when management and incentives systems can be devised to permit it. See Frederick W. Crook, "The Commune System in the People's Republic of China, 1963–74," U.S. Congress, Joint Economic Committee, Joint Committee Print, *China: A Reassessment of the Economy,* 94th Congress, 1st session, 1975. Also Prybyla, *Political Economy,* pp. 286–93; and William L. Parish, "China—Team, Brigade, or Commune?," *Problems of Communism* 25 (March-April 1976).

* The basic production units are the following: the state farms, in which individual farmers, like industrial workers in a factory, are hired for wages; the collective, which sells production primarily to the state, either freely or under compulsion, and whose members take their incomes out of whatever the collective manages to earn (and are sometimes paid minimum wages plus a share of earnings); the private farm (in Cuba, Poland, and Yugoslavia); and the private plot, which is the small piece of land for each member of a collective on which the family can produce for its own consumption and for sale. The collective is usually organized as a cooperative but, regardless of legal form, it is controlled by party and state.

In the U.S.S.R. less than half the heavily cultivated land is in state farms, more than half in collectives. In the Soviet Union, the average size of a state farm is about 600 workers, of a collective, 400 households; and work is organized by production teams each more or less permanently assigned to some section of the farm (Paul Dibb, "Soviet Agriculture since Khrushchev: An Economic Appraisal," in *Comparative Economic Systems: A Reader,* ed. Marshall I. Goldman, 2nd ed. [New York: Random House, 1971], p. 385). In China only 4 percent of the heavily cultivated land is in state farms (Audrey Donnithorne, *China's Economic System* [New York: Praeger, 1967], p. 96). Neither country permits private farms. In Cuba, in which sugar plantation agriculture is dominant, state farms account for 70 percent of cultivated land, leaving 30 percent for private farms often so closely controlled by government as to reduce the owner-cultivator to something close to a salaried manager or farm employee. (Leo Huberman and Paul M. Sweezy, *Socialism in Cuba* [New York: Monthly Review Press, 1969], p. 128; and Archibald R. M. Ritter, *The Economic Development of Revolutionary Cuba: Strategy and Performance* [New York: Praeger, 1974], pp. 236–40.) Cuba's declared policy is gradually to eliminate the private farms. (Mesa-Lago, *Cuba in the 1970's,* pp. 88–92.)

Today in all the communist systems, state and collective farms are organized much like enterprises or industry. Inputs to state and collective farms are for the most part authoritatively assigned to the farms much as inputs are assigned to industrial enterprises. Farm managers are, however, allowed some discretionary funds for purchase of inputs. They also engage in barter and other transactions which, although mostly illegal, are in fact permitted them so that they can achieve their output goals.

As for outputs from farm enterprises, state farms deliver quotas, as do factories. Collectives and private farms are compelled, prodded, and induced in a variety of ways which are often combined in any one country at any one time. They include: simple compulsory delivery to the state; taxes in kind, which are roughly equivalent to compulsory deliveries to the state; incentive prices for sales to the state; and free sale of a portion of output.[21] In European communism until recently a trend seemed clear: away from compulsion toward market-induced output. But, responsive to internal policy conflict, China moves for a time in one direction, then in the other.

Private Plots

The dependence of communism on market rather than moral incentives in agriculture is all the more conspicuous in the small private plots. They are assigned in most communist systems by the collective farm for the private use of the family. Families grow products (and sometimes raise livestock) for their own use. The family is usually also permitted to sell in organized peasant markets, although from time to time China has tried to eliminate sales from private plots and may do so again.[22]

Productivity in the private plots has always been much higher than in the state farm or collective, and not only because vegetables and other high productivity outputs are largely given over to private plots. The incentive to produce on the private plot is high, and it continuously saps the peasants' incentives to work for the collective. Variously estimated, between a fifth and a third of gross value of agricultural output as a whole in the Soviet Union comes from private plots, embracing only about 3 percent of sown land.[23] In China private plots, which cover perhaps 5 percent of sown land, have been estimated to account for as much as a third of agricultural output.[24]

The productivity of the private plots is, of course, the other side of the coin of low productivity in farms operating on quotas and targets and subject to the generalized exhortations of communist "education." Organized Soviet agriculture stagnated under Stalin, stagnated again after 1968. Thirty-five years after the revolution, Khrushchev himself acknowledged that grain production and numbers of cattle were below the figures for 1916.[25] Not a single communist system has met with much success in agriculture, even by its leaders' own admission, without reverting in great degree to market-system inducements to produce. Agriculture has been not the bright future but the big failure of communist authority.

Moral Incentives for Rural and Urban Labor

The story of moral incentives in rural and urban wage employment is somewhat brighter that the history of agriculture, at least in China.[26]

Controls over Labor

In communist systems labor has been and still is allocated and energized in largest part by a combination of authoritative direction and market incentives. Moral incentives need to be seen against that background. As in the market-oriented systems, workers in most communist systems are recruited into jobs or induced to move from one job to another by the offer of a job for pay. In all communist systems market incentives for the labor force are manipulated by top leadership and planners in order to induce the labor force to do what is centrally planned for them to do, although market manipulation may be of little significance in China today. For example, wages are kept lower in nonpriority occupations. In agriculture and trades, wages are lower than for industry, transport, and construction.[27]

Authoritative assignment of labor supplements the market. Until recently the U.S.S.R. attempted to use a passport system to control movement from farm to city. In World War II and variably at other times, the Soviet Union has frozen workers into their jobs, permitted movement only with government permission, or allocated scarce kinds of labor. The current situation is relatively free movement and free choice of jobs. Today the principal authoritative assignment remaining—and widely evaded—may be of graduates of technical training schools and universities after graduation, as well as of members of the Communist Party and youth organizations. The Eastern European systems are in these respects much like the U.S.S.R.[28]

China differs in that job assignments are more often compulsory. Since the Cultural Revolution perhaps all industrial employment is administratively assigned.[29] Workers are not free to leave their jobs without permission. And controls on movement and job changes are generally imposed to prevent movement of rural workers into the cities, as well as to compel urban workers to move into rural areas.[30] As especially in the Great Leap Forward, China has drafted millions of students, office workers, and teachers along with peasants and soldiers in special work projects, particularly in water conservation projects.[31]

In Cuba workers are not allowed to leave their jobs without government permission.[32] In addition, a great amount of part-time labor is compulsory—sometimes labeled voluntary. Labor has been required of students as well as ordinary job holders. Estimates are that 8 to 12 percent of tasks that would ordinarily be done by paid labor have been done by unpaid labor of one kind or another in Cuba.[33] But "voluntary" labor is now being restricted in favor of wage labor.[34] Another distinctive use of authority to organize the labor force has been compulsory military conscription. The army, part of which is unarmed, has served as a large administratively allocable work force.[35] "In normal times, all for production. In times of danger, all for defense."[36] However, although the army's labor brigades are now being separated from the army, they continue to be organized on military lines.[37]

Communist governments do not share their control of labor with labor unions. Although they were temporarily disbanded in China during the Cultural Revolution, unions ordinarily exist in communist systems. But their role is that of an agency of the government, and their principal functions are to increase worker productivity and to scrutinize managerial performance.[38]

Training programs are another method of allocation of labor. Although all politico-economic systems use such an allocative mechanism, communist systems appear to do so more deliberately and ambitiously. Thus, by one estimate, in nine years after the Liberation, Chinese enrollment in specialized vocational-technical schools was quadrupled. Moreover, better than 90 percent of China's higher-educated engineers and scientists have been trained since the Liberation. The growth in higher education was twice as fast as India's, even though the less deliberately planned Indian growth rate since Independence in 1947 was itself extraordinary.[39]

Professing an antagonism to the market system and in fact sharply reducing its functions in industry, the Soviet Union and China alike have nevertheless driven or induced millions of women into the labor market. It is estimated that from the Liberation in 1949 up to 1960, women workers in the Chinese labor market, excluding most rural agricultural workers, rose from 600,000 to 8 million; and by 1963 women constituted one-fourth of urban employment. The Soviet Union has gone even further;

there roughly half of industrial employment is female.[40] Paradoxically, for urban women, life in a labor market milieu is more typical of communism than of the market-oriented polyarchies.

The Introduction of Moral Incentives

Experiment with moral incentives does not simply disestablish the labor market controls just outlined. Instead it has taken two modest supplementary forms: first, reducing wage differentials, bonuses, piece rates, overtime pay and other monetary distinctions; and, second, substituting the devices of "education" to induce the worker to respond to government appeals and do his best in his job without thought of monetary reward. The full panoply of preceptoral methods is brought to bear.

Compared to European communist systems, China uses bonuses, piece rates, overtime pay, and other special monetary rewards sparingly; and it has narrowed wage differentials, as we saw in the preceding chapter.[41] At the peak of the movement toward moral incentives, Cuba may have gone further than China. Even if it has now leaned far from them in a reinstitution of monetary incentives, the earlier experience in Cuba remains significant.

According to one view, the key moral incentive is the inducement in the Maoist slogan to "Serve the people!" and, in Castro's words, in the "sense of solidarity and brotherhood among men." The pleasure of work itself is another major, though secondary, theme. Castro has said:

> And if we want all men to work some day with such spirit, it will not suffice just to have a sense of duty. [That kind of] moral motivation will not be enough. It will be necessary for the marvelous nature of the work itself, work directed by man's intelligence, to be one of the basic motivations.[42]

In both Cuba and China, moral incentives owe something to the pursuit of equality, which calls for the reduction of market incentives. They owe something to austerity, which calls for incentives that are less costly than real income. They also owe something to Marxian antimarket ideology. Finally they owe something to leadership's desire to instill a sense of responsibility in the national community.

Yet in actual practice, in Cuba and China—less so in European communist systems—a common form of moral incentive has been competition: for a badge, banner, or title of rank, like the Soviet "Hero of Labor, the Cuban May Day banner or Heroic Guerrilla award, and the Chinese Labor Hero award. Workers could also compete for travel opportunities, expensive consumer goods, attendance at prestigious meetings, even an interview with Premier Castro or Chairman Mao.[43] Notice that the "moral" incentives are not in fact always intangible.[44]

The awards are usually won through "socialist emulation," which is competition of an institutionalized form. In Cuba points were given to workers and work groups according to degree of plan fulfillment, as well as for quality, assistance, punctuality, and professional improvement. In this respect, the moral incentive system substituted intangible score points for pesos, and operated as a kind of price system, in which points rather than money amounts were varied to induce specific kinds of performance.[45] In recent years socialist emulation has been tied to wage bonuses and distribution of consumer goods.

Emulation was first greatly publicized in the Soviet Union. In a massive effort beginning in 1935, individual workers—but more often groups of workers—were induced to compete, and exceed if possible, Alexei Stakhanov's feat of producing 102 tons of coal in one shift.[46] But emulation campaigns had origins at least as early as 1930.[47]

Socialist emulation looks much like a halfway house between market rivalry and the incentives of service to the society. After Castro was caught up with his ambition to create a "new man," the use of emulation declined in favor of less competitive motivation, and then perhaps was reinvigorated, though with more material and fewer moral rewards.[48] Emulation is disputed in China though still practiced.[49]

Another moral incentive is participation. In Cuba and China alike, workers are also brought into various kinds of meetings with officials, enterprise managers, or other workers to discuss ways of improving productivity, to deliberate on enterprise policy, and to evaluate each other's work. An economist reports from his visit to China an example that he thinks representative of what he found in industry.

> The Second Bicycle Factory in Tientsin received many complaints from customers that its product was too slow and heavy. The plant decided to replace scattered steel balls in the middle shaft by ball brackets to make the bike easier to ride, but it seemed that this would increase the cost. . . . Could this quality improvement be accomplished without increasing the cost? . . . Through an analytic struggle the plant aimed to carry out the "general line" of "greater, faster, better and cheaper."
>
> . . . All personnel attended various meetings and many formed problem-solving teams consisting of managers, technicians, and workers. Employees submitted more than three hundred "innovation" measures for practicing economy. . . .[50]

It is difficult to know just what to make of such a case as this. Is it a common practice? Many visitors to China, it is clear, are impressed by an innovative spirit.[51]

Meetings in the workplace do not put control of enterprises in the hands of employees. They are intended instead to create both a sense of participation and actual participation in implementation of plans made higher up. Production conferences in the Soviet Union perform some of these functions, but the careful cultivation of the worker through a variety of small group and mass assemblies is more distinctive to Cuba and China. Even in the Soviet Union, however, the production councils, together with other forms of interchange and instruments of mass propaganda, have succeeded in creating, as in Cuba and China, an ideology of production. Production comes to be a conspicuous and vivid collective goal as it perhaps never is in the market-oriented systems.[52]

Moral incentives, like preceptoral "education" generally, have often been in both China and Cuba a disguise for outright authority and often for coercive authority. In Cuba, for example, workers who have not responded to moral incentives are transferred, have sometimes been put in corrective labor camps, are publicly ridiculed through wall posters, or find their wages cut.[53]

The Record

"Money," Castro has said, "is a vile intermediary" to be eliminated as soon as possible.[54] Yet his interest in moral incentives has perhaps been more practical than principled. He was not won over to moral incentives by Che Guevara's highly moral espousal of them until he found Cuba unable to make satisfactory progress on two fronts simultaneously: consumption and investment in growth. It was then he opted for motivating the Cuban population, not with higher wages, with which they would want to buy more consumer goods which were not available, but with moral incentives.[55]

The pursuit of moral incentives in Cuba dates from the mid-1960s to about 1970. Since 1970, Castro has reinstated an earlier system of work norms and salary scales, measures of work performance, restriction on distribution of free goods, and distribution of consumer durables through work centers where they can be used as material incentives.[56] He has also explicitly reconsidered his earlier enthusiasm for the new man, recognizing that the development of the required new consciousness will take longer than he once thought.[57] Over the years too China has vacillated in its mixture of market and moral incentives.

Cuban leadership judged moral incentives to be not very successful. Cuba was plagued with low productivity, poor job discipline, and unusually high rates of absenteeism, all recognized by Cuban leadership itself to constitute grave problems. Agricultural and industrial productivity lagged, and industry turned out goods of low quality. Gross national product declined rather than grew in some years and it is quite possible that in as late as 1970 it was less than in 1959.[58]

Productivity of unpaid labor in Cuba has been especially low, not entirely for lack of incentive but also because it is wastefully used by managers who do not have to pay for it. Castro's frank acknowledgement of the problem indicates its magnitude. "Managers," he said,

> try to solve all their problems through the use of unpaid labor. . . . Often, they are employed to fill out the shift of agricultural laborers that only work three or four hours per day. . . . [Everybody] seeks the easier solution instead of attacking the problem at its roots.[59]

Other curious derangements suggest at least the transitional if not the permanent difficulties of moving away from money incentives; for example, liberal sugar rations at extraordinarily low prices have been fed to chickens and pigs.[60]

Cuba's emulation campaigns have been appraised—there is some room, however, for differences in judgment—as "rigid, complicated, formal, and bureaucratic"; they have not "generated mass support." Workplace meetings for the discussion of enterprise plans have been given various appraisals. Some observers are satisfied that such meetings do not much engage workers; others believe that they do.[61]

Cuba has been driven back more than once from heavier use of moral incentives in agriculture by their dampening effect on agricultural output and has had to cope with peasant slaughter of livestock when market incentives did not persuade the peasant to keep his stock alive.

China has not had Cuba's severe problem of failure of incentives in industry, yet has been able for twenty years to hold wages down to stimulate growth while achieving constantly rising productivity. It is a remarkable achievement either of moral incentives or of outright authoritative control over Chinese labor.[62] The continuation of moral incentives may also reflect a more pragmatic caution in experimenting with them and a restoration at several critical junctures of monetary incentives in agriculture.

Neither Cuba's difficulties nor China's caution with moral incentives constitute anything approaching proof that they cannot be made effective. In both systems, they were introduced concomitant with an attempt to create a new man rather than after. If in Cuba contemporary man will not respond sufficiently to moral incentives, it still remains a possibility that new men might. Moreover, the pressure of economic hardship has hardly permitted time for a fair trial; and the constant urgent attempt to do better than last year made leadership impatient. Castro stayed with his firm commitment to moral incentives for only five years. In both systems, too, the potential appeal of moral incentives has been weakened by some significant disorganization of management and work schedules, not surprising in a period of revolutionary transition and new responsibilities for inexperienced managers. Finally, moral incentives in both systems may also have been weakened by evidence apparent to ordinary workers and peasants of favors toward managers, bureaucrats, and party officials inconsistent with the egalitarian appeals of moral incentives.[63]

In a broad retreat from an appeal to national altruism in Cuba and perhaps in China, both continue to lean on altruism in participatory small groups. Thus the team (which is sometimes the clan or extended family) displaces the commune in Chinese agriculture. Each team is paid as a unit for its combined labor, and individual shares are for the team itself to decide.

* * *

"Money," the young Marx wrote, ". . . is the universal confusion and transposition of all things, the inverted world, the confusion and transposition of all natural and human qualities."[64] It is this theme, picked up in Cuba and China as in the early days of the U.S.S.R., that has stimulated the most revolutionary aspect of communism, the attempts to replace monetary with moral incentives. Yet, we have seen, it has never been more than a highly qualified attempt. And it has always been rivaled by practical exercises in setting monetary incentives aside not for moral ones but for nothing more novel than authoritative command, often highly coercive.

The Politics of
Business Enterprise

ALL communist systems use the market to distribute planned production. Most consumer goods and services are sold, not simply rationed without price. All communist systems use a labor market in order to attract labor into those lines of production that leadership has planned (although we have seen that in China administrative allocation of labor may have almost entirely supplanted market allocation). The market system also plays several roles in agriculture.

When communist systems are characterized as nonmarket systems, it is because the market system is not greatly employed in determining, outside of agriculture, what is to be produced and how inputs are to be allocated and used. These decisions are made authoritatively by top leadership and planners.

Thus, the unfolding possibilities of Chinese and Cuban egalitarianism aside, the principal innovation in communism has been administrative: a new form of business enterprise, together with a new method for setting its assignments, coordinating it with other business enterprises, and putting resources at its disposal. In that sense, communism has so far been more a technocratic or organizational revolution than a social one.

In a market-oriented enterprise, "domestic" affairs are organized largely by an internal hierarchy-bureaucracy. "Foreign" affairs—relations with other firms, input suppliers, and customers—are handled through a market system. Communism applies those authoritative, hierarchical, and bureaucratic controls that operate *within* large enterprises in all industrialized systems to relations *between* enterprises. In communist systems, both "domestic" and "foreign" affairs of the enterprise are managed by hierarchy-bureaucracy in a straightforward aspiration to achieve Model 1.

The Core Elements

In rough outline, control of nonagricultural production in communist systems takes the following form:

1. Top authorities and their planning staffs decide on what is to be produced and how resources are to be allocated. They then issue input quotas and output targets to production units. For regional or local production units, they issue quotas and targets to subsidiary functional or regional organizations, which in turn then plan and issue targets and quotas to production units under their jurisdictions.

2. To achieve some decentralization of lower order decisions, the productive agencies are organized as business enterprises (credited in monetary terms for their output, charged money costs for their inputs, and required to cover their money outlays through their receipts) rather than operated as ordinary government bureaus. Enterprise managers are often then paid premiums or bonuses tied to outputs, costs, and other performance indicators.

3. Although hypothetically a communist government could actively manipulate prices to induce output or input changes, with some exceptions for agricultural enterprises they do not do so. The evidence is that over long periods of years prices remain unchanged. Quotas and targets are immensely more important than prices in guiding enterprises. Even if not deliberately manipulated for control purposes, however, prices constantly press communist enterprises to avoid high-priced inputs and low-priced outputs. This is so because enterprises have to cover their costs and because bonuses are tied to performance measured in monetary terms.

4. In contrast to firms in market systems, the constant problem that enterprises face is not sales but supplies. Sales are usually assured. Allotments of inputs are always scarce.

5. For this reason and also because plans cannot foresee all possible contingencies (despite their Model 1 aspirations), the planners are in a constant interaction with enterprises in the style of Model 2, in which they

292

ceaselessly revise targets and quotas. Similarly, enterprises endlessly negotiate to obtain more inputs and to avoid high output targets.[1]

6. For the same reasons, enterprises engage heavily, again in the style of Model 2, in mutual help—trading inputs and outputs with other enterprises and seeking and granting favors in order to obtain supplies inadequately allocated by the planners. Although most of this mutually adjustive activity is illegal, it is in fact tolerated by planners and top authority. In some of this activity, enterprises operate in a crude black-market or grey-market system.

7. Being without adequate price information for achieving an efficient plan and largely occupied therefore with seeking only a consistent plan,[*] top authorities and planners try to insure that no more is assigned of any given input than is available and that no resources go unused (that is, they try to make sure that supplies will equal demands). To do this, planners employ an accounting in physical units of available supplies and uses of inputs. This is the method of planning by "materials balances."

In all these respects, communist systems differ somewhat among themselves. The Eastern European systems are largely modeled after the Soviet system, except for Yugoslavia and Hungary. After earlier experimentation with deviations from the Soviet model, Cuba now largely follows the Soviet model, although planning for so small and simple an economy is hardly comparable with the intricacies of Soviet economic administration.[†] China differs from the Soviet model in all the ways that would be predicted from the larger preceptoral element in Chinese communism: probably somewhat more autonomy for the enterprise, probably more unplanned buying and selling among Chinese enterprises, and greatly reduced use of financial incentives for enterprise managers accompanied by a greater dependence on moral appeals.[‡]

---

[*] For reasons given in chapter 7.

[†] Cuba's population is 9 million as against the U.S.S.R.'s 250 million and China's three-quarter billion or more. Its gross national industrial product is perhaps $6 billion compared with the U.S.S.R.'s $600 billion and China's possible $250 billion (World Bank, *World Bank Atlas* [Washington, D.C., 1975], pp. 28–29). It is not a highly diversified economy, like the other two, but overwhelmingly given to the production of sugar. On Cuban industrial planning, see Carmelo Mesa-Lago, *Cuba in the 1970's* (Albuquerque: University of New Mexico Press, 1974), pp. 30–32.

[‡] China is less technologically advanced than the U.S.S.R. Industry is a smaller sector of the economy in China than in the U.S.S.R., although the relatively greater modernization of the Soviet economy may have moved resources from conventional industry to the service "industries," thus leaving Chinese and Soviet conventional industry at about the same size relative to the whole economy. The economy is also much smaller than the Soviet. Output is about one-third to one-half of Soviet output. Moreover, a larger amount of industrial output in China is produced for internal use in small firms and workplaces attached to communes or other farm collectives. Similarly, because production methods are simpler than in the U.S.S.R., Chinese business enterprises go further than Soviet enterprises in making intermediate goods and

Characteristic Difficulties

Castro has said: "Inefficiency and low productivity are the bottomless pit that swallows up the country's resources."[2] We shall see that Soviet and Chinese leaders express similar concerns. Shortcomings of communist economic organization were once hotly debated, and some still are. But communists and noncommunists alike have gradually come to agree that communist systems, like market systems with their standard list of defects, are also plagued by a characteristic list of deficiencies.

The deficiencies are just those imperfections of hierarchy-bureaucracy outlined in chapter 5. They consist of general difficulties of rational choice in authority systems and of difficulties specific to economic choice in such systems. They include, consequently, both problems of over-centralization and failures in coordination of decentralized hierarchies. They include problems of inadequate criteria for input allocations and, more universally, inadequate measures of costs. They also include difficulties—some would say impossibilities—of finding a satisfactory performance measure or success indicator for the enterprise. All, it will be remembered, are problems for which efficiency prices and markets offer solutions. Or, to put it the other way around, all are problems that arise in the absence of efficiency prices and market system. The shortcomings do not constitute, however, a conclusive ground for rejecting communism any more than the standard defects of markets offer conclusive ground for rejecting the market system.

The Growth Record

Despite the characteristic difficulties of authoritative direction of industry, communist growth rates are comparatively strong. Very long-time per capita growth rates for the U.S.S.R. can be compared with "hundred year" rates for other systems, as in Table 22.1.

Soviet growth rates are, of course, much higher after the Revolution of 1917. They are matched by Sweden and Japan but are far greater than the

---

equipment for their own use. The national economy is thus less integrated. There is less to be centrally planned and less to be centrally coordinated. Chinese capacities for collecting and processing information, on which all central planning depends, are in any case inferior to Soviet. See Audrey Donnithorne, "China's Cellular Economy: Some Economic Trends since the Cultural Revolution," *China Quarterly* 52 (October-December, 1972); Yuan-li Wu, "Planning Management, and Economic Development in Communist China," in U.S. Congress, Joint Economic Committee, *An Economic Profile of Mainland China*, 90th Congress, 1st session, 1967; and Richman, *Industrial Society*, pp. 464–65.

TABLE 22.1

Growth Rates of New Developed Countries[3]

Developed country	Period	Average Per Capita Growth Per Decade of National Product (in constant prices)
United Kingdom	1780–1881	13.4%
	1855–1959	14.1
France	1840–1962	17.9
United States	1839–1962	17.2
Sweden	1861–1962	28.3
Japan	1879–1961	26.4
Russia/U.S.S.R.	1860–1913	14.4
	1913–1958	27.4
	1928–1958	43.9

United States, the United Kingdom, and France. But note the very high rate for the U.S.S.R. between 1928 and 1958.

A calculation of industrial growth rates comparing communist Eastern Europe from 1960 to 1968 with thirteen market-oriented systems and the United States shows an average aggregate annual industrial output growth of 7.6 percent for the former and 5.7 percent for the latter.[4]

China's growth is impressive whether measured against the communist or against market-oriented systems. The World Bank estimates China's annual growth rate per capita for the thirteen years from 1960 to 1973 at 3.8 percent, compared with 3.6 percent for the U.S.S.R. and 3.1 for the percent for the United States.[5] Another roughly consistent estimate for China shows an annual aggregate growth rate of gross national product of 5.2 percent from 1957 to 1974.[6] Table 22.2 below estimates China's aggregate growth at 5.6 percent, compared with 5.3 percent for the U.S.S.R. and 4.3 percent for the United States.

Table 22.2 displays an array of rates for a recent thirteen-year period—rougher estimates than the decimals imply. It shows that communist systems do not match the front-runners like Japan and Brazil. But this comparison is less favorable for the communist systems than the 1960–68 comparison of industrial growth and reflects in part the declining growth rates in European communist systems that became apparent in the 1960s. Since 1958, the Soviet Union's growth performance has not been distinguished when compared with other nations of similar per capita income.

Estimates of Cuba's growth rates are extremely rough. For the two years immediately following the revolution, gross national product may have grown 10 percent each year. The next few years are obscure, but

TABLE 22.2
Growth Rates of Total Product, 1960–73 in the Twenty-five Countries with the Largest 1974 Gross National Products[7]

Country	1960–73 Average Annual Aggregate Output Growth Rate (percent)
Japan	10.6
Iran	9.8
Spain	7.0
Mexico	6.9
Brazil	6.6
France	5.7
China	5.6
U.S.S.R.	5.3
Netherlands	5.3
Australia	5.1
Italy	5.0
Austria	4.9
Poland	4.8
Belgium	4.8
Denmark	4.6
West Germany	4.6
United States	4.3
Switzerland	4.3
Argentina	4.2
India	3.5
East Germany	3.0
United Kingdom	2.9
Czechoslovakia	2.9

gross national product may have dropped 30 percent between 1965 and 1970, the period of emphasis on moral incentives. Since then Castro has claimed annual gains of between 5 and 13 percent.[8]

The Special Problem of Technological Lag in European Communism

"Communism," said Lenin, "equals Soviet power plus the electrification of the whole country." It is engineers whom the Soviets train in large numbers and engineers whose careers sometimes come to a peak in the

Politburo. It might be expected, then, that communism would demonstrate an unusual capacity to find or invent and to install advanced technology. Indeed, in some circumstances communist systems do so. Soviet space and military technology and China's development of the atomic bomb are persuasive on the point.

Yet a shortcoming in European communism, which preceptoral elements in Chinese Communism may be able to avoid, has been technological backwardness. Communists themselves deplore it. Special circumstances aside, the general Soviet formula for development has not been a high level of technological proficiency. Instead, development has been achieved through a rapid shift of labor from agriculture to industry and an extraordinary mobilization of capital through forced savings (from 1928 to 1937), to create new industries. And by these methods the Soviet Union achieved in thirty years what the United States, Japan, and other Western nations took fifty to sixty years to achieve.[9]

The contemporary Soviet problem is that these methods have played out. No further great shift of manpower or mobilization of capital is possible. Leadership is also concerned because the productivity of capital and labor in the Soviet and European communist systems has been declining.[10] Technological advance does not offset diminishing returns from investment, as it does in other industrialized systems. Growth of man-hour labor productivity, once higher in the Soviet Union than in any of the most industrialized market-oriented systems, has (since 1958) fallen behind, as Kosygin lamented at the 1966 Party Congress.[11] The European communist systems have identified the same problem. Of Czechoslovakia, Ota Šik wrote: "In 1962–1963 the growth of productivity of labour actually stopped."[12] The communist systems of Europe have been faced with slowing growth rates* and find themselves dependent on the same sources of innovation as the market-oriented systems: inventions, adaptation of innovations from abroad, and rapid diffusion of inventions and innovations into actual production processes. All this is needed in addition to the improvements in planning that have been achieved over the years.

It is too early to say how successfully China, as it becomes more indus-

---

* From 1950 to 1955, Soviet gross national product rose by almost 7 percent each year. During the following five years, the average increase was only 6 percent. For the next following five years, 1960–65, the rate fell again down to 5 percent, where it remained into the 1970s (Cohn, "Analysis of the Soviet Growth Model," p. 248). And in Eastern Europe, for the period 1955–60, growth in half the Eastern European systems had fallen below 1950–55; and for 1960–65, except for Romania, they fell further (Frederick L. Pryor, *Property and Industrial Organization in Communist and Capitalist Nations* [Bloomington: Indiana University Press, 1973], p. 218). See also Joseph S. Berliner, "Prospects for Technological Progress," in U.S. Congress, Joint Economic Committee, *Soviet Economy in a New Perspective,* 94th Congress, 2d session, 1976.

trialized, will in its turn practice technological innovation; but both the Soviet Union and neighboring communist systems of Europe acknowledge alarm at their own technological incapacities. It has become an embarrassment to many Soviet leaders to have to admit that the principal source of past growth had been new inputs of industrial labor and investment capital made possible by forced savings. There is no evidence that eliminating the "anarchy" of the market and turning society toward a "scientific" organization of its productive resources in the style of Model 1 could claim the major credit for earlier successes of the Soviet system. In official pronouncements, the problem is sometimes "couched in terms usually reserved for major national emergencies."[13] The director of the Institute of Economics of the U.S.S.R. writes:

> . . . the planning of scientific and technical progress must, objectively, be the leading link of the whole system of national economic planning. Yet, hitherto, this link has perhaps actually been the most lagging link in the whole complex. . . .[14]

One major source of difficulty is that Soviet-style politico-economic organization was designed for a much simpler economy and society than those of the contemporary U.S.S.R. and Eastern Europe. The number of products—the Soviets sometimes say 20 million—is a large multiple of the number produced when the five-year plans were first inaugurated in 1928. The 3 million workers in industry in 1928 have now become roughly ten times that many. And the techniques of industrial production have become increasingly complex.

The problem is starkly put by communist difficulties in foreign trade. Because of technological clumsiness, other than armaments the Soviet Union can sell only a few of its industrial products abroad outside the communist orbit, except through special arrangements, such as foreign aid that compels recipients to buy Soviet goods. Its industrial products have not met international standards of quality. East Germany and Czechoslovakia, the most technologically advanced of the Eastern European systems, are only beginning to produce successfully for world industrial markets. A Czech study observes:

> The fact that Czechoslovak machinery can command on West European markets in general under two-thirds of the per-kilogram prices attained by capitalist competitors, although the factor inputs for the Czechoslovak goods are often higher, is due to a lower technological level, inferior quality in the widest sense, inadequate equipment and servicing, etc.[15]

Why does technological innovation lag? The simplest answer is that communist enterprises are without the incentives to innovate that propel enterprises in market-oriented systems. Innovation is dangerous to an enterprise manager in a system in which he is required to meet output quotas. If he experiments with new technology, he may fail to achieve his quota. If he succeeds, he fears that new quotas will be imposed on him.[16]

But that answer is incomplete. Presumably, in recognition of the weakness of innovative motives at the enterprise level, leadership will locate responsibility for innovation elsewhere. They do. Pressure for innovation comes down from above, from party and from specialized institutions for encouraging innovation, such as special plans (as a component of annual economic plans) drawn up for innovation, directives ordering production of new kinds of products, engineering design bureaus, technical publications, and canvassing of technical publications abroad. But these methods have not been generally successful.

The party as an innovating institution has lost its own innovating zeal with age (and never had the zeal in some of the smaller European countries). Increasingly it is specialized to ideological defense of the system—and of itself—and to supervision of personnel in government and industry. The engineering design bureaus are themselves deficient in incentives. The machine-building industry, through which innovation is actively promoted in market-oriented systems by machine salesmen who find users for new technologies, suffers from weakness in its own motivation to innovate. Formal planning for technological innovation is subject to all the defects of planning already identified above, and plan achievement in this sector is among the lowest of all sectors of the economy. It is also Soviet practice to skimp on allocations and funds for capital replacement. And for various institutional reasons, even after a decision is made to build a new plant or convert to a new technique of production, it takes two or three times as long to accomplish the task as it does in the market-oriented polyarchies.[17]

Reform and the Politics of Markets

As a result of deficiencies of the Soviet and East European communist systems, which it became possible to discuss there only after Stalin's death in 1953, reform was almost everywhere a serious prospect in the 1960s.[18] What European communists believed they needed was a cure for over-centralization and a release of initiatives and inventiveness for growth. Under Khrushchev, modest regional administration had been tried and had subsequently been abandoned as unsuccessful. The prospect of a greater and different kind of decentralization was appealing to many. But decentralized units still need some form of coordination. How to accomplish it? The market seemed a possibility. Could it be a new instrument for growth?

Except for Albania, all the European systems were caught up in the reform movement. Yugoslavia had already departed from the standard communist model and now departed further. Hungary began and has continued a significant restructuring in the direction of market socialism. Drawing on a liberal democratic tradition unique in Eastern Europe, Czechoslovakia's reformers went so far toward market and political liberalization as to provoke a Soviet invasion that imposed a return to the *status quo ante*.[19]

The key ideas in reform were liberalization, decentralization, and market system, and they can thus be viewed as a modest challenge of Model 2 to Model 1. At some risk of oversimplification, the reforms announced by Kosygin for the U.S.S.R. in 1965 can be described as attempting:

Some shift toward value targets rather than physical targets for enterprises: from a criterion of physical output maximization to one of profitability.

Some reduction in the number of targets imposed on the enterprise in order to give the enterprise more flexibility in efficient use of its inputs.

Some enlargement of enterprise authority to make its own arrangements for obtaining inputs, that is, some new use of interenterprise market transactions rather than administrative allocations of inputs.

Crediting firms (in some cases) with output only on successful sale of output rather than, as before, for output produced regardless of its acceptability to customers.

New financial incentives for managers and employees tied to enterprise profitability.

Limited price reforms that would have the effect of moving prices toward efficiency pricing.[20]

The "technical" appearance of these reforms hides what we shall see were far-reaching implications. No sooner did the reforms begin to take effect than the Soviet leadership drew back from them. By the 1970s, it was clear that in all the communist systems except Hungary and Yugoslavia, the reformer's expectations were being disappointed. In a poll of Soviet enterprise managers, almost 80 percent reported no actual change in the purportedly reformed supply system under which they operated, and 56 percent reported no such increase in their independence as the reforms promised.[21] Even at the time, the market reforms were challenged by reforms of a different spirit—those designed to make planning more scientific in the style of Model 1.[22]

If we determine why the market reforms were begun, why opposed, and why largely then aborted, we will better understand communism, especially the never-ending conflict between Models 1 and 2, which every kind of society resolves in its own distinctive way. We will also better understand the powerful implications of market systems for politics, especially for authority that aspires to rule as in Model 1, even when market systems are only timidly expanded as proposed in the reforms.

Supporting Currents of Thought

Independently of declining performance, various currents of thought supported reform. The existence of grey and black markets, as well as other interactions characteristic of Model 2, may have persuaded some leaders that, if these interactions could not be suppressed, they might better be made more systematically useful through market reform. As noted in chapter 2, a bureaucracy is sometimes very much like a badly organized market.

Economists were among the chief participants in the reform debate. Having been to a degree liberated from Stalinist constraints, they began to draw on Western economic theory and to let their views be heard on principles of economic choice, value, cost, and pricing. A long-standing obstacle to such a discussion had been the identification in communist thought of market system with capitalism. Economists drew a careful distinction, at great peril to themselves if they were misunderstood. Thus:

> From all these categories the smell of the capitalist spirit is very strong. Would it not be better to avoid these categories?
>
> No, it would not be better! When we are discussing the choice of methods for controlling our social production there exists only one choice criterion: to what extent they lead to raising its efficiency. . . .
>
> The market method of regulation, profit and flexible prices . . . can be criticised only because capitalism appeared on the earth before socialism, and to the extent that these can bring advantages to a socialist economy, they must find their place in it.[23]

Students of the controversy continue to disagree on whether ferment among enterprise managers and technicians was an important source of reform. In their inclination to set engineering and economic considerations above politics and in their professionalism, they are argued to have become an obstruction to monolithic party control. A considerable body of evidence, on the other hand, indicates that, taken as a whole, they remained docile and politically impotent.[24]

Yet as Soviet society advanced into industrial complexity and as an ever widening flow of highly educated persons took up specialist roles in Soviet society, a new intelligentsia of engineers, economists, scientists, students, artists and writers, professors, and other scholars began to argue the case for a less monolithic society. They had an effect beyond what they said when Soviet leadership began to fear that productive incentives for these new specialists would suffer without some degree of liberalization of the system.[25]

Some of them subsumed the demand for economic reform under a broader explicit demand for liberty and democracy. In the second of Sakharov's famous declarations, in 1970, in which he was joined by two other scientists, he urged "the further democratization of the social life of our country."[26] Earlier ideas of democratizing the workplace through employee participation in management, lost to Soviet thought after a flurry in the early days of the Bolshevik Revolution, were also resurrected. Even the mathematical economists interlarded their technical arguments on economic reform with such democratic demands as "democratization of management . . . for the development of creative activity of popular masses."[27]

Other currents were at work: for example, the attempt of the intelligentsia to win through economic reform higher incomes for themselves, a phenomenon especially important in Eastern European reforms.[28] A demand for "constitutional" rights for peasants in the collectives was also voiced.[29]

Resistance

Reform was resisted on small grounds and large, out of confusion and for good reason, opportunistically and in solemn regard for the society's future.

One large ground for resistance is that reform became broadly subversive. When economic reform came to be tied to demands for democracy and liberty—for example, in the underground circulation of the passage on civil liberties from the United Nations Universal Declaration of Human Rights—it challenged the whole system.[30]

In the light of an elite's claim to competence, appropriate to Model 1, the mere voicing of fundamental criticism is in a profound sense subversive, even beyond its technical illegality. And to criticize a communist state is to reveal a point of view different from the state's. That again is subversive in implying the legitimacy of a plurality of interests. The Olympian position of the state was also undercut by arguments that, just as industrial managers need targets and performance indicators, so also do party cadres and government officials.[31]

Some actual experiments in putting enterprise managers into market relations also became disturbing. The largest innovation was in agriculture, where the managers of the collectives had been given somewhat greater authority to operate as profit-seeking enterprises. Two consequences revealed how subversive a market-oriented management could be. It came to be alleged that the farm enterprise, the kolkhoz, now needed "rights" to guarantee its ability to operate in the market. And peasants began to show some signs of voicing demands as an interest group.[32] Model 2 threatened to displace Model 1.

Reform of Pricing

Yet it would seem that more restricted "technical" reforms of pricing and markets—far short of adoption of a market system as a whole— might have been possible without subversive implications. Why, we must ask, did a modest impetus toward technical reform and efficiency prices abort?

It is often said that the prices used by communist enterprises—specifically Soviet enterprise prices—are arbitrary. That is, they are not approximations to efficiency or scarcity prices that arise out of free buying and selling by enterprises in a market system. If, however, they are not efficiency prices in any degree and are wholly arbitrary, it does not help a planner or administrator to make any use of them at all. He might as well keep his accounts in tons or some other physical unit.

In fact, prices used by communist enterprises are rough—extremely crude—efficiency prices. Although not systematically tied to relative scarcities as in market systems and consequently exceedingly distorted, they are not simply random or arbitrary. They are in certain specific ways loosely related to relative scarcities.*

The evidence for this is that they bear a recognizable family resemblance to prices prevailing in market-oriented systems. Communist prices are inherited from market prices prevailing before communism. Moreover, communist price setting continues to be influenced by prices prevailing in the market-oriented systems, though it is hard to say how closely and systematically. Stalin referred approvingly, for example, to an opinion of Central Committee members that "cotton is altogether much dearer than grain, as the prices of cotton and grain in the world market testify."[33] In addition, prices are heavily influenced, because of the Marxian labor

---

* We are concerned here only with prices that are used by planners and managers to weigh their decisions. Prices at which consumer goods are actually sold to consumers are irrelevant to this discussion. In principle the prices set on consumer goods are set (often through the device of turnover tax) at whatever level necessary to dispose of consumer goods at a rate neither faster nor slower than the planners desire, but in fact prices are rarely changed and queues and informal rationing are often the consequence.

theory of value, by relative labor inputs. Other things being equal, a commodity with a high labor input is given a higher price than one with a lower or lower-skill labor input. Since labor is a major scarce input in any productive system, labor inputs also figure heavily in efficiency pricing. The prices most removed from efficiency prices are those on land and capital because Marxian doctrine forbids rent and interest. But at least in the Soviet Union and Eastern Europe, ideologically unobjectionable disguises are found for incorporating into prices various charges that replace—but not at all accurately—rent and interest.

Although communist prices are rough efficiency prices, it needs stressing how rough they are. In the case of the Soviet Union they have been characterized as a "monstrous irrationality." Chinese and Cuban prices are similarly defective.[34]

Let us put the question sharply. Since communist systems use prices, and since they use them because they are at least extremely crude efficiency prices, why would a modest movement to improve pricing abort?

One reason is that most Soviet engineers and other planners do not understand pricing. Pricing reforms were urged by economists on grounds of improving evaluation, substituting less scarce for more scarce resources, and adapting output targets to costs of achieving them. Engineers admired technological sophistication for its own sake without regard to cost. They therefore prized the technologically best way to produce rather than the way best adapted to cost. It was the same conflict that for many years in the United States divided military leadership, who wanted weapons of the most advanced technology, from the economists whom they hired as advisors. The economists wanted not extraordinarily expensive weaponry at the technological frontier but instead "the biggest bang for a buck."

Moreover, price reform is a big and discouraging job. There are perhaps 20 million Soviet prices. Another is that it is economically disruptive. The transition to a new set of prices would be difficult. Some industries would permanently suffer. When the anticipated dislocations were set against the anticipated gains in efficiency, the former seemed too large to many officials, who in any case do not understand efficiency prices well enough to be confident of their importance. The explanations are much the same as could be given for the continued disinclination of the U.S. government to revise the arbitrary prices that tariffs impose on many imports. Reformist arguments in the United States meet with the same indifference from officials who either do not understand or do not see any merit in efficiency prices; and the prospective losses to some industries are large enough to chill reform.

Another objection to improved pricing is that, although the purpose of introducing efficiency prices is to let value and scarcity considerations achieve a major influence on decisions on production, investment, technologies, industrial location, and the like, these are all decisions in which various groups had big stakes. Many local party leaders, for example, preferred to continue a system in which, say, location of an enterprise is determined not by economic evaluation but by political considerations important to their jobs. They are not much different from American senators and congressmen who disregard economics when they engage in pork-barreling.[35] The military was hostile to pricing reform because it feared a redirection of the economy toward the consumer and away from heavy industry.[36]

In its relations with the Eastern European systems, the Soviet Union might be described, moreover, as wishing to protect a vested interest of the whole Soviet system. In Eastern Europe market reform was seen as necessary for the success of the East European systems in trade with Western Europe. For that very reason, pricing reform posed a threat to Soviet domination of these nations and to trade relations between each of them and the Soviet Union. Soviet leaders knew that some pure reforms would remove these nations somewhat from dependency on the Soviet Union as their trade with Western Europe grew. They also knew that some Eastern European leadership wished to cultivate trade for just that reason.[37]

Implicit in moving toward efficiency pricing was a potential major readjustment of politico-economic structure and roles. Communists understand this better than we do in our society, where comprehensive price transformations have never been an issue. As early as 1938, for example, Molotov warned that "prices concerned politics not economics."[38]

A further particular objection to pricing reform was that the new prices would reflect consumer preferences rather than leadership's. Here lies a serious confusion shared by many Soviet leaders and foreign observers alike.[39] Price reforms need not be designed to reflect consumer preferences. They can be made to reflect leaders' preferences, we have seen, as in the model of a planned sovereignty market system.*

Still, there remains a problem. All the world's existing market systems are built around a core of consumer purchases. Prices in all of them largely reflect consumer preferences. No society has yet designed a set of prices to

---

* Or to reflect a combination of leaders' preferences and consumers' preferences, as would likely suit communist leadership in market-oriented reform. Over a wide area of consumer choice, communist leadership has everything to gain by accommodating consumer preferences. Insofar as leadership wants to limit the total amount of consumer goods production or the production of certain consumer goods that leadership thinks important, say, to health, it has at hand adequate instruments for constraining total consumer demand (through wage policy and taxation) and for discouraging or encouraging the consumption of particular commodities and services (through taxes on or subsidies to them). Thus it can achieve any combination it wishes of planner sovereignty and consumer sovereignty through the market. See Alec Nove, "Planners' Preferences, Priorities, and Reforms," *Economic Journal* 76 (June 1966).

reflect leaders' preferences. Understandably, then, it is not entirely clear to Soviet leadership or to anyone else, including Western economists, just how in actual practice it is to be done.

It is not enough that in the Soviet Union and Eastern European systems there are economists who grasp the concept of a planner sovereignty market system, any more than it was enough in the United States that economists after Keynes understood that new methods of economic stabilization were now possible. Keynesian insights into controlling depression and inflation, insights that called for only modest alterations in public policy, took between twenty and thirty years to move from the economics journals into widespread acceptance in Congress.

The idea of planner sovereignty in a market system is not easy to grasp —that by substituting a set of markets linked to end-product planning targets, central authority can direct an entire economy without conventional administrative controls. The idea was perhaps all the more difficult to grasp because the communist systems are all caught in a particular conflict between administrative control over the enterprise and a secondary control system effected through financial controls. In the Soviet Union a poorly designed set of prices constantly tempts enterprises, in pursuit of low input prices and high output prices, to make decisions contrary to their administrative instructions. The result is tighter and tighter administrative controls to close the loopholes.[40] Not surprisingly, top authority comes to see control through prices as an obstruction to its will rather than a potential instrument of its will.

A single final objection to pricing reform, for a few who understood the objection, is that the only known way to institute efficiency pricing according either to consumer preferences or planner preferences, is to create actual markets.* The practical implication of pricing reform is that the reformers have to stomach not simply a new set of prices but a market system as a whole. They have to establish an entire set of markets linking final demands from government back through intermediate industries to labor markets and markets for natural resources. Reform of pricing is no small alteration in economic organization. It goes to the heart of the roles of government and market.

Enterprise Autonomy

If what might be passed off as only a "technical" reform of pricing actually implied establishing a market system, it is even less surprising that the administrative changes proposed—more enterprise autonomy—turned out to have disturbing political implications.

* In contrast to synthetic markets with computed prices, which were shown in chapter 7 to be impossible, at least at existing and emerging levels of expertise.

306

Why did the reforms not go at least far enough to enlarge enterprise autonomy and win the advantages of decentralization? Among several reasons, one was that many enterprise managers actually feared the new responsibilities that would be thrust on them. They doubted they had the distinctive new skills that would be required.[41] And party officials whose careers had been given to administrative supervision, even "petty tutelage" of enterprises, feared for their careers.[42] While administrative decentralization had increased the authority of regional or provincial officials at the expense of central administrators, direct decentralization to enterprises would not have.[43]

More important, it appears that as the Soviets began to decentralize—to give enterprises some freedom as to how and with what inputs they would achieve their output targets—it became apparent that a reformed enterprise could make efficient decisions about inputs only if prices were not arbitrary. If they were arbitrary, the enterprises would underuse high-priced inputs and demand low-priced inputs excessively regardless of the real scarcity and productivity of the inputs. Such decentralist reforms as were actually implemented in Soviet and East European communism often worked very badly because the old prices prevailed and misdirected the enterprise. Reform of enterprise autonomy could not stand on its own feet. It required reform of pricing.

Duality of Leadership

Aside from that objection to enterprise autonomy is another: communist objections to the duality of leadership characteristic of market-oriented systems and to the privileged position of enterprise managers in them. At an extreme, and for good reason, they fear the rise of "industrial tsars."[44]

To establish a market system in a communist society requires that enterprise managers must be free to refuse to produce what top authority asks for unless it is willing to pay the price. A substantial duality of leadership is therefore as necessary in a communist market system as in any other. It is not merely a consequence of private property. Moreover, a rules system is required—rules to constrain higher officials from commanding what they are unwilling to pay for. To effect control at high level, top officials must agree that at a lower level their hands are to be tied. Such an arrangement may not have the "smell of capitalism," but it has a faint smell of constitutional liberalism for the managerial elite. Even assuming that communist leadership did not take a dim view of insolent bargainers, the new regime would be one of reciprocal control rather than unilateral control through command.

Soviet leadership would suffer its greatest loss of control to the new leaders on what we have called delegated decisions. Market systems, we noted in chapter 11, give consumers or planners a relatively immediate control over the end products to be produced but not over delegated decisions, such as those on plant location, technologies, organization of the work force, and executive recruitment, among others. Delegated decisions are controlled by purchases of consumers or planners only insofar as competition or some equivalent cost-reducing discipline forces managers to find least-cost solutions. We indicated grounds for doubting that any such discipline is effective. And if governmental leaders want, say, to locate plants in such a way as to equalize regional development or achieve some other specific purpose, the market system sends no such signal or instruction to enterprise managers.

As a device to implement top authority's control of the economy, a planner sovereignty market system differs from administrative controls in a critical way. As noted in chapter 11, the one controls through specifying end results, the other by specifying procedures. In a planner sovereignty market system, to achieve more effective control of enterprise responses to production targets in the plan, top authority has to surrender many of those controls it would otherwise use to regulate the whole production process. The problem is the emergence of a counterpart to the privileged position of business in private enterprise systems. It is not at all clear that even an informed and rational top leadership would accept such a state of affairs.[45]

Moreover, the establishment of a dual leadership on major matters of public policy might be expected to bring additional complications in its wake. One is the demand for more trade union autonomy. The market system commits enterprise managers to pursue a certain partisan efficiency in resource allocation—in disregard of other national objectives that might bear on, say, plant location or choice of technologies. As a result of market reforms, the enterprise manager would become therefore the first avowedly specialist or partisan leader in the style of Model 2—one who does not "in theory" pursue the one single collective national interest that at present all communist leadership, according to communist ideology, serves. Trade unions might be argued to be a necessary counterpoise to him. Even if the new partisan managers remain outside "politics" as "politics" is ordinarily conceived, they constitute on their own account and on account of counterpoise groups that can be expected to oppose them a significant pluralist innovation in the system.

* * *

It is not the resolution of the conflict of the 1960s over market reform but the conflict itself that is illuminating. Unable to live up to the aspirations of Model 1, in the 1960s Soviet leadership and technicians opened their minds more than they had for many decades to the possible advantages of a large admixture of Model 2. Eventually they drew back from taking a new course. The considerations that impelled them forward reveal fundamental problems in politico-economic organization by authority. The considerations that held them back reveal the powerful impact of market on politics. We saw that impact in the analysis of polyarchy. We have now seen it for communist systems.

PART

VII

OTHER ALTERNATIVES?

Policy Making and Planning

WHAT are the alternative methods of politico-economic organization that we have so far neglected? Looking about, we see three developments that suggest new possibilities. One is the attempt at more scientific policy making in the form of economic planning, which appears to be becoming increasingly conspicuous both in corporations and in the governments of the market-oriented polyarchies of Western Europe. A second is a new form of the corporation in Yugoslavia. A third is structural reform of polyarchy.

In this chapter, we shall consider the first of the three: economic planning. We can also use the exposition of planning in market-oriented systems to give us one further point of comparison with communist systems. To many thoughtful people, nothing seems more clear than that the future belongs to those who plan. They believe that the market-oriented polyarchies cannot survive if they cannot plan, even if in their own way, better than communist systems.*

---

* What is planning? We do not need a definition. For we shall enlarge our inquiry to encompass a variety of policy-making processes, without quibbling over which ones are to be labeled planning.

Two Kinds of Policy Making and Planning[1]

From the distinction between the two models of the humanitarian society, which differ in their estimate of man's intellectual capacities, we can make a distinction between two methods of planning and policy making. One—appropriate to Model 1—we shall call synoptic, calling attention to breadth and competence of analysis attempted in it. The other— appropriate to Model 2—we shall call strategic, calling attention to its limited intellectual aspiration and the consequent need for an intellectual strategy to guide an inevitably incomplete analysis.*

The need for an intellectual strategy needs to be precisely understood. Since people cannot intellectually master all their social problems in Model 2, they depend on various devices to simplify problem solving. Among them are trial and error and rules of thumb, as well as routinized and habitual responses to categories of problems. One commonplace strategy for a policy maker is to proceed incrementally and sequentially, with close interplay between end and means. In such a strategy, a policy maker is less concerned with "correctly" solving his problem than with making an advance. He is also less concerned with a predetermined set of goals than with remedying experienced dissatisfaction with past policy while goals and policies are both reconsidered.[2]

Consider two methods of policy making or planning for a twenty-year program of vastly expanded highway building. Synoptic theory requires that all the proposed highways be seen as part of an integrated grid and that no one highway be justified except in relation to the others. Strategic policy makers or planners will, however, operate on the assumption that they cannot see clearly twenty years ahead. They will also believe themselves incapable of grasping all the inter-connections of traffic that make the case for one route dependent on the design of other routes. They will therefore decide now on some of the required highways, then analyze the results before scheduling others.†

---

* To avoid confusion, I acknowledge that in earlier publications mentioned below I used the term "synoptic" to denote a certain pattern of decision making employed in the face of a given problem. I now enlarge the reference of the term to denote also a certain way of finding or defining the problem itself. Strategic policy making, it should also be noticed, is not synonymous with incremental or what elsewhere I call disjointed incremental policy making. They are particular strategies, among others, to be included in the category of strategic policy making.

† Many studies of the policy-making process do not appreciate the difference between the two kinds of policy making and planning. For example, Charles Schultze, former U.S. budget director and then chairman of the President's Council of Economic

Model 2 people also depend, we saw, on social interactions to reach outcomes that they are not competent to reach analytically. Market interactions, voting, and negotiation are among them. One such possibility among many others is drastic decentralization: to fragment the problem and its analysis. I do not mean by fragmentation the orderly division and subdivision of a problem into hierarchically arranged components, the parts all synthesized by a synoptic policy maker at the top of the hierarchy. I mean instead a breaking up of the problem and of its analytical tasks in such a way that the reintegration is achieved not by analysis but by interaction processes. Much of mutual adjustment among authorities, we have already noted, is problem-solving interaction of this kind.

Take the case, again, of policy on income distribution in the United States. No one policy-making organization is responsible for the distribution of income. Policy responsibility on income for the aged is assigned to or claimed by several organizations, among them the appropriate committees of Congress, Congress as a whole, and state and local governments. Policy on income redistribution in favor of families with schoolchildren comes under the responsibility of local taxing authorities, state governments, and local school boards. Market processes and taxing authorities are principal determinants of income shares for the gainfully employed. No organization or person coordinates these parts. They are coordinated, however, since the various policy makers obviously have to take account of each other in the interactions of Model 2 through all the possibilities of mutual adjustment discussed in the earlier chapter on patterns of authority.[3]

The use of interactions instead of analysis to solve problems is no mere occasional small aid to policy making and planning. We have seen that it is a mammoth possibility for substituting one kind of problem solving for another, as the single example of the market system as a substitute for centrally analyzed resource allocation and income distribution indicates.

Analysis is not excluded in Model 2, only limited in its aspiration. In

Advisers, sees strategic planning or policy making as no more than a substitution of bargaining or of "politics" for analysis. He misses the distinction between two forms of analysis, the one synoptic, the other limited and strategic; the one confident, comprehensive, and ambitious, the other selective, discriminating, economical of analytical talent (Charles L. Schultze, *The Politics and Economics of Public Spending* [Washington, D.C.: The Brookings Institution, 1968].)

In "The Decline of Politics and Ideology in a Knowledgeable Society" (*American Sociological Review* 31 [October 1966]), Robert E. Lane comes closer to the distinction we are drawing. He distinguishes two "pure" domains: knowledge and politics. But he agrees that politics is inescapable; and, although he does not make the point, his examples and categories of new forms of knowledge in policy making are overwhelmingly examples of knowledge tied to interactive processes, hence knowledge in strategic rather than synoptic policy making.

no way can we say that analysis is less frequent in the one model than in the other. We can only say that in Model 2 it is strategically adapted to its own limitations and to interactions. Strategic policy makers treat the competence to make intelligent policy or to plan as a scarce resource that must be husbanded and carefully allocated.

The Controlled Materials Plan of U.S. World War II economic mobilization is an example of making the most of a limited capacity to analyze. Unable to plan allocations for a large variety of industrial resources for war, planners decided to concentrate their planning on steel, copper, and aluminum on the assumption that if they planned an allocation of these three the use of many other resources would be adapted interactively to them without being planned.[4]

The adaptation of analysis to interaction takes at least three distinctive forms. One is analysis by any participant of how he can play his interactive role better to get what he wants—frankly partisan analysis asking "What shall I buy?" or "How shall I vote?" or (for a businessman) "How can I increase sales?" or (for a legislator) "How can I get this bill through the House?" The second is analysis of how to enter into existing interactions most successfully to achieve some public purpose which one, as a public official, has a responsibility to pursue. "Should taxes be cut to stimulate employment?" "Should criminal penalties for street crime be increased?" The third is analysis of possible changes in the basic structure of the interaction processes themselves: "Should markets be made more competitive by breaking up big business?" "Should the criminal justice system be revamped?" "What changes are required in parliamentary organization?"[5] Each of the three categories calls for feats of analysis less difficult than the comprehensive analysis required in Model 1.

The two methods of analysis—synoptic and strategic—also differ in that strategic policy makers allow for what in chapter 19 we called epiphenomenal solutions or outcomes. Resource allocation is the familiar example. It is achieved through market interactions as a by-product of individual decisions to buy and sell. Resource allocation itself is on the agenda of no decision maker. Strategic policy makers make use of interactive processes and their epiphenomena that are on some counts widely considered to be irrational. For example, we have seen that growth in market systems has always been to a large degree epiphenomenal—a consequence of the pursuit of profit, rather than a social goal pursued for its own sake.

In Model 2, analysis can be practiced as carefully and thoroughly as in Model 1. A corporation's analysis of its purchases or sales, for example, which is obviously an analysis adapted to market interactions, is not necessarily inferior in quality to analysis of all aspects of the allocation of capital in society.

316

Policy Making and Planning in the Polyarchies

In the polyarchies, policy making and planning are always—without exception—strategic, though there may be many attempts at synopsis. They are, for example, typically incremental, sequential, and dependent on feedback on both means and ends. Year after year, policies on growth, defense, income distribution, monopoly, taxation, wages, resource management, industrial relations, international economic cooperation, health, and social security are altered in endless sequences of trial-and-error steps.

Insofar as policy makers care about public opinion, as they must in a Model 2 society in which broadly willed rather than correct policies are sought, they will turn their limited analytical energies in some large part and sometimes exclusively to the analysis of citizen volitions rather than the substance of the policy problem at hand. This is a commonplace strategy for simplifying the analysis of a problem. Voting itself is a great simplifier. No official need analyze a policy problem to look for correct solutions if it can be settled by an election—thus by an expression of volitions.

Analysis of policy and plan making are also always tied to social interactions that bear part of the burden of problem solving. Economic policy making and planning revolve almost entirely around market interactions and consist of analysis of possibilities of altering market interactions. City planning similarly consists of analysis of possible interventions in the complex, interactive market and governmental processes through which cities are patterned.

Formal Economic Planning

In many of the polyarchies, a formal planning process has arisen since World War II as a reaction against the extreme fragmentation of economic decision making in a market system. It has appeared to promise a new scope for synoptic policy making and planning. In actual fact, however, planning by the new agencies remains strategic rather than synoptic. The planning process does not attempt a synoptic view of the entire economy or society.

The plans are, for the most part, no more than proposals for capital investment, although they may also propose certain limited institutional reforms. They therefore constitute a form of instruction or advice to private and governmental participants in various interactions, especially market interactions.[6] As has been observed of French planning, ". . . effective competition and intelligent planning are natural allies rather than

317

enemies."[7] Nor does planning replace any of the ordinary policy-making institutions or procedures of these societies. It is a far cry from an idealized synoptic planning such as Nehru once naively described in contemplating the transfer of planning techniques he thought he saw operating in the West:

> [Planning] and development have become a sort of mathematical problem which may be worked out scientifically. . . . [Planning] for industrial development is generally accepted as a matter of mathematical formula. . . . [Men] of science, planners, experts, who approach our problems from purely a scientific point of view [rather than an ideological one] . . . agree, broadly, that given certain pre-conditions of development, industrialization and all that, certain exact conclusions follow almost as a matter of course.[8]

Although there are dissenters and agnostics, the most discussed success story in planning in the polyarchies has been French investment planning through the Commissariat du Plan. This commission does not attempt a synopsis. Instead it greatly facilitates interaction among major private and governmental investors by arranging a collection and exchange of information among them with respect to their investment plans. It thus facilitates a substantial recalculation of investment plans by each participating private firm of government agency and, in addition, puts the French government in a position to bring its miscellaneous taxing and regulatory authority to bear incrementally on desired alterations in private investment decisions.[9]

Dutch planning is distinguished by the sophistication of the mathematical models it employs, as well as by the role given to governmental control of wages and prices, in consultation with employers and unions. Swedish planning is distinguished by a special system of government control over corporate funds held in reserve for investment and constrained or released to control inflation and unemployment. Both Dutch and Swedish planning are largely limited to achieving short-run stability rather than the long-run growth objectives of French planning. Both work through incremental interventions in market interactions.

In the United States, the most ambitious innovation has been monetary and fiscal planning for economic stability and growth through the President's Council of Economic Advisors. The council plans through programs to influence the interactive processes of the market. Its proposals are always incremental. Its proposals are adapted to the role that the president plays in interaction, especially to his interactions with Congress, Treasury, and Federal Reserve Board.

West Germany shares with the United States an ideological resistance to national economic planning, although both its parliamentary system and its more centralized banking system would permit it to go further than the United States. Its counterpart to the American President's Council is the Council of Economic Experts, established in 1964. It writes an annual report on economic trends, but neither it nor any other agency writes an investment or developmental plan for the economy.

After an unsuccessful attempt to establish development councils in a variety of industries after World War II, Britain retreated from a flurry of postwar interests in national economic planning. Only in 1962, with the establishment of the National Economic Development Council, did Britain turn again in the direction France has conspicuously taken. Even today, however, the United Kingdom does not engage administrators and business leaders in so ambitious a planning process as in France. Nor does the British government intervene as freely as the French government does, through taxes and subsidies, to influence the investment decisions of individual enterprises.

Aspirations toward Synopsis

Paradoxically, it is synoptic rather than strategic policy making that enjoys the highest esteem in the polyarchies. Thus, in the societies approximating Model 2, "planning" has come to be a word denoting policy making that aspires to Model 1. The theory of planning in the abstract has been written for the most part by scholars—usually those with scientific, engineering, economics, or mathematics training—who have taken it for granted that good planning is wholly intellectual or analytic. For them planning is attractive because they think of it as a way to substitute human intelligence for the crudities of politics.[10] They overlook the relation of analysis to social interaction.

Polyarchies make their longest reach toward synoptic policy making in their attempts to depoliticize decisions at intermediate and low levels. An early example was the Progressive movement in the United States at the beginning of the twentieth century with its advocacy of "good government" expressed in the city manager movement of that time. A professional city manager, so the argument went, could find competent, scientific, even "correct" solutions to municipal problems rather than "political" accommodations of warring interests. That same synoptic aspiration continues today in those who see politics as "a cooperative search for the concrete implications of a more or less objective public interest" and who consequently want authority to be exercised by technical experts, or at least by "statesmen" rather than "politicians."

Another specific manifestation of synoptic aspiration is the proliferating use of self-conscious formal techniques such as systems analysis, mathematical programming, and input-output analysis. These techniques are synoptic in intent insofar as they aspire to comprehensive analysis and to

319

scientific "correct" solutions. They go far to incorporate all relevant factors into a formal analysis. Enthusiasts sometimes see them as promising solutions to all of society's problems.

But one way to be strategic rather than synoptic in attacking large policy questions is to attempt synopsis through these techniques only for small problems or subproblems. Solutions to larger problems and the coordination of solutions to the subproblems then remain to be achieved strategically. In fact, this is how these techniques have made their great contribution to policy making—by solving small problems only. They are so far successfully applied not to problems of planning for a whole economy but to specific narrowly bounded problems of specific organizations: for example, choice of weapons systems by a branch of the military or a decision on plant size and location by a corporation.*

If not pushed to extremes, the use of these techniques can be reconciled with Model 2 and with strategic policy making, which need the techniques for appropriately bounded problems. At an extreme, however, their most ambitious use is hostile to strategic policy making, as well as to Model 2. Plato's philosopher-king, Rousseau's Legislator, and the Model 1 elite to which communist leadership at least once aspired, all join with some contemporary enthusiasts for formal systems analysis in their hostility toward strategic analysis adapted to social interactions.

Corporate and Governmental Planning

In the use of these formal techniques of planning the most successful planners are not government agencies but corporations.[11] Corporations do well with them because corporations play a well-defined role in market interactions. A corporation can set itself a specific problem—for example, what is the most profitable degree of product diversity?—without worrying about what is good for society or whether it has any responsibility other than making money. Corporate planning might be thought of as a limiting case of strategic planning in which planning is explicitly and wholly subordinated to an interaction process.

The opposite synoptic extreme would be one single central planning authority for the whole of society, combining economic, political, and social control into one integrated planning process that makes interaction unnecessary. No such authority exists or has ever been seriously considered

---

* The sort of simple, explicit model which operations researchers are so proficient in using can certainly reflect most of the significant factors influencing traffic control on the George Washington Bridge, but the proportion of relevant reality which we can represent by any such model or models in studying, say, a major foreign-policy decision, appears to be almost trivial. (Charles Hitch, "Operations Research and National Planning—A Dissent," *Operations Research* 5 [October 1957]:718.)

in any society. It follows then that for all planning, including governmental, some degree of adaptation of analysis to interaction is required.

Planning by government agencies is confused on that very point. Frequently agencies bear broad responsibility for functioning "in the public interest." In their formal planning they are thus drawn into impossible synoptic attempts to define it, or into heavy-handed attempts to pursue, or at least avoid obstructing, all the many values or social objectives that appear in their version of the public interest.[12] President Johnson's effort to tie systems analysis to program budgeting in the PPB formula (planning-programming-budgeting) ran aground in just this way.

Polyarchal Differences

In their approximations to Model 2 and their practice of strategic policy making, the polyarchies are not all alike. Their interaction processes differ. The American system is marked by a wide dispersion of veto powers so that policy initiatives are relatively easy to abort. The Congress has roughly 250 subcommittees, each with important veto authority; but veto authority is scattered everywhere. Consequently, in the American system and others like it, each successful policy requires a mobilization of widespread support specific to that policy. The contrast is the British system, in which voters choose among relatively disciplined parties and the winning party delegates substantial decision-making authority to prime minister and cabinet. They need not then mobilize a fresh supporting coalition on each desired policy.[13] The one system proceeds through a succession of ad hoc legislative majorities (or even larger coalitions necessary to overcome vetoes); the other through a longer lasting majority that empowers a strong decision-making authority to act until removed.

Similarly, interest groups play their roles differently in the interactions characteristic of Model 2. They may participate at many points in the system, as in the United States, or largely through close relations with the civil service, as in the United Kingdom and France. Moreover, most polyarchies are multiparty systems that tend to elect representatives of specific religious, ethnic, or ideological groups, whose elected representatives must thereafter come to terms with each other in parliamentary negotiation.[14] A few others, the United Kingdom and the United States among them, operate through parties that conduct relatively more negotiation with various interests before the election, so that at elections each party offers voters a combination of policies rather than representation on a single issue.[15] At an extreme, a two-party system permits the voters to decide who will constitute the cabinet—the leaders of the winning party. In a multiparty system the cabinet's composition is decided by parliamentary negotiation.

Widespread fragmentation of authority, separation of powers, checks and balances, multiple vetoes, low development of party discipline, a multiplicity of relatively autonomous legislative committees rather than one single committee playing the role of a cabinet—all these characteristics of the American system make it an extreme version of Model 2 in contrast, say, to some slight coloration of Model 1 and synoptic policy making through prime minister and cabinet in the United Kingdom. But both are approximations to Model 2, both far from Model 1.

While different forms of polyarchy have strong advocates, we have no solid evidence to connect differences in structure with differences in performance. The British system is widely admired because it appears to avoid many of the excesses of fragmentation of authority, weak initiative, easy vetoes, and proliferated partisanship in the American system. But the British record for many decades now is one of immobilism and economic retardation.

Barriers to Synopsis

We can understand the inevitability that planning will remain strategic rather than synoptic in the market-oriented polyarchies by looking back to certain differences between Models 1 and 2, from which the two concepts of planning are derived. Synoptic planning, it would seem to follow from those models, will be possible (1) if the problem at hand does not go beyond man's cognitive capacities *and* (2) if there exist agreed criteria (rather than social conflict on values) by which solutions can be judged *and* (3) if the problem solvers have adequate incentives to stay with synoptic analysis until it is completed (rather than resort to rules of thumb, decision routines, guesstimates, and the like). All three conditions are required for synoptic planning or policy making.

For none of the big politico-economic problems of the contemporary nation can the first condition be met. As for the second condition, given emerging problems of nuclear weaponry, world order, environmental protection, and energy conservation, it may be that citizens and leaders all over the world will increasingly come to believe that we shall all live or die together. If so, some agree criteria might emerge. On the third condition, disincentives to synoptic analysis constitute a powerful obstruction to synoptic policy making and planning. Although electronic computation and other new devices for augmenting man's intelligence have given new zest to analysis in many circumstances, most complex problems that legislators and executives must face are still "solved" by only cursory analysis, far from synoptic.

Synoptic analysis is impossibly costly. A public official simply has no time and patience for exhaustive analysis, nor staff large enough to carry it through even if we wished. Hence, most ostensibly synoptic decision making is in fact accomplished by intuitive acts of judgment, the analytical component of which is not yet well understood. Or decisions are reached by the application of ideological guidelines, often inappropriate if not actually foolish. Or by appeals to common sense, which bring both old prejudices and old insights to bear. Or by the invocation of moral principles, which on a closer look would be disclosed as insufficient for the problem at hand. Or by reference to all manner of beliefs representing inherited prejudices, myths, misunderstandings, conventions, questionable rules of thumb, and the like, not excluding some serviceable insights. In any case, no synopsis.

Sometimes it is suggested that synopsis can be more closely achieved if—it is a big if—the solution to each of the system's subproblems is largely independent of solutions reached on each of the others. An inference is then drawn that conventionally conceived central planning in the style of Model 1 is then possible and appropriate. A more correct inference is that it is possible but inappropriate because then unnecessary. Independence among subproblems calls for no central coordination of solutions. For independent subproblems and their independent solutions, if in fact they exist, decentralized market decision making and pluralistic politics would do quite as well as central synopsis.

Man's inability to satisfy the three conditions under which synopsis would be possible does not mean, however, that strategic policy making and planning display encouraging prospects. Everywhere around us are evidences that his mistakes in strategic policy making are large and frequent.

Many thoughtful people seek an escape from the dismal conclusion that the polyarchies cannot rise above the untidy mixture of social interaction and limited analysis that we have described as the characteristic style of polyarchal policy making and planning. They fruitlessly push for synopsis, which remains impossible. It may clarify the alternatives that are possible to point out that improvements are presumably available in strategic problem solving.

Among them, one is noteworthy because its advocates sometimes discredit it by confusing it with utopian aspirations toward synopsis.[16] It is the introduction into interactive processes, especially those of polyarchal politics, of a voice for efficiency, specifically an advocate of solutions that achieve at least a Pareto optimum. Such a participant in interaction specializes in the search for policies that are acceptable to all participants and positively advantageous to at least some. In, for example, the contemporary struggle in the polyarchies between those who push for policies to control inflation and those who push for policies to increase employment, policy making will be greatly improved if there are participants who specialize in the search for amendments that to some degree do both.

Such a specialist, the voice for efficiency, is likely to become also a voice for some of the absentees. One of the conspicuous imperfections in interactive processes is that many people are not engaged at all, or only peripherally, in them. When, for example, interactions between unions and corporations set wage rates for the economy, a large public is not an effective participant. Hence, the search for efficient solutions usually incorporates at least some attempt to identify possible gainers and losers whose interests would otherwise be neglected.

Do such specialists actually exist? They are to be found among city planners hired by the city councils and mayors, budget analysts in the U.S. Office of Management and Budget, the staff of the French Planning Commission, or tax experts in the U.K. Treasury. Such "professionals"—and many others like them—can and often do perform an indispensable function as the voice for efficiency and for at least some of the absentees.

Curiously, they themselves often misperceive their role. They think they are synoptic planners. They do not see that they are partisan participants in the interactive process of Model 2.[17]

Policy Making and Planning in Communist Systems

In their ideal world, Communists would suppress politics and other interactions in their attempt to construe social reconstruction as synoptic policy making and planning.[18] Insofar as the "correct" policy is not yet known, communist ideologues see their task as analytically seeking the correct line rather than falling back on problem-solving interactions. Mao, for example, acknowledges that Marxism-Leninism "has in no way put an end to the discovery of truth."[19] There is always a correct course of action if it can only be found. Although struggle plays a central role in Mao's thinking, it is a struggle between what is true and what is false. It is an internal ideological struggle through which men purge themselves of the errors of presocialist thinking, not at all the struggling interactions of polyarchal politics.[20]

In actual fact, how are policy making and planning accomplished in communist systems? How synoptic are they? How close are they to Model 1?

Economic Planning

The most conspicuously apparent pattern of synoptic planning is in formal economic planning. Yet we have seen that market-system interactions play an important policy-making role in agriculture, in the distribution of consumer goods and services, and in the allocation of the labor force. In these areas, party and governmental policy making is consequently strategic not synoptic. Strictly speaking, therefore, the ambition to make policy synoptically is largely limited to investment and production decisions.

Within that restricted—though major—area of policy making, planning is now recognized to be less synoptic than was once believed. In large part, communist economic planning, we have seen, consists of remedial, sequential, incremental alterations of the production scheduled for the previous period.[21] We have also seen that production schedules and input allocations are endlessly reconsidered and altered in a variety of interactions: among enterprises, between enterprises and planning authorities, and among planning authorities at various levels.

Formal planning is pursued through such methods as material balances and iterative procedures. These methods, we have noted, aim at no more than balance or consistency in economic plans, so far are they from achieving synopsis. In the words of a report to the Presidium of the Soviet Academy of Sciences, the Soviet system "can barely attain even a balanced plan."[22]

Communist planners acknowledge that they have not achieved synoptic economic planning. Yet their continued aspiration to do so is revealed in the administrative reforms that arose in the Soviet Union parallel to the aborted market reforms of the 1960s. Having timidly approached and then recoiled from an experiment in less synoptic planning, the Soviets perhaps increased their efforts to achieve an intellectual mastery of the economy as a whole. Planning, they have declared, is to become more "scientific." More computers, more mathematical models. More detailed plans. More centralization. More long-range forecasting. One result so far is that in seven years the administrative bureaucracy grew by a third.[23]

Policy Making in Other Areas

For economic policy more complex than production planning, as well as for social, military, and other policies, communist systems have made almost no attempt at synoptic planning, despite the rhetoric of Model 1. Communist policy is arrived at through a political interactive process, as witness Soviet, Cuban, and Chinese party purges at the top level. The governing elite is neither wholly stable nor homogenous in its beliefs on what constitutes a correct solution to a complex problem. Hence it has to substitute for analysis and theory a whole range of problem-solving inter-actions. They include voting or bargaining within a politburo; negotiation among party leadership, the military, and the high levels of the civil service; and adaptation of party-made policy to meet the challenges of mass unrest and dissent from the intelligentsia.[24]

On their large problems, communists systems, like polyarchies, are driven by ignorance and uncertainty to endless improvisation rather than synoptic plans. Since the Liberation of 1949, China, for example, has intended to eliminate small-scale private agriculture in favor of collectives. In the first years of communism, leadership concluded that expediency required that private family agriculture be left largely intact. From 1953 to 1955, however, it moved to organize peasants into "lower level" agri-cultural producers' cooperatives, in which land was pooled and unified management practiced, although leaving supplementary private plots of limited size at the disposal of each peasant. In 1956–57, in another change of policy, it organized the peasants into "advanced" cooperatives in which payment to each peasant for his pooled land was abolished. Supplementary private plots were still allowed. (In 1955, however, they had in effect closed down free markets in which peasants could sell produce from their private plots. A year later, in 1956, the free markets were again permitted, and private plots were enlarged.) In 1958, the cooperatives were combined into communes and free markets were curbed, and the private plots were legally eliminated. Communal dining and free supply of basic commodities were instituted with the communes. By 1959, one year later, free supply and communal dining were already on their way out. Free markets and private plots were reintroduced in 1959. Later in the same year, private plots were again eliminated. But they were again reintroduced in 1960.

Subsequently, communes were reduced, on the average, to less than half their former size; and they were divested of their earlier status as the major economic organization for agriculture and local industry. Responsibility for agricultural production was moved back to organizations of the size of the earlier "advanced" cooperatives and to even smaller production teams.[25]

Similarly, the U.S.S.R. experimented with worker control of produc-tion and the elimination of money in the period of War Communism; recoiled in 1921 from its disastrous effects on production into the partial restoration of "capitalism" in the period of the New Economic Policy until 1928; then began a sequence of five-year plans for industry and agriculture that persisted with remarkable stability until the death of Stalin in 1953. Since then policy has again moved at varying pace and with reversals toward a slightly enlarged use of the market system and reduction of the physical controls of the Stalin period. It would be hard to find a record of any greater improvisation in U.S. policy making.

Because, however, policy making is less fragmented in communist systems than in pluralist polyarchal systems, one might expect policy-making authorities to go further than the Western profit-seeking corporation or specialized governmental agency in comprehensively surveying the consequences of its policies. Communist ideology helps and encourages it to do so. Yet it has been observed that

> The characteristic Soviet approach to problems is that of "storming," i.e., tackling (on the domestic scene) one or a limited number of objectives at a time and hitting them hard, largely ignoring side effects. The regime's notion of how to effect social change is still based on a direct *assault* on goals with only a secondary consideration of cost and consequences.*

It is true that, more often in the polyarchies, communist leaders do on occasion pursue extraordinarily ambitious policies, as in the collectivization of Soviet agriculture in 1930 or the Great Leap Forward (and with concomitant risk of disorganization in both cases). They decide upon these goals, however, not in any planning or policy-making process different from the processes employed by decision makers who do not plan.

Moreover, like Castro's ambition to create a new Cuban man, most ambitious policy goals call not for big steps but for sequences of incremental adjustments in policy as in the polyarchies.[26] To create a new man required hundreds of policy steps to change schooling, job discipline, wages, leisure-time activity, political participation, and a multiplicity of other factors. Although in the U.S.S.R. agriculture was collectivized in a few large steps, in China and Cuba it is being pursued through many small steps.

Instead of nonincremental change, communist societies often demonstrate a capacity for extremely rapid sequences of incremental change. In 1929, for example, at the beginning of the five-year plans in the Soviet

* Raymond A. Bauer, Alex Inkeles, and Clyde Kluckhohn, *How the Soviet System Works* (Cambridge, Mass.: Harvard University Press, 1957), p. 51. Even formal economic planning displays such a characteristic. Input allocations are assigned to major high-priority uses, leaving lower priority uses to adapt to remaining availabilities, on the assumption that, if a serious bottleneck develops in a lower priority use, it can then be itself "stormed." Moreover, where assigned inputs, even to high-priority uses, cannot be made to match requirements, the planner's solution is simply to demand more output from given inputs. See Hardt et al., *Mathematics and Computers,* p. xii; Lewin, *Political Undercurrents,* p. 143; Herbert S. Levine, "Pressure and Planning in the Soviet Economy," in *Industrialization in Two Systems,* ed. Henry Rosovsky (New York: John Wiley & Sons, 1966); and Thomas G. Rawski, "China's Industrial System," in U.S. Congress, Joint Economic Committee, *China: A Reassessment of the Economy,* 94th Congress, 1st session, 1975, pp. 181ff. Within the individual enterprise too, "storming" and "shock work" are characteristic of European and Chinese communism alike.

Union, light manufacturing was roughly 30 percent above, and heavy manufacturing roughly 35 percent below, normal levels for a country with the same income, population, and natural resource level. In only eight years, a deliberate program of stimulating heavy industry through incremental adjustments brought it to 20 percent above normal.[27]

Science in Policy Making

Science is essential to Model 1 and to synoptic policy making. Not surprisingly, therefore, European communist systems may spend more on research and development than European market-oriented systems at the same levels of per capita income.[28] But they have little use for social science. As they have developed in the world, the social sciences are largely committed to the study of interactions, hence are adapted to Model 2 rather than Model 1, and to strategic rather than synoptic policy making. Economics, for example, is largely the study of market interactions, political science the study of governmental and political interactions. Take away the problem-solving interactions of government and politics, and all that is left of political science is the study of some aspects of administration. Parts of economics, all once tightly suppressed under Stalin, are now given greater scope only because of their affinity to engineering. Political science as distinct from law and managerial studies hardly exists at this date in the U.S.S.R. "The Soviet communist party has not produced a *single* creative and influential Marxist thinker in the fifty years since it seized power in 1917."[29]

China has been hostile to professional intellectuals because of their tendency to be no better than lukewarm to revolutionary change. The result has been a disparagement of science of all kinds. The universities have been converted from scientific centers to schools of revolutionary ideology and practical technology.[30] Alleging that the masses are capable of scientific innovation, Mao declared a specialized set of scientific institutions and scholars to be unnecessary.[31]

More in communist than in liberal democratic systems, therefore, ideological propositions substitute for social science. The substitution is increasingly of committee work and political pronouncements for research and analysis. Ideological discussion becomes a monopoly of party officials, as in the U.S.S.R. and perhaps China. It becomes increasingly protective of the party, and "ideological petrification" appears to set in.[32]

Hence, although ideology continues to play its role in preceptoral "education" and thus in implementing policies, its contribution to top authority's analysis of problems has probably greatly declined. It was never more than a substitute for social science in policy making. As a poor substitute for a social science that would itself have been inadequate to the task, it has in turn been displaced by a more experimental, pragmatic, and incremental style of policy making with less of a scientific component than in the polyarchies.[33]

In the militarily imposed communist systems of Eastern Europe and in Cuba, ideology has never played the policy-making role it may once have played in the U.S.S.R. In China, its role (other than its preceptoral role) is unclear, although Maoists give evidence of their dependence on it in their struggles with an opposition that stresses pragmatic and conventional gradualism for China's development.

But ideological or not, and Maoist or not, Chinese leadership has been conspicuous in a particular aspiration toward synoptic policy making. This aspiration is evidenced in the leaders' disposition to debate and analyze all the great issues of policy to an extraordinary degree. In doing so, they do not develop a supporting social science; however, the habit of debate is not merely applied ideology. Among top leaders the debate seems to be an exercise, as Mao would claim, in the "discovery of truth." Observers have noted that "Chinese Communists have a habit of analyzing everything."[34]

China's leaders apparently attempt a map of the social problems of an entire society. Their effort is possibly part of a historic attempt to bring intellect to bear directly on solving social problems in a more comprehensive way than has ever been attempted in any other society. Whether such an intellectual ambition will survive Mao and the superficiality that attends such breathtaking scope can hardly be predicted. The Soviets had something of the same faith in reason in the 1920s when they often claimed that "science is the religion of the Soviet Union."[35]

Corporate Governance and the Yugoslav Innovations

A REMARKABLE development in industrial organization in recent decades has been the small cooperating work group in the business enterprise, a face-to-face group on which responsibility is devolved for the assignment of tasks and sometimes for the distribution of wage income paid to the group as a collectivity. Quietly and gradually, workplace committees have come to play an important role in British industry. Roughly half of British trade unionists are members of one. The authority of the groups is informal, but they have become important participants in the determination of wages and working conditions, sometimes at the expense of the traditional authority of the unions, of which they remain a part. Similar work groups have been developing in other Western European systems and in the United States, and are sometimes called for by law.[1] They join the many interactive processes of Model 2.

On the whole, the movement and its advocates remain somewhat insensitive to the larger political issues about workplace organization. They do not raise such questions as: Why does or should authority rest with property rather than with employees? How could welfare and productive incentives be affected by disestablishing conventional authority entirely?

Other new voices raise these larger issues. More in Europe than in the

United States, new forms of employee participation in corporate management hint at a possibility—still remote, however—of an eventual drastic transformation of corporate governance.[2] This new wave, lapping gently at the shores of corporate governance in several West European systems, is curiously in fullest tide in Yugoslavia, which has forsaken conventional communist central planning to become a market-oriented system.

Industrial Democracy

Industrial management has by no means been as exploitative as its critics often allege. If it had been, wages would never have risen. In fact they have risen in all industrialized countries since the earliest development of industry and long before unionism. Nor would working conditions have steadily improved, as historically they have. In the polyarchies, the mechanism for improvement—for limiting employer exactions—has been the market system, specifically labor markets in which employers must bid for workers with better wages and working conditions. (In prosperous times the bidding can become highly competitive.) If competition for employees is rigorous, a labor market in effect permits some degree of worker control over employers.

A labor market is, however, a grossly imperfect instrument of worker control, despite its long-time success in pushing wages and working conditions upward. Its effectiveness often plummets in periods of unemployment. Even in good times, an employer can easily victimize any given employee. Democratization of the workplace requires more than competition for workers.

A number of forces strengthen contemporary demands for more democracy in the workplace. In May 1968 the French economy was paralyzed. Almost all major enterprises were shut down for several days by an unplanned spasm of worker rebellion not connected with a wage dispute or any other specific issue. It was an extraordinary event, and it is to be wondered if it did not foreshadow an increasingly troubled future for industrialized societies. One hypothesis is that the episode was a crisis of alienation.

Although scholars dispute just what Marx meant by "alienation," his term at least conjures up a picture of a worker distressed on several counts. He takes neither pleasure, nor incentive, nor self-improvement from his task. Nor from the product he produces. Because of the structure of authority in the workplace and his rivalry with his workmates, he is also separated from a rewarding intimacy of association with his fellows. The literature on alienation is large. The evidence that these problems exist is reasonably conclusive to skeptics and overwhelming to others. So also is the evidence that even modest forms of democracy in the workplace often bring relief.[3] They afford opportunities to discuss and understand purposes, to organize tasks that carry obvious purpose, to enjoy accomplishment, and to associate in mutually respectful ways with one's workmates.

Much the same points are made by those who formulate the chronic problem not as alienation but as the decline of the work ethic. At least for many forms of repetitive industrial task, some segments of society are returning to the older view—as in ancient Greece and among other times and civilizations—that most work is degrading. Work is not necessarily or typically a challenge that enlarges a man's capacities, nor an experience that fosters character and virtue. At an extreme, some industrial tasks kill, more than a few are disabling, and millions of jobs are stultifying. Greatly as he extolled the division of labor as a major source of productive efficiency, Adam Smith nonetheless confessed that "the man whose whole life is spent in performing a few simple operations . . . becomes as stupid and ignorant as it is possible for a human creature to become."[4]

Out of the concern for alienation and the decline of the work ethic come the specific claims that industrial democracy will make workers happier and better people—and will also stimulate production by improving their incentives.[5] Traditional work disciplines are under fire: both market incentives (pay, promotion, discharge) and authoritative instructions. In this respect many contemporary business managers find a surprising kinship with Maoist thought on incentives, with its insistence that incentives of participation among others can to some degree replace conventional incentives.

Some of the new interests in industrial democracy and participatory incentives arise out of a deeper challenge to a long-standing preoccupation of social scientists and managers alike with coordination as the key to efficiency. Energy, resourcefulness, and inventiveness are increasingly argued to be grossly underutilized sources of efficiency. The reduction of individual and organizational slack through tapping individual productivity is now often alleged to promise a great deal more than increased meticulous attention to coordination. Maoist thought, we have seen, is willing to trade coordination for resourcefulness, but so also are innovators in Western business management.

That worker control experiments are afoot in both the liberal democratic and communist worlds suggests that private property and private enterprise are not, as socialists used to believe, the principal targets of democratization of the workplace. The target is instead a hierarchical and authoritarian structure of authority in the enterprise, whether resting on private property or not.

Participatory Democracy

In some countries the worker control movement is part of a broader movement toward participatory democracy in every aspect of group life. As a movement for democratic reform, its roots go back to such faith as Mill had in democracy for the citizen's "advancement in intellect, in virtue, and in practical activity and efficiency"* and to doubts that *representative* government is enough. Rousseau thought democracy impossible in the nation-state because so large a system could not constitute a participating community. Mill feared "the sinister interests of kings and aristocracies"[6] and speculated on a variety of forms of participation to restrain that interest. Older concerns are now supplemented by a new antagonism to bureaucracy. Everywhere today, large numbers of scholars, businessmen, administrators, students, and employees either question or protest it. In particular some believed that personality is stifled in impersonal organizations in which tasks are authoritatively assigned and minutely divided. Tasks could be self-assigned, they believe, by collective decision, through which tasks could be varied and made whole.

Some critics allege that participation is an activity that is valuable for its own sake.[7] Participation is also sometimes intended to weaken contractual relations and strengthen relations of kinship, neighborliness, affection, loyalty, or commonality of purpose. In 1887, Ferdinand Tönnies marked the contrast between formal organization and more "natural" forms in the title of his *Gemeinschaft und Gesellschaft.* The contrast has a long history in political philosophy. Emile Durkheim, Lord Acton, Léon Duguit, and others have examined some of its aspects. The advocates of participatory democracy in effect propose a recovery of the older values of community.[8] It has even been argued that a frustrated longing for community has at an extreme driven whole nations into that hideous caricature of community called totalitarianism.[9]

* See chapter 10.

Doubts

Grounds for skepticism about participatory democracy are not in short supply among those who fear too frantic a participation, too tight a rein on leadership, or too great a public preoccupation with politics. In ancient Athens, "the more perfect their democracy became, the poorer the citizens became."[10] Moreover, the participatory democrats have allies who may one day betray them: They are the antibureaucratic intellectuals and technical experts who propose knowledge instead of conventional authority, collegiality instead of hierarchy, decentralized initiatives instead of imposed coordination, and planning instead of administraton by exigency.[11] On first sight, theirs is a laudable set of proposals. But a not unreasonable interpretation is that in effect their proposals would displace one elite with another. They would give freer rein (and reign) to a highly educated and professional elite as successors to an older "lay" bureaucracy.

We do not now have to weigh the aspirations against the doubts. It is enough for the moment that we see in participatory democracy a new movement of potential but not unchallenged revolutionary significance. The decline of the town meeting suggests that participatory democracy is a lost cause in modern society. But its reinvigoration in the Israeli kibbutz, as well as in new community action and community development groups in the United States under the Economic Opportunity Act of 1964, suggests a different inference. In Tanzania, a possibility for participatory democracy is pursued through the establishment of what is intended to be a new form of politico-economic community: the *Ujamaa* rural cooperative movement. And some elements of it sprout in the Chinese commune.

The most fertile soil for a more participatory democracy appears to be in industry, perhaps because the potential for democracy is large in an arena in which authoritarianism has been for so long universally practiced and little questioned. Movements toward industrial democracy and participatory democracy fuse as new agitation for worker control of management.

Worker Control

That the democratization of industry has not long ago been accomplished lends credence to the Marxian hypothesis that property owners see democracy in government as less threatening by far than democracy in industry. They yield to the one when they will not to the other. It is not surprising that they should. In constitutional orders that protect property, political democracy turns out to challenge the prerogatives of property ownership only marginally. By contrast, democratization of industry immediately, directly, and categorically strikes at them. Although worker control is offered as a method of democratizing industry (and government), its boldest bid has so far been in an authoritarian nonpolyarchal state in which private property in industry was already abolished.*

In Yugoslav self-management, the rule is that all nonagricultural enterprises employing more than five persons are socially rather than privately owned. They are placed in the custody of the employees of the enterprise, including blue collar and white collar alike. For smaller firms, all employees are members of a workers' council. For enterprises with more than thirty employees, workers elect a representative council. In many large enterprises various identifiable production units within the enterprise each elect a council. In their formal authority the councils are supreme in the enterprises. Although they delegate the immediate tasks of management to a management committee and a manager, the management committees are usually drawn from council members. Since 1968 the councils have had authority to recruit, choose, and depose managers. Since 1968 the enterprises have not been subject, as in Soviet-style organization, to comprehensive governmental instructions from higher up. They are to a great degree regulated by government and party, but somewhat in the style of American, French, or British corporate regulation.

All this is established in an authoritarian system under the tutelage of a communist party, the League of Communists, and a government that frequently practices severe repression. But more than in any other communist country, the media enjoy some significant freedom, individual movement domestically and abroad is almost wholly free, the legislature holds some genuine authority, citizens participate in a variety of elections more genuine than in other communist systems, and the party is not monolithic or efficient as a monitor of the society. Yugoslav leadership has in theory granted two noteworthy principles foreign to Model 1: legitimacy of special interests, and some organizational autonomy (for communes, legislatures, enterprises, unions, workers' councils, and other organizations).[12] Elections of workers' councils are therefore not simply sham, although party and union control over them, as well as other imperfections, seriously compromise a democratic choice.[13]

The Yugoslav experience suggests that an authoritarian regime weak

---

* In Germany, worker participation in management may, like other similar reforms elsewhere, turn out to be more of a device for pulling the teeth of worker control than for effecting it. To put employee representatives on corporate supervisory boards may turn out to co-opt employees into management rather than bring effective control into their hands.

on some counts and loath, for several reasons, to claim the omniscience of a Model 1 elite may find advantages in permitting some significant development of worker control. So great are the historical, ethnic, and cultural divisions in Yugoslav society and so weak the sense of nationhood that leadership cannot accomplish a firm central control. Worker control is both a method of acknowledging powerful centrifugal forces in Yugoslav society and simultaneously a method of devolving authority on many small enterprise units instead of on large geographic units, the six Yugoslav "republics." It is feared that large grants of devolved authority to the "republics" would make subversion possible. A greatly fragmented decentralization is safer than a more limited one.[14]

Certain characteristic problems in Yugoslav self-management further illuminate it. One is the possibility of managerial incompetence, a problem in any nation growing rapidly into industrialization. In some cases, workers choose indulgent rather than competent managers. And in some cases electoral politics within the enterprise permit a director to use his position to build up a following.[15] Loyalty to the party may generally count for more than managerial skill.[16] Many work groups, however, show a strong interest in managerial competence. The employees' own incomes depend on it. Worker councils typically look for professional managers. They do not make one of their own fellows—untrained and inexperienced—their manager.[17]

The employee's short time horizon may turn out to be more troublesome than managerial incompetence. Any worker or other group managing an enterprise can deprive the enterprise of growth capital by making excessive wage payments or other distributions in the form of dividends or bonuses. In the same way it can diminish its working capital. Excessive distributions do appear in fact to pose a frequent though not disabling problem in Yugoslavia, for the Yugoslav formula grants the employee no share either to hold or to sell on leaving the firm. All he can take from the enterprise, he must take while he is an employee.[18]

Yugoslav enterprises are wasteful of labor, often slack on discipline.[19] Yet possibly no more so than in many developing countries with conventional management. We do not yet have enough data to know what the connection is, if any between self-management and employee discipline. Another difficulty is that self-management in all but small firms is through representative rather than direct democracy, and hence it partly fails to enlarge direct participation.* Even in large firms, however, there may be some gains through rotation of membership in management committees.

---

* Membership on the representative councils is rotated, however; and there is more interchange between members and constituents than, say, for local government in the United States. And on major policy questions in the enterprise, referenda are used. (Neuberger and James, "Self-managed Enterprise," pp. 259–60.)

Like many market-oriented systems, the system is also plagued by both inflation and unemployment, some of the inflation almost certainly attributable to the excessive wage distributions voted by the workers' council.[20] There are also, inescapably in the present system, inequitable differences in employee income from enterprise to enterprise.[21] Worker control itself is often weakened by apathy as well as by a tendency for white collars to exclude blue from participating in the councils or for better educated blue collars to dominate councils and elections. One indication of the persisting influence of inegalitarianism is a structure of wage differentials much like that of the Western European market system.[22]

Party control over the enterprise inimical to worker control has persisted in the attempt to combine some central control with decentralization.[23] Illegal private enterprises operate openly in construction, trucking, restaurants, and many other fields. And the system is heavily burdened with monopoly since, in the absence of adequate domestic or foreign competition, enterprises can easily raise prices.[24] For all these reasons worker control remains in large part an aspiration.

It may be largely an aspiration on another count: the sometime capture of the worker control system by management. Managers and their staffs, armed with their own technical knowledge of the enterprise's affairs, sometimes reduce the workers' councils to rubber stamps.[25] A 1960s study in depth of two enterprises concluded that worker control "has primarily benefited management, giving it more freedom and room for initiative."[26] A later study in depth of two firms concluded that management consulted widely within the enterprise, took initiatives, responded to initiatives from employees and "walked a tightrope" between obtaining a high level of commitment through consensus, on one hand, and manipulating worker participation, on the other.[27] Opinions on the distribution of authority and other power between management and workers are of wide variety. It seems clear that self-management makes a big difference to consultation and participation, more now than in the 1960s. Yet it may be true that "the traditional lines of authority have not been, in fact, decisively altered."[28]

Coordination of Decentralized Decision Making

A generic problem is the coordination of the decentralized enterprises. A root difficulty in any system of participatory democracy is that a high level of participation is possible only in small groups. But interdependencies prohibit giving each small decision-making group a license to go its own way. An enterprise is of concern not only to its employees but to the persons, ordinarily far more numerous than its employees, for whom it produces a product or service. Lenin was early aware of the problem when he rejected worker control as "syndicalist."[29]

Solutions are obvious, but none are wholly satisfactory. One is to limit participatory democracy to those issues on which interdependencies are insignificant. But that means gutting participation of any serious consequence. Another solution is to establish a discretionary central authority to supervise the decentralized units, much as state governments in the United States supervise municipal government. That solution perpetuates many of just those elements of authority, hierarchy, and bureaucracy against which the participatory democratic movement is a protest.

In principle, for any decentralized autonomous organization, there is often a more satisfactory solution. It is a method characteristic of Model 2. Let the decentralized units, without any superior coordinating authority, negotiate and in other ways adapt themselves mutually to each other. Let them agree on what they will do for each other and what they will not do to each other.

In many actual circumstances, however, the number of other decision-making units with which any one small group would have to cope is impossibly large. The complexity of negotiation participated in by thousands of independent parties would reduce the whole mutually adaptive process to paralysis. And the enormous task of mutual adaptation itself would require full-time specialists, with the result that the ordinary citizen would again find himself shoved away from participation.

Nevertheless, in one distinctive set of circumstances mutual adjustment among thousands, even millions, of small groups will work. I refer of course to the circumstances in which it can be organized through markets. And this the Yugoslavs have understood. Despite their ideological hostility to the market system, despite their immersion in the Marxian identification of the market system with private property, capitalism, and chaos, the Yugoslav communists were able to perceive that decentralized units could be coordinated by the market rather than through the bureaucratic instruments of a central government. They were able to break market system and private enterprise apart in their minds and thus use the market system in a new way, without private enterprise and instead with worker control.

Market Socialism in Yugoslavia

Yugoslavia's move to market socialism can now be better understood. Its leadership has reacted to those pervasive inefficiencies of communist central planning that have led communists in the Soviet Union and Eastern Europe to experiment with some elements of the market system. And it has also reacted to what it has perceived to be an appalling discrepancy between historical communist aspirations for the liberation of man, on one hand, and a stultifying bureaucratization of Soviet-style communism. Its hostility to the Soviet model was rooted, to be sure, in nationalism, indeed in the several nationalisms of Yugoslavia. But at least in support of desires for national independence, it raised its objections to Soviet-style communism to issues of major principle. Both for general efficiency and for making good on theoretical communist commitments to working-class control, it found new merit in the market system.

Yugoslav communism and Maoism both turn against what they perceive to be a bureaucratic degeneration of communism in the U.S.S.R. Both see the need for drastic decentralization. For Mao, though he never carried decentralization as far as did Tito, coordination is to be achieved through preceptoral "education"; for Yugoslavia, through a new form of market system. Other than the possibility of a Maoist path, there appeared to be no other route that Yougoslavia could have taken in its antipathy to Soviet-style bureaucratic communism.

Until the Soviet suppression of 1968, market socialism was in process of development in Czechoslovakia too. It continues to attract some political leaders and administrators in all the European communist systems and has in the last few years been to a degree established in Hungary, despite some anxiety there about possible Soviet intervention if it goes too far. In some ways, many Eastern European communists are rediscovering classical economic liberalism, as well as Model 2. In explaining why Yugoslavia has developed market socialism, Tito, for example, returned to the theme of the division of labor, on which Adam Smith erected his argument for a market system in *The Wealth of Nations*. Tito writes:

> . . . backward, weak and small enterprises cannot participate in the international division of labor. That is why integration and complete specialization in production are necessary so that production can be as inexpensive as possible, of the widest possible assortment, and of the highest quality.[30]

Such liberalization as the Yugoslavs achieved through the market system they matched for a time with political liberalization. This they did on several fronts: party and governmental decentralization,[31] stimulation of direct citizen participation in local government,[32] some new scope for public discussion of politics and for interest groups,[33] some strengthening of due process and constriction of arbitrary arrest and punishment,[34] and, finally, the development of a significant, even if still small, independent governing role for parliament[35] and electorate.[36] In recent years internal conflict among the "republics" led Tito to revoke some of these reforms. The future is uncertain.

The Market and the Enterprise

Since first turning its back on Stalinist central administration in 1952, Yugoslavia moved in a series of steps toward reduction of central direction, with substantial central direction intermixed with market direction until the implementation of the major reform of 1965. Since then, central administrative control has been roughly of the same sort as is found in the market-oriented polyarchies. It is achieved not through a compulsory central production plan but by ad hoc interventions through taxation, occasional subsidies, specific regulations binding on particular industries, and both central and "national" (that is, provincial) control over major new investment.

The Yugoslav enterprise produces what it finds profitable to produce. Its new investment funds are routinely obtained, if not from internal enterprise savings or investment by local government, from commercial banks. The banks are instructed to lend not by administrative plan but on considerations of profitability of investment, although there continues to be some governmental and party supervision of the pattern of bank lending. The firm buys its inputs freely on the market, usually, of course, from other firms selling freely on the market. It rents land from government and private owners. It hires labor, but with a difference. Above minimum wages, workers receive income in the form of shares in profits, which vary according to job.

Like a private enterprise in the U.S. economy, the Yugoslav enterprise must cover its costs, including the minimum level of wages, to stay afloat. It is free to look for new markets, to diversify its production, and to apportion its profits between wages, including collective benefits to its workers, and reinvestment in the growth of the enterprise.

New firms can be started by any individual or group and are in fact most often undertaken by units of local government (communes) or existing firms. Except for small private enterprises of less than five employees, enterprises must, once founded be turned over to social ownership. At least experimentally, some enterprises are constructed as joint ventures combining partial social ownership on the Yugoslavian side and partial private ownership to represent the participation of foreign corporations. The hybrids are required to practice employee self-management.

To curb monopoly, government has used a variety of methods, including tariff reduction and removal of import restrictions. It intends thus to stimulate foreign competition with domestic enterprises, both to hold prices down within Yugoslavia and to compel exporting firms to hold their own costs and prices down to levels that make exports possible.

The trade union is an important participant in the enterprise, often vying in importance with the workers' council. Far more than in any other communist system, it is an instrument through which employees can defend their own occupational interests, even though it is still also an instrument of party and government direction of enterprise and work force. Whether strikes should continue to be legal has been debated, and they are at least on the fringe of illegality. In actual fact, strikes were once common. Almost 1,400 were reported between 1958 and 1966.[37] None has been officially reported since 1968.

A potential for expansion of the social enterprise lies in agriculture. An earlier collectivized agriculture has now in large part given way to private holdings and private farming, although the 10–15 percent of arable land now in the hands of state farms or collectives is especially prominent in providing marketed supply for domestic and foreign markets. The retreat from collective to private farming in 1953 was defended as an expedient, necessary until such time as the development of the communist new man would once again make collective agriculture possible. It is probable that the potential superior efficiency of large-scale mechanized agriculture still appeals to Yugoslav leadership. Official doctrine still declares that private farming, already curbed in size of farm, will someday be brought to an end, not to be replaced by planned farming, however, but by market-oriented self-managed farm enterprises.[38]

Duality in Leadership

How Yugoslavia will cope with the duality of leadership and privileged position of enterprise management that are characteristic of market systems is not yet clear. Because on the whole enterprises are small, the authority and other power of their managers is less of a challenge to the authority of government than in the more industrialized systems. Managers are also subject to party control. Through both party and government they are authoritatively instructed to pursue profits even under circumstances in which a private enterprise would be willing to do so only if granted indulgences sufficient to motivate it. Managers are also subject to control through local government, banks, industrial chambers, professional associations, and youth organizations.[39]

341

If these controls over management achieve desired objectives yet simultaneously respect market criteria for managerial decisions—if they do not, for example, impose decisions that drive the firm into high cost or debilitating losses—they must be administered with skill and restraint. That Yugoslavia has not yet, however, found a wholly satisfactory way to control business leadership is indicated in severe unemployment and inflation. Yugoslav difficulties illustrate how little we yet know about how to make use of business leadership in market systems without, on the one hand, failing to establish sufficient control over that leadership or, on the other hand, establishing such controls as destroy the enterprise or make it inefficient.

It is possible too that the prerogatives of businessmen in the private enterprise systems will become the prerogatives of groups of employees in each firm. They may settle into comfortable monopoly privilege, each extracting from government, such benefits as they find necessary to their efficient performance, as businessmen do in private enterprise systems. They rather than businessmen will enjoy a privileged position.

Such a development is obviously far from ideal. If a transfer of privilege from management to employees is, by many democratic and egalitarian standards, a gain, the division of the economy into islands of monopoly is not. Nor is its division into workers' control groups each operating its enterprise in its own interest with little regard for the rest of the nation.

Prospects

Market socialism and self-management after 1952 were accompanied by extremely rapid if erratic growth and a remarkable rise in the standard of living.[40] Between 1954 and 1964, national income increased by almost 9 percent per year and put Yugoslavia among the very few fastest growing economies of the world. Growth then slowed for a few years—partly because of anti-inflation measures. Since 1969, growth has been rapid, though not at the earlier phenomenal rate. For 1969 through 1973, the average growth rate was 6.6 percent (compared to thirteen-year roughly estimated average rates for the United States of 4.3 percent; China, 5.6; U.S.S.R., 5.3; and Mexico, 6.9).[41]

The growth prospects for a market socialism cannot be judged, however, by any one case, even less so by the first stable historical venture into market socialism.* Similarly, one has to be cautious about arguing that the identifiable problems of the Yugoslav system are inherent in all ventures in market socialism. No nation—we have said it before—has yet used

* The U.S.S.R. from 1921 to 1928, the period of the New Economic Policy, operated a form of market socialism.

the market system skillfully; and Yugoslavia is inexpert in doing so. It has not yet even developed good accounting, financial, and managerial procedures. And as a newcomer to industrialization, it is without the long experience of the market-oriented polyarchies in regulating and tuning the market to cope with monopoly, monetary disturbances, employment fluctuations, inflation, labor relations, and the like.

Its present ineptness in using the market may persuade Yugoslavia once more to turn away from it. Or, if legal and illegal private enterprise grow, as they have been, and if managers capture workers' councils as in the United States they capture stockholders' meetings, the system may revert in fact if not in name to a conventional private enterprise system with a more or less authoritarian government. On the other hand, Yugoslavia may presage the gradual development of a greatly more efficient and equitable economic order. In destroying the historical connection between market system and private enterprise, Yugoslavia may—it is at least a possibility—have set itself and the world on a new course.

A Future for Democracy?

IN this final chapter, many of the themes of earlier chapters are brought together to clarify possibilities for the further pursuit of the democratic tradition in national government. The possibilities are presumably not limited to those imperfect approximations to democracy which are the existing polyarchies. Variation from one existing polyarchy to another is small. Their differences are not enough to reveal many opportunities for new directions in potentially democratic politico-economic organization.

Boldly conceived major new democratic alternatives have not yet been designed. They may never be, even if their design may someday become necessary to the survival of polyarchy. In egalitarian vision, the democratic movement has rarely looked forward bravely—as it did briefly in the French Revolution. It has been cautious, reluctant to invent new political forms, and pushed from the rear into an always obscured future. Parliamentary government owes its birth in England to the gradual enlargement of a royal council of nobles in order to accommodate not a new design for democracy but demands by a growing middle class for participation in the governing of their own affairs. In America the Constitutional Fathers saw their task as curbing, no less than implementing, popular control over government. In the United States as in the United Kingdom, widening of suffrage has repeatedly been undertaken by one party or another simply to win advantage over the other. Enfranchisement of blacks was reluctantly conceded only when continued refusal became scandalous and disruptive. A wider working-class participation in politics was an accident of the depression of the 1930s and the demands then generated for labor's right to organize for collective bargaining. In the same way, new polyarchal forms will presumably follow from new problems, political strategies, and historical "accidents" more than from democratic principles or theoretical design.

Yet new forms seem urgently necessary. In the United States, many citizens fear that social problems are running far ahead of government. We are losing control. Many of our children do not learn to read. Jobs are insecure. Money does not hold its value. On some days the air is not fit to breathe. The streets are not safe. And always the bomb—the likelihood of an accident if not a nuclear war.

The state of the nation points to three troublesome aspects of our politico-economic system, each of which we share in varying degree with the other polyarchies. The first is the pattern of problem-solving interactions, especially the degree and character of mutual adjustment in polyarchal politics. In no polyarchy are they satisfactory.

Disabilities of Mutual Adjustment

One common diagnosis of our difficulties in problem solving by mutual adjustment is that responsibility is excessively fragmented. Policy making is ostensibly a legislative responsibility. Decades ago it became clear that the initiative actually lies with the president. But he can hardly make policy without the cooperation of Congress, and Congress often goes its own way. For that matter, individual committees and their chairmen go their own ways. And the federal government denies responsibilities that it claims should be taken by the states. They reciprocate by throwing responsibilities onto the federal government. The fragmentation goes even further. On some issues, a likely source of initiative might be a corporation, a union, or some other private organization. But an ordinary citizen often does not know where to look for action. Many of us come to despair that anyone will act, or we believe that if anyone acts, some other person or organization will stand in the way.

One is tempted to jump to the conclusion that Model 1 is, after all, the appropriate model for society. Indeed, for each of the new collective problems, scientific and technical questions that are components of the larger problem require "correct" answers. Incorrect answers can be too costly for the future of mankind.[1] It is therefore required that the polyarchies find new methods for putting scientific and technical competence to use.

345

Although that is an old problem in all government, it is growing exponentially in importance as social problems become increasingly the product of scientific and technical development. Nuclear accident, air pollution, and energy shortage are all the offspring of science and technology.*

But for larger problems the omniscient elite postulated in Model 1 is still not available. An alternative conclusion, then, to which to jump—or to which to proceed in an orderly manner—is Model 2 with greatly improved strategic policy making, both analytical and interactive. The disabilities of mutual adjustment do not logically imply that there should be less of it. Restructuring it is an obvious alternative.

Everyone understands that market interactions may be restructured— say, by antitrust legislation or some other change in industrial organization. But as a general formula for improving policy making, restructuring of mutual adjustment has been given little attention. An example of how it can be done we can take from the preceding chapter. Planners can be brought into policy making either in a fruitless effort to raise decision making to the style of Model 1 or to provide a voice, as we said, for efficiency and for the absentees in mutual adjustment processes. The latter is a feasible role for experts to play in Model 2 interactions and one that we have only begun to disentangle from their ostensible synoptic role.

Just what is it that is wrong with the fragmented interaction through which policy is made in the United States? Pinpointing the trouble may point in the direction of a solution.

One defect may be pivotal. It is the ease with which opponents of any positive policy to cope with a problem can obstruct it. In one way and another, formal and informal, vetoes are widely distributed in polyarchal systems. They are conspicuous in the United States. Although the president of the United States cannot force any initiatives on Congress, he can veto anything that Congress initiates. Although a minority of members cannot act positively on any policy, in House or Senate, it can stop either house from acting. Although neither house in Congress can force any policy on the other, each can veto the other simply by inaction. Although within each house dozens of committees cannot compel any initiatives or any forward motion, each can stop or delay legislation. Because ours is a federal system, the states can stop federal legislation in certain areas. The federal government can call a halt to state action in others. In polyarchal politics, to move, to initiate, or to innovate requires the cooperation of a coalition. To stop or to block a change is a legal privilege granted to many.

* If popular control is even to survive, it may become necessary to find appropriate new controls for the potentially most overpowering elite with which a citizenry has ever had to cope: the emerging new elite of knowledge, the meritocracy.

In our day, the veto appears even more threatening because of a change in the character of public problems and a consequent change in the impact of blockages. In one of the main traditions of democratic thought, government has been conceived of as presiding over a constant redistribution of benefits like wealth and power. At any time, some claimants are in process of demanding more, and other claimants are in process of yielding some of their disproportionately large shares to the newcomers. One man's gain is another man's loss. On a newer view that now restores an old tradition in political philosophy, distributional issues are fading. All citizens are now joined in a concern for peace, the conservation of energy, protection of the environment, economic stability, and other common or collective purposes. A failure of policy making leaves the entire society in peril. One person's loss is now every person's loss.

The emerging peril to the survival of polyarchy is that vetoes are increasingly cast not simply against proposed redistributions but against proposed solutions to collective problems. A veto of a redistribution— say, of new school budgets—is disappointing to some groups. A veto of a solution to a collective problem—say, of an energy policy—may put society on the road to catastrophe.

Outside the complex procedures of government proper, veto authority is elsewhere even more widely distributed. The foundation of these vetoes is largely the autonomy of the business enterprise. This is a point that conventional political science has been neglecting. A market system requires that on many points the enterprise be legally protected in a right to say no to the state. More important, its privileged position permits it to obstruct policies such as those on environmental pollution and decay, energy shortage, inflation and unemployment, and distribution of income and wealth. As we have seen, businessmen need do no more than persuade government officials that reforms will damage business. Their vetoes are powerful and ubiquitous.

How little we understand vetoes and the larger phenomenon of mutual adjustment is indicated by our failure—as in the literature of social science—to envision mutual adjustment or a pluralistic polyarchy free of business privilege. None of the market-oriented polyarchies has ever practiced pluralism without the lopsided participation of businessmen in their double role as leaders of enterprises and as members of disproportionately strong electoral and interest-groups. A pluralism without business vetoes or with greatly reduced business vetoes has hardly been explored.

How far then to go in restructuring? What vetoes to suppress? Which to allow? Here a comparison with market decision making can change the whole character of our thinking about vetoes. As we earlier noted, market systems operate with at least one major bias toward innovation. Buyers and sellers are ordinarily free to engage in transactions without regard to adverse effects on third parties. Hence, business enterprises are free to introduce new products and new technologies without regard for the skills, enterprises, or communities they destroy in doing so. Market systems are thus characterized by the very opposite of a veto. In market systems tiny minorities of one or a few can innovate, but they cannot veto.

It is a curious situation. If vetoes are as necessary to polyarchy as tradition claims them to be, there is almost certainly a comparable case for them in the market system. If, on the other hand, the relative absence of vetoes in the market system and the ease of innovation are desirable in the great market decisions taken by corporations, might they not be desirable features worth expanding in polyarchy? Market-oriented societies have hardly begun to think through this discrepancy in the value placed on initiatives and vetoes in the two different arenas. There are both fundamental similarities and dissimilarities to be explored.

Since our task is not to write prescriptions, this is as far as we shall take the veto problem. It is a problem that throws a great deal of light on the possibility of restructuring an unsatisfactory pattern of mutual adjustment. It also tells us that restructuring goes to fundamentals of the politico-economic order.

The Trade-off

There is a second major problem bearing on the future of democracy. In all market-oriented polyarchies there remains a fundamental structural problem posed by the privileges that businessmen need as a condition of their performance. It is in some part to business privilege that many contemporary problems can be traced, among them monopoly, inflation, unemployment, environmental decay, and obstruction to polyarchy, especially, we have just seen, through a skewed pattern of mutual adjustment. Is it possible to reconcile the minimum privileges required by business with a withdrawal of business privilege, including privileges to veto, that might help solve these problems?

This is an old, fundamental, continuing, inescapable problem in public policy making from which no market-oriented system can escape for a year, month, day, or hour. It is not a problem to be solved, as many critics of the corporation would tell us, simply by curbing the giant corporations and giving them their marching orders, without regard to their consequent performance. Nor is it a simple problem, as friends of the corporation would tell us, of protecting through no more than the most delicate of regulations their productive virtuosity. Nor is it a relatively uncomplicated problem that can be solved by compromise between these two views, requiring simply that we give corporations half of what they want. Half of what they want may be too much to give them in a world in which corporate discretion even thus reduced remains an insufficiently controlled source of the new chemically produced diseases of progress. And, yet, on the other hand, only half of what they want may be insufficient to induce them to produce.

In what direction, then, might there be a solution? We can sketch out one possibility as an example of strategies that need to be considered. Governments might take on the meticulous task of designing a highly discriminating mixture of financial inducement to business with governmental control over them. It is a particular way of creating a hybrid form of market and polyarchal controls such as was mentioned in Chapter 11. The key strategy is, in effect, to pay businesses to waive some of their privileges.

A clue on how government might proceed in such a venture lies in an unlikely place: aerospace and other industries that produce for defense contracts. They have come to accept, we noted in Chapter 8, what is by ordinary standards an extraordinary detail of control. For all the much professed indispensability of corporate autonomy, the military contractors have been willing to part with much of it. The government contracts they eagerly seek require that they do so. They do so because it pays. These industries are not ideal models, since they have in turn achieved, through what President Eisenhower named the military-industrial complex, an inordinate intimacy with and control over government officials responsible for military contracting. But the clue is clear enough. Businessmen may be willing to sell many of their privileges.

But can ordinary business be made so profitable that businessmen will, in return for profits, accept a great deal of regulation? Can it be done in the case of enterprises producing for ordinary markets rather than for government contracts? Again, a clue on possibilities is to be found in the aerospace and military industries. Government provides much of their capital and underwrites much of their risk. The largest defense contractors produce their products in facilities and with equipment roughly half of which are provided by the U.S. government.[2] The facilities are not provided free of charge, but their provision by government frees the enterprises from the need for large and risky capital expenditure. The U.S. government also bears a great share of the cost of research and develop-

349

ment. Of all research in the U.S., about two-thirds is at governmental expense. Government also provides some of the industry's working capital, and it underwrites risks with loans and loan guarantees. And the government guarantees profitable sales.

Clearly governments have not in the past carefully distinguished between two types of privilege: those that directly assure profitability and those that give the corporation autonomy to pursue profits with little constraint. Corporations have insisted on both, hardly distinguishing between the two. Policy makers have uncritically accepted the necessity for both. A policy based on a fundamental distinction between the two would seem a possibility worth examining.

One can of course imagine a broad public indisposition to indulge the corporation with financial benefits designed to compensate them for accepting a reduction of their freedom of action. Why, it might be asked, must the government and the public pay for the privilege of imposing controls the imposition of which presumably lies within the authority of government? But it is not a question of rights or authority. It is a practical question of combining social control over business enterprises with inducements for business.

In actual fact the common pattern is that financial benefits to the corporation do not remain locked up there. They reappear in the form of increased production or lower prices. It is a long-standing public misconception that corporations can be fined or taxed without usually shifting the charge onto a broader public. It is also a misconception that corporations can be financially indulged without normally at the same time indulging the wider public that uses their products.

Might, however, managers of corporations enrich themselves and shareholders by not passing their financial benefit on in the form of increased production and lower prices? It remains indeed a possibility. But it may be well within the capacity of tax policy to control. Assuming the veto problem can be overcome, tax and transfer policies can perhaps cope with any adverse income consequences of assuring the profitability of corporations.

But then why should corporate management be motivated to give up autonomy for financial benefits? The benefits to management turn out to be illusory. They appear on the corporate books as profits. But they are not channeled into managerial and stockholder incomes as attractive additions to their incomes. Or, if they are, they are soon taxed away. The answer is, as noted in chapter 3, that corporate profit making is a kind of game, habit, or custom. Corporate profits may be like scores in a game, indices of success, without respect to their implications for personal income. And if that is not true for all corporate managers, it seems increasingly true for a new breed of professional salaried managers, whose numbers are ever growing as increasingly open access to positions in corporate management enlarges the number of persons who want to be privileged to play the game.

A strategy of financial indulgence to offset regulatory severity does not promise guaranteed success, for it may be that at some point it awakens business leadership, passive as it appears to be in the defense industries, to a new universal threat to its influence in nation and world. But the strategy points to a road down which policy could possibly travel for some great distance. Our point is that there exists a possibility largely yet unexplored in public debate and policy experiments. In such exploration, we may find a future.

Socioeconomic Class

A third problem bearing on the future of polyarchy is the apparent decline of class indoctrination.

Consider the problem of economic instability. It is in part attributable to an excess of demands made on the resources of each nation. Most typically, inflation follows from an excess of market demand for goods and services. But inflationary demands of many kinds are these days pressed in public welfare programs, in collective bargaining, and in the multiplicity of ways in which corporations and the professions use their own exchange power in the market and employ the aid of government to raise prices and fees.[3] The simultaneous appearance of unemployment and inflation in recent years may reflect corporate demands for levels of profitability that, despite inflation of their selling prices, still do not induce them to produce at high levels of employment.

It is now a possibility that the market-oriented polyarchies cannot much longer reconcile the necessary privileged demands of business with the demands of strong unions and the welfare state. Indeed, lagging economic performance in Britain is enough to convince many observers that at least one nation has already succumbed to a fundamental problem in irreconcilable demands. Swedish unionism and welfare programs are as well developed as the British, but these observers would explain Sweden's escape from the problem as an only temporary respite in a period in which Swedish business has been able to profit from unusual resources of timber and minerals and other vanishing special opportunities in international trade.

351

The puzzle is: Why these difficulties—in the United States and much of Western Europe—now rather than twenty, or fifty, or even a hundred years ago? What is new? What has changed?

One common answer is rising expectations, a change in what people think they deserve.[4] Not only workers, investors, and managers but women, blacks, consumers, and youth have been pressing demands earlier non-existent, as a variety of "liberation" movements attest. But why have expectations risen? The evidence is not that these groups lacked the authority or the means to press demands in earlier years. With the possible exception of blacks in the United States, there have been no great changes in the options open to these groups for at least forty years.

The new expectations, it might be offered, are nothing more than would eventually be expected in societies rhetorically committed to democratic equality. Blacks want equality with whites, women with men; and the poor want a little more of what the rich enjoy. Nothing more. There are, therefore, no oddities in these demands that require special explanations.

But the question remains: Why now? What happened to release the demands. The answer may lie in the decline of class indoctrination. A reasonable hypothesis is that the old indoctrinations of class and leadership are losing effect. Although the old indoctrinations have muted demands for many long decades, acquiescence, deference, and compliance are now waning.

Consider as further evidence the problems of alienation and the decline of the work ethic, complex phenomena of obscure roots. We cannot dismiss the possibility that one cause is that the indoctrinations of class and leadership are no longer persuasive. Workers no longer are persuaded that industrial jobs are rewarding, challenging, or in any other way good for character development, as they have been taught to believe at least since the Reformation.

Or consider the signs of loss of confidence in government and in poiltical leadership. That the nation's institutions are sound, that the nation's leaders know what they are doing, are among the most common messages in the indoctrination of the citizenry. Perhaps they are no longer believed.

Other evidence has been available for decades in the growth of union participation in politics. A more important evidence is the increasing number of persons who attend universities and technical training institutes. In the single generation since 1940, the number of 25-to-29-year-olds who completed high school jumped roughly from 40 percent to 80 percent; and the proportion of college graduates among young citizens tripled.[5] The result is a rise both of a new elite of knowledge that in some important ways disassociates itself from class affiliation with other leadership and a new public more capable of resisting indoctrination. The decline of class is also revealed in studies of the measurable decline of deference of working class Englishmen to their "superiors."[6]

If class and leadership indoctrination is in fact declining in effectiveness, the consequences may entail surprises for a generation of citizens that has forgotten, if it ever knew, the older arguments for indoctrination as a constraint on the excesses of universal suffrage and democracy. From the decline of the traditional indoctrination may arise demogoguery, the extremes of opportunism, and a variety of forms of political incompetence as power shifts to citizens who reject the guidelines of their earlier indoctrination yet have little to put in their place. One can even easily imagine the evaporation of some currently prized liberties. A potentially rebellious, skeptical, nondeferential citizenry may display some of the same tendencies to challenge the law as have recently been displayed by youth and other minorities. Or a fearful citizenry may repress the dissidents.[7]

This is a problem that has been with society for a long time. It lies in Hobbes' vision of society as a "war of all against all," over "men's person, wives, children, and cattle." The sources of intense conflict remain. In the less concrete language of contemporary social science, men struggle for at least two prizes: for resources that are insufficient for all, and for authority that cannot be granted to everyone.

For Hobbes, the solution was political authority repressive enough to maintain civil order. In the "age of democracy" the solution may in fact have been—and may have to be—the constraints of class or of leadership's control over popular volitions. Either the one or the other may be necessary to achieve the consensus often alleged to be necessary to democracy.[8] In the decline of that indoctrination looms the possibility of the renewal of the war of all against all.

These strains may be exacerbated by the steady tendency of polyarchal governments to move certain decisions out of the market into government. The distribution of income, for example, is increasingly decided by government decisions on taxes, public education, public housing, health care, pensions, disability and unemployment compensation, and other transfer payments. As these decisions move from market to government, there is more to fight about in politics and a greater burden, consequently, on whatever political devices there are to keep the peace.[9]

The Impossibility of Democratization?

It may follow, then, that it is impossible for democracy to develop significantly beyond what is found in crippled form in existing polyarchy. More democracy means less. To bring popular control out of the constraint of indoctrinated volitions is to plunge the attempt at popular control into divisiveness and disorder.

353

One possibility is that the citizenry will fall into divisive conflict as indoctrination recedes. A second is that the citizenry, never very firmly attached to the polyarchal rules, will quickly abandon them under stress, for which there is some evidence in the followings achieved by Senator Joseph McCarthy, in mass enthusiasm for Hitler, in Peronism in Argentina. A third possibility is that elites or leadership groups, no longer themselves united by a common indoctrination, will fall into bitter dispute ending in coup or civil war. A final possibility is that leadership, no longer indulged by a deferential population, will no longer be motivated to hold to the polyarchal process.[10] For any of these reasons, democracy may devour itself before it is full-grown.*

Disturbing as is the hypothesis that democracy in its crippled polyarchal form is the best we can do, it is a comfortable one to some minds. It suggests that polyarchy in roughly its existing form is a kind of practicable compromise in democratic aspiration. One might even compare the constraints on polyarchy with the constraints that a stable personality imposes on the choices of the adult individual. His life is forever full of secondary choices (like the secondary political choices that are relatively unconstrained by indoctrination in a polyarchy), but his grand choices are closed. He is what he is. He could not retain his sanity if he were to consider as open all the fundamental alternatives of life style, of method of judgment, and of characteristics of perception. These are fixed through the development of what is recognized as his unique personality.

Others will find neither the suggestion of a compromise nor the analogy with personality development anything more than a complacent rationalization. Societies, they will say, are composed of many individuals. Even if each tends toward a rigidity in choice, the interplay among them should nevertheless, according to democratic aspiration, forever hold open all the important choices among social institutions and policies. And since men learn and individuals who can no longer themselves learn can pass on the learning to new generations, democracy remains forever a movement rather than an equilibrium.

When we contemplate the possibility that a decline in class and leader indoctrinations will undermine polyarchy, we need to remind ourselves that these are the same dire consequences that have often been predicted for democracy, as, for example, on the many occasions when an extension of the franchise has been debated.[11] Up to this date in history, democratization has not produced the predicted effects. We have had to look at very

---

* A parallel analysis, and one that confirms these possibilities, has to do with the thesis that many leaders in the less developed countries are antagonistic to democracy because it entails demands and responses that leadership judges to be incompatible with the demands of economic growth (Karl de Schweinitz, Jr., *Industrialization and Democracy* [New York: Free Press of Glencoe, 1964]).

recent developments to find hints of democratic decay. The longer historical story has been one of repeated invalidation of predictions of the impossibility of democracy.

There is one specific ground for believing that a decline of indoctrination, even though it introduces new conflict into the society, may not threaten polyarchy. Less indoctrinated minds may be more flexible and conciliatory. Hence disagreements, though more frequent, may be manageable under polyarchal procedures.

It is also true that, in principle at least, there exists an alternative to social order through repression, on one hand, or through class and leader indoctrination, on the other. It is the development of self-restraint both by individuals and groups in society. An unlikely prospect, one might say. But then again, no more unlikely than those out of which in an earlier period polyarchy itself arose and stabilized. Men learn. Societies, with their succession of generations, learn even more.

It is therefore possible that the democratic movement, freed of such indoctrinated opinion as now cripples it, was—and still is—a revolutionary force that remains realizable beyond any present accomplishment. Even Karl Marx at one time so believed. On the Chartist movement, he wrote:

> Universal Suffrage is the equivalent of political power for the working classes of England, where the proletariat forms the large majority of the population. . . . The carrying of Universal Suffrage in England would, therefore, be a far more socialistic measure than anything which has been honoured with that name on the Continent. Its inevitable result, here, is the political supremacy of the working class.[12]

Are the prospects to be taken seriously? So far, something has blocked, we have seen, the revolutionary force of the democratic movement. It is a cautious, constrained movement. For an explanation, shall we turn back to our earlier discussion of class indoctrination as a constraint on polyarchy? Perhaps class indoctrination, even if necessary for maintaining a low level of polyarchy is, after all, the main obstacle to a fuller democracy.

We need to caution ourselves against overestimating the effect of class in retarding a fuller democracy. The extension of suffrage was, as Marx understood, a powerful weapon to weaken the constraining influence of class on democracy. We also know that on other grounds the influence of class had already in his time somewhat declined. Vastly enlarged educational opportunities had made a difference. Other developments were the establishment of new societies that were broken loose from a feudal tradition, as in America; the decline of extremes of deference as the democratic movement spread; and new formal legal guarantees— important even if often defaulted on—of free speech and of the other civil liberties granted to all without respect to class. Important as class is in skewing popular control, it does not necessarily explain sufficiently the only very slow course of democratization.

We therefore come back to the corporation. It is possible that the rise of the corporation has offset or more than offset the decline of class as an instrument of indoctrination. That the corporation is a powerful instrument for indoctrination we have documented earlier. That it has risen to prominence in society as class lines have muted is clear enough. That it creates a new core of wealth and power for a newly constructed upper class, as well as an overpowering loud voice, is also reasonably clear. The executive of the large corporation is, on many counts, the contemporary counterpart to the landed gentry of an earlier era, his voice amplified by the technology of mass communication. A single corporate voice on television, it has been estimated, can reach more minds in one evening than were reached from all the platforms of all the world's meetings in the course of several centuries preceding broadcasting. More than class, the major specific institutional barrier to fuller democracy may therefore be the autonomy of the private corporation.

It has been a curious feature of democratic thought that it has not faced up to the private corporation as a peculiar organization in an ostensible democracy. Enormously large, rich in resources, the big corporations, we have seen, command more resources than do most government units. They can also, over a broad range, insist that government meet their demands, even if these demands run counter to those of citizens expressed through their polyarchal controls. Moreover, they do not disqualify themselves from playing the partisan role of a citizen—for the corporation is legally a person. And they exercise unusual veto powers. They are on all these counts disproportionately powerful, we have seen. The large private corporation fits oddly into democratic theory and vision. Indeed, it does not fit.

NOTES

Chapter 1

Comparing Systems

1. See the estimates and sources in Robert L. Heilbroner, *An Inquiry into the Human Prospect* (New York: Norton, 1974), chapter 2.

2. John K. Galbraith, *The New Industrial State* (Boston: Houghton Mifflin, 1971), chapter 1; and Daniel Bell, "Labor in the Post-industrial Society," in *The World of the Blue-collar Worker*, ed. Irving Howe (New York: Quadrangle, 1972), pp. 164–65, 192–93.

3. Paul Baran and Paul Sweezy, *Monopoly Capital* (New York: Modern Reader, 1966), p. 53.

4. Daniel Bell, *The Coming of Post-industrial Society* (New York: Basic Books, 1973). For another forecast of emergent society, see Zbigniew Brzezinski, *Between Two Ages* (New York: Viking, 1970). For caution against overstating the decline of industry, the growth of "service" activities, and the decline of conventional bureaucracy, see Robert L. Heilbroner, *Business Civilization in Decline* (New York: Norton, 1976), chapter 3.

5. For a thoughtful, informed, and illuminating example of prediction in the Marxist style, see John G. Gurley, *Challengers to Capitalism* (San Francisco: San Francisco Book Company, 1976), chapter 6.

6. Victor R. Fuchs, *The Service Economy* (New York: National Bureau of Economic Research, 1968), pp. 1–2.

7. For a good but still imperfect classification, see John C. Harsanyi, "Measurement of Social Power, Opportunity Costs, and the Theory of Two-person Bargaining Games," in *Behavioral Science* 7 (January 1962); and Amitai Etzioni, *A Comparative Analysis of Complex Organizations* (New York: Free Press, 1961), pp. 3–22.

Chapter 2

Authority and State

1. Robert A. Dahl and Charles E. Lindblom, *Politics, Economics, and Welfare* (New York: Harper & Brothers, 1953), p. 106.

2. New York *Times*, 16 January 1970, p. 1.

3. For a formal definition, see Herbert A. Simon, *Models of Man* (New York: John Wiley & Sons, 1957), p. 184.

4. William H. McNeill, *The Rise of the West* (Chicago: University of Chicago Press, 1963).

5. Peter H. Merkl, *Modern Comparative Politics* (New York: Holt, Rinehart, and Winston, 1970), pp. 123–24.

357

6. Max Weber, *Wirtschaft und Gesellschaft* (Tübingen: Mohr, 1922), of which Part I is translated by A. M. Henderson and Talcott Parsons as *The Theory of Social and Economic Organization* (New York: Free Press, 1947). See pp. 324–29.

7. William Bradford Huie, *The Execution of Private Slovik* (New York: Dell, 1970).

8. Quoted in Jerome M. Gilison, *The Soviet Image of Utopia* (Baltimore: Johns Hopkins University, 1975), p. 121.

9. Merle Fainsod, *How Russia Is Ruled,* rev. ed. (Cambridge, Mass.: Harvard University Press, 1963), pp. 141–42.

10. Zbigniew Brzezinski, "The Soviet Political System: Transformation or Degeneration?" in *Dilemmas of Change in Soviet Politics,* ed. Zbigniew Brzezinski (New York: Columbia University Press, 1969), pp. 16–19.

11. Robert Conquest, *Power and Policy in the U.S.S.R.* (New York: St. Martin's, 1961), p. 33.

12. Louis M. Kohlmeier, *The Regulators* (New York: Harper & Row, 1969), p. 276.

13. *Newsweek,* 15 March 1976, p. 30.

14. For a supportive but different formulation, see Arthur L. Stinchcombe, *Constructing Social Theories* (New York: Harcourt, Brace, and World, 1968), p. 150.

15. Richard E. Neustadt, *Presidential Power* (New York: John Wiley & Sons, 1960), p. 9.

16. The fountainhead of most contemporary thinking about bureaucracy continues to be Weber, *Wirtschaft und Gesellschaft.* An excellent very brief characterization of bureaucracy is Robert K. Merton, *Social Theory and Social Structure,* rev. ed. (New York: Free Press, 1957), pp. 195–206. On why bureaucracies develop, see S. N. Eisenstadt, "Bureaucracy, Bureaucratization, and Debureaucratization," *Administration Science Quarterly* 4 (1959), and Michel Crozier, *The Bureaucratic Phenomenon* (Chicago: University of Chicago Press, 1964), pp. 296–314. These have been gathered together, along with other writings on bureaucracy and formal organizations in Amitai Etzioni, ed., *A Sociological Reader on Complex Organizations* (New York: Holt, Rinehart, and Winston, 1961).

On consequences of bureaucracy for the analysis of policy problems see Harold L. Wilensky, *Organizational Intelligence* (New York: Basic Books, 1967).

17. Robert C. Fried, *Performance in American Bureaucracy* (Boston: Little, Brown, 1976), pp. 23ff and 39.

18. Jerry F. Hough, "The Bureaucratic Model and the Nature of the Soviet System," *Journal of Comparative Administration* 5 (August 1973).

19. Warren G. Bennis, "Beyond Bureaucracy," in *American Bureaucracy,* ed. Warren G. Bennis (Chicago: Aldine, 1970), p. 13. For an argument that hierarchial forms are inevitable in biological and social organizations, see Herbert A. Simon, *The Shape of Automation* (New York: Harper & Row, 1965), p. 110.

20. New York *Times,* 21 January 1951, p. 1; and 7 February 1951, p. 20.

21. Charles Peters and Timothy J. Adams, eds., *Inside the System* (New York: Praeger, 1970), p. 178.

22. In Marshall I. Goldman, ed., *Comparative Economic Systems: A Reader,* 2nd ed. (New York: Random House, 1964), p. 420.

Chapter 3

Exchange and Markets

1. Adam Smith, *An Inquiry into the Nature and Causes of the Wealth of Nations* (London, 1776), book 4, chapter 9.

2. William H. McNeill, *The Shape of European History* (New York: Oxford University Press, 1974), p. 114.

3. U.S. Department of Labor, Bureau of Labor Statistics, *Occupational Employment Statistics, 1960–67* (Washington, D.C., 1970), pp. 4ff.

4. E. Phelps Brown, *The Economics of Labor* (New Haven, Conn.: Yale University Press, 1962), p. 102.

5. Karl Polanyi, *The Great Transformation* (New York: Rinehart & Company, 1944), part 2, section 1.

6. David Macarov, *Incentives to Work* (San Francisco: Jossey-Bass, 1970), especially chapters 4, 6, and 7 for a survey of studies.

7. For empirical evidence, George F. Break, "Income Taxes and Incentives to Work," *American Economic Review* 47 (September 1957): especially pp. 539–41.

8. The full argument is in Martin Bronfenbrenner, *Income Distribution Theory* (New York: Aldine-Atherton, 1971), chapter 9. See also Robin Barlow, Harvey E. Brazer, and James N. Morgan, *Economic Behavior of the Affluent* (Washington, D.C.: Brookings Institution, 1966), chapter 10, "Working Behavior."

9. Ibid., p. 150. See p. 130 for the other studies, all of which, in a "record of unanimity," agree that income-tax work disincentives are minor.

10. Ibid., chapter 10; William H. Whyte, *The Organization Man* (New York: Simon & Schuster, 1956), pp. 144–45.

11. For example, Milton Friedman, *Capitalism and Freedom* (Chicago: University of Chicago Press, 1962), pp. 13–15; and Friedrich A. Hayek, *The Road to Serfdom* (Chicago: University of Chicago Press, 1944), pp. 14–17, 36.

12. In both Friedman, *Capitalism and Freedom,* and Hayek, *Road to Serfdom,* the possible coerciveness of the distribution of property is not discussed. Frank H. Knight argues that the history of the distribution of property undermines the claim that freedom leads to desirable results, but he does not consider the possibility that it may itself undercut the claim that market relations are free ("Freedom as fact and as Criterion," in *Freedom and Reform,* Frank H. Knight [New York: Harper & Brothers, 1947], p. 9). Some recent liberal explorations of questions on liberty are: James M. Buchanan, *The Limits of Liberty* (Chicago: University of Chicago Press, 1975); Robert Nozick, *Anarchy, State and Utopia* (New York: Basic Books, 1974); and John Rawls, *A Theory of Justice* (Cambridge, Mass.: Harvard University Press, 1971).

13. William Townsend, *Dissertation on the Poor Laws* (London: Ridgways, 1817; first published 1786), p. 15.

14. Exclusive of pension rights and cumulations. Dorothy S. Projector and Gertrude S. Weiss, *Survey of Financial Characteristics of Consumers* (Washington, D.C.: Federal Reserve System, 1966), p. 100.

Chapter 4

Persuasion and Preceptoral Systems

1. Karl W. Deutsch, *The Nerves of Government* (New York: Free Press, 1963); and John D. Steinbruner, *The Cybernetic Theory of Decision: New Dimensions of Political Analysis* (Princeton, N.J.: Princeton University Press, 1974).

2. Norbert Wiener, *Cybernetics* (Cambridge, Mass.: MIT Press, 1948).

3. On concepts of totalitarianism, see Carl J. Friedrich, Michael Curtis, and Benjamin R. Barber, *Totalitarianism in Perspective* (New York: Praeger, 1969).

4. Alexis de Tocqueville, *Democracy in America,* vol. 3 (New York: Vintage Books, 1945), pp. 336–37.

5. Richard Grunberger, *The 12-Year Reich: A Social History of Nazi Germany, 1933–1945* (New York: Holt, Rinehart, and Winston, 1971) 401–2.

6. Hannah Arendt, *The Origins of Totalitarianism* (Cleveland: World Publishing Company, 1958), p. 306.

7. Karl Dietrich Bracher, *The German Dictatorship* (New York: Praeger, 1970), p. 342.

8. Jean Jacques Rousseau, *Émile* (London: Everyman's Library, J. M. Dent and Sons, 1969), pp. 84–85; and *The Social Contract* (New York: Hafner Publishing Company, 1947), p. 36.

9. E. L. Wheelwright and Bruce McFarlane, *The Chinese Road to Socialism* (New York: Monthly Review Press, 1970), p. 147. See also Raymond A. Bauer, *The New Man in Soviet Psychology* (Cambridge, Mass.: Harvard University Press, 1952).

10. From an official Cuban newspaper, *Granma,* as quoted in Richard R. Fagen, *The Transformation of Political Culture in Cuba* (Stanford, Calif.: Stanford University Press, 1969), p. 17.

11. Frederick C. Barghoorn, *Politics in the U.S.S.R.* (Boston: Little, Brown, 1972), p. 94; Raymond A. Bauer, Alex Inkeles, and Clyde Kluckhohn, *How the Soviet System Works* (Cambridge, Mass.: Harvard University Press, 1957), p. 138; James Hsiung, *Ideology and Practice* (New York: Praeger, 1970), p. 8; Fagen, *Political Culture in Cuba,* p. 14.

12. On obedience to authority in Cuba, see Fagen, *Political Culture in Cuba,* p. 14; for China, see Hsiung, *Ideology and Practice,* p. 8.

13. Ezra F. Vogel, "Voluntarism and Social Control," in *Soviet and Chinese Communism,* ed. Donald W. Treadgold (Seattle: University of Washington Press, 1967).

14. Quoted in Alex Inkeles and Raymond A. Bauer, *The Soviet Citizen* (Cambridge, Mass.: Harvard University Press, 1959), p. 67.

15. Franz Schurmann, *Ideology and Organization in Communist China,* 2nd ed., enl. (Berkeley: University of California Press, 1971), p. 233.

16. James R. Townsend, *Political Participation in Communist China* (Berkeley: University of California Press, 1967), p. 184.

17. In Schurmann, *Ideology and Organization,* pp. 47–48. See also Robert Jay Lifton, *Thought Reform and the Psychology of Totalism* (New York: W. W. Norton, 1961).

18. Schurmann, *Ideology and Organization,* p. 32.

19. Bauer, *The New Man,* p. 177.

20. Schurmann, *Ideology and Organization,* pp. 47–53.

21. Ibid., p. 20.

22. Hsiung, *Ideology and Practice,* p. 157; and Schurmann, *Ideology and Organization,* p. 57.

23. John G. Gurley, "Capitalist and Maoist Economic Development," *Bulletin of Concerned Asian Scholars* 2 (April-July 1970): 39.

24. Schurmann, *Ideology and Organization,* pp. 162ff; Barry M. Richman, *Industrial Society in Communist China* (New York: Random House, 1969), pp. 229ff.

25. Schurmann, *Ideology and Organization,* pp. 100, 233.

26. Émile Durkheim, *The Division of Labor in Society* (first published 1893; New York: Free Press, 1933).

27. For example, Harvey Leibenstein, "Allocative Efficiency *vs.* 'X-Efficiency,' " *American Economic Review* 56 (June 1966).

28. William Foote Whyte and Melville Dalton, *Money and Motivation* (New York: Harper & Row, 1955), p. 259.

29. Alexander Eckstein, "Economic Development and Political Change in Communist Systems," *World Politics* 22 (July 1970): 486.

30. Ibid., p. 485.

Chapter 5

Authority Systems: Strong Thumbs, No Fingers

1. On the fateful discrepancy between cognitive capacity and complexity of social problem, see Herbert A. Simon, *Administrative Behavior* (New York: Macmillan,

1949), pp. 80–84; and David Braybrooke and Charles E. Lindblom, *A Strategy of Decision* (New York: Free Press, 1963), chapters 2 and 3.

2. On the U.S.S.R., Abram Bergson, *The Economics of Soviet Planning* (New Haven, Conn.: Yale University Press, 1964), p. 138; and Joseph S. Berliner, "Managerial Incentives and Decision Making," in U.S. Congress, Joint Economic Committee, Joint Committee Print, *Comparisons of the United States and Soviet Economies,* 86th Cong., 1st sess., 1959, part 1. On China, Barry H. Richman, *Industrial Society in Communist China* (New York: Random House, 1969), pp. 464ff; on Cuba, Carmelo Mesa-Lago and Luc Zephirin, "Central Planning," in *Revolutionary Change in Cuba,* ed. Carmelo Mesa-Lago (Pittsburgh: University of Pittsburgh Press, 1971), p. 170.

3. Quoted in Alexander Balinky et al., *Planning and Market in the U.S.S.R.* (New Brunswick, N.J.: Rutgers University Press, 1967), p. 52.

4. John Lindbeck, ed., *China: Management of a Revolutionary Society* (Seattle: University of Washington Press, 1971), p. 298. For extended discussion see Harold Wilensky, *Organizational Intelligence* (New York: Basic Books, 1967).

5. From a document of the German Central Planning Office in the Nazi period in Walter Eucken, "On the Theory of the Centrally Administered Economy," *Economica* N.S. 58 (May 1948): 86–87.

6. J. S. Prybyla, *The Political Economy of Communist China* (Scranton, Pa.: International Textbook, 1970), p. 306.

7. Ibid., p. 230. On the problem in China, see Richman, *Industrial Society,* p. 466. For Cuba, see Mesa-Lago and Zephirin, "Central Planning," pp. 158ff.

8. For more on the consequent inefficiencies, see J. M. Montias, *Central Planning in Poland* (New Haven, Conn.: Yale University Press, 1962), p. 188 and passim.

9. U.S. Bureau of the Budget, *The United States at War* (Washington, D.C., 1946), p. 437.

10. Quoted in Heinz Kohler, *Scarcity Challenged* (New York: Holt, Rinehart, and Winston, 1968), p. 507.

11. Audrey Donnithorne, *China's Economic System* (New York: Praeger, 1967), pp. 158ff; Prybyla, *Political Economy,* p. 305; Mesa-Lago and Zephirin, "Central Planning," p. 176.

12. R. W. Davies, "Planning a Mature Economy in the U.S.S.R.," *Economics of Planning* 6 (1966): 147.

13. Barrington Moore, *Terror and Progress in the U.S.S.R.* (Cambridge, Mass.: Harvard University Press, 1954), p. 22.

14. The design of improved incentives for authority systems is in its infancy. Most authority systems are full of disincentives, as well as distorted incentives that positively motivate the wrong kind of action. For a view of the problem, see Charles L. Schultze, "The Role of Incentives, Penalties, and Rewards in Attaining Effective Policy," in *Public Expenditures and Policy Analysis,* eds. Robert H. Haveman and Julius Margolis (Chicago: Markham, 1973).

15. *Beyond Freedom and Dignity* (New York: Alfred A. Knopf, 1971) pp. 61–66.

Chapter 6

The Limited Competence of Markets

1. Karl Polyani, *The Great Transformation* (New York: Rinehart and Company, 1944).

2. Erich Fromm, *Escape from Freedom* (New York: Rinehart and Company, 1941).

3. Leo A. Orleans, "China's Environomics," in U.S. Congress, Joint Economic Committee, Joint Committee Print, *China: A Reassessment of the Economy,* 94th Congress, 1st session, 1975.

4. The complexity of imposing charges to make prices better represent all costs are

discussed in R. H. Coase, "The Problem of Social Costs," *Journal of Law and Economics* 3 (October 1960). On a relatively successful program of pollution control using charges, see Allen V. Kneese, "Water Quality Management by Regional Authorities in the Ruhr Area," *Papers and Proceedings of the Regional Science Association* 11 (December 1963), ed. Morgan D. Thomas.

5. R. H. Coase, "The Nature of the Firm," *Economica* N.S. 4 (November 1937).

6. Edward Hallett Carr, *The New Society* (Boston: Beacon Press, 1957), p. 57.

7. Wassily Leontief, "Notes On a Visit to Cuba," *New York Review of Books* 13 (21 August 1969): pp. 16ff.

8. See Graham Wootton, *Workers, Unions, and the State* (New York: Schocken Books, 1967), p. 107.

9. George E. Berkley, *The Administrative Revolution* (Englewood Cliffs, N.J.: Prentice-Hall, 1971), pp. 44ff.

10. George J. Staller, "Fluctuations in Economic Activity: Planned and Free Market Economics, 1950–1960," *American Economic Review* 54 (June 1964).

11. Or, in China, assignment of the unemployed urban worker to farm labor. Carl Riskin, "Workers' Incentives in Chinese Industry" in Joint Economic Committee, *China*, p. 206.

12. For an overview of the difficulties, see James Tobin, "Inflation and Unemployment," *American Economic Review* 62 (March 1972).

13. John Ruskin, *Unto This Last*, ed. Lloyd J. Hubenka (Lincoln: University of Nebraska Press, 1967), pp. 74–75.

14. For examples, see the collection of articles in David Mermelstein, ed., *Economics: Mainstream Readings and Radical Critiques* (New York: Random House, 1970).

Chapter 7

Alternative Market Systems

1. U.S. Department of Commerce, *Survey of Current Business* 56 (January 1976) part 1, p. 30; U.S. Department of Labor, Bureau of Labor Statistics, *Employment and Wages, First Quarter 1974* (1975), p. 98.

2. Robert C. Fried, *Performance in American Bureaucracy* (Boston: Little, Brown, 1976), p. 39; and Ralph Nader and Mark J. Green, eds., *Corporate Power in America* (New York: Grossman Publishers, 1973), pp. 90–93.

3. See, for Europe, M. M. Postan, *American Economic History of Western Europe, 1945–1964* (London: Methuen, 1967), chapter 8. See also "The *Fortune* Directory of the 500 Largest Industrial Corporations," *Fortune* 83 (May 1971) and "The *Fortune* Directory of the 200 Largest Industrials Outside the U.S.," *Fortune* 84 (August 1971).

4. Robert Heilbroner, *Business Civilization in Decline* (New York: Norton, 1976), p. 83.

5. Raymond Vernon, ed., *Big Business and the State* (Cambridge, Mass.: Harvard University Press, 1974), chapter 2.

6. For the history of the idea and of the controversy, Abram Bergson, "Socialist Economics," in *A Survey of Contemporary Economics*, ed. Howard W. Ellis (Philadelphia: Blakiston, 1948).

7. Alexander Balinky et al., *Planning and the Market in the U.S.S.R.* (New Brunswick, N.J.: Rutgers University Press, 1967), pp. 64, 93. See also Willem Keizer, *The Soviet Quest for Economic Rationality* (Rotterdam: Rotterdam University Press, 1971), p. 199.

8. Estimate is by I. Malyshev, Deputy Director, Central Statistical Administration, "Cybernetics, Economic Planning, and the Social System," *U.S.S.R.*, no. 9 (September 1964): 15.

9. On Soviet data requirements and capacities for meeting them, see Richard W. Judy, "Information, Control, and Soviet Economic Management," in *Mathematics and Computers in Soviet Economic Planning,* ed. John P. Hardt (New Haven: Yale University Press, 1967).

10. Heinz Kohler, *Scarcity Challenged* (New York: Holt, Rinehart, and Winston, 1968), p. 494.

11. On Soviet experience, see Vladimir G. Treml, "Input-Output Analysis and Soviet Planning," in *Mathematics and Computers.*

12. For fresh thinking on these lines, see Janos Kornai, *Mathematical Planning of Structural Decisions* (Amsterdam: North Holland, 1967); and Janos Kornai and T. Liptak, "Two-Level Planning," *Econometrica* 33 (January 1965). See also Jeffrey B. Nugent, "Linear Programming Models for National Planning," *Econometrica* 38 (November 1970).

13. On the U.S.S.R., see Gertrude E. Schroeder, "Recent Developments in Soviet Planning and Incentives," in U.S. Congress, Joint Economic Committee, Joint Committee Print, *Soviet Economic Prospects for the Seventies,* 93rd Congress, 1st session, 1973; and Keizer, *The Soviet Quest,* p. 203.

14. Eli Ginzberg, Dale Hiestand, and Beatrice G. Reubens, *The Pluralistic Economy* (New York: McGraw-Hill, 1965), p. 87. If churches, fraternal orders, interest groups, political parties, and many other private nonprofit organizations are counted as enterprises, which on many counts they are, then private nonprofit organization receipts account for as much as a quarter or third of gross national product. For estimates, see Burton A. Weisbrod, "Some Collective-Good Aspects of Non-governmental Activities," (mimeo) Prepared for 32nd Congress, International Institute of Public Finance (Edinburgh, September 9, 1976). For an impressive analysis of inefficiencies not uncommon in nonprofit institutions, see Donald A. Schon, "The Blindness System," *The Public Interest* 18 (Winter 1970).

15. Frederic L. Pryor, *Property and Industrial Organization in Communist and Capitalist Nations* (Bloomington: Indiana University Press, 1973), p. 389.

16. Compare P. J. D. Wile's models in his *Political Economy of Communism* (Oxford: Basil Blackwell, 1962), p. xiii and chapter 4.

17. R. W. Davies, *The Development of the Soviet Budgetary System* (Cambridge: University of Cambridge Press, 1958).

Chapter 8

The Market-oriented Private Enterprise System

1. William Nordhaus and James Tobin, "Is Growth Obsolete?" in National Bureau of Economic Research, Fiftieth Anniversary Colloquium V, *Economic Growth* (New York: National Bureau of Economic Research, 1972); and Ismail Abdel-Hamid Sirageldin, *Non-Market Components of National Income* (Ann Arbor: University of Michigan Institute for Social Research, 1969).

2. For a systematic comparative survey and study of government economic policy in nine market-oriented systems, see E. S. Kirschen et al., *Economic Policy in Our Time,* 3 vols. (Amsterdam: North-Holland, 1964).

3. Expenditures of all kinds, at all levels of government, including expenditures of governmentally owned business enterprises, government capital investment, and social security and other welfare expenditures. Bruce M. Russett et al., *World Handbook of Political and Social Indicators* (New Haven, Conn.: Yale University Press, 1964), p. 63.

4. Not all public enterprises included.

5. Not all public enterprises included.

6. All figures for 1968, derived from United Nations, *Yearbook of National*

Accounts Statistics, 1969 (New York: United Nations, 1970), except for the Austrian, Indian, and Nigerian figures, which are derived from the 1972 *Yearbook.*

7. For United States: U.S. Bureau of the Census, *Statistical Abstract of the United States, 1975* (Washington, D.C.: Government Printing Office, 1975).

France: France, Ministère de l'Economie et des Finances, *Annuaire Statistique de la France 1972* (Paris: Institut National de la Statistique et des Études Économiques, 1972).

India: India, Department of Statistics, *Statistical Abstract 1969* (New Delhi: Government of India Press, 1970).

Japan: Robert E. Ward and Roy C. Macridis, eds., *Modern Political Systems: Asia* (Englewood Cliffs, N.J.: Prentice-Hall, 1963), p. 100.

West Germany: Roy C. Macridis and Robert E. Ward, eds., *Modern Political Systems: Europe,* 2nd ed. (Englewood Cliffs, N.J.: Prentice-Hall, 1968), pp. 428, 380.

Britain: Great Britain, Central Statistical Office, *Annual Abstract of Statistics, 1975* (London: Her Majesty's Stationery Office, 1975). Richard Pryke, *Public Enterprise in Practice* (London: MacGibbon & Keek, 1973), p. 22.

8. Murray Weidenbaum, *The Modern Public Sector* (New York: Basic Books, 1969), pp. 10–11.

9. Derived by subtracting "compensation of employees" from "general government final expenditures" in United Nations, *Yearbook of National Account Statistics, 1974* (New York: United Nations, 1975).

10. Seymour Melman, *Pentagon Capitalism* (New York: McGraw-Hill, 1970); idem, *The Permanent War Economy* (New York: Simon & Schuster, 1974). See also Michael Kidron, *Western Capitalism since the War,* rev. (Harmondsworth, England: Penguin Books, 1970). "Significantly, in so far as planning exists in the U.S. . . . its most sophisticated practitioner is the Department of Defense whose methods have long since abandoned any pretence at tendering on large contracts in favour of strict physical controls over quality and quantities." (p. 30).

11. Melman, *Pentagon Capitalism,* pp. 38ff.

12. M. M. Postan, *An Economic History of Western Europe, 1945–1964* (London: Methuen, 1967), p. 226.

13. Henry W. Ehrmann, *Organized Business in France* (Princeton, N.J.: Princeton University Press, 1957), p. 346; and Roy Harrod, *Are These Hardships Necessary?* (London: Hart-Davis, 1947), Appendix.

14. Ehrmann, *Organized Business,* pp. 349ff. See also Andrew Shonfield, *Modern Capitalism* (London: Oxford University Press, 1969), pp. 140, 167–68, 171.

15. New York *Times,* 25 March 1967, pp. 31ff.

16. U.S. Department of Commerce, *Survey of Current Business* 54 (July 1974), pp. 17, 34. For more detail on government enterprises, market and nonmarket, in the United States, see William G. Shepherd, *The Treatment of Market Power* (New York: Columbia University, 1975), especially table p. 13.

17. More detail, including listings of the most important public corporations in the United States, is in Lloyd D. Musolf, *Government and the Economy* (Chicago: Scott, Foresman, 1965), pp. 134ff.; and Clair Wilcox and William G. Shepherd, *Public Policies Toward Business* (Homewood, Ill.: Irwin, 1975) part V.

18. Robert H. Haveman, *The Economics of the Public Sector* (New York: John Wiley & Sons, 1970), p. 8.

19. Frédéric François-Marsal, *Le Dépérissement des Entreprises Publiques* (Paris: Calmann-Lévy, 1973), p. 16.

20. Figures are derived from rough estimates and have been rounded. For Argentina, Chile, and Mexico: U.S. Bureau of International Affairs, *Directory of Labor Organizations: Western Hemisphere, rev. ed.* (Washington, D.C.: Government Printing Office, 1964). For India: U.S. Bureau of International Labor Affairs, *Directory of Labor Organizations: Asia and Australia,* rev. ed. (Washington, D.C.: Government Printing Office, 1964). For Sweden: U.S. Bureau of International Labor Affairs, *Directory of Labor Organizations: Europe,* rev. ed. (Washington, D.C.: Government Printing Office, 1965). All other figures are from: Phillip A. Klein, *The*

Management of Market-Oriented Economies (Belmont, Calif. Wadsworth, 1973) pp. 111–15.

21. In Israel, however, the national union, Histadrut, owns and manages a large number of major businesses, accounting for perhaps a fifth of total employment in Israel.

22. Kidron, *Western Capitalism,* chapter 7.

23. Allan M. Cartter and F. Ray Marshall, *Labor Economics* (Homewood, Ill.: Irwin, 1972), p. 88.

24. George E. Johnson, "Economic Analysis of Trade Unionism," *American Economic Review* 65 (May 1975): 26.

25. For a fuller statement see John T. Dunlop, "The Social Utility of Collective Bargaining," in *Challenges to Collective Bargaining,* ed. Lloyd Ulman (New York: Columbia University, The American Assembly, 1967).

26. Johnson, "Economic Analysis," pp. 26–28; Frederick M. Scherer, *Industrial Market Structure and Economic Performances* (Chicago: Rand McNally, 1971), pp. 298–303.

27. For a program of market reforms, see James E. Meade, *The Intelligent Radical's Guide to Economic Policy* (London: George Allen & Unwin, 1975). For new thinking and theory on specific organizational alternatives—in which market enterprise and government agency are systematically compared—see Oliver E. Williamson, *Markets and Hierarchies* (New York: Free Press, 1975); and William A. Niskanen, *Bureaucracy and Representative Government* (Chicago: Aldine, 1971).

Chapter 9

Politics: The Struggle Over Authority

1. Percival Spear, *India, Pakistan, and the West,* 4th ed. (London: Oxford University Press, 1967), p. 59.

2. Maxime Rodinson, "The Political System," in *Egypt since the Revolution,* ed. P. J. Vatikiotis (London: Allen & Unwin, 1968).

3. W. A. C. Adie. "China's 'Second Liberation' in Perspective," in *China After the Cultural Revolution* (New York: Random House, 1969), p. 44.

4. See also Frederic L. Pryor, *Public Expenditures in Communist and Capitalist Nations* (Homewood, Ill.: Irwin, 1968), chapter 7.

5. Cyril E. Black, "Soviet Society," in *Prospects for Soviet Society,* ed. Allen Kasoff (New York: Praeger, 1968), p. 52.

6. Evidence of Soviet responsiveness to public opinion is in A. H. Brown, "Policy-Making in the Soviet Union," *Soviet Studies* 23 (July 1971): 140–43.

7. James Chich Hsiung, *Ideology and Practice* (New York: Praeger, 1970), p. 293.

8. Hugh Heclo, *Modern Social Politics in Britain and Sweden* (New Haven: Yale University Press, 1974), p. 291.

9. Frederick C. Barghoorn, *Politics in the U.S.S.R.,* 2nd ed. (Boston: Little, Brown, 1972), p. 224.

10. See *International Encyclopedia of the Social Sciences,* s.v. "Constitutions and Constitutionalism," by Carl J. Friederich.

11. Franz Schurmann, *Ideology and Organization in Communist China* (Berkeley: University of California Press, 1966), p. 188.

12. Jan S. Prybyla, *The Political Economy of Communist China* (Scranton, Pa.: International Textbook, 1970), p. 9.

13. Its gradual emergence in Yugoslavia up to about 1970 is significant, even if since then it has in some respects receded (Winston M. Fisk, "The Constitutional Movement in Yugoslavia," *Slavic Review* 30 (June 1971).

14. New York *Times,* 30 May 1976, section 4, p. 4.

15. New York *Times,* 14 May 1976, p. A 11.

16. *Time,* 19 April 1976, p. 65. New York *Times,* 3 June 1976, p. 2.

Chapter 10

Polyarchy

1. Amended from a list of R. A. Dahl, *Democracy in the United States,* 3rd ed. (Chicago: Rand McNally, 1976), p. 47. Dahl would add Sri Lanka (Ceylon) and Colombia to the list. A similar classification in Harold Wilensky, *The Welfare State and Equality* (Berkeley: University of California, 1975), p. 138, adds Ecuador, Guyana, and Turkey; and removes Venezuela.

2. In Richard McKeon, ed., *Democracy in a World of Tensions* (Chicago: University of Chicago Press, 1951), p. 174.

3. Carole Patemen, *Participation and Democratic Theory* (Cambridge: Cambridge University Press, 1970), pp. 18, 20.

4. Frank H. Knight, "The Meaning of Democracy," in his *Freedom and Reform* (New York: Harper & Brothers, 1947), p. 190.

5. Theorists of this stripe are listed, summarized, and compared with "contemporary" theorists in Lane Davis, "The Cost of Realism," *Western Political Quarterly* 17 (March 1964): 29.

6. John Stuart Mill, *Representative Government* (London: Dent, 1910), p. 195.

7. From the use of the term in Robert A. Dahl and Charles E. Lindblom, *Politics, Economics, and Welfare* (New York: Harper & Brothers, 1953).

8. The list is from R. A. Dahl, *Polyarchy* (New Haven, Conn.: Yale University Press, 1971), p. 3; and such a list varies somewhat from author to author. If fully satisfied, the list would characterize democracy not polyarchy.

9. For thoughtful speculation on the most critical secondary rules governing the behavior of leaders in a polyarchy, see V. O. Key, Jr., *Public Opinion and American Democracy* (New York: Alfred A. Knopf, 1961), p. 536–39.

10. Dahl, *Polyarchy,* pp. 1–2.

11. On the concept of a volition, see Robert E. Emmer, *Economic Analysis and Scientific Philosophy* (London: Allen & Unwin, 1967), p. 31.

12. This is not to say that basic values have to be agreed to in a democratic or other society. For brief summary and a bibliography on various views on just what has to be harmonized, see Michael Mann, "The Social Cohesion of Liberal Democracy," *American Sociological Review* 35 (June 1970).

13. The term "integrated" as distinguished from "compromised" is from Mary Parker Follett (Henry M. Metcalf and L. Urwick, *Dynamic Administration: The Collected Papers of Mary Parker Follett* [New York: Harper & Brothers, 1942], pp. 65–66.) In the language of preferences, what is required is not compromises but Pareto optima; but that terminology is inappropriate, given that the language of preference is itself questioned here.

14. Mill, *Representative Government,* pp. 277ff.; James Bryce, *The American Commonwealth,* 2 vols. (London: Macmillan, 1904), 2: chapter 76.

15. Susan Blackall Hansen, "Participation, Political Structure, and Concurrence," *American Political Science Review* 69 (December 1975).

16. From Charles E. Lindblom, *The Policy-Making Process* (Englewood Cliffs, N.J.: Prentice-Hall, 1968), p. 103.

17. A vivid concrete description of the process is in Robert E. Lane, *Political Ideology* (New York: Free Press, 1962), pp. 442–46.

18. Sidney Verba and Norman H. Nie, *Participation in America* (New York: Harper & Row, 1972), p. 31.

19. Ibid., pp. 25, 26.

20. For detail, see Charles E. Lindblom, *The Intelligence of Democracy* (New York: Free Press, 1965), esp. pp. 63, 84.

21. E. E. Schattschneider, *The Semisovereign People* (New York: Holt, Rinehart, and Winston, 1960), p. 35.

22. In American political science, the 1960s marked a wave, perhaps only the

beginning of a wave, of reconsideration of pluralist theories of polyarchy. Some representative pluralist theories are: David Riesman, *The Lonely Crowd* (New Haven, Conn.: Yale University Press, 1950); R. A. Dahl, *A Preface to Democratic Theory* (Chicago: University of Chicago Press, 1956), chapter 5. For other pluralist estimates of the efficacy of popular control, see V. O. Key, Jr., *Public Opinion and American Democracy,* esp. chapter 21; David Truman, *The Governmental Process* (New York: Knopf, 1951) and Truman, "The American System in Crisis," *Political Science Quarterly* 59 (December 1959), pp. 481–98. Critics include: Henry Kariel, *The Decline of American Pluralism* (Stanford, Calif.: Stanford University Press, 1961); Theodore Lowi, *The End of Liberalism* (New York: Norton, 1969); Peter Bachrach, *The Theory of Democratic Elitism* (Boston: Little, Brown, 1967).

23. It has even been suggested that the cleavage between organized and unorganized has displaced cleavage between organized economic groups as a major feature of the American system. Bruce C. Johnson, "The Democratic Mirage," *Berkeley Journal of Sociology* 13 (1968).

24. Robert V. Presthus, *Men at the Top* (New York: Oxford University Press, 1964), esp. pp. 408–9.

25. Dahl and Lindblom, *Politics, Economics, and Welfare,* pp. 504–5.

Chapter 11

Polyarchal and Market Controls

1. On the first alternative, "exit," and the second, "voice," see Albert O. Hirschman, *Exit, Voice, and Loyalty* (Cambridge, Mass.: Harvard University Press, 1970).

2. On the elected official's different understandings of his role in the United States, see John C. Wahlke et al., *The Legislative System* (New York: John Wiley & Sons, 1962), pp. 282–86; and Raymond A. Bauer, Ithiel de Sola Pool, and Lewis Anthony Dexter, *American Business and Public Policy* (New York: Atherton, 1963), chapters 29 and 30. For the United Kingdom see Samuel H. Beer, *British Politics in the Collectivist Age* (New York: Alfred A. Knopf, 1966).

3. Robert A. Levine, *Public Planning: Failure and Redirection* (New York: Basic Books, 1972), p. 67.

4. F. M. Scherer, *Industrial Market Structure and Economic Performance* (Chicago: Rand McNally, 1970), pp. 55ff.

5. T. O. Lloyd, *Empire to Welfare State* (London: Oxford University Press, 1970), pp. 267–68; Alfred F. Havighurst, *Twentieth Century Britain,* 2nd ed. (New York: Harper & Row, 1962), pp. 366–67; Henry Pelling, *Modern Britain, 1885–1955* (Edinburgh: Thomas Nelson & Sons, 1960), pp. 154–55.

6. Christopher D. Stone, *Where the Law Ends* (New York: Harper & Row, 1975), p. 238.

7. Walter Adams and Joel B. Dirlam, "Big Steel, Invention, and Innovation," *Quarterly Journal of Economics* 80 (May 1966).

Chapter 12

Market and Democracy

1. Sir Ernest Barker, *Reflections on Government* (London: Oxford University Press, 1942), p. 188.

2. Hans Kelsen, *Vom Wesen und Wert der Demokratie* (Tübingen: Verlag von J. C. B. Mohr, 1929), p. 93, this author's translation.

3. George Sabine, "The Two Democratic Traditions," *The Philosophical Review* 61 (October 1952). See also Kelsen, *Vom Wesen und Wert der Demokratie*.

4. Karl Marx, *Capital,* ed. Frederick Engels (New York: Modern Library, 1906), p. 786.

5. Barker, *Reflections,* p. 191.

6. C. B. Macpherson, *The Real World of Democracy* (London: Oxford University Press, 1965), p. 46.

7. For a fuller discussion on wartime organization, see R. A. Dahl and C. E. Lindblom, *Politics, Economics, and Welfare* (New York: Harper & Brothers, 1953), pp. 402–12; and Tibor Scitovsky, Edward Shaw, and Lorie Tarshis, *Mobilizing Resources for War* (New York: McGraw-Hill, 1951), esp. pp. 135–39.

8. U.S. War Production Board, *American Industry in War and Transition, 1940–1950,* Part II (WPB Document No. 27, 1945).

9. For description of the plan, see David Novick, Melven Anshen, and W. E. Truppner, *Wartime Production Controls* (New York: Columbia University Press, 1949), chapter 8.

Chapter 13

The Privileged Position of Business

1. U.S. Congress, Senate, Subcommittee on Antitrust and Monopoly of the Committee on the Judiciary: Hearings, Egon Sohmen testimony in *Economic Concentration,* 90th Congress, 2d session, 1968, p. 3446.

2. For a long list of U.S. business subsidies, see Clair Wilcox, *Public Policy toward Business,* 4th ed. (Homewood, Ill.: Irwin, 1971), chapter 33. On the variety of promotions, see Murray Weidenbaum, *The Modern Public Sector* (New York: Basic Books, 1969), esp. the table on p. 137.

3. Quoted in Heinz Hartmann, *Authority and Organization in German Management* (Princeton, N.J.: Princeton University Press, 1959), p. 229.

4. Harold Brayman, *Corporate Management in a World of Politics* (New York: McGraw-Hill, 1967), p. 57.

5. On the adjustment of protesting businessmen to the reduction of their privileges, see Robert E. Lane, *The Regulation of Businessmen* (New Haven, Conn.: Yale University Press, 1954).

6. On tax policy support, see Robert E. Hall and Dale W. Jorgenson, "Tax Policy and Investment Behavior," *American Economic Review* 57 (June 1967): 410.

7. For detail, see James O'Connor, "The Private Welfare State," in Milton Mankoff, ed., *The Poverty of Progress* (New York: Holt, Rinehart, and Winston, 1972), pp. 96–101.

8. Christopher D. Stone, *Where the Law Ends* (New York: Harper & Row, 1975), pp. 54–56.

9. Mark Green and Peter Petkas, "Nixon's Industrial State," *New Republic* 167 (16 September 1972): 20.

10. Ibid., p. 19.

11. Joseph LaPalombara, *Interest Groups in Italian Politics* (Princeton, N.J.: Princeton University Press, 1964), p. 278.

12. Stephen Blank, *Industry and Government in Britain* (Lexington, Mass.: D. C. Heath, 1973), pp. 67–70, 211.

13. Chitoshi Yanaga, *Big Business in Japanese Politics* (New Haven, Conn.: Yale University Press, 1968), pp. 3, 34, 95–96, 308. See also Hugh Patrick, "An Introduction to the Japanese Economy," mimeographed (October 1973); Ryutaro Komiya, "Economic Planning in Japan," in *Economic Planning, East and West,* ed. Morris Bernstein (Cambridge, Mass.: Ballinger, 1975); and T. F. M. Adams and N. Kobayashi, *The World of Japanese Business* (Tokyo: Kodansha International, 1969).

14. Brayman, *Corporate Management,* p. 110.

15. *Time,* 29 December 1975, p. 61.

16. Stone, *Where the Law Ends,* pp. 192–93.

17. U.S. Congress, Senate, Committee on Armed Services, draft report of the National Stockpile and Naval Petroleum Reserves Subcommittee, *Inquiry into the Strategic and Critical Material Stockpiles of the United States,* 88th Congress, 1st session, 1963, pp. 4–5, 36–46.

18. Gilbert M. Sauvage, "The French Businessman in His Milieu," in *The Business Establishment,* ed. Earl F. Cheit (New York: John Wiley & Sons, 1964), p. 236.

19. Andrew Shonfield, *Modern Capitalism* (London: Oxford University Press, 1965), p. 139.

20. Ibid., p. 164.

21. Ibid., p. 241; and Chitoshi Yanaga, *Big Business in Japanese Politics,* pp. 35–36.

22. Shonfield, *Modern Capitalism,* p. 188.

23. Henry W. Ehrmann, *Organized Business in France* (Princeton, N.J.: Princeton University Press, 1957), pp. 103ff.

24. Green and Petkas, "Nixon's Industrial State," p. 19.

25. Shonfield, *Modern Capitalism,* p. 335.

26. Louis A. Kohlmeier, *The Regulators* (New York: Harper & Row, 1969), p. 49.

27. Brayman, *Corporate Management,* pp. 68–69.

28. U.S. Congress, House, hearings before a subcommittee of the Committee on Government Operations, *Amendment to the Administrative Expense Act of 1946,* 85th Congress, 1st session, 1957, pp. 2, 23.

29. Grant McConnell, *Private Power and American Democracy* (New York: Knopf, 1967), p. 271.

30. New York *Times,* 8 June 1975, p. 1.

31. Henry W. Ehrmann, *Politics in France* (Boston: Little, Brown, 1971), p. 178; Ehrmann, *Organized Business,* pp. 259ff.

32. For details on a case, see Ehrmann, *Organized Business,* p. 262.

33. Shonfield, *Modern Capitalism,* pp. 128 and 232n.

34. J. Blondel, *Voters, Parties, and Leaders* (Harmondsworth, Middlesex, England, 1966), pp. 223, 222–31.

35. Shonfield, *Modern Capitalism,* p. 243n.

36. Gerard Braunthal, *The Federation of German Industry in Politics* (Ithaca, N.Y.: Cornell University Press, 1965), p. 239.

37. Ryutaro Komiya, "Economic Planning in Japan," in *Economic Planning, East and West,* ed. Morris Bornstein (Cambridge, Mass.: Ballinger, 1975).

38. Woodrow Wilson, *The New Freedom* (New York: Doubleday, Page, 1913), p. 58.

Chapter 14

The Consequences for Polyarchy

1. Tom Wicker, New York *Times,* 21 November 1976, Section 4, p. 17.

2. Andrew Shonfield, *Modern Capitalism* (London: Oxford University Press, 1965), pp. 186–87.

3. Ibid., pp. 131, 160ff.

4. The revisionist studies are summarized and documented in Kenneth Prewitt and Alan Stone, *The Ruling Elites* (New York: Harper & Row, 1973), chapter 2.

5. On the discrepancy, with respect to regulatory processes, between democratic symbolism and a contrasting reality, see Murray J. Edelman, "Symbols and Political Quiescence," *American Political Science Review* 54 (September 1960).

6. Matthew Josephson, *The Politicos* (New York: Harcourt, Brace, 1938), p. 526.

7. For documentation on the range and intensity of business activities in politics, see: for the United States, Edwin M. Epstein, *The Corporation in American Politics* (Englewood Cliffs, N.J.: Prentice-Hall, 1969); for West Germany, Gerard Braunthal,

The Federation of Germany Industry in Politics (Ithaca, N.Y.: Cornell University Press, 1965); for France, Henry W. Ehrmann, *Organized Business in France* (Princeton, N.J.: Princeton University Press, 1967); for Italy, Joseph LaPalombara, *Interest Groups in Italian Politics* (Princeton, N.J.: Princeton University Press, 1964); on the United Kingdom, Stephen Blank, *Industry and Government in Britain* (Lexington, Mass.: D. C. Heath, 1973); and for Japan, Chitoshi Yanaga, *Big Business in Japanese Politics* (New Haven, Conn.: Yale University Press, 1968).

8. In some systems, some legal restrictions are placed on corporate political spending. In the United States a few kinds of corporate contribution are illegal. The prohibition is widely evaded by arrangements through which the contribution appears to come from the personal income of an individual officer of the corporation. See Alexander Heard, *The Costs of Democracy* (Chapel Hill: University of North Carolina Press, 1960), pp. 199ff; and Epstein, *The Corporation in American Politics*, pp. 93ff.

9. The sales promotion figure is an extrapolation from Julian L. Simon, *Issues in the Economics of Advertising* (Urbana: University of Illinois Press, 1970), pp. 26–27. The electoral expenditures figure is from Herbert E. Alexander, *Financing the 1972 Election* (Lexington, Mass.: Lexington Books, 1976).

10. Alexander, *Financing the 1972 Election*, pp. 93, 95, 506, 386, 389.

11. Epstein, *The Corporation in American Politics*, p. 158.

12. Francis X. Sutton et al., *The American Business Creed* (Cambridge, Mass.: Harvard University Press, 1956), p. 292.

13. Richard Rose, *Influencing Voters* (New York: St. Martin's, 1967), p. 171.

14. On West German party financing by business, see Braunthal, *The Federation of German Industry*, chapter 5.

15. U.S. Bureau of the Census, *Statistical Abstract of the United States, 1975*, pp. 372, 497.

16. U.S. Department of Commerce, *National Associations of the United States*, 1949, p. viii.

17. Patrick Rivers, *Politics by Pressure* (London: George G. Harrap and Co., 1974), p. 40; Norman Kogan, *The Government of Italy* (New York: Thomas Y. Crowell, 1962), pp. 65–66; and Epstein, *The Corporation in American Politics*, pp. 51–53, 90.

18. Henry W. Ehrmann, *Organized Business in France* (Princeton, N.J.: Princeton University Press, 1957), pp. 224–25, 233, 235. Raymond A. Bauer, Ithiel de Sola Pool, and Lewis Anthony Dexter, *American Business and Public Policy* (New York: Atherton, 1963).

19. On the practice in the United States, see Ralph Nader and Mark Green, eds., *Corporate Power in America* (New York: Grossman, 1973), p. 34; Robert Engler, *The Politics of Oil* (Chicago: University of Chicago Press, 1961), p. 318; Morton Mintz and Jerry S. Cohen, *America, Inc.* (New York: Dial Press, 1971), p. 247. For Japan, see Yanaga, *Big Business*, p. 108; Patrick, "An Introduction to the Japanese Economy," chapter 8, p. 19. For France, see Ehrmann, *Organized Business in France*, pp. 267ff. For Italy, see Shonfield, *Modern Capitalism*, p. 197.

20. Wolfgang Hirsch-Weber, "Some Remarks on Interest Groups in the German Federal Republic," in *Interest Groups on Four Continents*, ed. Henry W. Ehrmann (Pittsburgh: University of Pittsburgh Press, 1960), p. 106. On labor's weakness in the United States see Epstein, *The Corporation in American Politics*, pp. 151–71.

Chapter 15

Circularity in Polyarchy

1. C. Wright Mills, *The Power Elite* (New York: Oxford University Press, 1956).

2. Ferdinand Lundberg, *The Rich and the Super-Rich* (New York: Lyle Stuart, 1968).

3. John Kenneth Galbraith, *The New Industrial State,* 2nd ed. (Boston: Houghton Mifflin, 1971), chapter 6.

4. Gabriel Kolko, *Wealth and Power in America* (New York: Praeger, 1962), p. 69.

5. Ibid., pp. 56–57.

6. Gaetano Mosca, *Sulla Teorica dei Governe e sul Governo Parlementare* (1884); Roberto Michels, *Zur Soziologie des Parteiwesens in der Moderne Demokratie* (1911); and Vilfredo Pareto, *Trattato di Sociologia Generale* (1916).

7. For example, G. William Domhoff, *Who Rules America?* (Englewood Cliffs, N.J.: Prentice-Hall, 1967); Michael Tanzer, *The Sick Society* (New York: Holt, Rinehart, and Winston, 1968); Victor Perlo, *The Empire of High Finance* (New York: International Publishers, 1957); Thorstein Veblen, *Engineers and the Price System* (New York: Augustus M. Kelley, 1965); and James Burnham, *The Managerial Revolution* (New York: John Day, 1941). But Ralph Miliband, *The State in Capitalist Society* (New York: Basic Books, 1969), has a great deal to say.

8. Francis X. Sutton et al., *The American Business Creed* (Cambridge, Mass.: Harvard University Press, 1956), p. 302.

9. A. A. Rogow, *The Labour Government and British Industry* (Ithaca, N.Y.: Cornell University Press, 1955), p. 146.

10. New York *Times,* 8 June 1976, p. 51.

11. Stephen S. Cohen, *Modern Capitalist Planning: The French Model* (London: Weidenfeld & Nicolson, 1969), pp. 230–31; and John Sheahan, *An Introduction to the French Economy* (Columbus, Ohio: Charles E. Merrill, 1969), p. 79.

12. James C. Worthy, *Big Business and Free Men* (New York: Harper & Brothers, 1959), p. 3.

13. Robert Lowe, M. P., *Speeches and Letters on Reform* (London, 1867), pp. 52, 140–45, as quoted in Robert McKenzie and Allan Silver, *Angels in Marble* (Chicago: University of Chicago Press, 1968), p. 5.

14. McKenzie and Silver, *Angels in Marble,* p. 37.

15. Ibid., chapter 2.

16. Grant McConnell, *Private Power and American Democracy* (New York: Alfred A. Knopf, 1967), p. 19.

17. Joseph T. Klapper, *The Effects of Mass Communication* (New York: Free Press, 1965), pp. 17ff.

18. Ibid, pp. 17ff.

19. Paul Lazarsfeld and Elihu Katz, *Personal Influence* (Glencoe, Ill.: Free Press, 1955).

20. Bernard C. Hennessy, *Public Opinion* (Belmont, Calif.: Wadsworth, 1965), pp. 265–69.

21. Quoted in McKenzie and Silver, *Angels in Marble,* p. 48.

22. Michael Kidron, *Western Capitalism since the War,* rev. (Harmondsworth, Middlesex, England: Penguin, 1970), p. 20.

23. Robert E. Lane, "The Fear of Equality," *American Political Science Review* 53 (March 1959).

24. R. P. Kelvin, "What Sort of Incomes Policy," *New Society* 6 (April 1967).

25. McKenzie and Silver, *Angels in Marble;* and Eric A. Nordlinger, *The Working-Class Tories* (Berkeley: University of California Press, 1967).

26. Edwin H. Sutherland, *White Collar Crime* (New York: Dryden Press, 1949).

27. In Earl F. Cheit, ed., *The Business Establishment* (New York: John Wiley & Sons, 1964), p. 2.

28. Michael Mann, "The Social Cohesion of Liberal Democracy," *American Sociological Review* 35 (June 1970): 436.

29. *1971 Ayer Directory of Publications* (Philadelphia: Ayer Press, 1971).

30. On the role of the media in the politico-economic system, a useful bibliographical essay is Ithiel de Sola Pool, "Government and the Media," *American Political Science Review* 70 (December 1976).

Chapter 16

Circularity in Market Systems

1. Julian Simon, *Issues in the Economics of Advertising* (Urbana: University of Illinois Press, 1970), p. 27.

2. Jeremy Tunstall, *The Advertising Man* (London: Chapman & Hall, 1964), pp. 21–22.

3. William S. Comanor and Thomas A. Wilson, *Advertising and Market Power* (Cambridge, Mass.: Harvard University Press, 1974), chapters 3 and 5; and Lester D. Taylor and Daniel Weiserbs, "Advertising and the Aggregate Consumption Function," *American Economic Review* 62 (September 1972).

4. George E. Berkley, *The Administrative Revolution* (Englewood Cliffs, N.J.: Prentice-Hall, 1971), p. 137.

5. Taylor and Weiserbs, "Advertising."

6. Stuart Ewen, "Advertising as Social Production," *Radical America* 3 (May-June 1969).

7. Graham Bannock, *The Juggernauts* (New York: Bobbs-Merrill, 1971), p. 218.

8. Sidney Verba, "The Silent Majority: Myth and Reality," *University of Chicago Magazine* 63 (December 1970): 13–14.

9. An estimate by Louis Harris. (Richard Rose, *Influencing Voters* [New York: St. Martin's, 1967], p. 236).

10. For varied evidence, see Howard Flieger, "Where It Never Leaks," *U.S. News and World Report*, 9 February 1976, p. 76; *Time*, 6 May 1974, p. 56; and *Time*, 13 October 1975, p. 87.

11. Marlen H. Seiden, *Who Controls the Media* (New York: Basic Books, 1974), pp. 93–94.

12. Henry W. Ehrmann, *Politics in France* (Boston: Little, Brown, 1971), pp. 135–38.

Chapter 17

Socioeconomic Class

1. In recent years, among many others, Nico Poulantzas, *Political Power and Social Classes* (Atlantic Highlands, N.J.: Humanities Press, 1975); Ralph Miliband, *The State in Capitalist Society* (New York: Basic Books, 1969); Charles H. Anderson, *The Political Economy of Social Class* (Englewood Cliffs, N.J.: Prentice-Hall, 1974); and Ralf Dahrendorf, *Class and Class Conflict in Industrial Society* (Stanford, Calif.: Stanford University Press, 1959).

2. For example, leading democratic theorists like Robert A. Dahl, *A Preface to Democratic Theory* (Chicago: University of Chicago Press, 1956), and Giovanni Sartori, *Democratic Theory,* 2nd ed. (New York: Praeger, 1965), make only sparing reference to effects of class. And many scholars dispense with the concept in favor of concepts such as elite, stratum, and status. For a useful summary of controversy on the concept, by a scholar who believes the concept to be pivotal, see H. Frankel, *Capitalist Society and Modern Sociology* (London: Lawrence & Wishart, 1970), chapters 1, 2, 3.

3. For a survey of concepts of class, see Stanislaw Ossowski, *Class Structure in the Social Consciousness* (London: Routledge & Kegan Paul, 1963), pp. 121–44.

4. See the vivid summary statement describing what is here called "packaging" in A. B. Hollingshead, *Elmtown Revisited* (New York: John Wiley & Sons, 1975), pp. 383–85. On intergenerational continuity (father's and son's occupation, education, and income), see Otis Dudley Duncan, David L. Featherman, and Beverly Duncan, *Socioeconomic Background and Achievement* (New York: Seminar Press, 1974), chapter 3.

5. For such concepts, see Oscar Lewis, *The Children of Sanchez* (New York: Random House, 1961); and Edward C. Banfield, *The Moral Basis of a Backward Society* (New York: Free Press, 1958).

6. Among them, Robert D. Hess and Judith V. Torney, *The Development of Political Attitudes in Children* (Chicago: Aldine, 1967); Fred I. Greenstein, *Children and Politics* (New Haven, Conn.: Yale University Press, 1965); and Edgar Z. Friedenberg, *Coming of Age in America* (New York: Random House, 1963).

7. Alfred C. Kinsey, *Sexual Behavior in the Human Female* (Philadelphia: Saunders, 1953). Alfred C. Kinsey, Wardell B. Pomeroy, and Clyde E. Martin, *Sexual Behavior in the Human Male* (Philadelphia: Saunders, 1948).

8. Thousands of citations are possible. See, for example, Robert E. Lane, *Political Life* (Glencoe, Ill.: Free Press, 1959). Even those social scientists who do not give the concept of class an important place in their own conceptualization routinely acknowledge the existence of American social classes. See, for example, Zbigniew Brzezinski and Samuel P. Huntington, *Political Power: U.S.A./U.S.S.R.* (New York: Viking Press, 1963), pp. 98ff; and Arnold M. Rose, *The Power Structure* (New York: Oxford University Press, 1967), pp. 202ff.

9. On ethnicity as possibly more important than class, see Dennis H. Wrong, "How Important Is Social Class?" in *The World of the Blue-Collar Worker*, ed. Irving Howe (New York: Quadrangle Books, 1972). On producer-consumer: J. David Greenstone, *Labor in American Politics* (New York: Knopf, 1969), p. 387ff. On cosmopolitical-provincial: Everett Ladd, Jr., *Ideology in America* (Ithaca, N.Y.: Cornell University Press, 1969). On sophisticated versus scientifically illiterate, see Apter in David E. Apter, ed., *Ideology and Discontent* (New York: Free Press, 1964), pp. 30–31.

10. J. Blondel, *Voters, Parties, and Leaders* (London: Penguin, 1965), pp. 136, 195ff, 239ff; Andrew Hacker, "The Elected and the Annointed," *American Political Science Review* 55 (September 1961); Gilbert M. Sauvage, "The French Businessman in His Milieu," in *The Business Establishment*, ed. Earl F. Cheit (New York: John Wiley & Sons, 1964); Chitoshi Yanaga, *Big Business in Japanese Politics* (New Haven, Conn.: Yale University Press, 1968), esp. pp. 9–26 and passim.

11. Christopher Jencks, *Inequality* (New York: Basic Books, 1972) and passim, esp. pp. 213ff; Samuel S. Bowles and Herbert Gintis, *Schooling in Capitalist America: Educational Reform and the Contradiction of Economic Life* (New York: Basic Books, 1976); Hess and Torney (on "acquisition of more active and initiatory aspects of political involvement" by children), *Development of Political Attitudes,* chapter 7; and, for a summary of a number of studies, as well as an additional one, see Greenstein, *Children and Politics,* chapter 3. See also, for other dimensions of class-related treatment of children in the school system, Edgar Litt, "Civic Education, Community Norms, and Political Indoctrination," *American Sociological Review* 28 (February 1963); A. B. Hollingshead, *Elmtown's Youth* (New York: John Wiley & Sons, 1949); and William L. Warner, *Who Shall Be Educated?* (New York: Harper & Brothers, 1944).

12. Edwin H. Sutherland, *White Collar Crime* (New York: Dryden Press, 1949).

13. In addition to studies of schools cited above, see the results of a Louis Harris *Life* poll of 2,500 teachers, parents, and school administrators in 100 schools (*Life,* 16 May 1969, esp. p. 34). Harmon Ziegler, *The Political Life of American Teachers* (Englewood Cliffs, N.J.: Prentice-Hall, 1967), esp. p. 22; V. O. Key, Jr., *Public Opinion and American Democracy* (New York: Knopf, 1967), p. 316; and M. Kent Jennings and Richard G. Niemi, "The Transmission of Political Values from Parent to Child," in *Power and Change in the United States,* ed. Kenneth M. Dolbeare (New York: John Wiley & Sons, 1969).

14. Nathan M. Pusey, *The Age of the Scholar* (Cambridge, Mass.: Harvard University Press, 1963), p. 171.

15. Lane, *Political Life,* chapter 16; and Sidney Verba and Norman H. Nie, *Participation in America* (New York: Harper & Row, 1972), pp. 100, 336, 339–40. For Europe, Norman H. Nie, G. Bingham Powell, Jr., and Kenneth Prewitt, "Social Structure and Political Participation," *American Political Science Review* 63

(September 1969); and Lester W. Millbrath, *Political Participation* (Chicago: Rand McNally, 1965), p. 116.

16. E. E. Schattschneider, *The Semisovereign People* (New York: Holt, Rinehart, and Winston, 1960), pp. 30–35; and W. Lloyd Warner, Darab B. Unwalla, and John H. Trimm, eds., *The Emergent American Society* (New Haven, Conn.: Yale University Press, 1967), pp. 279–86. On how political leaders of socialist parties in Europe tend to be recruited from, or acquire the beliefs of, the class that wishes to perpetuate the existing politico-economic order, see Frank Parkin, *Class, Inequality, and Political Order* (New York: Praeger, 1971), pp. 128–36.

17. In a 1969–1970 survey, only 5 percent of American academics classified themselves at left (Everett Carll Ladd and Seymour Martin Lipsett, *The Divided Academy* [New York: McGraw-Hill, 1975], p. 26).

18. See citations referred to in footnote 11 above.

19. For analysis and bibliography on *embourgeoisement,* John H. Goldthorpe, David Lockwood, Frank Bechhofer, and Jennifer Platt, *The Affluent Worker in the Class Structure* (London: Cambridge University Press, 1971), chapter 1.

20. David Butler and Donald Stokes, *Political Change in Britain* (New York: St. Martin's, 1971), pp. 126–34.

21. Goldthorpe et al., *The Affluent Worker,* chapter 6.

22. On *embourgeoisement* of American workers see Edwin M. Epstein, *The Corporation in American Politics* (Englewood Cliffs, N.J.: Prentice-Hall, 1969), pp. 161–65.

23. Talcott Parsons, *Societies* (Englewood Cliffs, N.J.: Prentice-Hall, 1966), p. 113.

24. Peter M. Blau, ed., *Approaches to the Study of Social Structure* (New York: Free Press, 1975), pp. 15–17, chapters 3 and 5.

25. Abram Kardiner, *The Psychological Frontiers of a Society* (New York: Columbia University Press, 1945).

Chapter 18

Communist Systems

1. U.S. Congress, Joint Economic Committee, Joint Committee Print, *China: A Reassessment of the Economy,* 94th Congress, 1st session, 1975, p. 35.

2. Franz Schurmann, *Ideology and Organization in Communist China* (Berkeley: University of California Press, 1966), p. 11.

3. Ibid., p. 125.

4. T. H. Rigby, "Traditional, Market, and Organizational Societies and the U.S.S.R.," *in Communist Studies and the Social Sciences,* ed. Frederic J. Fleron (Chicago: Rand McNally, 1969), p. 176; and Jerome M. Gilison, *The Soviet Image of Utopia* (Baltimore: Johns Hopkins University Press, 1975) and passim, esp. p. 52.

5. Andrés Suárez, "Leadership, Ideology, and Political Party," in *Revolutionary Change in Cuba,* ed. Carmelo Mesa-Lago (Pittsburgh: University of Pittsburgh Press, 1971), pp. 8ff.

6. On his various lines of authority, see Rigby, "Traditional, Market, and Organizational Societies and the U.S.S.R.," p. 181.

7. Paul Hollander, *Soviet and American Society* (New York: Oxford University Press, 1973), pp. 44–55.

8. Jerry F. Hough, *The Soviet Prefects* (Cambridge: Harvard University Press, 1969), pp. 111ff.

9. Frederick Barghoorn, *Politics in the U.S.S.R.,* 2nd ed. (Boston: Little, Brown, 1972), pp. 34, 55, 185.

10. Raymond A. Bauer, Alex Inkeles, and Clyde Kluckhohn, *How the Soviet System Works* (Cambridge, Mass.: Harvard University Press, 1957), p. 39.

11. Schurmann, *Ideology and Organization,* p. 109.

12. Hough, *Soviet Prefects,* pp. 98ff.

13. Ibid., chapter 4.

14. Rigby, "Traditional, Market, and Organizational Societies and the U.S.S.R.," p. 182.

15. Hough, *Soviet Prefects,* chapters 5 and 7; and Rigby, "Traditional, Market, and Organizational Societies and the U.S.S.R.," p. 182.

16. On party as implementer rather than policy maker, see Robert Conquest, *Power and Policy in the U.S.S.R.* (New York: St. Martin's, 1961), p. 30. See also Chalmers Johnson, "Comparing Communist Nations," in *Change in Communist Systems,* ed. Chalmers Johnson (Stanford, Calif.: Stanford University Press, 1970), p. 11.

17. James Chieh Hsiung, *Ideology and Practice* (New York: Praeger, 1970), p. 156.

18. For an excellent brief statement on ideology in the Soviet Union, see Bauer, Inkeles, and Kluckhohn, *How the Soviet System Works,* pp. 31–35.

19. Jerry Hough, "The Soviet System," *Problems of Communism* 2 (March-April 1972): 31.

20. See Daniel Bell "Ideology and Soviet Politics," *Slavic Review* 24 (December 1965): 602.

21. See Schurmann, *Ideology and Organization,* pp. 109ff, esp. p. 111, on party as innovator in China.

22. The complex and subtle ways in which an innovating elite loses its innovative zeal is examined in Vernon V. Aspaturian, "Social Structure and Political Power in the Soviet System," in U.S. Congress, House, Committee on Foreign Affairs, Subcommittee on Europe, Hearings, *Recent Developments in the Soviet Bloc, Part II,* 88th Congress, 2d session, 1964.

23. V. I. Lenin, *State and Revolution* (New York: International Publishers, 1932), p. 84.

24. Donald R. DeGlopper, "Recent Changes in Chinese Society," *The Annals* 402 (July 1972): pp. 21ff; and William L. Parish, "China—Team, Brigade, or Commune," *Problems of Communism* 25 (March-April 1976).

25. Schurmann, *Ideology and Organization,* pp. 479ff.

26. Robert M. Bernardo, *The Theory of Moral Incentives in Cuba* (University, Ala.: University of Alabama Press, 1971), pp. 66–67.

27. Schurmann, *Ideology and Organization.* On the reaffirmation of "society" over organization, see p. 542.

Chapter 19

Two Models

1. An earlier version of the two models, from which I have taken some passages, is Charles E. Lindblom, "The Sociology of Planning," in *Economic Planning East and West,* ed. Morris Bornstein (Cambridge, Mass.: Ballinger, 1975).

2. Zbigniew Brzezinski, *Between Two Ages* (New York: Viking, 1970), p. 72, for example. And although he dissents on many counts from communist faith in man's intellectual competence, Andrei Sakharov revealed a Model 1 confidence in 1971 when he recommended the establishment of an "International Council of Experts on the Problems of Peace, Disarmament, Economic Aid to Needy Countries, the Defense of Human Rights, and the Protection of the Environment"!

3. Quoted in Jerome M. Gilison, *The Soviet Image of Utopia* (Baltimore: Johns Hopkins University Press, 1975), p. 120.

4. Talmon distinguishes "a sole and exclusive truth in politics" from "pragmatic contrivances" for "trial and error" (J. L. Talmon, *The Origins of Totalitarian Democracy* [New York: Praeger, 1960], p. 1).

5. Harry Harding, Jr., "Maoist Theories of Policy-Making and Organization," in *The Cultural Revolution in China,* ed. Thomas W. Robinson (Berkeley: University of California Press, 1971), p. 123.

6. Talmon distinguishes "an all-embracing and coherent philosophy" from "pragmatic precepts" (*The Origins of Totalitarian Democracy,* p. 2).

7. On Soviet concern for correctness, see Abraham Katz, *The Politics of Economic Reform in the Soviet Union* (New York: Praeger, 1972), p. 120 and passim; and Raymond A. Bauer, Alex Inkeles, and Clyde Kluckhohn, *How the Soviet System Works* (Cambridge, Mass.: Harvard University Press, 1957), p. 49.

8. Robert A. Dahl, *Polyarchy* (New Haven, Conn.: Yale University Press, 1971), pp. 1–2.

9. Michael Polanyi, *Science, Faith, and Society* (London: Oxford University Press, 1946), chapter 3.

10. Harding, "Maoist Theories," p. 123.

11. Donald V. Schwartz, "Recent Soviet Adaptations of Systems Theory to Administrative Theory," *Journal of Comparative Administration* 5 (August 1973): 236.

12. Benjamin I. Schwartz, "A Personal View of Some Thoughts of Mao Tse-tung, in *Ideology and Politics in Contemporary China,* ed. Chalmers Johnson (Seattle: University of Washington Press, 1973), p. 359.

13. Talmon, *The Origins of Totalitarian Democracy,* p. 2.

14. Gregory Grossman, "The Solidary Society" in *Essays in Socialism and Planning in Honor of Carl Tandauer* (Englewood Cliffs, N.J.: Prentice-Hall, 1970).

15. Derek Bryan, "Changing Social Ethics in Contemporary China," *Political Quarterly* 45 (January-March, 1974): 50.

16. See Ralf Dahrendorf, *Class and Class Conflict in Industrial Society* (Stanford, Calif.: Stanford University Press, 1959). pp. 157–65.

17. Frank Knight, *Freedom and Reform* (New York: Harper & Brothers, 1947), p. 190. Ernest Barker, *Reflections on Government* (London: Oxford University Press, 1942), p. 40.

18. Carl L. Becker, *New Liberties for Old* (New Haven, Conn.: Yale University Press, 1941), p. 106.

19. Edmund Wilson, *To the Finland Station* (Garden City, N.Y.: Doubleday, 1940), p. 283.

20. J. L. Talmon, *The Rise of Totalitarian Democracy* (Boston: Beacon Press, 1952).

21. See also the argument that knowledge displaces politics in Robert E. Lane, "The Decline of Politics and Ideology in a Knowledgeable Society," *American Sociological Review* 31 (1966): 649–62.

22. Grossman, "The Solidary Society," p. 191.

23. Alfred North Whitehead, *Science and the Modern World* (New York: Free Press, 1967), p. 186. In the Model 2 tradition, social scientists have explored the useful functions of social conflict at length. See, for example, Lewis Coser, *The Functions of Social Conflict* (Glencoe, Ill.: Free Press, 1964) in which he follows Georg Simmel's 1908 work on conflict.

24. See Mary Parker Follett on integrated versus compromised solutions to problems and the role of conflict in motivating the search for integration, H. M. Metcalf and L. Urwick, eds., *Dynamic Administration* (New York: Harper & Brothers, 1942), pp. 239ff. See also Coser, *The Functions of Social Conflict.*

25. John Stuart Mill, *Representative Government* (London: Dent, 1910), p. 195.

26. C. B. Macpherson, *Democratic Theory* (London: Oxford University Press, 1973), pp. 1–23, draws such a distinction.

27. Quoted in Allen Kassof, "The Administered Society," *World Politics* 16 (July 1964), p. 558.

28. Michel Oksenberg, ed., *China's Developmental Experience* (New York: Praeger, 1973), p. 29.

29. As envisioned by some behavioralists. See, for example, B. F. Skinner, *Beyond*

Freedom and Dignity (New York: Alfred A. Knopf, 1971). See also Raymond Bauer, *The New Man in Soviet Psychology* (Cambridge, Mass.: Harvard University Press, 1952); E. L. Wheelwright and Bruce McFarlane, *The Chinese Road to Socialism* (New York: Monthly Review Press, 1970), p. 147; and Richard R. Fagen, *The Transformation of Political Culture in Cuba* (Stanford, Calif.: Stanford University Press, 1969), p. 14.

30. Émile Durkheim, *The Division of Labor in Society,* trans. George Simpson (New York: Free Press, 1933).

31. Robert S. McNamara, *The Essence of Security* (New York: Harper & Row, 1968), pp. 109–10.

Chapter 20

Democracy, Freedom, and Equality

1. J. L. Talmon, *The Origins of Totalitarian Democracy* (New York: Praeger, 1960), C. B. Macpherson, *The Real World of Democracy* (London: Oxford University Press, 1966), and others use the term "democracy" to include both communism and liberal democracy, on the ground, roughly speaking, that both are in theory "for" the people.

2. On the degeneration of the mass line, see Victor C. Funnell, "The Metamorphosis of the Chinese Communist Party," *Studies in Comparative Communism* 4 (April 1971).

3. Mao Tse-tung, *Selected Works,* vol. 4, 1941–1945 (New York: International Publishers, 1956), p. 113.

4. For an identification of continuing patterns of conflicts over authority in the U.S.S.R., see T. H. Rigby, "The Extent and Limits of Authority," *Problems of Communism* 12 (September-October 1963).

5. On Cuba, see James M. Malloy, "Generation of Political Support and Allocation of Costs," in *Revolutionary Change in Cuba,* ed. Carmelo Mesa-Lago (Pittsburgh: University of Pittsburgh Press, 1971).

6. For a case study of cooperation between education officials and scientists to change a Khrushchev policy, see Philip D. Stewart, "Soviet Interest Groups and the Policy Process: The Repeal of Production Education," *World Politics* 22 (October 1969).

7. Frederick Barghoorn, *Politics in the U.S.S.R.,* 2nd ed. (Boston: Little, Brown, 1972), pp. 198–99.

8. James R. Townsend, *Political Participation in Communist China,* new ed. (Berkeley: University of California Press, 1969), pp. xiii–xiv.

9. Andrew C. Janos, "Group Politics in Communist Society," in *Authoritarian Politics in Modern Society,* Samuel P. Huntington and Clement H. Moore (New York: Basic Books, 1970), pp. 446ff; T. H. Rigby, "Crypto-Politics," *Survey* 50 (January 1964); and Michel Oksenberg, "Occupational Groups in Chinese Society and the Cultural Revolution," in *Communist Systems in Comparative Perspective,* eds. Lenard J. Cohen and Jane P. Shapiro (New York: Doubleday, 1974).

10. For a brief identification of some themes in contemporary interpretations of pluralist tendencies in the U.S.S.R. (with bibliography), see Moshe Lewin, *Political Undercurrents in Soviet Economic Debates* (Princeton, N.J.: Princeton University Press, 1974), p. 268.

11. Jerry F. Hough, "The Soviet System," *Problems of Communism* 2 (March-April 1972): 27–32.

12. Jerry F. Hough, "The Brezhnev Era," *Problems of Communism* 25 (March-April 1976), p. 10.

13. A. H. Brown, "Political Change in Czechoslovakia," *Government and Opposition* 4 (Spring 1969).

14. New York *Times,* 19 September 1976, p. 1.

15. On limits on dissent, see Rudolf L. Tökés, ed., *Dissent in the U.S.S.R.* (Baltimore: Johns Hopkins University Press, 1975).

16. Barry H. Richman, *Industrial Society in Communist China* (New York: Random House, 1969), pp. 369ff; J. A. Cohen, "The Criminal Process in China," in *Soviet and Chinese Communism,* ed. Donald W. Treadgold (Seattle: University of Washington Press, 1967); and, for the U.S.S.R., Telford Taylor, *Courts of Terror* (New York: Alfred A. Knopf, 1976).

17. One estimate is 600 executions when Castro first came to power. Herbert Matthews, *Fidel Castro* (New York: Simon & Schuster, 1969), p. 145.

18. Alexander Dallin and George W. Breslauer, *Political Terror in Communist Systems* (Stanford, Calif.: Stanford University Press, 1970).

19. John W. Lewis, *Leadership in Communist China* (Ithaca, N.Y.: Cornell University Press, 1963), p. 5.

20. Robert Conquest, *The Great Terror* (New York: Macmillan, 1973), pp. 702–13.

21. Yuri P. Frantsev, "The Individual under Communism: A Soviet View," in *The Challenge of Politics,* eds. Alvin Z. Rubenstein and Garold W. Thumm, 3rd ed. (Englewood Cliffs, N.J.: Prentice-Hall, 1970), p. 231.

22. See Jeremy R. Azrael, "Soviet Union," in *Education and Political Development,* ed. James S. Coleman (Princeton, N.J.: Princeton University Press, 1965), pp. 250–54, and, for bibliography, S. M. Lipset, "Equity and Equality in Public Wage Policy" in *Public Employee Unions,* ed. A. L. Chickering (San Francisco, Calif.: Institute for Contemporary Studies, 1976), pp. 112–13.

23. Barbara Wolfe Jancar, "Women and Soviet Politics," in *Soviet Politics and Society in the 1970's,* eds. Henry W. Morton and Rudolf L. Tökés (New York: Free Press, 1974), pp. 118, 141–42; and Paul Hollander, *Soviet and American Society* (New York: Oxford University Press, 1973), p. 247.

24. Jonathan Mirsky, "China after Nixon," *Annals* 402 (July 1972): 85–86.

25. Recently, however, the Soviet Union has been reducing wage differentials and has also reduced urban-rural wage and social security differentials (Hough, "The Soviet System," p. 39).

26. Herbert L. Matthews, *Revolution in Cuba* (New York: Scribner's, 1975), p. 370; Carl Riskin, "Workers' Incentives in Chinese Industry," in U.S. Congress, Joint Economic Committee, *China: A Reassessment of the Economy,* 94th Congress, 1st session, 1975, p. 206.

27. On Chinese social security and medical care, see Riskin, "Workers' Incentives in Chinese Industry." Also Jan S. Prybyla, *The Political Economy of Communist China* (Scranton, Pa.: International Textbook, 1970), pp. 92, 196–97; and *Time,* 10 January 1972, pp. 60–61. On Cuba, see Matthews, *Revolution in Cuba,* chapter 16.

28. Nicholas R. Lardy, "Economic Planning in the People's Republic of China," in Joint Economic Committee, *China.*

29. Hough, "The Brezhnev Era," pp. 11–12.

30. J. Wilczynski, *The Economics of Socialism* (London: George Allen & Unwin, 1970). The U.S. provision of these services is less than in Western Europe for many historical reasons and for reasons referred to in chapter 17, "Socioeconomic Class."

31. Frederick L. Pryor, *Public Expenditures in Communist and Capitalist Nations* (Homewood, Ill.: Richard D. Irwin, Inc., 1968), chapter 7. On details of social security systems, see Jack Minkoff and Lynn Turgeon, "Income Maintenance in Eastern Europe," *Social Policy* 6 (March-April, 1976).

32. Harold L. Wilensky, *The Welfare State and Equality* (Berkeley: University of California Press, 1975), pp. 30–31.

33. Robert B. Semple, Jr., "Income Inequity in Britain Found to Change Little in Decade," New York *Times,* 2 August 1975. Semple's article is based on: Royal Commission on the Distribution of Income and Wealth, *Initial Report on the Distribution of Income and Wealth* (London: Her Majesty's Stationery Office, 1975). On U.S. figures, James D. Smith and Stephen D. Franklin, "The Concentration of Personal Wealth, 1922–1969," *American Economic Review* 64 (May 1974): 162–67.

In the United States many extremely wealthy people show no taxable income on their returns. On evasions and other confusions in measuring income in the United Kingdom, see H. Frankel, *Capitalist Society and Modern Sociology* (London: Laurence & Wishart, 1970), pp. 83–86.

34. Source: Harold Lydall, *The Structure of Earnings* (London: Oxford University Press, 1968), p. 153, except for the U.S.S.R. figures which are from Frederic R. Pryor, *Property and Industrial Organization in Communist and Capitalist Nations* (Bloomington: Indiana University Press, 1973), p. 83. Pryor's calculations are directly comparable because he explicitly sets out to supplement Lydall's list, using Lydall's methods.

35. Peter Wiles, *Distribution of Income: East and West* (Amsterdam: North-Holland, 1974), pp. 25, 48.

36. In the U.S.S.R., some collective farms appear to have average wages of only one-third to one-half the average pay for industry. Robert Conquest, *Agricultural Workers in the U.S.S.R.* (London: Bodley Head, 1968), pp. 99–100. On income discrimination against agriculture, see Robert E. Miller, "The Future of the Soviet Kolkhoz," *Problems of Communism* 25 (March-April 1976). For China, one estimate is that the agricultural average is only one-quarter the industrial average for wages. (Charles Hoffman, *Work Incentive Practices and Policies in the People's Republic of China, 1953–1965* [Albany: State University of New York Press, 1967], p. 13). Hoffman is not including the monetary equivalent of in-kind pay (crops) given agricultural workers. An estimate that does incorporate such compensation sees the gap as substantially smaller, but still sizable: agricultural workers are seen as receiving 74 to 85 percent of the wages of urban workers (Riskin, "Workers' Incentives in Chinese Industry," p. 205).

37. Pryor, *Property and Industrial Organization*, p. 83.

38. For various estimates of wage differentials in China see A. Doak Barnett, *Uncertain Passage* (Washington, D.C.: Brookings Institution, 1974), pp. 132–33; Alexander Eckstein, *China's Economic Development* (Ann Arbor: University of Michigan Press, 1973), pp. 346–50; Richman, *Industrial Society*, pp. 804–5; and Christopher Howe, "Economic Trends and Policies," *Political Quarterly* 45 (January-March 1974): 23.

39. Riskin, *"Workers' Incentives."*

40. Joseph A. Kahl, "Cuban Paradox," in *Cuban Communism*, ed. Irving L. Horowitz (New Brunswick, N.J.: Transaction, 1972), p. 288.

41. Bruce M. Russett et al., *World Handbook of Political and Social Indicators* (New Haven, Conn.: Yale University Press, 1964), p. 243. A confirming estimate is in P. J. D. Wiles, *The Political Economy of Communism* (Cambridge, Mass.: Harvard University Press, 1964), p. 48.

42. W. Irwin Gillespie, "Effect of Public Expenditures on the Distribution of Income," in *Essays in Fiscal Federalism*, ed. Richard A. Musgrave (Washington, D.C.: Brookings Institution, 1965), pp. 164–65.

43. Further detail on inegalitarian public expenditure is in William C. Mitchell, *Public Choice in America* (Chicago: Markham, 1971), chapter 4.

44. Morton Paglin, "The Measurement and Trend of Inequality," *American Economic Review* 65 (September 1975). But remember that the data are grossly imperfect. Richard Titmucs sees evidence of a movement away from equality, at least in the United Kingdom: *Income Distribution and Social Change* (London: George Allen & Unwin, 1962), p. 198.

45. James E. Meade, *Efficiency, Equality, and Ownership of Property* (Cambridge, Mass.: Harvard University Press, 1965), pp. 38–39.

46. "The Private Lives of Russia's Rulers," *Atlas* (July-August 1971): 20–27; Andrei D. Sakharov, *My Country and the World* (New York: Alfred A. Knopf, 1975), pp. 25–27; and, on China and the U.S.S.R., Jacqueline R. Kasun, "United States Poverty in World Perspective," *Current History* 64 (June 1973): 251–52.

47. Matthews, *Revolution in Cuba*, pp. 380–81; and Archibald R. M. Ritter, *The Economic Development of Revolutionary Cuba: Strategy and Performance* (New York: Praeger, 1974), pp. 288ff.

48. Arthur G. Ashbrook, Jr., "China: Economic Overview, 1975," Joint Economic Committee, *China*, p. 51.

49. David P. Barkin and Nita R. Manitzas, eds., *Cuba: The Logic of the Revolution* (Andover, Mass.: Warner Modular Publications, 1973), p. M261–9.

Chapter 21

Preceptoral "Education" and Moral Incentives

1. Franz Schurmann, *Ideology and Organization in Communist China*, 2nd ed., enl. (Berkeley: University of California Press, 1971), p. 46. See also James Chieh Hsiung, *Ideology and Practice* (New York: Praeger, 1970), p. 155. For comparison with the U.S.S.R., see Merle Fainsod, "Transformations in the Communist Party of the Soviet Union," in *Soviet and Chinese Communism*, ed. Donald W. Treadgold (Seattle: University of Washington Press, 1967).

2. On the Cultural Revolution, see Schurmann, *Ideology and Organization*; Jürgen Domes, "Party Politics and the Cultural Revolution," in *Communist China, 1949–1969*, eds. Frank N. Trager and William Henderson (New York: New York University Press, 1970); and A. Doak Barnett, *Uncertain Passage* (Washington, D.C.: The Brookings Institution, 1974), pp. 6–8.

3. James R. Townsend, *Political Participation in Communist China*, 2nd ed. (Berkeley: University of California Press, 1969), pp. 39, 45, 83.

4. Schurmann, *Ideology and Organization*, p. 32.

5. Derek J. Waller, "Revolutionary Intellectuals or Managerial Modernizers," *Political Quarterly* 45 (January-March 1974): 12.

6. Barry M. Richman, *Industrial Society in Communist China* (New York: Random House, 1969), pp. 258, 766.

7. Harvey Leibenstein, "Allocative Efficiency vs. 'X-Efficiency,'" *American Economic Review* 56 (June 1966).

8. Hsiung, *Ideology and Practice*, p. 297.

9. Ibid., p. 282.

10. Barnett, *Uncertain Passage*, pp. 139–41.

11. Ezra F. Vogel, "Voluntarism and Social Control," in *Soviet and Chinese Communism*, ed. Treadgold, p. 178.

12. From Teng Hsiao-p'ing as quoted in J. M. H. Lindbeck, "Transformations in the Chinese Communist Party," in *Soviet and Chinese Communism*, ed. Treadgold, p. 103.

13. Richard H. Solomon, *Mao's Revolution and the Chinese Political Culture* (Berkeley: University of California Press, 1971), p. 506.

14. Schurmann, *Ideology and Organization*, p. 48.

15. Ernesto Guevara, "Man and Socialism in Cuba," in *Che: The Selected Works of Ernesto Guevara*, eds. R. E. Bonachea and N. P. Valdes (Cambridge, Mass.: MIT Press, 1970), p. 159.

16. Richard R. Fagen, *The Transformation of Political Culture in Cuba* (Stanford, Calif.: Stanford University Press, 1969), p. 146.

17. James M. Malloy, "Generation of Political Support and Allocation of Costs," in *Revolutionary Change in Cuba*, ed. Carmelo Mesa-Lago (Pittsburgh: University of Pittsburgh Press, 1971), p. 41.

18. Carmelo Mesa-Lago, *Cuba in the 1970's* (Albuquerque: University of New Mexico Press, 1974), chapter 3.

19. In the Soviet Union agriculture employs a fourth of the nation's work force and produces about a fifth of the gross national product. In China agriculture employs perhaps 70 percent of the work force and produces perhaps from a fourth to near half of gross national product. In Cuba about 30 percent of the labor force is in agriculture, producing perhaps 25 percent of gross national product. U.S. Congress, Joint Economic Committee, *Soviet Economic Prospects for the Seventies*, 93rd Congress, 1st session,

1973, p. 341; United Nations, *Yearbook of Labour Statistics 1975* (Geneva: International Labour Office, 1975), pp. 71, 89, 157; Charles L. Taylor and Michael C. Hudson, *World Handbook of Political and Social Indicators,* 2nd ed. (New Haven, Conn.: Yale University Press, 1972), p. 338; Jan Deleyne, *The Chinese Economy* (New York: Harper & Row, 1974), p. 62; David P. Barkin, "Cuban Agriculture: A Strategy of Economic Development," in *Cuba: The Logic of the Revolution,* eds. David P. Barkin and Niki R. Manitzas (Andover, Mass.: Warner Modular Publications, 1973), pp. R261–10 to R261–13. In the United States agriculture employs roughly only 4 percent of the work force and produces about 4 percent of gross national product.

20. Jan S. Prybyla, *The Political Economy of Communist China* (Scranton, Pa.: International Textbook, 1967), p. 159.

21. Paul Dibb, "Soviet Agriculture since Khrushchev: An Economic Appraisal," in *Comparative Economic Systems: A Reader,* ed. Marsall I. Goldman, 2nd ed. [New York: Random House, 1971], p. 372. J. Wilczynski, *The Economics of Socialism* (London: Allen & Unwin, 1970), pp. 120ff, esp. p. 123; Frederick W. Cook, "The Commune System in the People's Republic of China, 1963–1974," U.S. Congress Joint Committee Print, *China: A Reassessment of the Economy* 94th Congress, 1st session, 1975, pp. 399ff; and Carmelo Mesa-Lago, "The Revolutionary Offensive," *Trans-Action* 6 (April 1969): 23.

22. Dwight H. Perkins, *Market Control and Planning in Communist China* (Cambridge, Mass.: Harvard University Press, 1966), pp. 33–93. For incentive reasons, in China, probably much less so in the U.S.S.R., individual peasants or production teams are permitted to engage in small-scale private enterprise, as, for example, in pottery making and woodcrafts. Policy varies on the limits of these activities (Crook, "The Commune System," p. 332).

23. Dibb, "Soviet Agriculture," p. 363; Wilczynski, *The Economics of Socialism,* p. 123; Robert Conquest, ed., *Agricultural Workers in the U.S.S.R.* (London: Bodley Head, 1968), p. 114.

24. Prybyla, *Political Economy,* pp. 350–51; Barry H. Richman, *Industrial Society in Communist China* (New York: Random House, 1969), p. 544.

25. Conquest, *Agricultural Workers,* pp. 8–9.

26. North Korea too is experimenting with moral incentives. See Byung Chul Koh, "North Korea: Profile of a Garrison State," *Problems of Communism* 18 (January–February 1969): 22; Joungwon Alexander Kim, "The 'Peak of Socialism' in North Korea: The Five and Seven Year Plans," in *Comparative Economic Systems,* ed. Jan S. Prybyla (New York: Appleton-Century-Crofts, 1969), pp. 417, 423.

27. Wilczynski, *The Economics of Socialism,* pp. 107–8, 164.

28. Emily Clark Brown, "Continuity and Change in the Soviet Labor Market," in *The Soviet Economy,* eds. Morris Bornstein and Daniel R. Fusfeld, 4th ed. (Homewood, Ill.: Irwin, 1974); Wilczynski, *The Economics of Socialism,* p. 99; E. H. Phelps Brown, *The Economics of Labor* (New Haven, Conn.: Yale University Press, 1962), pp. 122–23; and Merle Fainsod, *How Russia Is Ruled,* rev. ed. (Cambridge, Mass.: Harvard University Press, 1963), pp. 106–7.

29. Alexander Eckstein, *China's Economic Development* (Ann Arbor: University of Michigan Press, 1975), pp. 362–64.

30. Carl Riskin, "Workers' Incentives in Chinese Industry," in Joint Economic Committee, *China.*

31. Prybyla, *Political Economy,* pp. 261–62.

32. Carmelo Mesa-Lago, *The Labor Sector and Socialist Distribution in Cuba* (New York: Praeger, 1968), chapter 3.

33. Mesa-Lago, "Economic Significance of Unpaid Labor in Socialist Cuba," *Industrial and Labor Relations Review* 22 (April 1969).

34. Mesa-Lago, *Cuba in the 1970's,* p. 48.

35. James M. Malloy, "Generation of Political Support and Allocation of Costs," in *Revolutionary Change in Cuba,* ed. Carmelo Mesa-Lago (Pittsburgh: University of Pittsburgh Press, 1971), p. 35.

36. Raul Castro in New York *Times,* 8 December 1972, p. C 11.

37. Mesa-Lago, *Cuba in the 1970's,* p. 70.

38. Frank N. Trager and William Henderson, eds., *Communist China, 1949–1969* (New York: New York University Press, 1970), p. 50; Donald DeGlopper, "Recent Changes in Chinese Society," *The Annals* 402 (July 1972): 25; Frederick C. Barghoorn, *Politics in the U.S.S.R.,* 2nd ed. (Boston: Little, Brown, 1972), p. 70; and Roberto E. Hernández and Carmelo Mesa-Lago, "Labor Organization and Wages," in *Revolutionary Change,* ed. Mesa-Lago, pp. 210ff.

39. Richman, *Industrial Society,* pp. 147, 163.

40. Ibid., p. 304.

41. Riskin, "Workers' Incentives," pp. 214ff; and Ritter, *Revolutionary Cuba,* pp. 327–29.

42. Richard R. Fagen, *The Transformation of Culture in Cuba* (Stanford, Calif.: Stanford University Press, 1969), p. 142.

43. Robert M. Bernardo, *The Theory of Moral Incentives in Cuba* (University, Ala.: University of Alabama Press, 1971), pp. 54–55; Riskin, "Workers' Incentives," p. 215.

44. In China, material rewards for emulators have been terminated (Riskin, "Workers' Incentives," p. 222).

45. Bernardo, *Moral Incentives,* pp. 60–61.

46. Arvid Brodersen, *The Soviet Worker* (New York: Random House, 1966), p. 135.

47. Richard Lowenthal, "Development *vs.* Utopia in Communist Policy," in *Change in Communist Systems,* ed. Chalmers Johnson (Stanford, Calif.: Stanford University Press, 1970).

48. Mesa-Lago, *Cuba in the 1970's,* pp. 44–45.

49. Archibald R. M. Ritter, *The Economic Development of Revolutionary Cuba: Strategy and Performance* [New York: Praeger, 1974], pp. 264–69. Riskin, "Workers' Incentives," p. 215.

50. Richman, *Industrial Society,* p. 53.

51. For example, Eckstein, *China's Economic Development,* p. 366.

52. Charles Hoffman, "Work Incentives in Chinese Industry and Agriculture," in U.S. Congress, Joint Economic Committee, *An Economic Profile of Mainland China,* 90th Congress, 1st session, 1967, vol. 2, pp. 491–92; and Brodersen, *The Soviet Worker,* pp. 132–38.

53. Bernardo, *Moral Incentives,* pp. 67–68.

54. Ibid., p. 120.

55. Malloy, "Political Support," pp. 37ff.

56. Ritter, *Revolutionary Cuba,* pp. 326ff.

57. Ibid., p. 326.

58. Bernardo, *Moral Incentives,* pp. 102–14; see also Ritter, *Revolutionary Cuba,* chapters 7 and 8.

59. Mesa-Lago, "Unpaid Labor," p. 347.

60. Bernardo, *Moral Incentives,* pp. 89, 121.

61. Hernández and Mesa-Lago, "Labor Organization and Wages," pp. 238ff., are more dubious than Maurice Zeitlin, "Inside Cuba," *Ramparts* 8 (March 1970).

62. Hoffman, "Work Incentives," p. 494; Richman, *Industrial Society,* pp. 260ff.

63. For evidence on Cuba, see Ritter, *Revolutionary Cuba,* pp. 288ff.

64. Karl Marx, *Early Writings,* trans. and ed. T. B. Bottomore (New York: McGraw-Hill, 1964), p. 193.

Chapter 22

The Politics of Business Enterprise

1. Raymond P. Powell, "Plan Execution and the Workability of Soviet Planning," *Journal of Comparative Economics* 1 (March 1977); Barry H. Richman, *Industrial Society in Communist China* (New York: Random House, 1969), p. 462.

2. Archibald R. M. Ritter, *The Economic Development of Revolutionary Cuba: Strategy and Performance* (New York: Praeger, 1974), p. 224.

3. Simon Kuznets, *Modern Economic Growth* (New Haven, Conn.: Yale University Press, 1966), pp. 64–65.

4. Harry G. Shaffer, "Economic Performance under the Plan," in *Current Problems of Socialist Economics,* ed. William D. G. Hunter, mimeographed (Hamilton, Canada: McMaster University, 1971), p. 58.

5. World Bank, *World Bank Atlas* (Washington, D.C., 1975). Comparisons with other nations are in Table 22.2.

6. Arthur Ashbrook, "China: Economic Overview, 1975," U.S. Congress, Joint Economic Committee, *China: A Reassessment of the Economy,* 94th Congress, 1st session, 1975, p. 44.

7. Claire Wilcox et al., *Economies of the World Today,* 3rd ed. (New York: Harcourt Brace Jovanovich, 1976), p. 19. Based largely on *World Bank Atlas* 1975.

8. For 1959 and 1960, Ritter, *Revolutionary Cuba,* p. 111. On the drop in the 1960s and on recent claims, Carmelo Mesa-Lago, *Cuba in the 1970's* (Albuquerque: University of New Mexico Press, 1974), 53–54.

9. Stanley H. Cohn, "Analysis of the Soviet Growth Model" in *The Soviet Economy,* eds. Morris Bornstein and Daniel Fusfeld, 4th ed. (Homewood, Ill.: Irwin, 1974); and Cyril E. Black, "Soviet Society: A Comparative View," in *Prospects for Soviet Society,* ed. Allen Kassof (New York: Praeger, 1968), p. 32.

10. J. Wilczynski, *The Economics of Socialism* (Chicago: Aldine, 1970), p. 82. U.S. Congress, Joint Economic Committee, *Current Economic Indicators for the U.S.S.R.,* 89th Congress, 1st session, 1965. See also other indices in Abram Bergson, *Soviet Post-War Economic Development* (Stockholm, Sweden: Almqvist & Wiksell International, 1974).

11. Cohn, "Soviet Growth Model," p. 250; and Shaffer, "Economic Performance," p. 38. For an attempt, with many pitfalls, to measure factor productivity in the U.S.S.R., the United States, France, West Germany, and the United Kingdom in which the United States comes out the most productive and the U.S.S.R. the least, see Abram Bergson, "Productivity under Two Systems," in *Optimum Social Welfare and Productivity,* eds. Jan Tinbergen et al. (New York: New York University Press, 1972).

12. A. H. Brown, "Political Change in Czechoslovakia," *Government and Opposition* 4 (Spring 1969) : 180.

13. Gregory Grossman, "Soviet Growth: Routine, Inertia, and Pressure," *American Economic Review* 50 (May 1960): 69.

14. Quoted in Gregory Grossman, "Innovation and Information in the Soviet Economy," *American Economic Review* 56 (May 1966): 126–27.

15. Joseph Goldmann and Karel Kouba, *Economic Growth in Czechoslovakia* (Prague, 1969), pp. 83–91ff.

16. On innovation in market and authoritarian systems, see Benjamin N. Ward, *The Socialist Economy* (New York: Random House, 1967), pp. 149–57.

17. For a summary of difficulties, see Grossman, "Innovation and Information." See also Joseph S. Berliner, *The Innovation Decision in Soviet Industry* (Cambridge, Mass.: MIT Press, 1976). For analysis in depth of political implications, see Moshe Lewin, *Political Undercurrents in Soviet Economic Debates* (Princeton, N.J.: Princeton University Press, 1974), pp. 153–54. On implications for internal reform and for relations of the European systems to each other, see R. V. Burks, "Technology and Political Change in Communist Systems," in *Change in Communist Systems,* ed. Chalmers Johnson (Stanford, Calif.: Stanford University Press, 1970).

18. The regional decentralization of Soviet economic administration first undertaken by Khrushchev in the mid-1950s was generally regarded as a failure. (Abraham Katz, *The Politics of Economic Reform in the Soviet Union* [New York: Praeger, 1972], chapter 5.) The issue in the new reform movement was decentralized directly to the enterprise itself. (J. M. Montias, "East European Reforms in Retrospect," U.S. Senate, Committee on the Judiciary, Subcommittee on Antitrust and Monopoly, *Hearings on Economic Concentration,* 90th Congress, 2nd session, 1968, part 7.)

19. Galia Golan, *The Czechoslovak Reform Movement* (London: Cambridge University Press, 1971) and *Reform Rule in Czechoslovakia* (London: Cambridge University Press, 1973); and Brown, "Political Change in Czechoslozakia."

20. For a more detailed summary of the reforms, see Gertrude E. Schroeder. "Soviet Economic Reform at an Impasse." *Problems of Communism* 20 (July-August 1971).

21. Katz, *Economic Reform*, p. 179.

22. Gertrude E. Schroeder, "Recent Developments in Soviet Planning and Incentives," in U.S. Congress, Joint Economic Committee, *Soviet Economic Prospects for the Seventies*, 93rd Congress, 1st session, 1973.

23. Quoted in Michael Ellman, *Soviet Planning Today* (Cambridge: Cambridge University Press, 1971), p. 53, from A. and N. Kobrinskii, *Mnogo li cheloveku nuzhno?* (1969), p. 173.

24. Jeremy R. Azrael, *Managerial Power and Soviet Politics* (Cambridge, Mass.: Harvard University Press, 1966). For a summary of the variety of views, see Willem Keizer, *The Soviet Quest for Economic Rationality* (Rotterdam: Rotterdam University Press, 1971), pp. 291ff.

25. For a good discussion of the effect of social complexity on relaxation of government control, on which social science so far produces more hypothesis than empirical confirmation, see Chalmers Johnson, "Comparing Communist Nations," in *Change in Communist Systems*, pp. 15–26, esp. 23–24.

26. Quoted in Morris Bornstein, ed., *Plan and Market* (New Haven, Conn.: Yale University Press, 1973), p. 383.

27. Quoted in Moshe Lewin, *Political Undercurrents in Soviet Economic Debates* (Princeton, N.J.: Princeton University Press, 1974), pp. 230ff.

28. Michael Ellman, *Planning Problems in the U.S.S.R.* (Cambridge: Cambridge University Press, 1973), pp. 141ff.

29. Lewin, *Political Undercurrents*, pp. 222ff.

30. Ellman, *Planning Problems*, p. 140.

31. See Lewin, *Political Undercurrents*, chapter 8.

32. Ibid., pp. 223, 226–27.

33. Peter Wiles, *The Political Economy of Communism* (Cambridge, Mass.: Harvard University Press, 1964), p. 111.

34. Ibid., p. 122. On Chinese prices, see Richman, *Industrial Society*, pp. 381, 463. On Cuban prices, see Carmelo Mesa-Lago and Luc Zephirin, "Central Planning," in *Revolutionary Change in Cuba*, ed. Carmelo Mesa-Lago (Pittsburgh: University of Pittsburgh Press, 1971), p. 176.

35. Wiles, *Economy of Communism*, p. 152.

36. Katz, *Economic Reform*, pp. 197–98 and passim.

37. For a discussion of the impact of economic reform on the relations among the communist systems, see R. V. Burks, "The Political Implications of Economic Reform," in Bornstein, ed., *Plan and Market*.

38. Wilczynski, *Economics of Socialism*, p. 127.

39. As, for example, in much of the debate on the Liberman proposals in the Soviet Union. (In the mid-1960s, Yevsei G. Liberman's name was associated with proposals to use market procedures in the Soviet economy.) See Katz, *Economic Reform*, pp. vii, 63–71; and Keizer, *Soviet Quest*, p. 125.

40. Katz, *Economic Reform*, pp. 193 and 201.

41. Ibid., p. 200. Jerry F. Hough, "The Party Apparatus," in *Interest Groups in Soviet Politics*, eds. H. G. Skilling and F. Griffiths (Princeton, N.J.: Princeton University Press, 1971), p. 70.

42. Alec Nove, *Economic Rationality and Soviet Politics* (New York: Praeger, 1964), p. 62. But see the caution on overestimating managerial and bureaucratic resistance in Montias, "East European Reforms."

43. See Franz Schurmann, *Ideology and Organization in Communist China*, 2nd ed., enl. (Berkeley: University of California Press, 1971) and passim, especially pp. 195ff. For Soviet-Chinese comparisons on the point, see his "Politics and Economics in Russia and

China," in *Soviet and Chinese Communism,* ed. Donald W. Treadgold (Seattle: University of Washington Press, 1967).

44. Keizer, *Soviet Quest,* p. 222. See also John N. Hazard, "The Politics of Soviet Economic Reform" in *Planning and the Market in the U.S.S.R.,* eds. Alexander Balinky et al. (New Brunswick, N.J.: Rutgers University Press, 1967), pp. 79–80.

45. But an imaginative and yet carefully considered set of proposals is outlined in Ellman, *Planning Problems,* chapter 7, "What Kind of Economic Reform Does the Soviet Union Need?"

Chapter 23

Policy Making and Planning

1. An earlier version of the two, from which I have taken some passages, is in Charles E. Lindblom, "The Sociology of Planning," in *Economic Planning, East and West,* ed. Morris Bornstein (Cambridge, Mass.: Ballinger, 1975).

2. Such a strategy is laid out in detail and evaluated in David Braybrooke and Charles E. Lindblom, *A Strategy of Decision* (New York: Free Press, 1963).

3. Various forms of fragmentation and mutual adjustment are analyzed in further detail in Charles E. Lindblom, *The Intelligence of Democracy* (New York: Free Press, 1965).

4. David Novick, Melven Anshen, and W. C. Truppner, *Wartime Production Controls* (New York: Columbia University Press, 1949), chapter 8.

5. For examples of the third, see any items in the literature on governmental reform, as well as theoretical studies like Kenneth J. Arrow, *Social Choice and Individual Values* (New York: John Wiley & Sons, 1951), or Douglas Rae, *The Political Consequence of Electoral Laws* (New Haven, Conn.: Yale University Press, 1967).

6. For a comprehensive study of these plans, see Albert Waterston, *Developmental Planning* (Baltimore: Johns Hopkins Press, 1965). See also Jack Hayward and Michael Watson, *Planning, Politics, and Public Policy: The British, French, and Italian Experience* (London: Cambridge University Press, 1975); and Andrew Shonfield, *Modern Capitalism* (London: Oxford University Press, 1966). Tabular comparisons of formal structure, participants in, and techniques of formal planning in various systems are in Jan Tinbergen, *Central Planning* (New Haven, Conn.: Yale University Press, 1964).

7. John Sheahan, *Promotion and Control of Industry in Postwar France* (Cambridge: Harvard University Press, 1963), p. 44.

8. R. K. Karanjia, *The Mind of Mr. Nehru* (London: George Allen & Unwin, 1960), pp. 49ff.

9. Stephen S. Cohen, *Modern Capitalist Planning: The French Model* (London: Weidenfeld & Nicolson, 1969).

10. For an example of the distinction in the literature between analytical and political policy making (but without advocacy of one or the other), see James G. March and Herbert A. Simon, *Organizations* (New York: John Wiley & Sons, 1958), pp. 129ff.

11. Neil W. Chamberlain, *Private and Public Planning* (New York: McGraw-Hill, 1965), chapter 1.

12. A good exposition of simplification through fragmentation as an alternative to conventional planning, with excellent illustration in detail, is Bertram M. Gross, "The Managers of National Economic Change," in *Public Administration and Democracy,* ed. Roscoe C. Martin (Syracuse, N.Y.: Syracuse University Press, 1965), pp. 101–27.

13. S. A. Walkland, *The Legislative Process in Great Britain* (London: George Allen & Unwin, 1968), pp. 21–27, 35.

14. Giovanni Sartori, "The Typology of Party Systems," in *Mass Politics,* eds. Erik

Allardt and Stein Rokkan (New York: Free Press, 1970), pp. 322–52. Even in two-party systems there may be occasional or peripheral third parties.

15. For an illuminating brief comparison of two-party and multiparty systems, see Leon D. Epstein, *Political Parties in Western Democracies* (New York: Praeger, 1967), chapter 3.

16. Charles L. Schultze, *The Politics and Economics of Public Spending* [Washington, D.C.: The Brookings Institution, 1968].

17. For clarification on their role, I am indebted to Professor David Cohen, Harvard University.

18. Chalmers Johnson, "Comparing Communist Nations," in *Change in Communist Systems,* ed. Chalmers Johnson (Stanford, Calif.: Stanford University Press, 1970), pp. 12–16.

19. Mao Tse-tung, *On Practice: On the Relation between Knowledge and Practice—between Knowing and Doing* (Peking: Foreign Languages Press, 1951 [1937]), p. 22.

20. Richard H. Solomon, *Mao's Revolution and the Chinese Political Culture* (Berkeley: University of California Press, 1971), p. 516.

21. R. W. Davies, "The Soviet Planning Process for Rapid Industrialization," *Economics of Planning* 6 (1966).

22. John P. Hardt et al., eds., *Mathematics and Computers in Soviet Economic Planning* (New Haven, Conn.: Yale University Press, 1967), p. 32.

23. Gertrude Schroeder, "Recent Developments in Soviet Planning and Incentives," in U.S. Congress, Joint Economic Committee, *Soviet Economic Prospects for the Seventies,* 93d Congress, 1st session, 1973, esp. p. 521; and Moshe Lewin, *Political Undercurrents in Soviet Economic Debates* (Princeton, N.J.: Princeton University Press, 1974), pp. 275–76.

24. On "bargaining attitudes" and "incremental perspective," see Jerry F. Hough, *The Soviet Prefects* (Cambridge, Mass.: Harvard University Press, 1969), pp. 285–86 and 312–13; and Hough, "The Brezhnev Era," *Problems of Communism* 25 (March-April 1976).

25. Details on these changes in policy, and on others related to them, are in Jan Prybyla, *The Political Economy of Communist China* (Scranton, Pa.: International Textbook, 1970), pp. 148–350, esp. 148–49, 233–34, 283–89, 298, 350.

26. See for evidence and analysis, A. H. Brown, "Policy-Making in the Soviet Union," *Soviet Studies* 23 (July 1971), esp. pp. 129, 145; and Jerry F. Hough, "The Soviet System," *Problems of Communism* 2 (March-April 1972).

27. Paul Gregory, *Socialist and Nonsocialist Industrialization Patterns* (New York: Praeger, 1970), p. 140.

28. Frederic L. Pryor, *Public Expenditures in Communist and Capitalist Nations* (Homewood, Ill.: Irwin, 1968), pp. 284–85. But the emphasis in European communism is more on engineering than pure science, and in China reconstruction of the universities may have put an end to basic research.

29. Zbigniew Brzezinski, *Between Two Ages* (New York: Viking, 1970), p. 78.

30. Charles M. Martin, "China: Future of the University," *Bulletin of the Atomic Scientists* 27 (January 1971): 11–15.

31. C. H. G. Oldham, "Science Travels the Mao Road," *Bulletin of the Atomic Scientsts* 25 (February 1969): 80–83.

32. Brzezinski, *Between Two Ages,* p. 153, and Daniel Bell, "Ideology and Soviet Politics," *Slavic Review* 24 (December 1965): 602.

33. Hough, "Soviet System," p. 30.

34. Franz Schurmann, *Ideology and Organization in Communist China,* 2nd ed., enl. (Berkeley: University of California Press, 1971), p. 48.

35. Raymond A. Bauer, *The New Man in Soviet Psychology* (Cambridge, Mass.: Harvard University Press, 1952), p. 49.

Chapter 24

Corporate Government and the Yugoslav Innovations

1. Michael Kidron, *Western Capitalism since the War* (Harmondsworth, England: Penguin Books, 1970), pp. 129ff. Among the advocates of new forms of small-group cooperation in the enterprise are many of the social scientists who have given, in roughly the last two decades, a new richness to the understanding of organizations and incentives: among others, Chris Argyris, *Personality and Organization* (New York: Harper & Brothers, 1957); Douglas McGregor, *The Human Side of Enterprise* (New York: McGraw-Hill, 1960); Rensis Likert, *New Patterns of Management* (New York: McGraw-Hill, 1961); Abraham Maslow, *Motivation and Personality* (New York: Harper & Row, 1970).

2. On innovations in West Germany, Britain, France, Scandinavia, and Israel, see David Jenkins, *Job Power* (New York: Doubleday, 1973).

3. For a summary of it, see Paul Blumberg, *Industrial Democracy* (New York: Schocken Books, 1969), chapters 5 and 6.

4. Adam Smith, *The Wealth of Nations,* 2 vols. (Chicago: Irwin, 1963), vol. 2, p. 284.

5. Important early insights on alternative incentives were developed by the Guild Socialists in early twentieth century England. For bibliography and comment, see Graham Wootton, *Workers, Unions, and the State* (New York: Schocken Books, 1967), pp. 106ff. Blumberg, *Industrial Democracy,* summarizes in detail the impressive empirical evidence now accumulated that participation in control is a powerful incentive.

6. John Stuart Mill, *Considerations on Representative Government* (London: George Routledge & Sons, 1905), p. 114.

7. For a summary of evidence from several countries on participation for its own sake, see Carole Pateman, *Participation and Democratic Theory* (London: Cambridge University Press, 1970), pp. 56ff.

8. Such a proposal follows upon Robert A. Nisbet's history and analysis in his *Quest for Community* (New York: Oxford University Press, 1953).

9. For example, Karl Polanyi, *The Great Transformation* (New York: Rinehart & Company, 1944); and Erich Fromm, *Escape from Freedom* (New York: Rinehart & Company, 1941).

10. Giovanni Sartori, *Democratic Theory* (New York: Praeger, 1965), p. 254.

11. The advocates of such a cluster of antibureaucratic reforms are now many: see, for example, George E. Berkeley, *The Administrative Revolution* (Englewood Cliffs, N.J.: Prentice-Hall, 1971); Warren G. Bennis, "Beyond Bureaucracy" in *American Bureaucracy,* ed. Warren G. Bennis (Chicago: Aldine, 1970).

12. Andrew C. Janos, "Group Politics in Communist Society," in *Authoritarian Politics in Modern Society,* eds. Samuel P. Huntington and Clement H. Moore (New York: Basic Books, 1970), p. 444.

13. For good summaries and studies of the Yugoslav experience with worker control, including in some cases interview material, see Joel B. Dirlam and James L. Plummer, *An Introduction to the Yugoslav Economy* (Columbus, Ohio: Charles E. Merrill, 1973); Jenkins, *Job Power;* Pateman, *Participation and Democratic Theory;* Ichak Adizes, *Industrial Democracy: Yugoslav Style* (New York: Free Press, 1971); and Egon Neuberger and Estelle James, "The Yugoslav Self-managed Enterprise," in *Plan and Market,* ed. Morris Bornstein (New Haven, Conn.: Yale University Press, 1973).

14. In decentralizing both to enterprises and to the "republics," Yugoslavia has cautiously mixed the two forms of decentralization. Just how conscious policy makers have been of the trade-off between the two is not clear. See Paul Shoup, *Communism and the Yugoslav National Question* (New York: Columbia University Press, 1968), pp. 252–60.

15. Dirlam and Plummer, *Yugoslav Economy,* p. 28.

16. Adizes, *Industrial Democracy: Yugoslav Style,* p. 198.

17. Dirlam and Plummer, *Yugoslav Economy*, p. 33.

18. Neuberger and James, "Self-managed Enterprise," pp. 260ff.

19. Dirlam and Plummer, *Yugoslav Economy*, pp. 32–38.

20. Blumberg, *Industrial Democracy*, pp. 210ff.

21. Neuberger and James, "Self-managed Enterprise," p. 282.

22. Frank Parkin, *Class Inequality and Political Order* (New York: Praeger, 1971), pp. 118, 172–78.

23. Blumberg, *Industrial Democracy*, pp. 198–205, 230.

24. Dirlam and Plummer, *Yugoslav Economy*, pp. 73–86.

25. Pateman, *Participation and Democratic Theory*, pp. 98ff; Blumberg, *Industrial Democracy*, pp. 218, 226; and Neuberger and James, "Self-managed Enterprise," pp. 275ff.

26. Jiri Kolaja, *Workers' Councils* (New York: Praeger, 1966), p. 75.

27. Adizes, *Industrial Democracy*, chapter 4.

28. Jenkins, *Job Power*, p. 104. See his chapter 7 for the variety of opinion, among both participants and observers.

29. Richard Lowenthal, "Development vs. Utopia in Communist Policy," in *Change in Communist Systems*, ed. Chalmers Johnson (Stanford, Calif.: Stanford University Press, 1970), p. 55.

30. In Stephen S. Anderson, "Economic 'Reform' in Yugoslavia," *Current History* 52 (April 1967): 215.

31. Paul Shoup, "The National Question in Yugoslavia," *Problems of Communism* 21 (January-February 1972): pp. 19, 25ff.

32. George W. Hoffman and Fred Warner Neal, *Yugoslavia and the New Communism* (New York: Twentieth Century Fund, 1962), chapter 13; and M. J. Broekmeyer, ed., *Yugoslav Workers' Self-management* (Dordrecht, Holland: D. Reidel Publishing, 1970), pp. 6–7.

33. Paul Shoup, "The Evolution of a System," *Problems of Communism* 18 (July-October 1969): pp. 71ff; Hoffman and Neal, *Yugoslavia and the New Communism*, pp. 399ff.

34. Hoffman and Neal, *Yugoslavia and the New Communism*, pp. 385ff.

35. Anderson, "Economic 'Reform,'" p. 218; and Fred W. Neal and Winston M. Fisk, "Yugoslavia: Towards a Market Socialism," *Problems of Communism* 15 (November-December 1966): 33ff.

36. Hoffman Neal, *Yugoslavia and the New Communism*, p. 397. Public discussion of the possible desirability of a two-party system has been possible for some years, and some leaders favor it. Shoup, "Evolution of a System," p. 73.

37. Shoup, "Evolution of a System," p. 73. See also Hoffman and Neal, *Yugoslavia and the New Communism*, pp. 398–99.

38. Hoffman and Neal, *Yugoslavia and the New Communism*, pp. 171f.

39. Kolaja, *Workers' Councils*, p. 4.

40. Dirlam and Plummer, *Yugoslav Economy*, chapter 6.

41. For the Yugoslav figure, United Nations, *Statistical Yearbook*, 1975, p. 603. For the other nations, see table in chapter 22.

Chapter 25

A Future for Democracy?

1. On problems posed by increasingly important technical aspects of policy making see Daniel Bell, *The Coming of Post-industrial Society* (New York: Basic Books, 1973), pp. 311–12.

2. Seymour Melman, *Pentagon Capitalism* (New York: McGraw-Hill, 1970), pp. 47–48.

3. On tensions arising from welfare demands, see Morris Janowitz, *Social Control of the Welfare State* (New York: Elsevier, 1976). On a variety of demands, see Samuel Brittan, "The Economic Contradiction of Democracy," *British Journal of Political Science* 5 (April 1975).

4. Ibid. Also John H. Goldthorpe, David Lockwood, Frank Bechhofer, and Jennifer Platt, *The Affluent Worker in the Class Structure* (London: Cambridge University Press, 1969), chapter 5.

5. Michael Harrington, "Old Working Class, New Working Class," in *The World of the Blue-collar Worker,* ed. Irving Howe (New York: Quadrangle, 1972), p. 153.

6. Robert McKenzie and Allan Silver, *Angels in Marble* (Chicago: University of Chicago Press, 1968), pp. 256ff, 183–190.

7. On strains on democracy from democratic aspiration, see Samuel P. Huntington, "The Democratic Distemper," *Public Interest* (Fall 1975): especially pp. 35–38.

8. For pertinent comment, see Crawford Brough Macpherson, *The Political Theory of Possessive Individualism* (Oxford: Clarendon Press, 1968), pp. 93ff. For a careful analysis of how certain class-related phenomena induce the acceptance of authority in varying degrees in different countries, see Eric Nordlinger, "A Theory of Stable Democracy," in his *Working Class Tories* (Berkeley: University of California Press, 1967).

9. On related possibilities of increasing conflict, disorder, and violence, see Samuel P. Huntington, "Post-Industrial Politics: How Benign Will It Be?" *Comparative Politics* 6 (January 1974).

10. For a good, brief analysis, with bibliography, of elite consensus as a requirement of polyarchy, see Peter Bachrach, *The Theory of Democratic Elitism* (Boston: Little, Brown, 1967), chapter 4. See also, on threats to polyarchy from unindoctrinated mass, his chapter 3.

11. For a brief account of the traditional fears and predictions, with bibliography, see Robert E. Lane, *Political Life* (New York: Free Press, 1959), pp. 27–37. See also McKenzie and Silver, *Angels in Marble,* chapter 1.

12. Karl Marx as quoted in McKenzie and Silver, *Angels in Marble,* p. 4.

INDEX

Index

397

Index

401